THE COMPLETE GUIDE TO
THE NATIONAL PARK LODGES

EIGHTH EDITION

DAVID L. SCOTT AND KAY W. SCOTT

gpp®

Guilford, Connecticut

An imprint of Rowman & Littlefield

Distributed by NATIONAL BOOK NETWORK

British Library Cataloguing-in-Publication Information Available

Library of Congress Cataloguing-in-Publication Data Available

ISBN 978-1-4930-0647-2 (paperback)

∞™ The paper used in this publication meets the minimum requirements of American National Standard for Information Sciences—Permanence of Paper for Printed Library Materials, ANSI/NISO Z39.48-1992.

All the information in this guidebook is subject to change. We recommend that you call ahead to obtain current information before traveling. The dollar cost of rooms and meals is for summer 2014. Taxes are not included unless noted.

Maps provided are for reference only and should be used in conjunction with a road map or official park map. Distances suggested are approximate.

CONTENTS

PREFACE

This eighth edition of *The Complete Guide to the National Park Lodges* includes several important changes. The Argonaut Hotel and the Inn at the Presidio are new entries. Each of these upscale San Francisco hotels is tied to a theme associated with an important chapter in the city's history. The two lodging facilities are both quite nice but offer guests very different experiences in terms of size, atmosphere, and location.

Sadly, Bluffs Lodge on the Blue Ridge Parkway remains closed as the National Park Service continues its search for a concessionaire. Over the years the lodge and its associated coffee shop became a favorite stop for travelers driving the parkway. Its fans, including the two of us, are hoping the National Park Service is successful in locating someone interested in reopening Bluffs. One of the parkway's other four lodges, Rocky Knob Cabins, is closed and unlikely to reopen as a regular lodging operation. With only seven cabins available for guests, Rocky Knob is simply too small to attract a concessionaire.

The cabins and main lodge at Big Spring Lodge in Ozark National Scenic Riverways are scheduled for a major overhaul that is expected to result in the entire facility being closed until spring 2018. At least that was the plan at the time we submitted the manuscript. In Badlands National Park, all of the quaint cabins at Cedar Pass Lodge have been replaced with modern wooden cabins. The lodge manager indicates the upgrade has resulted in guests choosing longer stays in this South Dakota park. In Florida, Everglades National Park officials continue to consider new lodging to replace the old Flamingo Lodge that was destroyed in 2005 by hurricanes.

Big changes for lodging are a possibility for several parks. The motel units in the Maswik South lodging area of Grand Canyon's South Rim are to be demolished and replaced with lodge-style buildings. The beginning and completion dates for this are uncertain. The Canyon area of Yellowstone National Park is undergoing substantial changes with new lodging replacing several hundred of the aging Frontier cabins. Replacement cabins are expected at Log Cabin Resort in Olympic National Park. Major improvements, mostly structural, have been completed on Many Glacier Hotel in Montana's Glacier National Park. Portions of this popular hotel had been closed for several summers. Extensive work on the annex portion of the hotel is anticipated, but the dates are uncertain.

Major changes have occurred with regard to the companies that operate the lodges. All the lodging facilities in Glacier National Park, Kings Canyon National Park, and Shenandoah National Park have new concessionaires. Kalaloch Lodge and Log Cabin Resort in Olympic National Park, plus Peaks of Otter Lodge on the Blue Ridge Parkway are each under new management.

Even with these and other changes noted in this book, much about America's national park lodges remains a constant. The lobby of Glacier Park Lodge is still awe-inspiring, the meals at Far View Lodge in Mesa Verde are still delicious, the canyon views from Grand Canyon Lodge on the North Rim are still amazing, and evening music from a string quartet at Lake Yellowstone Hotel continues to soothe the soul. It is time to make a reservation and join the fun.

INTRODUCTION

Have you ever thought of waking up, peering out your window, and viewing the morning sun shining on the north face of the Grand Canyon? How about an evening stroll down a dirt road from the historic hotel where you just enjoyed a dinner of walleye pike, and standing where French fur trappers portaged canoes around a waterfall? Maybe you would enjoy relaxing on a wooden deck outside your room while listening to the roar of a mountain stream. Perhaps you are a closet cowboy who has longed to spend a week riding horses at a dude ranch. These are dreams that can be brought to life during a stay at a national park lodge.

The two of us have devoted more than 30 summers and numerous winter vacations to exploring America's national parks. Most took place in a series of 4 Volkswagen campers that logged nearly a quarter of a million miles. Seven summers and numerous shorter trips have been dedicated to experiencing national park lodges. At each lodge we walk the property, view different types of rooms, talk with employees, and sample the food. We gather information that we believe will be of value in planning a trip. Most national park lodges are in well-known and heavily visited parks, such as Grand Canyon, Death Valley, Yosemite, Yellowstone, Grand Teton, Olympic, and Glacier. However, several lesser-known parks, including Oregon Caves National Monument, Isle Royale National Park, Big Bend National Park, and Lassen Volcanic National Park, each offer interesting lodge facilities. Some of the biggest and busiest parks do not have lodges. For example, Great Smoky Mountains National Park, Rocky Mountain National Park, and Acadia National Park do not offer conventional lodging inside their boundaries.

Staying in a lodge during a national park visit will almost certainly enhance your vacation experience. It certainly has ours. Spend time talking to employees and learning about the history of the building where you are staying. Most of all, travel and enjoy.

CONSIDERATIONS IN PLANNING A STAY AT A NATIONAL PARK LODGE

National park lodges offer a different vacation experience. Most lodges are in close proximity to things you want to see, places you want to visit, and facilities you want to utilize during a visit. At Crater Lake Lodge, you can sleep in a room with windows overlooking the crater rim. In Yellowstone's Old Faithful Inn, you can walk out the entrance and view an eruption of Old Faithful geyser. At Grand Canyon's El Tovar, you can step outside the hotel and gaze in wonder into the magnificent canyon. Many park lodges have large rustic lobbies where you can relax and converse with other guests, often in front of a blazing fireplace. The mammoth fireplaces at each end of the lobby in Mount Rainier National Park's Paradise Inn are simply amazing. The lodges are frequently near National Park Service visitor centers or campgrounds where guided walks originate and natural history programs are presented. Evening programs or other entertainment can be enjoyed in many of the lodges.

Most national park lodges are owned by the government but managed by private firms

NATIONAL PARKS AREAS WITH LODGING FACILITIES

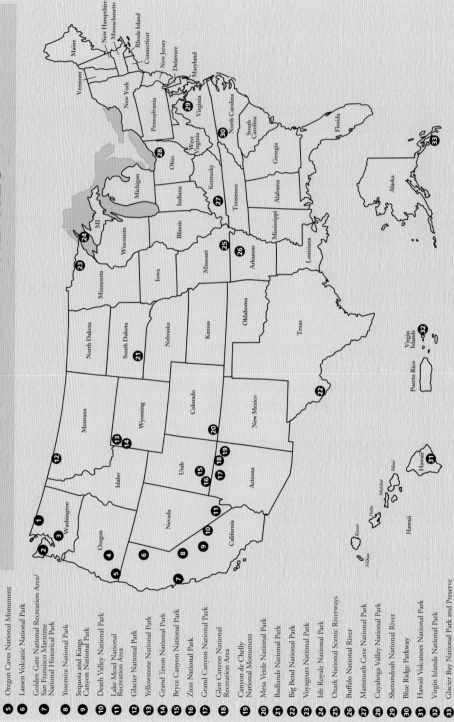

1. North Cascades National Park
2. Olympic National Park
3. Mount Rainier National Park
4. Crater Lake National Park
5. Oregon Caves National Monument
6. Lassen Volcanic National Park
7. Golden Gate National Recreation Area/ San Fransisco Maritime National Historical Park
8. Yosemite National Park
9. Sequoia and Kings Canyon National Park
10. Death Valley National Park
11. Lake Mead National Recreation Area
12. Glacier National Park
13. Yellowstone National Park
14. Grand Teton National Park
15. Bryce Canyon National Park
16. Zion National Park
17. Grand Canyon National Park
18. Glen Canyon National Recreation Area
19. Canyon de Chelly National Monument
20. Mesa Verde National Park
21. Badlands National Park
22. Big Bend National Park
23. Voyageurs National Park
24. Isle Royale National Park
25. Ozark National Scenic Riverways
26. Buffalo National River
27. Mammoth Cave National Park
28. Cuyahoga Valley National Park
29. Shenandoah National River
30. Blue Ridge Parkway
31. Hawaii Volcanoes National Park
32. Virgin Islands National Park
33. Glacier Bay National Park and Preserve

Volcano House at Hawaii Volcanoes National Park

subject to oversight by the park in which they are located. Managements operate as concessionaires and must obtain approval of the National Park Service for room rates, improvements, activities, and prices charged for everything from food to gasoline. Some lodges remain under private ownership on private property within a park. For example, both the Inn at Furnace Creek and the Ranch at Furnace Creek in Death Valley National Park are privately owned. In general, lodges under private ownership were in operation prior to the establishment or expansion of a park. Lodges on private property are subject to less government oversight regarding what they offer and prices they charge.

Basic information regarding reservations, facilities, and policies can be helpful if you have never stayed in a national park facility or have stayed in only one or two lodges. Most lodges experience large public demand for a limited number of rooms, especially during peak season.

Consider that additional accommodations have not been added to most national parks in decades, and it is easy to understand why there are often insufficient rooms to meet demand. In Yosemite Valley hundreds of guest rooms have been lost due to flooding and rock slides. Thus, make a reservation as early as possible, especially if your planned vacation coincides with the park's busiest period. Try to book rooms at a popular lodge at least 6 months before your expected arrival. Several lodges in very busy locations such as Yosemite Valley should, if possible, be booked nearly a year in advance. Choosing to vacation in off-peak periods, normally spring and fall, makes it more likely that you will successfully obtain a reservation for the desired dates.

Facilities

National park lodges range from luxurious and expensive facilities, such as Yosemite National Park's Ahwahnee and Death Valley National

Park's Inn at Furnace Creek, to rustic cabins without bathrooms, such as those in Kings Canyon National Park. Some facilities call themselves lodges but are not what most of us picture when thinking of a lodge. Old Faithful Lodge Cabins (not the more famous and nearby Old Faithful Inn) offers only cabins as overnight accommodations. Likewise, Signal Mountain Lodge in Grand Teton National Park does not include a main lodge building with overnight accommodations; rather, it is comprised of several types of cabins that rent at a fairly wide range of prices. The variation in facilities between and within parks makes it important to understand exactly what types of accommodations are being reserved.

Most national park lodging facilities lack amenities such as spas, exercise rooms, swimming pools, game rooms, and other niceties you may expect at commercial facilities outside the parks. In fact, rooms in many park lodges don't have a telephone or television. Several older lodges, including Old Faithful Inn in Yellowstone National Park, Wawona in Yosemite National Park, and Lake Crescent Lodge in Olympic National Park, offer some guest rooms in which occupants are required to use community bathrooms. Tent cabins make up a portion of the lodging at some parks including the Curry Village area of Yosemite National Park and the Grant Grove area of Kings Canyon.

Rooms

Rooms in many national park lodges vary considerably with regard to size, bedding, view, and rate. Likewise, a lodging facility may offer rooms in the main building, rooms in nearby motel-type buildings, and a variety of cabins. This is the case for Lake Crescent Lodge in Olympic National Park and Big Meadows Lodge in Shenandoah National Park. Potential differences in rooms

make it essential to learn what options are available at a particular location. Waiting to make a reservation near your planned arrival date makes it likely you will find a limited variety of accommodations available. For example, you may discover that all rooms with a private bath are taken. Call early and a wide choice of rooms at a broad range of rates are likely to be offered. Ask about a view room, for example. Sometimes rooms with an excellent view are more expensive, and sometimes they are not. Some multiple-story buildings lack elevators, so the floor you are assigned may be important. Higher floors tend to offer better views but may require more climbing. Rooms near the lobby may be noisy. Some lodges allow you to reserve a specific room, but most guarantee only a particular class of room. Even when a particular room can't be guaranteed, a lodge will often make note of your preferences and attempt to satisfy the request when rooms are assigned.

Accessibility

Most national park facilities offer some type of wheelchair accessibility, but the degree varies considerably among the lodges and among different types of accommodations at the same lodge. It isn't that lodge operators don't care, but rather that many national park lodging facilities are historic and restrictions exist with regard to modifications that are permitted. Keep in mind that lodging facilities are sometimes a distance from parking, and many facilities with 2 or more stories do not have elevators. In addition, some national park accommodations do not have telephones in the rooms. Be certain to have a clear understanding about the extent of accessibility when booking a room. Also consider other special medical issues that may be encountered. For example, will there be a need to refrigerate medication or plug in medical equipment? With

The Old Faithful Snow Lodge at Yellowstone National Park

regard to the latter, rooms in historic structures may not have electrical outlets for 3-prong plugs so you should pack an adapter.

Reservations

Reservations can generally be made by telephone and the Internet.

Using the telephone allows you to discuss with the reservation agent the types of facilities that are available. It is a good idea to study the lodge website so as to gain a basic understanding of the facilities and rates prior to calling. This will allow you to know which type of room and building to request and what to expect regarding rates. Be aware that it is often difficult to get through to a reservation agent via telephone, especially if you call late in the spring. Try calling at odd hours, such as weekend mornings.

Most lodges require a deposit of at least 1 night's lodging. When sending a deposit check or giving a credit card number, request an e-mail or written confirmation that can be taken with you on your vacation. In the event your plans change, refund of a deposit requires advance notice, usually 48 hours, but this varies by concessionaire.

Rates

In general, accommodations in the national parks aren't cheap. Expect to pay $150 and up for most double rooms, although some rustic cabins are less expensive, while a room at one of the nicer facilities can run $250 and up. Discounts for seniors, AAA members, government employees, and other special groups are generally unavailable but it never hurts to ask. Most lodges quote rates for two adults. Additional adults pay extra, although young children are generally free when staying with adults. Some lodges allow children 12 years and under to stay free, while other facilities limit free stays to children 3 and under. Lodges sometimes offer reduced off-season rates or have special packages that include meals and tours or a lower rate for multi-day stays. Check the website or ask about specials when booking a reservation. The dollar cost of rooms and meals for summer 2014 is used in this book. Expect somewhat higher prices in subsequent years.

Obtaining a Room without a Reservation

National park lodges often have available rooms, especially during off-peak periods. Even busy lodges experience cancellations or early departures that free up rooms. For example, you may find rooms available in a busy park like Yellowstone during peak summer months just by dropping in at one of the 9 lodges and asking about a vacancy. If rooms are available, they are unlikely to be the exact configuration, location, or price category you would choose. You may have to accept a room without a private bathroom or a room that is more expensive than you would ordinarily choose. In a large park like Yellowstone or Glacier, the only available rooms may be in a different facility many miles from the lodge where you are making the request. Taking a chance on a vacancy is risky. Being unsuccessful may result in a long drive to a distant location where you are likely to overpay for an inferior room. Save a possible headache by calling ahead.

Pets

National park lodges generally prohibit pets of all kinds except for service animals. There are exceptions, but not many. Some larger lodges, including those in Mammoth Cave National Park, the South Rim of Grand Canyon National Park, and Yosemite National Park, have kennels available,

but don't count on this convenience at the park you plan to visit. Ask about the pet policy when making a reservation. Some lodges allow pets, but only in a particular type of room. National parks require that pets be kept on a leash at all times. In addition, pets are normally prohibited from park trails. The bottom line: Pets are best left at home when making a trip to a national park.

Reducing Expenses

National park lodges are pricey. However, it is possible to take steps to reduce your expenditures. Choosing a room without a private bathroom (if available) can often save $40 to $70 per night compared to rooms with a private bath.

Another money-saving strategy is to spend each second or third night camping. Parks with lodges usually have campgrounds that charge $16 to $30 per night. Arrange campground stays into your schedule when making reservations. For example, spend 2 nights in a lodge, then move to a campground the third night. Keep in mind that some national park campgrounds operate under a reservation system, and unoccupied or unreserved sites may be difficult to find.

Spend the night prior to arrival at a less expensive commercial facility within an hour or two of the park. The close proximity permits you to enjoy most of a full day in the park before checking in at the lodge. Likewise, obtain a reservation at a motel a couple of hours outside the park on your departure date so that you can spend most of an extra day finishing your park sightseeing. Take along a cooler with food and drinks. Buy groceries outside the park, where they are likely to be cheaper. Eat a breakfast of fruit and cereal in your room, and have a picnic lunch or supper. If you choose to eat in a restaurant, keep in mind that lunch is often less expensive than dinner. In parks with several restaurant facilities, examine the menus, as prices can vary a great deal from one restaurant to another. In general, cafeterias are considerably less expensive than dining rooms.

Take advantage of the many free things offered at most parks. National Park Service personnel offer guided walks and programs, generally at no charge. Parks with campgrounds typically provide evening history and nature programs offered without charge. Park visitor centers have exhibits and audiovisual programs to help you understand what you will see and experience in the park. Some of the lodges even offer free tours of their building. Many parks offer Junior Ranger programs for children. Stop at the park visitor center and request a list of daily activities.

Park Fees

Most areas operated by the National Park Service charge an entry fee that covers everyone inside a noncommercial vehicle. Hikers, motorcyclists, bicyclists, and visitors entering in commercial vehicles pay a separate fee applicable to individual entry. Entrance fees range from $10 to $25 per private vehicle, with the higher price charged at large national parks, including Yellowstone, Glacier, and Grand Canyon. The fee generally provides unlimited exit and entrance for 3 to 7 days. The National Park Service and several other federal agencies sell 3 types of passes providing free entrance at federal recreation areas including national parks. The America the Beautiful–National Parks and Federal Recreation Lands Pass ($80) allows unlimited entry to all federal recreation sites for 1 year from the month of purchase. For seniors (age 62 and over), the America the Beautiful Senior Pass provides lifetime free entrance for a one-time fee of $10. A lifetime pass is available at no charge to the disabled. Passes for seniors and the disabled also allow a 50 percent reduction in fees for parking, boat launching, and most tours. All 3 passes are available at most National Park Service entrance stations and visitor centers and can be purchased by mail or online. Visit www.nps.gov/findapark/passes.htm for more information.

Cell Phones and Wi-Fi

Communications with the outside world can be spotty or nonexistent, depending upon the park or location within a particular park. More park lodges have started offering Wi-Fi, a trend that will certainly continue, but access may be limited to a single building or even a limited area within a building. Still, for good or for bad, Wi-Fi access is improving. Cell phone functionality depends not only upon the park, but also upon the provider. If use of a cell phone or Wi-Fi capability is important, call the lodge in which you are planning to stay and ask about the services in which you are interested. We have heard numerous visitors complain they can't get their cell phones to work. They should have called ahead.

Getting the Most from a National Park Visit

Staying in a national park lodge should enhance your visit to a park, but don't let it be your main activity. National park areas offer numerous activities in which you can participate. Your first order of business should be to learn about the park areas you will be visiting. We have included addresses, phone numbers, and websites for each park unit that has lodging facilities. Read about the parks so you will have a basic understanding of the history, geology, and activities prior to arrival. At parks with an entry station, you will be given a park newspaper and a mini-folder with a park map. These can be obtained at the visitor centers of parks without an entry station. Stop at a visitor center to determine what activities are scheduled during your stay. Visitor centers generally have excellent video presentations that provide either an overview of the park or insight about some particular facet of history or geology. Visitor centers also generally post a list of daily activities including talks, demonstrations, guided hikes, and campfire programs. Take advantage of as many of these activities as time permits, for they are nearly always enjoyable and educational. You will have an opportunity to ask questions of an expert at the same time that you share information with other visitors who have interests similar to yours.

Most parks offer Junior Ranger programs for children. These programs allow kids to earn a Junior Ranger patch or badge while they learn about the park and its environment. Information on these programs is available at the visitor center.

For more information about national park lodging, visit http://mypages.valdosta.edu/dlscott/Lodges/lodge.html.

Glacier Bay National Park and Preserve

1 Park Rd. • Gustavus, AK 99826 • (907) 697-2230 • www.nps.gov/glba

Glacier Bay National Park and Preserve comprises approximately 3.3 million acres including some of the world's most impressive tidewater glaciers, rivers of ice that flow to the sea. The park is rich in plant and animal life and is home to moose, black bears, grizzly bears, mountain goats, sea lions, sea otters, puffins, bald eagles, humpback whales, and porpoises. A 9-mile paved road links the small town of Gustavus and its airport with the lodge, but most natural features of the park can be seen only by boat or airplane. The park is in southeastern Alaska, approximately 60 miles northwest of Juneau. Access to the park is only via plane or boat.

Park Entrance Fee: No charge.

Lodging in Glacier Bay National Park: Glacier Bay Lodge offers the only overnight accommodations in the park. The rustic 48-room lodge is located near the mouth of Glacier Bay in the southeastern section of the park.

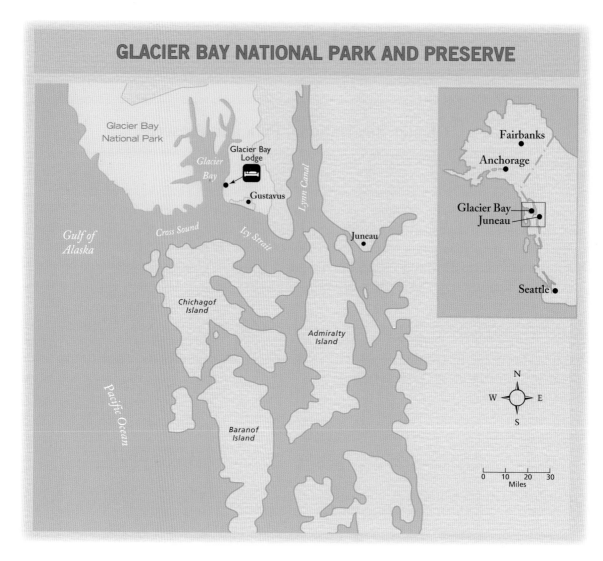

GLACIER BAY NATIONAL PARK AND PRESERVE

Glacier Bay National Park

Glacier Bay Lodge

Glacier Bay

Gustavus

Lynn Canal

Gulf of Alaska

Cross Sound

Icy Strait

Juneau

Chichagof Island

Admiralty Island

Pacific Ocean

Baranof Island

Fairbanks

Anchorage

Glacier Bay
Juneau

Seattle

N
W E
S

0 10 20 30
Miles

GLACIER BAY LODGE
179 Bartlett Cove • Gustavus, AK 99826 • (907) 697-4000 • www.visitglacierbay.com

Glacier Bay Lodge is a wilderness resort situated on Bartlett Cove in a Sitka spruce rain forest. The complex includes an attractive two-story wooden chalet-type lodge that houses a lobby with a cathedral ceiling and wood beams, a large gas fireplace, registration desk, dining room with great vistas, and a gift shop. A National Park Service visitor center on the lodge mezzanine offers interpretive displays and an auditorium where films are shown and programs are presented by park rangers. Boardwalks connect the main lodge with 19 nearby one-story wooden structures that house the guest accommodations.

The lodge offers 48 guest rooms that are near but separate from the main lodge. Approximately a dozen rooms are utilized as housing for management and interpreters. The buildings each have from 2 to 6 rooms. The rooms all

Guest rooms at Glacier Bay Lodge

have radiant heat, a coffeemaker, a hair dryer, a telephone, and a private bathroom. There are no televisions. All but 4 of the rooms are the same size, and most have 1 double bed plus a twin bed. A limited number of rooms have 2 double beds. The rooms have attractive interiors with rough-hewn wood walls and a vaulted ceiling. Sixteen rooms classified as "view rooms" offer window views of Bartlett Cove and rent for about $25 per night more than rooms that offer forest views. If a water view is important, we suggest rooms 9 through 21. Keep in mind water views are at least partially obscured by spruce trees. If a water view isn't important, save $25 by requesting rooms 43 through 52. Steps are required to reach some rooms, especially those with a view. Mention if steps will be a problem when making a reservation.

Glacier Bay Lodge is a place to enjoy spectacular scenery and abundant wildlife in a wild

Glacier Bay Lodge, constructed from 1965 to 1966 by the National Park Service, opened in June 1966 with the main lodge plus 20 cabins. The concessionaire constructed an additional 35 cabins plus 2 utility cabins and a service building (the current shower and laundry) 6 years later. The added buildings were subsequently purchased by the National Park Service from the financially distressed concessionaire. During the winter of 1984–85, the National Park Service enlarged the lodge basement and provided exhibit space on the second floor that currently houses the National Park Service visitor center. The lodge and its boat tours have operated under a succession of firms, including one that filed for bankruptcy in 1989. The lodge contract was awarded in 2004 to a joint venture of Aramark Leisure Services and a subsidiary of HUNA Totem Native Corporation. The contract was extended by 2 years in late 2013.

environment. The lodge is in a rain forest with cool temperatures and plentiful moisture, so pack rain gear and clothing appropriate for daytime summer temperatures that range from 45° to 65° Fahrenheit. We suggest at least 3 nights at the lodge to allow sufficient time to enjoy and explore the surrounding area. Most guests choose to take the daylong Glacier Bay cruise that departs at 7:30 a.m. from the dock behind the lodge. We saw mountain goats, wolves, sea otters, sea lions, puffins, and a grizzly bear during our cruise. We also witnessed a huge chunk of ice split off a tidewater glacier and crash into Glacier Bay. The next day can be spent kayaking Glacier Bay or hiking 1 or more of 4 trails that begin near the lodge. The 1-mile Forest Loop Trail begins from the beach below the lodge and winds through the rain forest where the trees, ground, and logs are covered in green. Bicycle rentals are available at the lodge. On the second evening consider the whale-watching tour that cruises to a popular feeding area for humpback whales. The tour is available with or without dinner. Whale-watching tours

Nearly everyone visiting Glacier Bay, be it by boat or plane, travels by way of Juneau. Alaska's capital offers a variety of things to see and do that make a layover of several days worthwhile. As you might expect in a capital city, Juneau is home to an interesting state museum and offers state capitol tours. Perhaps you would enjoy a 1,800-foot tram ride up Mount Roberts. Scenic seaplane flights over the Juneau Icefield and its many glaciers leave from a downtown dock. A short distance north of Juneau, a US Forest Service visitor center offers exhibits near a viewing area for the famous Mendenhall Glacier. Nearer downtown a salmon hatchery and its small aquarium offer insights on one of the state's important industries. After all this, it may be time for a tour of the Alaska Brewing Company, where visitors can sample fine brews. For information contact the Juneau Convention & Visitors Bureau. Call (800) 587-2201, or visit www.traveljuneau.com.

are not offered every night, so inquire about schedules when making a lodge reservation.

Rooms: Singles, doubles, triples, and quads. Rollaways are available. All rooms have private baths.

Wheelchair Accessibility: Two rooms are ADA compliant. An elevator is available to transport guests to the second floor of the lodge, where the national park visitor center is located.

Reservations: Glacier Bay Lodge & Tours, 3000 C St., Ste. 101, Anchorage, AK 99503. Phone (888) 229-8687; www.visitglacierbay.com. Rooms must be prepaid. A fee of 10 percent of the total reservation is charged for any cancellation at least 31 days prior to arrival. Later cancellations result in a forfeit of deposit.

Rates: View rooms ($230); regular rooms ($205). Rates quoted are for 2 adults. Each additional person is $25 per night. Children under 12 stay free with adults. Packages are offered and nonrefundable rates are sometimes available.

Location: Approximately 9 miles northwest of Gustavus, on the shore of Bartlett Cove.

Season: Late May through early Sept.

Food: A dining room specializing in fresh Alaskan seafood, such as halibut and salmon, serves breakfast ($6–$14); lunch ($8–$13); and dinner ($15–$30). The lunch menu is served on the deck during the afternoon and evening hours. A small grocery is in Gustavus.

Transportation: Alaska Airlines operates scheduled jet service to Gustavus during summer months. Charter airlines (Wings of Alaska and Alaska Seaplanes) and air taxis provide service between Glacier Bay and several Alaska towns. Alaska Marine Highway System stops in Gustavus 1 or 2 times per week. Call (800) 642-0066 for schedules and fares. A lodge shuttle (fee) operates between the lodge and Gustavus. A private taxi service is also available. Service and schedules are subject to change, so check with the lodge or review Gustavus transportation information at www.gustavus.com/gethere/index.html.

Facilities: Restaurant, cocktail service, gift shop, bike and kayak rental, national park visitor center. A ranger station and boat dock are nearby.

Activities: Hiking, guided walks, biking, kayaking, guided kayak trips, fishing, fishing charters, all-day wildlife and glacier cruises, and whale-watching dinner cruises. A 9-hole golf course is in Gustavus (rental clubs are available).

Canyon de Chelly National Monument

PO Box 588 • Chinle, AZ 86503 • (928) 674-5500 • www.nps.gov/cach

Canyon de Chelly (pronounced "d' SHAY") National Monument comprises nearly 84,000 acres of Navajo land that include ruins of Indian villages built between AD 350 and 1300 in steep-walled canyons. The visitor center is near the park entrance. Excellent views of Canyon del Muerto are available from scenic overlooks along North Rim Drive (36 miles round-trip) and Canyon de Chelly along South Rim Drive (34 miles round-trip). White House Ruin is accessible via a 2.5-mile (round-trip) trail that begins at a trailhead on South Rim Drive. All other trails and all 4-wheel-drive travel within the park require a park ranger or authorized guide. Canyon de Chelly is in northeastern Arizona, approximately 85 miles northwest of Gallup, New Mexico, near the town of Chinle.

Monument Entrance Fee: No charge.

Lodging in Canyon de Chelly National Monument: Sacred Canyon Lodge, near the monument entrance, is the monument's only lodging facility. The lodge is on Navajo Route 7, 3 miles east of the intersection with Highway 191 in the town of Chinle.

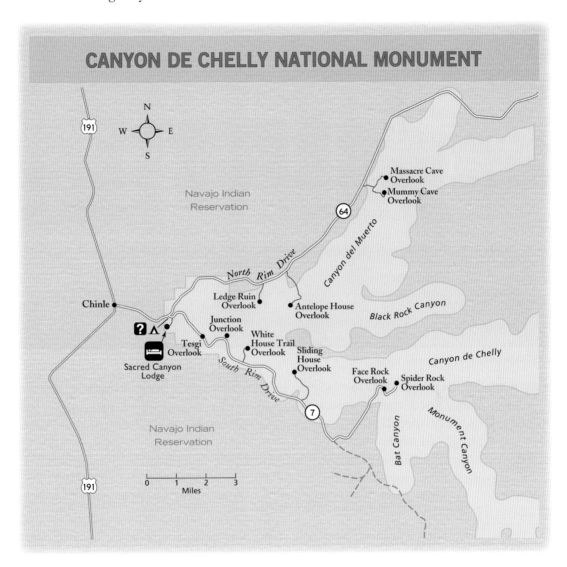

CANYON DE CHELLY NATIONAL MONUMENT

Sacred Canyon Lodge
Rural Route 7 • Chinle, AZ 86503 • (800) 679-2473 • www.sacredcanyonlodge.com

Sacred Canyon Lodge is an attractive, well-maintained motor lodge, offering 70 rooms just inside the entrance to Canyon de Chelly National Monument. The lodge, situated in a grove of cottonwood trees, comprises a complex of several adobe and stone buildings, including 4 adobe units that contain most of the guest rooms. The adobe registration building is separate but

A De Chelly building at Sacred Canyon Lodge

adjacent to the buildings with guest rooms. Separate stone buildings house a small number of rooms, a gift shop, and a cafeteria.

The lodge offers 2 major categories of rooms. All are decorated in an attractive Southwestern style and have air-conditioning, heat, ceiling fans, television, and a telephone. They do not have a coffeemaker or hair dryer.

Forty-one adobe motel-type rooms were constructed in 1984, and most have 2 queen beds and a full bath. Adobe rooms have beamed ceilings and are housed in 2 long buildings built into the back of a hill. Parking is directly in front of a covered walkway stretching across the front of the buildings. Twenty-eight De Chelly rooms were built in the 1960s and most contain 2 double beds and a full bath, although one has 3 full beds, and a few are available with a king bed. All but 4

De Chelly rooms are in 2 buildings constructed around a grassy courtyard. These rooms back up to one another, with half facing the courtyard and half facing the parking lot. Four De Chelly rooms are in 2 buildings, 1 stone and 1 adobe, situated in the center of the complex. One suite in a stone building has a separate bedroom with 1 king bed, a living room area with a queen sofa bed and a refrigerator, and a full bathroom. We recommend choosing from De Chelly rooms 14 through 18 or 25 through 29, all of which face the courtyard and front on a nice grassy area.

Sacred Canyon Lodge is an exceptionally well-maintained facility offering a relaxing atmosphere where guests sometimes visit from porch chairs directly outside their rooms. The green lawns are immaculate and the building exteriors always appear as if they were recently redone.

Guests from a neighboring room told us during one of our visits that Sacred Canyon Lodge was their favorite stay during a 2-week trip to the Southwest. The lodge cafeteria has an attractive interior with decorative Navajo rugs and offers inexpensive food, including the house specialty Navajo taco, from early morning to evening. The lodge gift shop features a large selection of hand-woven Navajo rugs. The National Park Service visitor center is an easy half-mile walk from the lodge. Interpretive programs at the visitor center include ranger presentations and guided walks. The lodge is near the monument's campground, where evening campfire programs are offered.

Rooms: Doubles, triples, and quads. All rooms have a full private bath.

Wheelchair Accessibility: Four De Chelly rooms are wheelchair accessible.

Reservations: Sacred Canyon Lodge, Rural Route 7, Chinle, AZ 86503. Phone (800) 679-2473; www.sacredcanyonlodge.com. Cancellation must be made 24 hours in advance for a full refund.

Rates: Summer rates (Mar 1 to Oct 31) for 2 people: Adobe rooms ($109); De Chelly rooms ($99); Suite ($169). Each additional person is $7. Winter rate for 2 persons: Adobe rooms ($83); De Chelly rooms ($73); Suite ($99). Rollaway, crib, and each additional person is $7. Special packages are available during winter months. Senior discounts and government rates are offered.

Sacred Canyon Lodge (formerly Thunderbird Lodge) was originally constructed in 1902 as a trading post on the Navajo Reservation. The post served as a store, bank, post office, community meeting place, and courtroom. The owner began offering rooms and food service to accommodate an increasing number of tourists, who came to view the cliff dwellings and spectacular scenery. The present-day cafeteria is in the original trading post, while the building housing the gift shop originally served as home for the trading post's owner.

Location: A short distance inside the park entrance.

Season: Open year-round. Heaviest season is from Apr through Oct, when reservations are advised.

Food: A lodge cafeteria offers basic food at reasonable prices from 6:30 a.m. to 8 p.m. during the summer months, with shorter hours the remainder of the year. Breakfast ranges from $4 to $7, while lunch and dinner cost from $6 to $15.

Facilities: Cafeteria, gift shop, National Park Service visitor center. Three miles west, Chinle has fast-food outlets, service stations, grocery stores, laundries, and a bank.

Activities: Hiking, canyon tours are offered by private guides, National Park Service interpretive programs, horseback riding.

Glen Canyon National Recreation Area
PO Box 1507 • Page, AZ 86040 • (928) 608-6200 • www.nps.gov/glca

Glen Canyon National Recreation Area comprises 1.25 million acres of high desert surrounding and including Lake Powell and its nearly 2,000 miles of shoreline. Lake Powell is formed by Glen Canyon

Dam near Page, Arizona, which backs up the Colorado River for nearly 200 miles. Most activities here, including boating, fishing, and waterskiing, are water-related. Houseboat rentals are offered at several locations. Although nearly all the recreation area is in southern Utah, the most accessible section is along US 89 near Page, Arizona, where the Glen Canyon Dam is located.

Entrance Fee: $15 per vehicle or $7 per person, good for 7 days.

Lodging in Glen Canyon National Recreation Area: Three locations in the recreation area offer guest accommodations. The largest and nicest by far is Lake Powell Resort, 6 miles north of Page, Arizona, on US 89. The resort also has a large marina. Overnight accommodations are offered by the same concessionaire at Bullfrog Resort and Halls Crossing, 2 smaller facilities in the recreation area's Utah

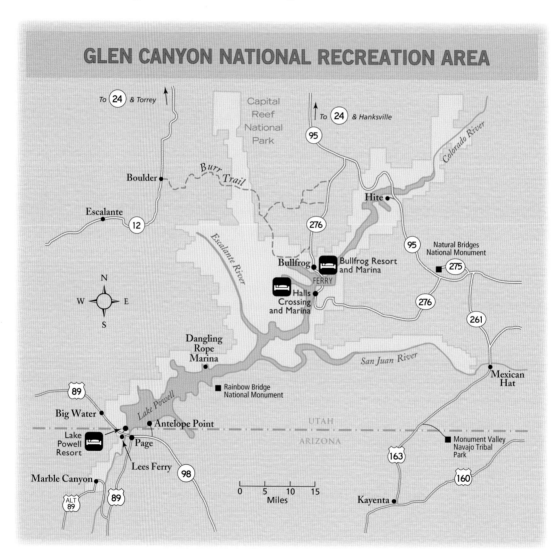

section. Reservations are made using the address and phone number listed for Lake Powell Resort. All the locations permit pets.

Bullfrog Resort and Marina
PO Box 4055 • Lake Powell, UT 84533 • (435) 684-3000

Bullfrog Resort and Marina offers 48 rooms at Defiance House Lodge plus 8 family units. Lodge rooms range from $81 to $177. These are in a stucco building that sits atop a high bluff overlooking Bullfrog Bay. Both the building, constructed in the early 1980s, and rooms within are similar in appearance to those at Lake Powell Resort. Eight freestanding prefabricated family units rent for $172 to $330 depending upon the season. Each unit contain 3 bedrooms, 2 full baths, living room, full kitchen, microwave,

coffeemaker, toaster, dishes and utensils for 8 people, linens, and a television but no telephone. A gas grill and picnic table are outside each unit. All units have heat, air-conditioning, and attractive interiors.

The resort is at Bullfrog Basin on UT 276 on the west side of Lake Powell. A toll ferry at Bullfrog crosses the lake. Bullfrog Resort and Marina offers a restaurant, cocktail lounge, gift shop, liquor store, and gas station. Although the resort is open year-round, the restaurant operates from early Apr through early Nov. It offers cocktails and 3 meals a day (breakfast is seasonal). The marina store sells basic food supplies and beverages. Ranger programs are offered during summer. A National Park Service visitor center adjacent to the resort contains exhibits concerning the Colorado Plateau and the evolution of Glen Canyon plant and animal life. A concessionaire offers half- and full-day boat tours during summer. Boat rental is available.

HALLS CROSSING AND MARINA
PO Box 5101 • Lake Powell, UT 84533 • (435) 684-7000

Halls Crossing and Marina, on UT 276 between Blanding and Hanksville, offers 12 freestanding family units identical to those at Bullfrog Resort and Marina. Halls Crossing has auto service, a marina, and a store with limited supplies. Boat rentals and tours are offered. A toll ferry provides continuation of UT 276. Transportation is available from a small airport 10 miles from Halls Crossing. Rates are the same as at Bullfrog Resort and Marina.

LAKE POWELL RESORT
PO Box 1597 • Page, AZ 86040 • (928) 645-2433 • www.lakepowell.com

Lake Powell Resort offers 348 rooms as part of an attractive marina resort complex on Lake Powell. The resort comprises a registration building plus 8 nearly identical two-story lodge buildings on a peninsula of Lake Powell. The landscaped stucco buildings are finished and decorated in a Southwestern design. The complex also includes 2 swimming pools, a well-equipped fitness room with sauna, gas station, upscale restaurant, coffee bar, lounge, grill, sports shop, and a gift shop. A variety of boat tours can be arranged at the lobby registration desk. Special packages combining a boat tour and lodge room are available. A large marina complex is down the hill from the lodge.

All rooms other than 10 suites are of nearly identical size. The majority have 2 queen beds, while others have a king bed. Each room has heat, air-conditioning, television, telephone, mini-refrigerator, coffeemaker, hair dryer, and a full bath. Second-story rooms each have a private balcony while first-story rooms enjoy a patio. Second-floor rooms require climbing a flight of stairs, as buildings do not have an elevator.

Four categories of rooms are available. The least expensive Traditional rooms on both the first and second floors face the large parking area with views pretty much confined to asphalt, vehicles, and other buildings, especially from first-floor rooms. Marina View rooms face Wahweap Marina and an attractive landscape. Lake View rooms generally offer good views of the lake and surrounding mesas and buttes. Rooms in the 2 newest buildings (the 700 and 800 buildings) have superior balconies and patios that allow guests to more easily enjoy a view of the lake and surrounding landscape without standing. The other 6 buildings have relatively high outside balcony and patio walls that require second-floor guests to stand in order to view the landscape. The lodge offers 6 suites, some of which face the lake while other face the marina. Each is twice the size of a regular room. Suites include a wet bar, a microwave, 2 televisions, a king bed, and a sofa bed in the sitting room. Four Junior Suites are somewhat smaller than a suite and lack a lake view and wet bar.

Lake Powell Resort lodge buildings

Lake Powell Resort is an upscale place to spend one or several nights in a scenic lakeside setting. The type of room to choose is best determined by how you plan to spend your stay. Choose the less-expensive Traditional room if you expect to arrive late and leave early or immediately after a morning boat tour. On the other hand, spend the extra money for a Lake View room if you will be staying a couple of days and plan to spend time enjoying the patio or balcony. Request a second-floor room that provides better views if you don't mind climbing a flight of stairs. Relaxing on a lakeside balcony with a hot cup of coffee and watching the sun rise over the distant mesa was a high point we experienced during one stay here.

The resort is a center for water-based recreation, and we suggest at least one boat tour during your stay. The Rainbow Bridge Cruise provides access to the world's largest natural stone bridge at Rainbow Bridge Natural Monument. This giant water-eroded sandstone arch is even more impressive than we imagined. Boat tour information is available at the resort registration desk.

Houseboat rentals are big business on Lake Powell, a huge body of water where boaters can wander at leisure and anchor in isolation among some of America's most spectacular landscapes of brilliant red canyons, mesas, and buttes. Houseboats ranging from 50 to 75 feet, sleeping from 6 to 22 people, with multiple bedrooms, multiple bathrooms, a complete kitchen with full-size appliances, satellite television, upscale furniture, and a Jacuzzi on the top deck, are available for rent. Two major players in houseboat rentals near Page are Lake Powell Resort and Antelope Point Marina (800-255-5561; antelopepointlakepowell.com). Rentals range from $4,000 to $15,000 per week, depending on season and boat size. Ski boats, kayaks, and deck cruisers are also available.

Rainbow Room restaurant at Lake Powell Resort

Guided fishing excursions and kayaking tours are also available.

Rooms: Doubles, triples, and quads. All rooms have private baths.

Wheelchair Accessibility: Twelve rooms are ADA compliant.

Reservations: Lake Powell Resorts & Marinas, PO Box 56909, Phoenix, AZ 85079. Phone (800) 528-6154 or, from the greater Phoenix area, (602) 278-8888; www.lakepowell.com. A deposit of 1 night's lodging is required. Cancellation notice of 24 hours is required for a refund.

The stunning landscape surrounding Lake Powell Resort has served as a location for more than 40 movies, including 1962's *The Greatest Story Ever Told,* starring Charlton Heston, Carroll Baker, Pat Boone, and Jose Ferrer. *Maverick,* with Mel Gibson, Jodie Foster, and James Garner, was filmed here in 1993. Other movies filmed in the Lake Powell area include *Planet of the Apes, Sergeants Three, The Outlaw Josey Wales, Superman III,* and *Anasazi Moon.* John Travolta stayed in Lake Powell Resort suite 274 for a month during the 1995 filming of *Broken Arrow.*

Rates: Guest room rates vary considerably during the year. Prime time is summer, especially Aug, when rates are generally highest. Winter months typically offer the lowest rates. Traditional ($93–$313); Marina View ($109–$323); Lake View ($124–$344); Junior Suite ($145–$375); Suites ($187–$427). Cribs are free and rollaways are available for a fee. Children under 18 years of age stay free. Discounts are available for advance purchase (no refunds), AAA, and seniors. Check the website for special packages.

Location: On US 89, 6 miles north of Page, Arizona.

Season: Open all year.

Food: A full-service restaurant with a tiered circular dining area and wall of windows offers diners a panoramic view of the lake and surrounding countryside. The restaurant serves breakfast ($7–$15), lunch ($8–$14), and dinner ($16–$33). Alcoholic beverages are available in the restaurant and an adjacent lounge that serves appetizers, salads, sandwiches, and limited dinners. A coffee bar in the lobby serves gourmet coffee and prepackaged foods. A grill with indoor/outdoor dining serves pizza, pasta, hamburgers, sandwiches, salads, and ice cream from Mar through Sept. A floating restaurant is at Wahweap Marina. *The Canyon Princess* offers weekend dinner cruises seasonally depending on demand. Advance reservations are required.

Facilities: Sport shop (with limited groceries), lounge, gift shop, gas station, restaurant, grill, and marina with rentals. Two swimming pools, a hot tub, and a fitness room with a sauna and showers. A coin-operated laundry is at the nearby campground.

Activities: Swimming; walking and hiking; boating; waterskiing; fishing; boat tours.

Pets: A fee of $20 per night is charged per pet. Pets are allowed only in Traditional rooms.

Grand Canyon National Park

PO Box 129 • Grand Canyon, AZ 86023 • (928) 638-7888 • www.nps.gov/grca

Grand Canyon National Park covers 1,904 square miles and is one of our most popular national parks. The Grand Canyon itself is so spectacular that first-time visitors are likely to think they are viewing a painting. The canyon has been created by massive uplift and the cutting effect of the Colorado River, which originates in the Rocky Mountains. The river now flows nearly a mile below the South Rim and even farther below the higher North Rim. Although developed areas of the North and South Rims are separated by only about 10 miles, the distance by road is 215 miles. A daily shuttle service (fee charged) is offered between the South and North Rims. An alternative is the 21-mile Kaibab Trail, which leads from Yaki Point on the South Rim to within 2 miles of Grand Canyon Lodge on the North Rim.

North or South Rim? The 2 sides of the canyon are so different they share little other than the same canyon and river. The more popular South Rim is open year-round with easier access, more facilities, and many more visitors. The South Rim offers more eating facilities, more stores, more places to walk, and more people to bump into. Things move more slowly at the isolated North Rim, where services and visitors are limited. The higher elevation results in cooler temperatures and more trees. Vistas seem more intimate, and fewer people will be standing nearby straining for the same view. The North Rim is closed in winter.

Park Entrance Fee: $25 per vehicle or $12 per person, good for 7 days on both sides of the canyon.

Lodging in Grand Canyon National Park: The park has 8 lodges, 6 on the South Rim, 1 on the canyon floor, and 1 on the North Rim. Alternatives range from small lodge rooms without a private bath, to historic cabins, to rooms in a classic historic hotel. Rates vary depending on where you stay. The wide variation in accommodations means you should have a basic understanding of alternatives when making a reservation. On the South Rim, all lodges except for Yavapai are operated by the same concessionaire, and reservations are made using the same address, telephone number, or website. Reservation information for Yavapai is provided under the Yavapai heading. Reservation information for all other South Rim lodging is in the general information found below. The North Rim lodge is also operated by a different concessionaire and reservation information is available in the North Rim section. The lodges are all very popular, and reservations should, if possible, be made many months in advance. Keep

GRAND CANYON NATIONAL PARK

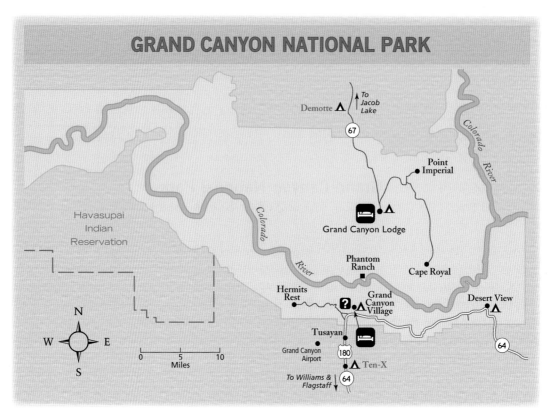

Demotte ▲

To Jacob Lake ↑

67

Colorado River

Point Imperial

Grand Canyon Lodge ▲

Havasupai Indian Reservation

Colorado River

Phantom Ranch

Cape Royal

Hermits Rest

Grand Canyon Village ?▲

Desert View ▲

Tusayan

180

Grand Canyon Airport

Ten-X ▲

To Williams & Flagstaff ↓

64

N
W E
S

0   5   10
Miles

GRAND CANYON VILLAGE

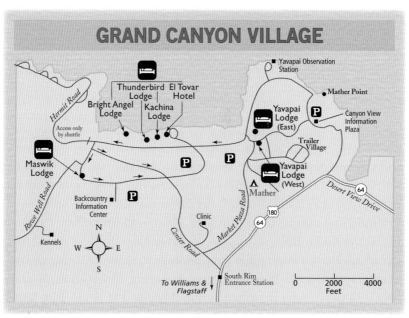

Yavapai Observation Station

Thunderbird Lodge El Tovar Hotel

Bright Angel Lodge

Kachina Lodge

Mather Point

Hermit Road

Access only by shuttle

Yavapai Lodge (East)

P

Canyon View Information Plaza

Maswik Lodge

Trailer Village

P

P

Yavapai Lodge (West)

Mather ▲

64A

Desert View Drive

Rowe Well Road

Backcountry Information Center

P

Market Plaza Road

Clinic

180

64

N
W E
S

Kennels

Center Road

To Williams & Flagstaff ↓

South Rim Entrance Station

0   2000   4000
Feet

in mind that if lodges in the park are full, several motels are a short distance outside the south entrance, 7 miles from Grand Canyon Village and the South Rim.

SOUTH RIM (6 LODGES)

Most visitors reach the South Rim of the Grand Canyon via AZ 180 and AZ 64 from Flagstaff, Arizona. Alternative route AZ 89 to AZ 64, through the east entrance, is longer and slower but offers excellent canyon views. The center of activity is Grand Canyon Village, which offers lodges, cabins, gift shops, restaurants, a large National Park Service visitor center, and the starting point for numerous tours.

The South Rim's 6 lodging alternatives (actually 8 because 2 lodges have separate units) include the classic El Tovar, directly on the rim and the park's top-of-the-line hotel. This historic hotel is in an ideal location, but nearby parking is scarce. Next door are Thunderbird and Kachina, 2 identical lodges with very nice guest rooms in buildings with the appearance of college dorms. North-facing rooms in both units have excellent canyon views. Bright Angel Lodge offers historic cabins with a flavor of the South Rim's history. Parking can be a problem, but Bright Angel's rim cabins with fireplaces are among the best accommodations on the South Rim. Maswik is a large lodging complex with 2 very different sections. Both offer plentiful parking and a nearby cafeteria. Maswik North has nice motel-type rooms a moderate walk from the canyon rim. Maswik South has smaller, less expensive cabins and motel rooms. Yavapai East offers relatively large rooms, while the rooms at Yavapai West are smaller and less expensive. Both sections of Yavapai offer plenty of parking and proximity to Market Plaza, the South Rim's commercial

center. Yavapai is about half a mile from the rim and 1 mile from the South Rim's other hotels and restaurants.

All the lodges are served by a free shuttle that stops at various points in the village. The main shuttle operates year-round and connects with 2 other shuttles that offer service to Hermits Rest on the West Rim and the Kaibab Trailhead on the East Rim. The village area can be quite congested, and it is advisable to park your vehicle and utilize the shuttle. The park newspaper available at entrance stations contains a map illustrating the shuttle routes.

Reservations for South Rim lodging other than Yavapai: Grand Canyon National Park Lodges, Xanterra South Rim, LLS, PO Box 699, 10 Albright St., Grand Canyon, AZ 86023. Phone (888) 297-2757; www.grandcanyonlodges.com. Cost of the first night's lodging is required as a deposit. Cancellation of 48 hours is necessary

for a full refund. Reservations may be made up to 13 months in advance. Try to make reservations 6 or more months in advance for busy summer months, especially for the popular El Tovar. Space is often available on short notice because of cancellations. For same-day reservations phone (928) 638-2631.

Food: A variety of restaurants and snack bars are scattered around Grand Canyon Village. Inexpensive food courts are near the registration areas of Maswik and Yavapai Lodges, while a classy restaurant is in the El Tovar. Excellent steaks are served in the Arizona Room connected to the Bright Angel Lodge. The Bright Angel complex also has a nice restaurant and a combination coffee shop/lounge. A deli/bakery and a full-service grocery store are at Market Plaza.

Facilities: Grand Canyon Village is truly a village. It includes a full-service grocery and general store, post office, full-service bank, laundry, gift shops, emergency medical and dental services, bookstores, ice cream shop, and an array of restaurants. Emergency auto service is available, and gasoline is sold in Tusayan and at Desert View, but not in Grand Canyon Village.

Activities: A variety of activities begin in the village including narrated motor coach tours of various sites along the South Rim. Additional activities, some of which begin outside the village, include river raft excursions, hiking, mule rides to Plateau Point and the canyon floor, horseback riding, and helicopter and airplane trips over the canyon. The National Park Service offers programs on history and geology throughout the day and evening. A fall chamber music festival takes place each Sept. Make Canyon View Information Plaza an early stop.

BRIGHT ANGEL LODGE

Bright Angel Lodge is a complex of a main registration building plus 18 cabins and dormitory-style buildings with 86 guest rooms. Buildings with lodging are separate from but adjacent to the main registration building, which houses a tour desk, gift shop, coffee shop/lounge, steak house, and restaurant. The complex is at the center of South Rim activity and handy to other hotels, eating facilities, and gift shops. This area of Grand Canyon Village is very busy with people and traffic, which creates a hectic setting for individuals and families intent on discovering nature. On the plus side, Bright Angel provides some of the South Rim's least expensive rooms in cabins that retain a flavor of the rim's historic past.

Bright Angel Lodge provides 4 types of rooms. All have heat but no air-conditioning. The least expensive "Standard," or "Lodge," rooms are in Powell Lodge and Buckey Lodge, 2 dormitory-style buildings. Most of the 38 rooms offer 1 double bed, while five have a double plus a single and two have 2 doubles. Some rooms have a full bath, while others have a shower or tub. Likewise, some have a sink and a toilet, while some have only a sink. Common bath and shower facilities are in the hallway. These rooms are particularly popular with hikers who desire a relatively inexpensive place to crash after returning from a trek through the canyon.

One step up are 34 guest rooms in 15 wooden or wood-and-stucco Historic cabins. Some buildings have a single cabin, while others have 2, 3, or 4 cabin-style rooms. Although the exteriors are rustic, interiors are nicely furnished and comfortable. Each cabin has a queen bed, ceiling fan, refrigerator, coffeemaker, hair dryer, television, and telephone. Some have a full bath, while others have a shower only. The most expensive Historic cabins are 15 Rim cabins that offer a canyon view. Each has a full bath and is situated in buildings beside a paved walking trail along the rim. Four have gas fireplaces. Two Rim cabins with fireplaces, 6151 and 6152, provide an outstanding view of the canyon and

Historic Cabin at Bright Angel Lodge

are 2 of our favorite accommodations on the South Rim.

The Bright Angel complex includes 3 suites. A two-room Historic cabin has a living room and a bedroom with 2 queen beds. Red Horse Cabin, an 1890s structure, was brought to the South Rim in 1902 and once saw service as a post office. The cabin was renovated and first offered as a suite in 2012. The Buckey Suite is the top of the line and sits on the canyon rim. It includes 2 large rooms, 1 bedroom with a king bed, and a living room with a large stone gas fireplace. This suite includes a wet bar and 2 televisions. This is by far the nicest and most expensive lodging accommodation in Bright Angel and one of the most desirable lodging facilities on the South Rim.

Bright Angel Lodge is a handy location for all South Rim activities and facilities. Although none of the rooms are directly on the rim and most don't offer a rim view, spectacular vistas of the canyon are only a few steps from any of the buildings. Other dining facilities, including a food court, 2 restaurants, and an elegant dining room, are a reasonable walk from any of the rooms. Parking can be a problem in the busy season. Parking spaces scattered among the cabins can generally be counted on to yield a few empty slots, although they may not be directly outside your room.

> Buckey O'Neill's cabin, constructed in the early 1890s, is the oldest surviving structure on the South Rim. O'Neill, a prospector-turned-tourism promoter, was killed in Cuba while serving as a member of Theodore Roosevelt's Rough Riders. The cabin was preserved by Mary Colter, architect of Bright Angel Lodge, who incorporated the structure into her design for one of the lodge buildings. Today the cabin is rented to guests as the "Buckey Suite."

Rooms: Singles and doubles. One two-room cabin can sleep up to 4, and rollaways are available. All except rooms in the 2 lodge buildings have full private baths. The 2 lodge buildings with Standard rooms have some rooms with private baths. Other rooms use common hallway baths and showers.

Wheelchair Accessibility: Four Historic cabins and 1 Rim cabin (with fireplace) are ADA compliant.

> The original Bright Angel Hotel was constructed in 1895 to serve stagecoach passengers passing through this area. In 1905 the hotel became Bright Angel Camp, which eventually included cabins and an adjoining tent village to serve tourists attracted by the canyon's spectacular scenery. In 1935 the Fred Harvey Company replaced the camp with today's Bright Angel Lodge.

Rates: Standard rooms ($73–$95); Historic cabins ($121–$184); two-room Historic cabin ($190); Rim cabins ($160–$188); Suite ($405). Each additional person is $9 per night. Children 16 and under are free with an adult.

Location: On the South Rim at the center of activity in Grand Canyon Village.

Season: Rooms at Bright Angel Lodge are open year-round.

Food: A full-service restaurant is inside the main registration building and convenient to all the rooms. The restaurant is open for breakfast ($6–$12), lunch ($7–$12), and dinner ($10–$26), and alcoholic beverages are available. The coffee shop/lounge offers specialty coffees and continental breakfast items beginning at 5:30 a.m. Appetizers are available after 11 a.m. The Bright Angel

Fountain, open May through Sept (10 a.m. to 6 p.m.), directly outside the registration building, offers sandwiches, soft drinks, and ice cream. The Arizona Room, offering steaks, poultry, and fish, is attached to the east end of the Bright Angel registration building. It is open for lunch ($8–$12) and dinner ($8–$30).

El Tovar Hotel

El Tovar is the regal hotel of the Grand Canyon's South Rim. Constructed in 1905 by the Santa Fe Railroad to promote the firm's transportation services, the hotel was named after Spanish explorer Pedro de Tovar, who led a 1540 expedition to this area. El Tovar is the type of hotel most people envision when they think about a national park lodge. It is a large wood-and-stone four-story structure that commands a hilltop vista on the canyon rim. The two-story lobby is complete with log beams, a large stone fireplace, and comfortable sofas and chairs for chatting with other guests. Several verandas and a large covered front porch have chairs for relaxing in the early morning or after dinner or an evening walk. A mezzanine with an overlook of the lobby has tables, stuffed chairs, a television, and a piano. Complimentary coffee and tea are provided here each morning for hotel guests. No elevators are in the building, but bell service is available to assist with luggage. A circular drive directly in front of the hotel entrance can be used

The El Torvar sits near the edge of the South Rim

for registration and baggage drop-off, but parking near the hotel is limited.

> The El Tovar has welcomed many famous guests, including Paul McCartney, who visited in fall 2001. With his room booked under a company name, the former Beatle spent the first night on the third floor in room 6474. The hotel upgraded him to the El Tovar Suite for the second and last night of his stay. Late one evening McCartney began playing the piano on the mezzanine until other guests, unaware the famous singer/songwriter was staying at the hotel, complained to the front desk about the noise. Instructed not to reveal that Mr. McCartney was staying at the El Tovar, employees were forced to ask that the famous musician stop playing. If the other guests had only known.

El Tovar offers 78 rooms in 5 classifications. Like many historic hotels, rooms in the same classification are of different sizes and shapes. Rooms are attractively decorated and have heat, air-conditioning, refrigerator, coffeemaker, telephone, television, and a hair dryer. Siting of the hotel results in only a few rooms having a canyon view. The least expensive lodging at El Tovar is a Standard Double with 1 double bed in a small room. Standard Queen rooms are also generally small but offer a variety of bedding options that includes 1 queen, 1 king, 2 doubles, and 2 queens. Deluxe rooms are larger and offer either a king or 2 queen beds with a small sitting area. Two Deluxe rooms, 6463 and 6465, have small balconies with chairs. Suites in the El Tovar are named and decorated to a particular theme. For example, the Zane Grey Suite is decorated western style with movie posters, several of the author's books, and framed first edition book jackets. All 12 suites have a bedroom with either a king or 2 queen beds, a sitting room with chairs and a couch (some convert into a bed), a full bath, and a dressing area. Four View suites each offer stunning canyon views and have a large porch with tables and chairs. The 2 third-floor View suites are smaller but offer more privacy from their porches than second-floor View suites. Eight Nonview suites on the south end of the hotel rent for slightly less than View suites. Four Nonview suites have a porch and 2 have a Jacuzzi (the Roof Garden Suite has both). Porches off the Nonview suites offer some views of the canyon, but not on the scale of the more expensive View suites.

Most of the things you will want or need during a trip to the Grand Canyon are available at or near the El Tovar. The ground floor has gift shops, a lounge, and an elegant dining room. The dining room fits perfectly in a national park. Murals on the walls reflect different Indian tribes, and a number of tables offer diners a view of the rim. A small private dining room with a capacity of up to 10 persons is available at no charge with a 72-hour advance reservation. The lounge has a bar and windows that overlook the canyon. Travel information is available, and tours can be booked at a small tour desk in the lobby. Service at El Tovar is a cut above that found at the

> El Tovar, built at a cost of $250,000, was to be a first-rate lodging facility, and at its completion, in 1905, many considered it the most elegant hotel west of the Mississippi. Designed as a cross between a Swiss chalet and a Norwegian villa, the hotel was constructed of stone and Oregon pine. The building was equipped with a coal-fired steam generator to provide electric lighting, and Santa Fe railroad tank cars brought fresh water from a distance of 120 miles. Water from the tank cars was pumped into a large metal container in the El Tovar's famous cupola, where gravity feed brought it to the rooms. Hens raised here supplied fresh eggs, and a dairy herd provided milk. Fresh fruit and vegetables were grown in greenhouses on the premises.

South Rim's other lodging facilities. For example, room service is available from the El Tovar dining room, and mints are placed on your bed each evening.

Rooms: Singles, doubles, triples, and quads. Some suites can sleep up to 6, and rollaways are available. All rooms have full baths.

Wheelchair Accessibility: Two rooms on the first floor are ADA compliant.

Rates: Standard double ($187); Standard Queen ($227); Deluxe ($305); Suites (Nonview $381–$421; View $465). Rates quoted are for 2 adults.

Each additional person is $14 per night. Children 16 and under are free with an adult.

Location: Center of Grand Canyon Village, directly east of Kachina Lodge and just up the hill from the train depot.

Season: Open year-round.

Food: A dining room off the hotel's lobby serves breakfast ($6–$14), lunch ($8–$17), and dinner ($13–$35). Alcoholic beverages are available, and reservations are recommended for dinner. A lounge offering appetizers and a limited menu is open from 11 a.m. to 11 p.m. Less expensive food service is within easy walking distance.

KACHINA LODGE/THUNDERBIRD LODGE

Kachina Lodge and Thunderbird Lodge are two virtually identical facilities that sit side by side between El Tovar and Bright Angel Lodge. The two-story stone buildings house a total of 104 rooms that, other than window views, are identical. Approximately half the rooms face the rim, while the remainder face the road and parking lot. No registration facilities are in either lodge. Registration for Kachina is at the registration desk of El Tovar Hotel, and registration for Thunderbird is at the registration desk of Bright Angel Lodge.

The exteriors of Kachina and Thunderbird resemble corporate administrative buildings, but the interiors with Southwestern decor have the appearance of fashionable hotel rooms. The interiors of both buildings were renovated in 2012. Each room has central heat and air, small refrigerator, coffeemaker, hair dryer, television, hair dryer, and a full tiled bath. Most rooms have 2 queen beds, while a few offer 1 king. Rollaways are available but result in a crowded room.

Rim-view rooms in both buildings rent for an extra $15 per day and are worth the additional cost. Two medium-size conference rooms in Thunderbird can be reserved.

Thunderbird and Kachina Lodges are in a convenient location at the center of South Rim activity. The central location results in insufficient parking during the busy summer season. No information desk or commercial facilities are in either building, but food service, gift shops,

Thunderbird Lodge on the Grand Canyon's South Rim

and anything else offered at the South Rim are a short walk from any of the rooms at these 2 lodges. Our choice in these lodges is a second-floor rim-view room in Kachina.

Rooms: Singles, doubles, triples, and quads. All rooms have full baths.

Wheelchair Accessibility: Two rooms in Thunderbird and 2 rooms in Kachina are ADA compliant.

Rates: Park-side (nonview) rooms ($195); Canyon-side rooms ($210). An extra $9 per person per night is charged for more than 2 persons. Children 16 and under stay free with an adult.

Location: On the Rim between El Tovar Hotel and Bright Angel Lodge.

Season: Open year-round.

Food: No eating facilities are in either building. Restaurants are within easy walking distance.

Maswik Lodge

Maswik Lodge (named for a Hopi kachina who guards the Grand Canyon) is a complex of modern apartment-type buildings and older cabins that provide 278 rooms in two large areas on each side of a centrally located registration building that houses the registration desk, food court, gift shop, pizza pub, and tour desk. All rooms and cabins have heat, telephone, television, and convenient parking.

Maswik North, the section nearest the canyon, offers rooms with air-conditioning, refrigerator, coffeemaker, hair dryer, and a full bathroom. These are the largest, nicest rooms in Maswik. Rooms have either 2 queens or 1 king bed. The rooms are in a cluster of 12 attractive wood and stone buildings. Most of the structures are two-story buildings (no elevators) with the appearance of an upscale apartment complex. Most rooms run the depth of the building with a front window and either a window or a sliding glass door in back. Those with a sliding door have either a balcony or patio. Eight end rooms are larger than average but rent for the same price as other rooms in this section. The larger rooms include 6803 through 6806 and 6831 through 6834. Try for a larger room or, failing this, a room with a balcony or patio.

Maswik South comprises 6 two-story, motel-type buildings (no elevators) at the end of the complex most distant from the rim. These relatively small rooms have 2 queen-size beds, refrigerator, coffeemaker, hair dryer, wall fan, and a full bathroom, but no balcony or rear window. They rent for considerably less than the more spacious rooms in Maswik North. The Maswik complex also includes 7 quad-style cabin buildings that house a total of 28 rooms, each with a vaulted ceiling, bathroom with a tiled shower, 2 double or queen beds, and a ceiling fan. The cabins offer the least expensive housing on the South Rim. Cabins with 2 queen beds are

The back side of lodge rooms at Maswik South

somewhat larger but rent for the same price as cabins with 2 full beds.

The lodge's location on the west side of the village, across the main road from the rim, is relatively peaceful. Staying in Maswik allows you to avoid the hustle and bustle of vehicles and crowds that roam over the rim area and yet remain within easy walking distance of the rim and most facilities in Grand Canyon Village. You are unable to view the Grand Canyon from the window of your room, but the same disadvantage exists with many rooms in other complexes closer to the rim. Maswik offers plentiful parking, a considerable advantage if you are driving, because other areas of the village are often very crowded.

Rooms: Singles, doubles, triples, and quads. Rollaways are available for all rooms except cabins. All rooms have private baths, most with a combination shower-tub.

Wheelchair Accessibility: Wheelchair-accessible rooms are available in both Maswik North and Maswik South, but not the cabins.

Rates: Cabins ($95); South Unit ($96); North Unit ($186). Additional person: $9. Children 16 and under stay free with an adult.

Location: West side of Grand Canyon Village, approximately a quarter-mile from the canyon rim.

Season: All rooms except cabins (closed in winter) are open year-round.

Many visitors to the Grand Canyon try a mule ride to the bottom of the canyon, where the views are spectacular and the temperature is considerably warmer than on the rim. Those with limited time are likely to choose the 4-mile, 3-hour Canyon Vistas Rim Ride along the East Rim. More adventurous souls may prefer the 2- or 3-day round-trip to Phantom Ranch on the canyon's bottom. The 10-mile ride down Bright Angel Trail takes 5½ hours. After an overnight at Phantom Ranch, the 4½-hour return trip follows the South Kaibab Trail. Advance reservations are required for mule trips and stays at Phantom Ranch. For information and reservations call (888) 297-2757.

Food: An attractive food court in the registration building serves a full breakfast ($4–$10), while lunch and dinner ($5–$12) offerings include Mexican and Asian dishes, hot and cold sandwiches, home-style meals, soups, salads, beer, wine, and ice cream. The food court is within easy walking distance of all Maswik rooms. A pizza pub is also in the building. Additional dining facilities on the rim are within walking distance of Maswik.

Yavapai Lodge is a complex of 16 buildings a distance from a separate registration building that houses a gift shop and large cafe. Yavapai Lodge is on the east side of Grand Canyon Village near Market Plaza about halfway between Yavapai Point and the rim hotels. It is a moderate walk from the rim of the Grand Canyon. Although the lodge is not in the center of Grand Canyon Village activity, free shuttle transportation to various points in the village is available.

Yavapai Lodge, with 358 rooms, is the park's largest lodging complex. The facility is divided into 2 separate complexes containing very different styles of buildings. The newest (constructed in the mid-1970s) and more expensive rooms are in Yavapai East. Six two-story wooden buildings (no elevators) each contain 33 spacious rooms that were renovated in 2011, have a king or 2 queen beds, telephone, television, full bath, heat, air-conditioning, small refrigerator, and a coffeemaker. The buildings have an outside staircase leading to an inside corridor with access to the rooms. A large window in each room provides a nice view of the pine and juniper woodlands in which the buildings sit. None of the rooms have a balcony or patio. The buildings, which sit well back from large parking areas, have the appearance of a nice apartment complex.

Ten buildings in less-expensive Yavapai West were constructed in the late 1960s and remodeled in 2010. These one-story brick buildings have a motel appearance, but the remodeled interiors are quite attractive. Each room has a full bath, heat, 2 queen beds, telephone, flatscreen television, small refrigerator, coffeemaker, hair dryer, and a ceiling fan. The rooms do not have air-conditioning. The rooms are considerably smaller than those in Yavapai East. Plenty of parking is in front of the buildings that are widely spaced in 2 large circles and surrounded by woodlands. Rooms in buildings 1 through 6 have a front window, which seems to result in a darker interior. Rooms in buildings 7 through 10 have back windows that provide more light and a pleasant outside view.

Yavapai is convenient to the Canyon View Information Plaza and to Market Plaza, a large commercial complex with a post office, bank, and general store with a large grocery selection. Meals are available at a cafe connected to the registration building and at a deli in the general store. The major downside of staying at Yavapai is that the distance from rim facilities will require you to take the shuttle or walk a considerable distance each time you visit the main area of the village. If you stay in Yavapai East, try to get into 1 of the first 2 buildings that are nearest Market Plaza and the shuttle stop.

Rooms: Doubles, triples, and quads. Rollaways are available. All rooms have a full bath.

Wheelchair Accessibility: Yavapai East has 4 first-floor rooms that are ADA compliant and a few have roll-in showers.

Lodge building at Yavapai East

Reservations: Phone (877) 404-4621 or visit www.theyavapailodge.com. A deposit of the first night's lodging is required. Visit the Yavapai website for cancellation information.

Rates: Yavapai East ($175); Yavapai West ($141). Rates quoted are for 2 adults. Each additional person is $9 per night. Children 16 and under stay free with an adult.

Location: On the east side of Grand Canyon Village, across from Market Plaza.

Season: Mid-Mar through Nov. Rooms are also available seasonally at Thanksgiving and Christmas.

At the bottom of Grand Canyon, Phantom Ranch provides food and overnight accommodations for hikers, rafters, and mule riders. Cabin accommodations are included with 2- or 3-day mule tours, while dormitory-style lodging and a limited number of cabins are available to backpackers. The ranch was originally constructed in 1922, and dormitories were added in 1976. Space is limited, so make reservations (phone 888-297-2757) well in advance for both lodging and food service.

Food: A large and attractive cafe connected to the registration building serves breakfast ($4–$10), lunch/dinner ($5–$16). Food selections include

Many visitors to Grand Canyon National Park decide to take an air tour of the canyon. Several airline and helicopter companies in the town of Tusayan and at the Grand Canyon Airport offer scenic canyon flights. The helicopter tours are generally shorter and somewhat more expensive than flights in fixed-wing aircraft but add extra excitement to the trip. Most firms offer several types of tours of various lengths. Any of the tours presents a very different perspective of the Grand Canyon. Prices for helicopter tours begin at about $170 per person.

salads, pasta, pizza, hamburgers, and chicken. Beer and wine are available. The general store has a deli that serves breakfast items, soups, salads, chicken, pizza, and large sandwiches. A large selection of grocery items, beer, wine, and other alcoholic beverages is available in the general store.

North Rim

Visiting the Grand Canyon's North Rim is an entirely different experience compared with a visit to the South Rim. You will actually feel you are in a different park, except, of course, for the Grand Canyon itself, which is the common thread dividing these 2 sections. With fewer visitors and facilities, plus a relatively short season, the North Rim provides a very different atmosphere. It is more peaceful and relaxing than the South Rim. The North Rim offers only a single lodge and the facilities are operated by a different concessionaire than South Rim facilities.

Grand Canyon Lodge
North Rim, AZ 86052 • (928) 638-2611 • www.grandcanyonforever.com

Grand Canyon Lodge is the only lodging facility at Grand Canyon National Park's North Rim. The lodge consists of a classic main lodge that houses the registration desk, lobby,

and dining room, plus more than 100 cabin units scattered along a peninsula of the Kaibab Plateau. The peninsula is surrounded by 2 spectacular canyons that snake off the Grand Canyon,

Pioneer Cabin at Grand Canyon North Rim

which can be viewed at the tip of the peninsula. All the rooms are in buildings that are separate from, but within walking distance of, the main lodge, which itself has no overnight rooms.

The North Rim lodge was constructed in 1936, after the original burned. This spectacular setting has been blessed with a nearly perfect building. It was designed by Gilbert Stanley Underwood, who also served as architect for the Ahwahnee at Yosemite National Park and the lodge at Bryce Canyon National Park. The U-shaped building, constructed of massive limestone walls and timber beams, is situated on the canyon rim near Bright Angel Point. Large windows in the beautiful high-ceilinged dining room offer diners scenic vistas of the canyon. A large sunroom just off the registration area

provides canyon views through 3 huge windows. A veranda next to the sunroom offers a place to enjoy equally spectacular views from chairs and benches scattered along the terrace. The building has 2 huge stone fireplaces, 1 in the sunroom and the other outside on the veranda. The lodge also houses a tour desk, deli, gift shop, post office, and coffee shop/saloon. An auditorium is available for evening programs.

More than 100 rustic log cabins constructed in the 1920s provide the majority of the 218 rooms for visitors to the North Rim. Forty rooms are in 2 motel-style buildings. The 4 basic types of rooms each have heat, telephone, coffeemaker, hair dryer, a private bath, and carpeted floors, but no air-conditioning (you don't need it) or television. All rooms with the exception of Frontier units have a refrigerator. Fifty-six Western cabins, the largest accommodations on the North Rim, are constructed 2 or 4 to a building. Each Western cabin has a finished interior, vaulted log-beam ceiling, and a private front porch with rocking chairs. These cabins have 2 queen beds, a full tiled bath, small dressing area, and gas fireplace. Four Western cabins sit directly on the North Rim and rent for $10 extra per day. Western cabins 310, 320, and 332 offer a nice view and rent for the regular rate.

Eighty-three Frontier cabins are constructed 2 units to a building. Each Frontier cabin has 1 double and 1 single bed and a bath with a shower. These cabins have an unfinished log interior, including a vaulted log ceiling, and are relatively small, so that beds consume most of the interior space. The bathroom is also quite small. Forty Pioneer cabins each have 2 bedrooms, 1 on each side of a central bathroom with a shower. One bedroom has a bunk bed, a futon, plus a sink, and the other bedroom has a queen bed. The Pioneer cabins farthest from the road (and parking) offer the best views. These are classified as Pioneer Rim cabins and cost $10 extra per night. The Pioneers have been renovated over the last decade and are quite nice. Frontier and Pioneer cabins do not have a porch or deck.

Two motel-type buildings with 40 rooms sit farthest from the main lodge and dining room. Rooms in each building back up to one another and each has a small front window and an outside bench beside the door. Rooms have a queen bed, ceiling fan, and small bathroom. These Motel rooms are of modest size and have a relatively dark interior. Rooms on the back side (410 through 420 and 431 through 440) provide the best views. Rooms 415, 416, 432, and 433 sit on the back side and are considerably larger than other rooms in these 2 buildings. End rooms 400, 409, 410, 420, 421, 430, 431, and 440 have windows on 2 sides and provide for a brighter interior. These rooms are also a little larger than most other rooms in these buildings. Rooms in the motel units have more room than Frontier cabins but are considerably smaller than Pioneer or Western cabins.

Western cabins offer a front porch, gas fireplace, larger interior, and a better location making one of these a good choice for a couple. They are also the units in greatest demand, so reservations should be made early. Pioneer cabins offer 2 bedrooms and have more space than a Western cabin, so these would be our choice for lodging on the North Rim. They are certainly the best choice for families with children. We stayed in a Pioneer during our last stay and utilized the second bedroom as a convenient place to park luggage and relax on the futon.

Limited short-term parking for registration or unloading and loading is near the lodge, but most lodging units are some distance from regular parking. Getting to the motel units involves descending 45 steps from the parking lot to the building. In addition, visitors (other than handicapped) are not permitted to drive to the main lodge that houses the registration desk. You should park in any open spot, walk down the road to the main lodge, and check in at the registration desk before removing luggage from your vehicle. Once you determine the location of your assigned unit, you may want to move your vehicle closer to your assigned cabin. Porters are available to assist with luggage.

The North Rim of the Grand Canyon is a special place. It is isolated, intimate, and unique. You may know of many friends who have visited the Grand Canyon, but it was most likely not the North Rim. The lodging facilities are rustic, but well maintained and a good fit for this location. The beauty of the lodge's dining room is surpassed only by that of Yosemite's Ahwahnee. On

Western Cabin at Grand Canyon North Rim

several stays we have risen early, fixed a cup of coffee, and walked to the lodge veranda to watch the rising sun paint the canyon with shades of orange. Each time there were no more than half a dozen people with whom to share such a special experience.

Rooms: Doubles, triples, and quads in the Western cabins. Doubles and triples in the Frontier cabins. Pioneer cabins can sleep up to 6. Doubles only in the motel units. Rollaways are available for the Western cabins and some motel units. All rooms have a private bath, although only Western cabins offer a combination shower-tub.

Wheelchair Accessibility: Four Western cabins, 2 Pioneer cabins, and 2 Frontier cabins are wheelchair accessible although they are some distance from disabled parking.

Reservations: Forever Resorts, 7501 E. McCormick Pkwy., Scottsdale, AZ 85258. Phone (877) 386-4383 or visit www.grandcanyonforever.com. One night's room charge is required as a deposit. Cancellations must be made at least 72 hours prior to scheduled arrival for a full refund.

Rates: Western cabins ($182); Western Rim cabins ($192); Motel units ($124); Frontier cabins ($132); Pioneer cabins, Standard View ($173); Pioneer cabins Rim View ($183). Rates are for 2 adults. Each additional person is $10 per night. Children 15 and under stay free. Rollaways available for Western cabins and some Motel rooms are $10.

Location: Forty miles south on AZ 67 from the town of Jacob Lake, Arizona.

Season: Mid-May to mid-Oct.

Food: An excellent restaurant with spectacular views offers 3 meals a day. Breakfast ($6 to $13 with a buffet available most mornings, $15), lunch ($10 to $17 and a buffet, $15), and dinner ($12 to $32). Mixed drinks, beer, and an extensive wine list are available. An evening Grand Canyon Cookout Experience ($30 per adult) offers guests a chance to ride a steam train tram to Outfitter Station for a meal and entertainment. The deli serves salads, sandwiches, pasta, pizza, ice cream, and beverages until closing at 9 p.m. The saloon offers gourmet coffee and fresh-baked bakery items beginning at 5:30 a.m. Alcoholic beverages are served in the saloon beginning at 11:30 a.m. Food from the deli may be taken into the saloon. Limited groceries, prepackaged sandwiches, and beverages are in the general store at the campground 1 mile away.

Facilities: A gift shop, information desk, post office, full-service restaurant, coffee shop/saloon, and deli are at the main lodge. A general store, bike rentals, laundry facilities, and combination gas/outfitters station are 1 mile north at the campground.

Activities: Hiking, mule rides, bicycling, daily interpretive programs, and guided hikes and nature walks. Several short- and intermediate-length trails originate near the lodge. Information about mule rides is available by calling (435) 679-8665 or visiting www.canyonrides.com.

Construction of the original Grand Lodge using Mormon craftsmen from surrounding towns began in 1927. The two-story lodge was completed at a cost of $350,000 in June 1928 and dedicated 3 months later. One year later the rustic North Rim Inn was constructed 1 mile north to offer less expensive accommodations. The second inn is now utilized as the camp store. Grand Lodge burned in September 1932, and construction of the current one-story lodge commenced on the same site in June 1936. It was completed 1 year later. Pictures of the original Grand Lodge are in the lodge Sunroom. Only a couple of cabins were lost to the fire. The current motel units were built later as employee housing. Interior corridors were later changed into small bathrooms when it was decided to convert employee housing into guest lodging.

ARKANSAS

State Tourist Information
(800) 628-8725 | www.arkansas.com

Buffalo National River

402 North Walnut St., Ste. 136 • Harrison, AR 72601 • (870) 365-2700 • www.nps.gov/buff

Buffalo National River is one of the most scenic, unpolluted, and undeveloped free-flowing rivers remaining in the lower 48 states. The 135-mile river flows eastward through forested hill country dominated by oaks and hickories. The river is especially popular for canoeing and floating. The park is in northwestern Arkansas in the Ozarks, across a 3-county area. The nearest sizable community is Harrison, Arkansas.

Park Entrance Fee: No charge.

Lodging at Buffalo National River: A single lodging facility is inside the national park boundaries. Buffalo Point Concessions offers cabins and a restaurant at Buffalo Point, 20 miles south of Yellville via AR 14 and an access road. Additional lodging facilities are in communities along the river but outside the park boundaries.

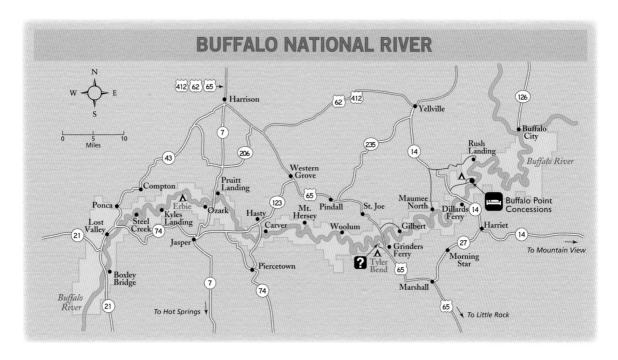

BUFFALO NATIONAL RIVER

BUFFALO POINT CONCESSIONS
2261 Hwy. 268 East • Yellville, AR 72687 • (870) 449-6206 • www.buffalopoint.net

Buffalo Point is a small lodging complex comprised of an office building, restaurant, and 10 wooden structures containing 17 cabins and lodge rooms. The complex is on a high ridge about a mile and a half from Buffalo National River. The restaurant sits on a bluff, and diners are treated to a view of the scenic river that snakes through the valley below. Lodging units are scattered along a road in a heavily wooded area. Four lodge units and 2 modern cabins offer an excellent view of the river. Other units are in a wooded area and do not offer a river view. The restaurant, open Memorial Day to Labor Day, is a short drive or moderate walk from most of the lodging units. A small National Park Service visitor center with exhibits and information is a short walk from the lodging office.

Three types of lodging units are available. Each has air-conditioning and a private bathroom with a shower. All offer a full kitchen with refrigerator, oven, stove, microwave, coffeemaker, and toaster. Cookware, dishes, and utensils are supplied. Units do not have a television or telephone. A picnic table and grill are outside each unit. The units vary in size, but each is set up to sleep from 5 to 7 people.

Five freestanding Rustic cabins with wooden floors and beamed ceilings were built by the Civilian Conservation Corps (CCC) in the 1940s. Each cabin has a large screened porch with 2 single beds, a separate bedroom with a full bed, and a large living area with a full bed, table, and chairs. These are the only cabins with a fireplace (firewood provided without charge), which serves as the only source of heat. Rustic cabins are nearest the office but most distant from the restaurant.

Eight Modern cabins were constructed in the 1960s as duplex units. Six of these sit side-by-side on a hill in the middle of the complex,

Buffalo Point Rustic Cabin

while the other 2 are on a bluff at the far end of the road. Modern cabins have larger windows with brighter interiors than Rustic cabins. Each Modern cabin has wooden floors, electric heat, a separate bedroom with a full bed, and a living area with a full bed, futon, table, chairs, and a nice back deck. The living area has ample space for the rollaway that is kept in a closet. Especially popular are cabins 13 and 14 with decks that provide a view of the Buffalo River. These 2 units are within easy walking distance of the restaurant.

The least expensive units are 4 Lodge rooms in a CCC-constructed building that sits on a bluff above the river. They are smaller in size than the cabins and do not have a separate bedroom. Each unit has a kitchen, electric heat, double bed, futon, table with chairs, and a shared deck that spans the back of the building. End units A and D are larger, have brighter interiors (due to a side window), and rent for the same price as units B and C. The 4 Lodge units offer good river views and are near the restaurant.

Buffalo Point is in a rural setting that offers nature, solitude, a beautiful river, inexpensive dining, and friendly people. We prefer Modern cabin units 13 or 14 for a party of 3 or more. The view from the deck is outstanding, and the more isolated location at the end of the road offers more privacy than other units in the complex. One person or a couple might consider Lodge units A or D, which offer good river views and are a little less expensive than the Rustic or Modern cabins. If an indoor fireplace is important, choose one of the Rustic cabins, preferably cabin unit 1, which offers more privacy. Our last choice would be Lodge units B and C, which have small, dark interiors.

Don't forget to bring a book and hiking shoes. Canoe rentals are available just outside the park.

Rooms: Lodge units can accommodate 2 occupants, while cabins can hold 5 to 7 people. All units have a private bath with a shower but no tub. Each unit has a full kitchen with utensils supplied.

Wheelchair Accessibility: One modern cabin is fully wheelchair accessible.

Reservations: Buffalo Point Concessions, 2261 Hwy. 268 East, Yellville, AR 72687. Phone (870) 449-6206. One night deposit required. Twenty days' cancellation notice required for a refund, less a $25 fee for cancellations or changes.

Rates: Rustic cabins ($86); Modern cabins ($86); Lodge units ($80). Rates are quoted for 2 adults. Extra persons are $10 each. Children 4 years and younger are free. Rates are reduced during winter.

Location: Twenty miles south of Yellville, Arkansas, on AR 14 and a paved access road.

Season: The 4 Lodge units and 4 Modern cabins, including those with a river view, are open year-round. The other cabins are open from Mar through Thanksgiving.

The last of the 6 Rustic cabins at Buffalo Point constructed by the Civilian Conservation Corps (CCC) were completed in 1942 as part of Buffalo River State Park. CCC workers quarried the rock, finished the lumber, and crafted the furniture used in the construction. The cabins retain their original design and most of the original material. They were placed on the National Register of Historic Places in 1988. Cabin 1, completed in 1940, is the only one of the 6 Rustic cabins that was built using log construction.

Food: A full-service restaurant serves breakfast ($4–$6), lunch ($3–$7), and dinner ($7–$13) from Mother's Day weekend through Labor Day. Groceries and restaurants are available in Yellville. No alcoholic drinks are available at Buffalo Point.

Facilities: Restaurant, National Park Service visitor center.

Activities: Hiking, canoeing, horseback riding, guided hunting and fishing trips. Daily ranger-led walks and programs during summer. The old mining town of Rush is nearby.

Pets: Pets are permitted at a nonrefundable fee of $30.

CALIFORNIA

State Tourist Information

(877) 225-4367 | www.visitcalifornia.com

Death Valley National Park

PO Box 579 • Death Valley, CA 92328 • (760) 786-3200 • www.nps.gov/deva

Death Valley National Park comprises 3.3 million acres of harsh desert environment that includes the lowest point in North America. The park features a desert mansion, ruins of mining towns, abandoned borax works, mountain peaks, volcanic craters, and some of the highest summer temperatures you have ever encountered. The visitor center is at Furnace Creek. The majority of the park is in southeastern California. The main road, CA 190, provides access to many of the major features and activity areas.

Park Entrance Fee: $20 per vehicle or $10 per person, good for 7 days.

Lodging in Death Valley National Park: Four separate lodging facilities provide accommodations that range from exquisite and expensive to quaint and moderately priced. We have stayed in all 4

DEATH VALLEY NATIONAL PARK

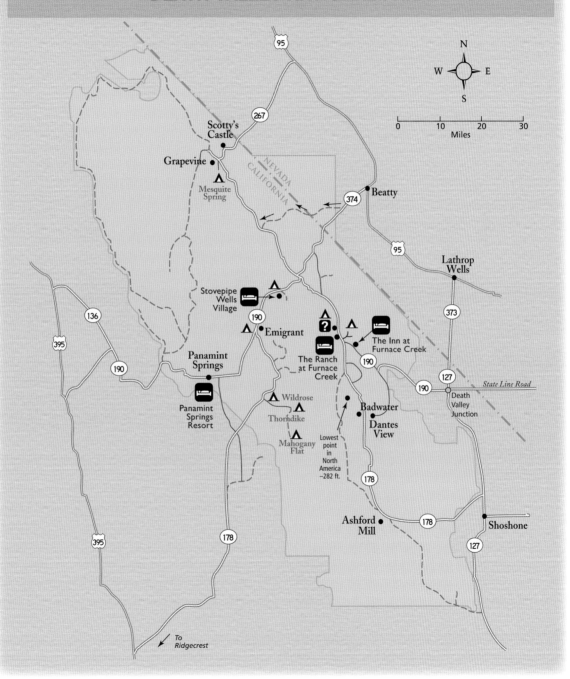

locations, and each provides a different desert experience. The Inn at Furnace Creek allows guests to experience the desert in luxury, with first-rate rooms plus excellent food and service. Nearby, the Ranch at Furnace Creek offers motel-type rooms in a desert oasis. This facility is less expensive and largely appeals to families and tour groups. Stovepipe Wells is isolated, with little surrounding vegetation, and provides a true desert experience. Panamint Springs Resort offers relatively small rooms in a location that is amazingly isolated. An evening sitting on the front porch nursing a cold beer while viewing the desert and distant mountains is an experience worth remembering. Panamint Springs sits approximately 2,000 feet higher than the 3 other lodging facilities, allowing guests to avoid some of the worst daytime heat.

THE INN AT FURNACE CREEK
PO Box 1 • Death Valley, CA 92328 • (760) 786-2345 • www.furnacecreekresort.com

The Inn at Furnace Creek

The Inn at Furnace Creek is one of the most elegant hotels in a national park, and it is certainly one of the most unusual lodging facilities in the country. Located in one of the country's most inhospitable environments, the AAA-rated, 4-diamond historic inn retains its original grandeur. The inn is built of stone and adobe in a Mission-style architecture. It sits on a hill overlooking a desolate but starkly beautiful desert that encompasses both the lowest point in North America (282 feet below sea level) and the Panamint Mountain Range, which soars to more than 11,000 feet. The inn is on the back side of an oasis of green grass and palm trees complete with stone walkways, a warm stream that feeds the pool and ponds on a terraced hillside. A large conference room with stone walls, beamed ceiling, and large windows is flanked by stone fireplaces.

The inn offers 66 upscale rooms of various shapes and sizes on 4 floors. Each room has heat, air-conditioning, ceiling fan, refrigerator, television, coffeemaker, hair dryer, and a telephone with data port and voice mail. Rooms are rented in 5 categories according to size, view, and amenities.

Eight relatively small Standard Hillside rooms on the back side of the hotel offer no view and are the least expensive accommodations. These rooms have 1 king bed and some bathrooms have a shower only. Thirty-four Standard Terrace rooms are slightly larger and offer varying views depending upon location. All 14 Standards in the main lodge building have a king bed, and those on the first or second floor have a terrace or deck. Twenty Standards on a U-shaped terrace above the pool have a double bed plus a twin bed. Several have connecting doors and some bathrooms have a shower, but no tub. Sixteen larger Deluxe rooms with a deck or terrace have either a king or 2 double beds. Five large Luxury Spa rooms have a spa tub, a deck or terrace, and either 2 double beds or 1 king bed. Two two-room suites each have a living room with a sofa bed plus a bedroom with a king bed. The suites have access to a very large deck.

An unusual room is the pool bungalow that is on the second floor of a separate building with a private outside staircase to the swimming pool. The room has stone walls and a beamed ceiling.

The Inn at Furnace Creek is perfect for a pampered and relaxing vacation. An attractive, hot-spring-fed swimming pool, 4 lighted tennis courts, an exercise room, a men's and a women's sauna, a nearby 18-hole golf course, horseback riding, and hiking are all available for sports-minded visitors. An upscale dining room serves 3 meals a day. A free shuttle connects the inn with nearby Ranch at Furnace Creek and the National Park Service visitor center.

Rooms: Doubles, plus a limited number of triples and quads. All rooms have a private bath.

Wheelchair Accessibility: One Standard Terrace room is wheelchair accessible. An elevator operates from the hotel's first floor to the third floor, where the room is located. The registration area, gift shop, and restaurant are also on the third floor.

Reservations: Furnace Creek Resort, PO Box 1, Death Valley, CA 92328. Phone central reservations (800) 236-7916 or on-site (760) 786-2345; www.furnacecreekresort.com. Cost of the first night's lodging is required as a deposit. Cancellation of 48 hours required for full refund.

The Inn at Furnace Creek was built by the Pacific Coast Borax Company, as part of what proved an unsuccessful attempt to save the firm's railroad following closure of the mines. Shoshone and Paiute working at the Ranch at Furnace Creek made adobe for the original inn that opened on February 1, 1927, 3 months after Bob Eichbaum's bungalows commenced business at Stove Pipe Wells. The first wing of 12 rooms, a dining room, and a kitchen were completed in 2 months. The 20-room Terrace Wing was added during 1927 and 1928, and a swimming pool, tennis courts, golf course, and airfield were completed a year later. The 20-room north wing was added in 1930. The female manager and staff from Yellowstone's Old Faithful Inn were brought down to manage the inn during the winter.

Rates: Standard Hillside ($325–$350); Standard Terrace ($345–$390); Deluxe ($365–$420); Luxury Spa ($425–$460); Suite and pool bungalow ($450–$470). Two- and 3-night minimums and higher rates apply during holidays and blackout periods. Rates are for two persons. A resort fee of $12 per room per night is added. Each additional person is $20; cribs and rollaways $20. Children 16 and under stay free. Senior discounts are available. Check the web for special packages.

Location: The inn is 120 miles northwest of Las Vegas and 300 miles northeast of Los Angeles.

Season: Open mid-Oct to Mother's Day (May).

Food: An elegant dining room with a scenic view of the Panamint Mountains offers a complete menu for breakfast ($9–$16), lunch ($14–$22), and dinner ($22–$48). Afternoon tea ($17) is served in the lobby. The Lobby Bar, open daily from noon to 11 p.m., serves espresso, liquor, wine, and light hors d'oeuvres. A bar at the end of the pool serves beverages and snacks. Less expensive restaurants are at nearby Ranch at Furnace Creek.

Facilities: The inn has a large, hot-spring-fed swimming pool (constant 82° Fahrenheit), a men's and a women's sauna, massage therapy, 4 lighted tennis courts, restaurant, lobby-bar, gift shop, and 4 meeting, banquet, and private event rooms. The resort has a concrete airstrip with lights for private planes. Transportation from the airstrip is available (contact the inn in advance). A gas station, general store, and bicycle rentals are at the Ranch at Furnace Creek. Jeep rentals are rented seasonally across from the inn.

Activities: Swimming, tennis, and golf (year-round); horseback riding, group hayrides, Jeep tours, bicycle tours, and carriage rides.

PANAMINT SPRINGS RESORT

PO Box 395 • Ridgecrest, CA 93556 • (775) 482-7680 • www.panamintsprings.com

Panamint Springs Resort is a small facility that, if not for the surrounding landscape, causes you to wonder if you are in Key West, Florida. Walk in the front door of the main building that houses the bar and dining room and you might expect to see Ernest Hemingway sitting on a stool at the bar made from a large slab of walnut supported by redwood roots. Most likely, he would be sampling one of the 150 varieties of beer and ale offered at the resort. A large porch wraps around the building, with the front and east sides serving as an outside dining area. Four wooden shake-roofed buildings directly behind the main building house guest rooms.

The resort offers 14 motel-type rooms and 1 two-bedroom cottage. The motel rooms are of varying size, but all are relatively small. Room rates are based on the number of beds in a room, not the number of occupants, although the number of occupants per room is limited. Rooms with 1 bed generally have a queen, although 1 has a king. Rooms with more than 1 bed have a queen plus either 1 or 2 double beds. Each room has heat, master cooling, a ceiling fan, and a private

The best-known man-made structure in Death Valley National Park is Scotty's Castle, which lies just inside the park's north entrance. This unique rock building, which cost nearly $2 million, was constructed in the 1920s as a vacation retreat for Albert Johnson, a partner and lifelong friend of Walter Scott, alias Death Valley Scotty, for whom the castle is named. Fifty-minute tours, conducted by Park Service rangers in period clothing, are offered daily from 9 a.m. to 5 p.m. Waits of an hour or two can be expected during busy times of the year. The castle includes a bookstore, a gift shop, an exhibit room, and a snack bar.

bathroom with a shower. Two rooms have tubs. Only the cottage has a television.

The cottage unit with a covered front porch has a living room with a television, a full bathroom, a refrigerator, a table and 4 chairs, but no cooking facilities. One large bedroom has a queen bed, and a second, smaller bedroom has a bunk bed with a double bottom and single top.

Panamint Springs Resort is a small, quaint facility where you will think you are a thousand miles from civilization, which isn't far from the truth. The resort generates its own electricity, and water is piped from a spring 5 miles away. The place isn't fancy, but it is fun and unique. The dining room serves homemade food with Angus beef hamburgers and gourmet pizzas being the house specialties.

Rooms: Two people in 1 queen or king bed to 6 people in rooms with 3 beds. Rooms have a private bath with a shower. The cottage and 1 guest room have a tub.

Wheelchair Accessibility: No wheelchair-accessible rooms are available. A ramp provides wheelchair access to the restaurant.

Reservations: Panamint Springs Resort, PO Box 395, Ridgecrest, CA 93556. Phone (775) 482-7680; www.panamintsprings.com. A credit card is required to guarantee a room. Cancellation of 48 hours is required. Lodge management prefers that travelers make reservation via the Internet because of limited phone service at the lodge. For questions e-mail the lodge at info@deathvalley.com.

Rates: Prices vary depending upon the season. One queen bed ($79–$99); 1 king bed

Lodging facilities at Panamint Springs Resort

($84–$104); 2 beds ($94–$114); 3 beds ($109–$129); cottage ($149–$169). Children under 12 are free if no additional bedding is required.

Location: The resort is on the western edge of Death Valley on CA 190, 48 miles east of Lone Pine. GPS devices are not always accurate with the given address.

Season: Open all year. The busiest season is mid-July through Aug.

Food: The dining room serves a breakfast buffet ($10), lunch and dinner ($10–$30). Beer, wine, and cocktails are available.

Facilities: Dining room, bar, and gas station with a limited selection of food and gift items, plus hand-scooped milkshakes and ice cream cones. An ATM is available.

Activities: Hiking, 4-wheel off-road driving, bird-watching, sightseeing.

Pets: Pet fee is $5 per night per pet.

Backside of Deluxe Units at The Ranch at Furnace Creek

The Ranch at Furnace Creek is the family alternative in an oasis area about 1.5 miles from the inn. The Ranch offers 224 rooms in 3 classifications in buildings that sit amid tall palm and tamarisk trees, with an 18-hole Pete Dye golf course at one end. All the rooms went through an extensive remodeling that was completed in 2010. Inside the gate and to the left in a western-style wooden building are a general store, saloon, and 2 restaurants. Lodging is in 6 one- and two-story motel-type buildings behind the restaurant, plus 14 duplex wood cabins near the registration building. All buildings with guest rooms are within walking distance of the store and restaurants. All rooms have heat, air-conditioning, television, refrigerator, coffee-maker, hair dryer, ceiling fan, and a telephone. Four two-story wooden buildings constructed in the 1960s house 164 Standard rooms. These buildings do not have elevators. Entrances at each end of the building provide room access through interior corridors. Second-floor rooms each have a balcony, while bottom-floor rooms have a patio. Standard rooms each have 2 queen beds. Half the 164 rooms face either the golf course or a grassy area surrounding the swimming pool. Rooms on the opposite side of each building face one another. All Standard rooms rent for the same price, so try for one with a view toward the golf course. These include even-numbered rooms in the 600 and 800 buildings and odd-numbered rooms in the 700 and 900 buildings.

Two one-story wooden buildings contain 32 Deluxe rooms, each with a large window and French door on the back side that opens to a patio and large grassy area near the swimming pool. Most of these rooms have 2 queen beds, are larger than Standard rooms, and have parking directly in front.

Twenty-eight Cabin units are constructed 2 to a building. Each has either 1 queen or 1 double plus a twin bed and a bath with a shower. The Cabin units with 2 beds are slightly larger than units with a single bed. They are nicely done but quite a bit smaller than Deluxe or Standard rooms.

The Ranch at Furnace Creek provides all you will need for an enjoyable stay in Death Valley. The golf course, the Borax Museum with interesting displays, and the National Park Service visitor center are within walking distance. For special meals take the free shuttle or drive to the nearby inn (mid-Oct to Mother's Day). Play golf or hike in the morning, enjoy a swim in the afternoon, have a beer in the saloon, take a nap, and walk to a restaurant without ever getting in your vehicle. Some activities are easier to handle in the spring, winter, and fall than during the summer heat.

Furnace Creek's golf course, situated 214 feet below sea level, qualifies as the world's lowest grass golf course. The course was opened in 1931 and, during the early years, closed each summer when it was leased to a cattle rancher. A small flock of sheep kept the course mowed during winter months. The 6,215-foot course was renovated in 1997 by Pete Dye. Although the course lies in the middle of a desert, 9 of its 18 holes have water hazards.

Rooms: Doubles, triples, and quads. All rooms have a private bath with a combination shower-tub except the cabins, which have only a shower.

Wheelchair Accessibility: Two Deluxe rooms and 4 Standard rooms are wheelchair accessible.

Water, the lifeblood for development in the Furnace Creek area, flows from 2 nearby hot water springs. The springs attracted forty-niners to camp here during their rush for riches and even resulted in ranchers giving this area a try. The water now flows from the springs to a holding tank that supplies the Inn at Furnace Creek, and eventually, the Ranch at Furnace Creek and the golf course. The National Park Service sells the water to the resort for irrigation and drinking water, as well as for the 2 swimming pools.

Reservations: Furnace Creek Resort, PO Box 1, Death Valley, CA 92328. Phone central reservations (800) 236-7916 or visit www.furnace creekresort.com. Cost of the first night's lodging is required as a deposit. Cancellation of 48 hours required for full refund.

Rates: Cabins ($142–$169); Standard ($172–$199); Deluxe ($192–$219). A resort fee of $12 per room per night is added. The higher rates apply during some holidays and special events. A 3-night minimum stay is required during New Year's. Rates quoted are for 2 adults. Children under 16 stay free when accompanied by an adult. Each additional person is $20 per night. Check the resort website for special packages.

Location: Furnace Creek is 120 miles northwest of Las Vegas and 300 miles northeast of Los Angeles.

Season: Open all year. The busiest seasons are mid-July through Aug, spring, and all holidays, when the facility is frequently full.

Food: The Wrangler offers a buffet breakfast ($12) and lunch ($15). Dinner (seasonally) is ordered from a menu that includes steaks, Italian, seafood, and poultry ($27–$48). The 49er Cafe offers breakfast (seasonally), lunch and dinner ($14–$29). The Corkscrew Saloon offers hot dogs, pizza, and snacks. Beer, wine, other beverages, and limited groceries are sold in the general store. The 19th Hole Veranda Bar & Grill at the golf course seasonally serves hamburgers, hot dogs, and sandwiches.

Facilities: A large, hot-spring-fed swimming pool, 2 lighted tennis courts, basketball court, children's playground, horseshoe area, volleyball court, 18-hole golf course, Borax Museum, coin-operated laundry, 2 restaurants, saloon, gas station, bicycle rental office, post office, and general store.

Activities: Swimming, tennis, golf, basketball, volleyball, horseshoes, bicycle tours, Jeep tours, and hiking. Horseback riding, group hayrides, and carriage rides are offered from mid-Oct to mid-May. The National Park Service seasonally offers interpretive programs throughout the park.

STOVEPIPE WELLS VILLAGE
Death Valley, CA 92328 • (760) 786-2387 • www.escapetodeathvalley.com

Stovepipe Wells Village is a complex of 11 wooden buildings that provide 83 overnight rooms and supporting services. A general store, small gas station, and National Park Service ranger station are directly across the road. The village has the appearance of a small western town, which in some respects it is. Six separate one-story buildings each contain from 8 to 23 rooms. The guest registration area is in a building that also houses an auditorium/meeting room, a gift shop, and a small guest lounge.

Stovepipe Wells offers 3 categories of rooms that range from a limited number of small, inexpensive Patio rooms to Deluxe rooms similar to those at the Ranch at Furnace Creek. All rooms have heat, air-conditioning, a coffeemaker, and a private bath, but no telephone. Forty-seven Deluxe rooms in 3 buildings each have 2 queens or 1 king bed. These rooms offer a full bathroom, television, small refrigerator, and ceiling fan. Rooms in the Roadrunner and 49er buildings facing east provide good views of

the valley, the Mesquite Sand Dunes, and distant mountains. Rooms on the west side have views obscured by other buildings. Less expensive and smaller Standard rooms have 2 double beds, a queen bed, or a queen plus a single bed. These rooms have a bathroom with a shower. The rooms do not have televisions. Standard rooms rent for about $25 less per night than Deluxe rooms. Eight smaller Patio rooms constructed in 1927 as part of the original building have 1 double or 1 double plus a single bed, and

Lodge building at Stovepipe Wells Village

General store at Stovepipe Wells Village

a bath with shower. These rooms are attached to the front of the registration building near the highway.

Stovepipe Wells is a convenient overnight stop for travelers seeking a true desert experience. The restaurant and saloon offer a western atmosphere with vaulted ceilings built with timbers from an old Death Valley mining operation. In fact, staying at Stovepipe Wells is itself a bit of the Old West, but in rooms that are comfortable and modern, and with access to a heated swimming pool. A general store offers supplies, souvenirs, limited groceries, soft drinks, beer, liquor, wine, and a microwave. A short distance east is a large area of sand dunes that is fun to explore.

Rooms: Doubles, triples, and quads. All rooms have a private bath.

Wheelchair Accessibility: Two Deluxe and 2 Standard rooms are fully wheelchair accessible.

Reservations: Stovepipe Wells Village, Death Valley, CA 92328. Phone (760) 786-2387. The first night's lodging is required as a deposit. Cancellation of 3 days prior to scheduled arrival is required for full refund.

Rates: Patio ($107–$117), Standard ($127–$146), and Deluxe ($156–$175). Rates quoted are for 2 adults. Children 12 and under stay free when accompanied by an adult. Each additional person is $10 per night. A crib is free, and a rollaway (Deluxe rooms only) is $10.

Location: Stovepipe Wells Village is on CA 190, near the middle of Death Valley National Park. It is approximately 25 miles northwest of Furnace

Creek and about 33 miles southwest of Beatty, Nevada.

Season: The facility is open all year. The busiest season is mid-Feb through Apr, when it is frequently full.

Food: The Toll Road Restaurant offers a buffet breakfast ($12) and dinner ($13–$25) is ordered from a menu. The Badwater Saloon offers lunch ($6–$15), draft beer, cocktails, and appetizers. Beer, wine, other beverages, and limited groceries are sold in the general store.

Facilities: Heated well water swimming pool, restaurant, saloon, guest lounge with TV and board games, business center with computers, auditorium/meeting room (fee charged), gift shop, gas station (regular only), and general store. An airstrip without lights is nearby.

> Stovepipe Wells served as the site for Death Valley's first tourist facility when, on November 1, 1926, Bob Eichbaum opened Stove Pipe Wells Hotel. Eichbaum built and operated a toll road franchise, and a daily stage line connected Los Angeles with various points in Death Valley. Often referred to as "Bungalette City," "Bungalow City," and "Stove Pipe Wells Hotel," the facility included 20 open-air bungalows and several larger buildings, supplemented by army tents, and a gas pump, all on the south side of the road. Later, additional bungalows were constructed along with another building on the north side of the road that served as the lobby, kitchen, and dining room.

Activities: Swimming, walking, and hiking. The National Park Service offers interpretive programs throughout the park except during summer.

Pets: Pets are permitted in all the rooms.

Golden Gate National Recreation Area &
San Francisco Maritime National Historical Park
Building 201 • Fort Mason, San Francisco, CA 94123-0022
(415) 561-4700 • www.nps.gov/goga & www.nps.gov/safr

Golden Gate NRA is a large, diverse urban park that spans the coastline north and south of San Francisco. The park includes beaches, redwood forests, wind-swept ridges, grasslands, historic military posts, a former airfield, a famous federal prison, a mammal center, an old lighthouse, and a Nike missile site. With over 75,000 acres it is one of the country's largest and most heavily used urban parks. San Francisco Maritime NHP was once part of Golden Gate NRA, but is now administered as a separate park that interprets maritime history rather than recreation.

Park Entrance Fee: No charge for entry to either park. The maritime park charges $5 to board the historic boats docked at the wharf.

Lodging in Golden Gate National Recreation Area and San Francisco Maritime National Historical Park: Cavallo Point Lodge at the north end of the Golden Gate Bridge and the Inn at the Presidio in San Francisco's Presidio are upscale lodging facilities in Golden Gate NRA. The Argonaut Hotel, at Fisherman's Wharf across from Hyde Street Pier, is part of San Francisco Maritime NHP. Golden Gate NRA also includes 2 youth hostels, 1 near Fisherman's Wharf in Fort Mason, and the other 4

GOLDEN GATE NATIONAL RECREATION AREA AND SAN FRANCISCO MARITIME NATIONAL HISTORICAL PARK

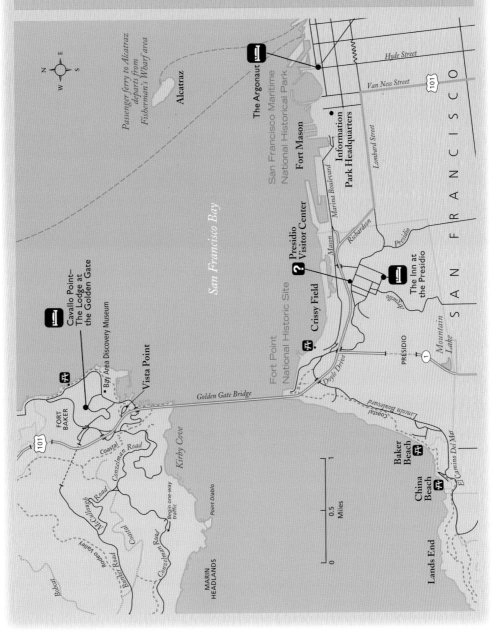

miles northwest of the Golden Gate Bridge in the Marin Headlands. Numerous lodging facilities ranging from luxury to budget are nearby.

THE ARGONAUT

495 Jefferson St. • San Francisco, CA 94109 • (415) 563-0800 • www.argonauthotel.com

The Argonaut is an upscale hotel salvaged by the major renovation of an old brick warehouse situated on San Francisco's famous Fisherman's Wharf. The hotel, rated four diamonds by AAA, has a nautical theme and is adjacent to the "Cannery," the old Del Monte canning factory that has been converted for commercial use. The Argonaut is across the street from Hyde Pier, the major element of San Francisco Maritime National Historical Park where the National Park Service keeps a group of restored historic boats and ships that are accessible to visitors. Although the hotel advertises itself as a boutique hotel, with 252 rooms it is considerably larger than what most of us would classify as "boutique."

The hotel is a four-story rectangle with rooms on each side of central corridors through the top 3 floors. Outside rooms are somewhat larger, more expensive, and offer better views compared to inside rooms, which basically offer views of inside room windows on the opposite side of the building. Outside rooms can also be noisier, especially on either Hyde Street or Beach Street, the latter of which is on the back side of the hotel. Outside rooms on the front of the hotel face San Francisco Bay. The east side of the hotel faces a courtyard beside the Cannery.

Guest rooms range in classification from Standard rooms that face the inside with a queen, king, or 2 queen beds, to Deluxe rooms on the outside that have either 2 queens or a king plus a soft sleeper. The price difference between Standard and Deluxe rooms is $30 to $45. Rooms on the front of the hotel that face San Francisco Bay cost from $30 to $50 more per night than other Deluxe rooms. The Argonaut also offers 13 King Suites, some of which have Bay views. Each suite is comprised of a combination living/dining room plus a separate bedroom. Suites enjoy a spa tub plus a large shower. Connecting bedrooms are available.

All rooms in the hotel have a combination shower/tub, large-screen LED television, coffee-maker, and a mini-bar. Rooms are decorated in keeping with the hotel's nautical theme and have large wooden beams, windows with interior shutters, and at least one exposed brick wall, adding to the ambience of a stay in the historic building.

The visitor center for San Francisco Maritime National Historical Park is on the hotel's first floor. The National Park Service's Hyde Street Pier and its restored ships are directly across the street from the hotel. The historical park's Maritime Museum is a short walk across the park.

The Argonaut is in a popular and touristy area of San Francisco. Fisherman's Wharf has many restaurants and gift shops that attract tourists but not residents, who typically avoid this area of the city. It can be a busy and noisy place, but that is part of the attraction for many visitors who encounter musicians, street vendors, and a variety of things to see and do. A Starbucks is in a backside corner of the hotel and an In-N-Out Burger is just down the street. Jake's Bar with 68 varieties of draft beer is next door. How can you do better than this?

The Argonaut

Rooms: Doubles, triples, and quads. All rooms have a private bathroom with a combination shower/tub.

Wheelchair Accessibility: Thirteen rooms, some in each classification, are ADA compliant. Several have roll-in showers.

Reservations: Argonaut Hotel, 495 Jefferson St., San Francisco, CA 94109. Phone (800) 790-1415 or visit www.argonauthotel.com. A credit card is necessary to guarantee a reservation. Cancellation required by 6 p.m. on the night prior to arrival.

Rates: Rates vary according to season and occupancy. Standard Queen or King ($240–$500); Standard 2 Queens ($250–$522); King Deluxe ($272–$546); 2 Queen Deluxe ($282–$569); Bay View King Deluxe ($303–$592); Bay View 2 Queen Deluxe ($313–$615); King Suite ($366–$674); Bay View King Suite ($418–$732). Rates are based on 2 adults. Additional adults are $20 each. AAA discounts are available. Check the hotel's website for specials.

Location: Corner of Jefferson and Hyde on San Francisco's Fisherman's Wharf. The hotel is directly across from Hyde Street Pier.

Season: Open all year.

The old warehouse in which the Argonaut is located was constructed in 1908 for the California Fruit Cannery Association, which packed fruit and vegetables for the Del Monte Company cannery located next door. At the time there were numerous canning operations in the Bay Area. Bricks used in construction of the warehouse were recycled from ruins of the great 1906 San Francisco earthquake.

The neighboring cannery closed in 1937 and the abandoned warehouse was purchased by the National Park Service in 1978. Kimpton Hotels was contracted in 2000 to renovate the warehouse into a luxury hotel. The company spent nearly $40 million on the renovation and opened the hotel in August 2003.

Food: The hotel's Blue Mermaid restaurant offers breakfast ($10–$15), lunch ($10–$24), and dinner ($18–$28). Many eating establishments from fast food to sit down are a short walk from the hotel. The hotel offers a complimentary wine and beer reception each evening. A famous Safeway is about a 20-minute walk from the hotel.

Facilities: Meeting rooms, restaurant, bar, fitness center, business center, in-room spa services, bicycles.

Activities: Walking, swimming (if you like cold water), bicycling, sightseeing cruises, tours.

Pets: Pets are permitted at no additional cost. Arrangements are available for dog sitters, day care, and dog walkers.

CAVALLO POINT—THE LODGE AT THE GOLDEN GATE
601 Murray Circle • Fort Baker, Sausalito, CA 94965 • (415) 339-4700 • www.cavallopoint.com

Cavallo Point Lodge is an upscale resort with 142 guest rooms in a combination of historic military quarters and newly constructed contemporary buildings. The complex, situated in a former US Army post, includes a spa, restaurant, bar, gift shop, fitness room, meeting facilities, and various maintenance and administrative buildings. The lodge has LEED Gold certification for environmentally sustainable design and operation. Additional buildings including a yacht club,

Cavallo Point – The Lodge at the Golden Gate

children's museum, and Coast Guard station are within the fort, but not part of the resort.

The lodge is situated in Fort Baker, an abandoned military post that occupies 335 acres flanking the Marin Headlands with magnificent views of San Francisco, San Francisco Bay, and the famed Golden Gate Bridge. Cavallo Point is located along the coast of central California just north of San Francisco and the Golden Gate Bridge. Driving north across the bridge, take the Alexander Avenue exit. Driving south on US 101, take the second Sausalito exit just before the Golden Gate Bridge.

Cavallo Point offers several room classifications in 2 basic categories: Historic and Contemporary. It also offers the Frank House, a 1,200-square foot historic home. The first floor has a living room, kitchen, bathroom, and a sun porch. The 2 upstairs bedrooms each have one queen bed and share a bathroom. The house sits on a hill and offers good views of the grounds.

Sixty-eight Historic rooms in former officers' quarters either line one side of the parade ground or border both sides of a road that climbs above the parade ground. These large white frame houses (a few are brick) were built in the early 1900s as duplex units, but subsequently converted into 4 to 12 rental units per building. Rooms in the Historic buildings are grouped into 5 classifications with the least expensive unit having a king or queen bed and no view. The most expensive are 2-bedroom suites with a separate living room containing a sofa bed. The interiors have been remodeled and modernized, but in a manner consistent with their history. Rooms differ in size and configuration, but each includes a gas fireplace, wood floors, original tin ceiling (first floor rooms only), ceiling fan, and a shared front porch. These two- and three-story buildings do not have elevators, meaning occupants of second- and third-floor rooms are required to climb stairways that are sometimes narrow and winding. On the plus side, parking is generally nearby and many of the porches and outside lawns offer good views of San Francisco.

Seventy-four Contemporary rooms in 13 two-story modern stucco buildings are scattered along a hillside above the parade ground. These rooms have tile and carpeted floors, ceiling fans, and gas fireplaces. Built with the environment in mind, units have radiant floor heating, utilize solar power, and are insulated with used denim. Rooms feature large windows, bamboo woodwork, and modern furniture that combine for a bright, pleasing interior. All but a few Contemporary units have either a balcony or patio with Adirondack chairs. Contemporary rooms are offered in 4 styles that vary in bedding and views. For example, Contemporary rooms with 2 queen beds do not have a balcony or patio. Kings, deluxe kings, and king suites are also available. The latter, with a double-sided fireplace and separate tub and shower, is the most expensive option. Rooms within a category are priced according to the view that is available.

Choosing between a Historic and a Contemporary room depends on your expectations. Some guests feel Historic rooms enhance a stay that is, after all, in a historic military post. In addition, nearby parking requires less walking when toting luggage or forgotten items from a vehicle. Historic buildings are especially convenient for occupants of first-floor rooms that have only porch stairs to climb. Rooms in these older but renovated buildings may be less desirable if you are on the second or third floor and must negotiate the stairways.

Contemporary rooms are bright, airy, and generally offer good views. Being on the hillside means climbing numerous steps or walking up and down paved roads to reach buildings that house the restaurant, bar, gift shop, and registration desk, and parking is some distance from most of these buildings. Bellmen with carts are available to transport you and your luggage, but some walking will almost certainly be necessary during your stay.

One employee told us he would choose a Historic unit, but only on the first floor. Otherwise, he would select a Contemporary unit. When choosing the latter, try for a second-floor room that generally offers a better view. Some of these buildings are constructed on the hillside so only a half flight of stairs is required to enter

The Fort Baker site was acquired in 1866 by the US government for defensive military purposes. Named for US senator Edward Baker, the fort was formally established in the 1890s with construction being essentially complete by 1910. Modern fortifications housing long-range cannons were in place prior to construction of the fort. An interest in offering soldiers improved living conditions resulted in the fort having a hospital, gymnasium, indoor toilet facilities, clean water, Colonial Revival–style officers' quarters, and decent barracks for enlisted men.

The fort was initially manned by the US Army's Coast Artillery Corps, whose mission it was to protect the harbor using long-range cannons. By World War II the obsolete cannons had been removed and the fort became a depot for the planting of underwater mines in San Francisco Bay. Following World War II the military became increasingly concerned about the possibility of an air assault. By the 1950s the fort served as headquarters for the US Army Air Defense Command responsible for Nike anti-aircraft missiles around the Bay Area.

By the 1960s and 1970s, Fort Baker was primarily utilized for training troops of the US Army Reserve. Today, it is manned only by the US Coast Guard.

second-floor rooms. Our experience with the staff was very positive. They are friendly, efficient, and know the rooms.

Cavallo Point Lodge is a different type of national park lodge. Rather than being in a destination park such as Glacier or Yellowstone, Cavallo is a destination lodge. Travelers choose to stay here because of the lodge, not the park. Of course, the lodge is just across the Golden Gate Bridge from one of the best cities in America. It is even closer to Sausalito, a great place to stroll. Dining is first class, which brings to mind one of our favorite amenities: complimentary coffee and homemade muffins and croissants each morning near the registration area. Pour a cup, select a muffin, and stroll to the front porch where you can sit in a rocker and gaze in awe at the Golden Gate Bridge. Life doesn't get any better.

Rooms: Most rooms are designed as doubles, however Historic 2-bedroom suites accommodate up to 6 persons. All units have a private bathroom, most with a combination tub/shower.

Wheelchair Accessibility: Three Historic units and 4 Contemporary units are ADA compliant.

Reservations: Cavallo Point, 601 Murray Circle, Fort Baker, Sausalito, CA 94965. Phone (888) 651-2003 or (415) 339-4700; www.cavallopoint .com. One night deposit required. Cancellation notice of 72 hours required for full refund.

Rates: Rates vary daily according to season, day of the week, and occupancy. Historic Rooms: Basic with king or queen ($300–$460); Separate sitting area ($320–$480); Queen suite ($400–$570); King suite ($490–$680); King suite with view ($535–$740); Two-bedroom suite ($600–$810); Suites include a queen sofa-sleeper. Contemporary rooms (price varies with view): Two queens without balcony, or 1 king with balcony ($320–$520); Deluxe king with separate sitting area ($420–$600); King suite ($650–$870); Frank House ($700–$920). The lodge charges a $25 daily resort fee in addition to the room rates noted above.

Location: Immediately north of San Francisco, at the northern end of the Golden Gate Bridge. The lodge is accessible from US 101.

Season: The lodge is open all year.

Food: Murray Circle, an AAA-rated 4-diamond restaurant, serves breakfast ($12–$17), lunch ($14–$29), and dinner ($15–$34). A chef's tasting menu of signature dishes with wine pairing is offered for lunch and dinner. A Sunday brunch is popular with locals. Farley Bar offers appetizers and snacks plus items off the restaurant menu during the hours Murray Circle is open. The spa's Tea Room offers salads, sandwiches, a soup, and wellness drinks. High tea is served on weekends. Complimentary coffee and breakfast rolls are offered each morning in the registration area. A nearby yacht club (unaffiliated with the lodge) offers a limited menu Thurs through Sun.

Transportation: The lodge provides a courtesy shuttle to the Sausalito ferry dock where ferry service is available to San Francisco's Ferry Terminal.

Facilities: Restaurant, bar, tea bar, gift shop, fitness room, meeting and banquet rooms, art gallery. A full-service spa offers complimentary eucalyptus steam rooms, whirlpool tubs, an outdoor basking pool, and a relaxation room with fireplace and library. A nearby children's museum is independent of the lodge.

Activities: Hiking, biking, fishing, kayaking, guided tours, yoga, spa treatments. A concierge can arrange for boat and bike rentals, and make reservations for tours, dinners, and shows in San Francisco.

Pets: Pets are permitted in first-floor rooms for a fee of $75 per visit. Pets receive welcome amenities such as a bed, food and water bowls, and treats.

INN AT THE PRESIDIO

Main Post, Presidio of San Francisco, 42 Moraga Ave. • San Francisco, CA 94129
(415) 800-7356 • www.innatthepresidio.com

Inn at the Presidio

The Inn at the Presidio offers 22 guest rooms in a newly renovated 1903 three-story brick building that once housed bachelor officers stationed at this former US Army post. An additional 4 guest rooms are available in a nearby historic 1860s frame house that once served as a home for an officer and his family. The buildings are situated in a relatively quiet area of the Main Post in San Francisco's Presidio, a 1,491-acre former military fort at the southern terminus of the Golden Gate Bridge. The Inn, which welcomed its first guests in 2012, is on the Presidio's east side and accessible via several gates from the city into the former army post.

The Inn is operated as a bed-and-breakfast that includes a complimentary continental breakfast and an evening wine and cheese reception. Chairs, sofas, and a gas fireplace are in the first-floor reception area that guests frequently utilize for reading and visiting. The breakfast and evening wine and cheese reception are in an adjoining dining area with tables and chairs plus a comfortable sitting area. Guests also have the option of eating on a small balcony outside the dining room or a large terrace highlighted with a fire pit. Parking is available directly behind the Inn.

All but 6 of the Inn's guest rooms are classified as King Suites, each of which has separate sitting and bedroom areas. The sitting areas are quite large and include a lounge chair, queen-size sofa bed, desk, large-screen TV, and a gas fireplace. The large, separate bedrooms have a king bed, lounge chair, large dresser, and a large-screen TV. These units have spacious tiled bathrooms with combination shower/tubs. The Inn's 6 other guest rooms consist of one Queen Suite and 5 Standard rooms with either one king or one queen bed. The Standard rooms are relatively small and do not have a fireplace. The Inn does not have an elevator, so if climbing stairs is a problem it is important to mention this when booking a reservation. Assistance with luggage is available.

Rooms on the first and second floors have larger windows than third-floor rooms. First-floor rooms have the problem of guests and visitors who can peer into the rooms when walking past on the front porch. Our choice of rooms would be 232 on the Inn's second floor and possibly 332 on the third floor, both of which are King Suites. These are corner rooms with an extra window in both the sitting area and the bedroom.

The separate one-story Funston House, a short distance down the street from the Inn, contains 4 guest rooms that include 1 Queen Suite, 2 Queen Standards, and 1 King Standard. The home has a common living room with a gas fireplace and dining room. The 4 bedrooms are rented individually, although a group might choose to book the entire house. Funston House guests enjoy access to both the continental breakfast and wine and cheese reception held at the Inn.

A stay at the Inn is a very different experience compared with stays in other lodging facilities in the San Francisco area. The natural setting and lack of crowds, noise, and traffic make the Inn an ideal place for those interested in nature, hiking, and enjoying one of California's special places. It's kind of like having a bed-and-breakfast in the middle of New York's Central Park, only better.

The Presidio contains many natural areas that are being continually expanded and improved through restoration. Although guests have relatively quick access to San Francisco's main attractions via either their private vehicles or public transportation, a day or two here is a nice respite from the hustle and bustle of the city. A major benefit of a stay here is the ability to get to know other guests. The limited number of rooms along with the breakfast and evening reception encourage conversations among guests.

Complimentary shuttle service throughout the Presidio allows guests to tour the former military post and take advantage of the many attractions and activities without the need of a private vehicle. Twenty-four miles of hiking trails are within the Presidio with one of the most popular beginning directly behind the Inn and leading to

The Inn at the Presidio is owned by the Presidio Trust and operated by a hotel management company. The Trust, interested in improving access to and enjoyment of the area, spent $11 million ($500,000 per room) on structural improvements and renovations over two years to what was once officers' barracks before opening the building in 2012 as a bed-and-breakfast. The building, once known as Pershing Hall, had been empty for 12 years prior to the renovations. The Inn is particularly popular with wedding parties of the many nuptials that take place in the Presidio.

Inspiration Point, which provides great views of the area. The Inn has a limited number of bicycles offered on a first-come, first-serve basis. A bike rental facility is at Chrissy Field. Food service is offered at several locations that are easily accessible by walking or using the free shuttle.

Rooms: Doubles, triples, and quads. All rooms have a private bathroom, most with a combination shower/tub.

Wheelchair Accessibility: The first floor of the Inn has one wheelchair-accessible King Suite. A Queen Suite in the Funston House is also wheelchair accessible.

The area now known as the Presidio was home to Native Americans for centuries prior to the 1776 arrival of the Spanish, who established it as one of numerous military outposts throughout present-day California. The Presidio subsequently fell under the control of Mexico following the country's independence in 1821, and later, the United States Army. The once-barren sand dunes were transformed by the US Army, which undertook a major tree-planting effort to make the area more habitable. The Presidio was included within the boundaries of newly created Golden Gate National Recreation Area in 1972 and transferred to the National Park Service in 1994 when the military base was closed. The Presidio Trust, which was created to partner with the National Park Service, is currently in charge of approximately 80 percent of the property while the National Park Service maintains 300 acres along the coastline.

Reservations: Inn at the Presidio, Main Post, Presidio of San Francisco, 42 Moraga Ave., San Francisco, CA 94129. Phone (866) 512-4571 or visit www.innatthepresidio.com. A credit card holds a reservation. Cancellation must be made within 72 hours of the arrival date. A block of 5 or more rooms requires a 30-day cancellation.

Rates: Standard Queen ($220); Standard King ($300); Queen Suite ($325); King Suite ($325–$375 depending upon the floor); Funston House ($1,000). Rates are quoted for 2 adults. Each additional person is $25 per night. Children 15 years and under stay free with an adult. Rates do not include the tax or a 14 percent park fee.

Location: Southern terminus of San Francisco's Golden Gate Bridge in the Main Post area of the Presidio.

Season: Open year-round.

Food: Continental breakfast and evening wine and cheese reception are included in the price of a room. The Officers' Club with a restaurant is within the block. Other restaurants and eating establishments are scattered throughout the Presidio.

Transportation: Two free shuttle routes offer access to most areas of the Presidio. One route includes a stop near the Inn. San Francisco municipal buses provide transportation from the Presidio Transit Center to various points in the city.

Facilities: Two basement meeting rooms can each accommodate up to 20 individuals. Complimentary bicycles. A nearby YMCA with exercise facilities and classes, plus a swimming pool is free to Inn guests. The Presidio includes a National Park Service visitor center, Fort Point National Historic Site, an 18-hole golf course, bicycle rentals, and the popular Walt Disney Family Museum.

Activities: Hiking, biking, golf, tennis, swimming, and bird watching.

Pets: Pets are permitted with a $40 per visit charge.

Lassen Volcanic National Park

PO Box 100 • Mineral, CA 96063 • (530) 595-4480 • www.nps.gov/lavo

Lassen Volcanic National Park comprises 106,000 acres of scenic and uncrowded mountainous country that centers on Lassen Peak, a 10,457-foot plug-dome volcano that last erupted during a 7-year period beginning in 1914. The park has other geothermal activity including boiling springs, mud pots, fumaroles, and sulfurous vents. A paved road connecting the southwest and north entrances provides scenic views and access to many features of this beautiful area. Lassen Volcanic National Park is located in north-central California, 42 miles east of Redding and 55 miles east of Red Bluff.

Park Entrance Fee: $10 per vehicle or $5 per person, good for 7 days.

Lodging in Lassen Volcanic National Park: The park has 1 lodging facility, and it is an out-of-the-way location for most visitors who drive through the park. Drakesbad Guest Ranch is in the southeast part of the park, 17 miles north of the small town of Chester.

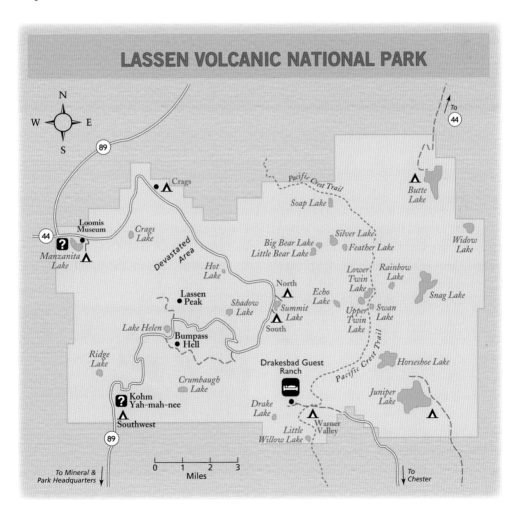

Drakesbad Guest Ranch

End of Warner Valley Road • Lassen Volcanic National Park • Chester, CA 96020
(866) 999-0914 • www.drakesbad.com

Drakesbad Guest Ranch offers 19 rooms in a complex of cabins, bungalows, and a two-story lodge. The ranch includes a central dining hall, a thermal heated swimming pool, and several service buildings. The isolated complex lies beside a meadow in the southeast portion of Lassen Volcanic National Park. It is at an altitude of 5,700 feet and surrounded by trees, hills, and mountains.

Several types of accommodations are available, all of which are relatively small. Rooms have propane heat but no telephone, air-conditioning, television, or electrical outlets. The two-story rustic lodge has 6 guest rooms, all on the second floor. Rooms are on each side of an interior corridor accessed via an inside stairway from the first-floor recreation room. No elevator is available. The 3 even-numbered Lodge rooms each have 1 double bed plus 1 bunk bed. Odd-numbered rooms on the opposite side of the building are somewhat smaller and have 1 double bed. Each Lodge room

Main lodge building at Drakesbad Guest Ranch

has electric lights and a private bath with a sink and toilet, but no tub or shower. Showers and bathtubs are in the swimming pool bathhouse, a short walk from the lodge.

The Northeast Annex, directly behind the dining hall, is the only other accommodation with electric lights. The one-story wooden annex has 2 rooms, each with 2 double beds and a bathroom with a sink, toilet, and shower. A porch spans the building's front. These rooms are somewhat larger and rent for a little more than rooms in the lodge.

The remaining rooms do not have electricity, and light is by means of kerosene lanterns. Four freestanding wooden cabins sit at the base of a hill across from the parking lot and the stable. Each has a double bed plus a single bed and a bathroom with a sink and toilet. Cabin guests must shower at the swimming pool bathhouse. Parking is directly in front of each cabin. Cabins rent for the same price and are somewhat larger than lodge rooms.

Six one-story Bungalows are constructed as duplex units. Each Bungalow has 2 double beds, a full bath with a shower, and a back porch that overlooks a large meadow. Parking is directly in front of each building. These are the nicest rooms at Drakesbad.

A single one-story wooden Duplex has 2 rooms on each side of a central bathroom. One room has 2 double beds; the other has a double bed plus a bunk bed. The Duplex is rented only as a single unit and is particularly desirable for families with 2 or more children.

Even frequent national park visitors are likely to find a stay at Drakesbad to be a very different experience. Don't expect a fancy lodge with room service, but rather a place to get away from the hustle and bustle of daily life while experiencing nature, but without giving up good food and fellowship. Facilities are comfortable but basic. A dinner bell rings 3 times daily to announce food is being served in the pine-paneled dining room.

The bottom floor of the lodge, filled with chairs, tables, and sofas, serves as a meeting place to read and chat with other guests. A wood stove is near the middle of the room, and a large stone fireplace occupies an end wall. Chairs are on the outside porch that wraps around the lodge. The ranch offers plenty to do including horseback rides and swimming in the naturally heated spring water pool. Equipment is provided for table tennis, volleyball, badminton, croquet, and horseshoes. Fly-fishing for trout is excellent for anglers. Several trails, both short and long, lead from the lodge to some of Lassen's best spots. Massage therapy is available. Campfires are held each evening when weather permits.

Best of all, employees and guests seem to be family members who have discovered a good

Lassen Volcanic National Park once housed another lodging facility, this one near Manzanita Lake in the northwest corner of the park. Manzanita Lake Lodge and 9 cabins were built by Lassen National Park Camp, Ltd. (which later became Lassen National Park Company) in 1933. A dining room and 10 wooden double housekeeping cabins were added in 1935. The lodging facility expanded yet again in 1940 when 40 tent cabins and a cafeteria, grocery store/gift shop, and gas station were added. The entire area was closed in 1974 when this area of the park was declared hazardous because of a potential rock avalanche. The lodge and cabins were removed in 1977. Photos of the lodge are in a loose-leaf binder kept at Loomis Museum near the park's northwest entrance station. Twenty camper cabins were added to the Manzanita area in 2011. The cabins have propane heat, but no electricity, running water, or linens. A battery-operated lantern is provided. A camping package including sleeping bags, stove, ice chest, and firewood is available for rent. Public restrooms, showers, and a Laundromat are at the nearby camper store. Call (877) 444-6777 or visit www.lassenrecreation.com for information about the camper cabins.

thing few others know about. The ease with which you will make friends is one of the great pleasures of staying here. Guests eat together in the dining hall and sit with one another around the evening campfire or on the porch of the lodge. Likewise, children have an easy time making friends among themselves. Drakesbad is a place where you can wind down and push your worries to another day.

Rooms: Singles, doubles, triples, and quads. A single Duplex holds up to 8 individuals. Cabins and Lodge rooms have half-baths. Other rooms have a full bath with shower.

Wheelchair Accessibility: One Bungalow is wheelchair accessible.

Reservations: Drakesbad Guest Ranch, 2150 North Main St., Ste. 5, Red Bluffs, CA 96080. Phone (866) 999-0914. Reservations should be made no later than the end of Feb to ensure a choice of rooms and dates. One night's deposit is required, and a 90-day cancellation is required for a full refund. A 10 percent fee is charged for cancellations of less than 90 days.

The valley in which Drakesbad Guest Ranch is located was first settled by Edward Drake, a trapper and guide who may have arrived here as early as 1875. Drake hosted occasional campers during summers but moved down the valley to Prattville during the harsh winters. In 1900 the 70-year-old Drake sold his 400 acres to Alexander Sifford, a schoolteacher from Susanville who traveled here to drink the healing soda water. Sifford later purchased an additional 40 acres and in 1908 renamed the valley Drakesbad, the original owner's name in combination with the German term for warm-water bath. Sifford and his family spent 60 years improving the property and providing visitor services, and in 1958 deeded the property to the National Park Service.

Rates: Rates are per person and include 3 meals daily. Lodge and Cabins (single, $189; double, $169; extra adult, $139); Bungalows and Northeast Annex (single, $209; double, $189; extra adult, $159); Duplex (double, $199; extra adult, $159). Weekly rate is approximately 6 times the daily rate. One child 6 and under is free with each paying adult. Additional children 6 and under are $49. Children ages 7 through 14 are $49. Ages 15 and over pay the adult rate. Rates for Lodge, Cabins, and the Duplex are reduced in early June and most nights from late Aug through closing. Check the lodge website for specials.

Location: Drakesbad is reached via a 17-mile road from Chester, California. The first 14 miles are winding and well-maintained. The last 3 miles are rough gravel.

Season: Mid-June to the second Mon in Oct, depending on the weather.

Food: Three meals daily are served in a rustic dining hall a short walk from the guest rooms. Breakfast includes fresh fruits, hot and cold cereals, and a hot entree. Lunch is buffet-style (sack lunches are available upon request), while dinner includes a choice of 1 of 2 entrees. Outdoor cookouts are sometimes offered. Beer and wine are available for purchase.

Facilities: Hot-spring swimming pool, dining hall, and stables.

Activities: Horseback riding (fee), fishing, swimming, hiking, guided walks, and a variety of games, including volleyball, croquet, ping-pong, horseshoes, archery, and badminton. Special activities are offered for children. Massage therapy (fee).

Sequoia National Park/Kings Canyon National Park

47050 Generals Hwy. • Three Rivers, CA 93271 • (559) 565-3341 • www.nps.gov/seki

Sequoia and Kings Canyon are separate but adjoining national parks that are nearly always visited together. The 2 parks comprise more than 865,000 acres, including groves of giant sequoias on plateaus surrounded by the scenic High Sierra. The magnificent sequoias are immense trees that can live for more than 3,000 years and grow until trunk diameters reach 40 feet. The wide range in elevation from 1,500 feet to nearly 14,500 feet results in a wide variety of wildlife and vegetation. The parks are in central California. Access from the west is via CA 180 from Fresno, which leads through the Grant Grove section of Kings Canyon to Cedar Grove. From the south, CA 198 leads to the Giant Forest area of Sequoia National Park, before connecting with CA 180 at Grant Grove.

Park Entrance Fee: $20 per vehicle or $10 per person, good for 7 days.

Lodging in Sequoia and Kings Canyon National Parks: Three locations within Sequoia and Kings Canyon National Parks offer overnight accommodations that range from tent cabins to modern lodges. Wuksachi Village and Lodge is just north of Lodgepole in Sequoia National Park. Lodging facilities in Kings Canyon National Park include rustic cabins and a lodge at Grant Grove, as well as a motel unit at Cedar Grove. Private lodging facilities are at Mineral King in the southern end of Sequoia National Park and in Sequoia National Forest on the road to Cedar Grove from Grant Grove. Two additional

SEQUOIA NATIONAL PARK/KINGS CANYON NATIONAL PARK

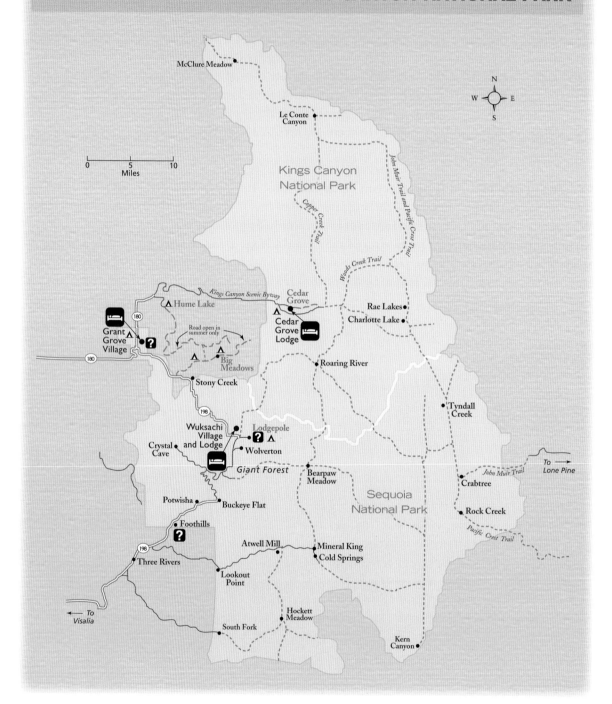

McClure Meadow

Le Conte Canyon

Kings Canyon National Park

John Muir Trail and Pacific Crest Trail

Copper Creek Trail

N
W — E
S

0   5   10
Miles

Kings Canyon Scenic Byway

Woods Creek Trail

Cedar Grove

Hume Lake

Rae Lakes

Charlotte Lake

Cedar Grove Lodge

Grant Grove Village

180

180

Road open in summer only

Big Meadows

Roaring River

Stony Creek

198

Tyndall Creek

Wuksachi Village and Lodge

Lodgepole

Crystal Cave

Wolverton

Giant Forest

Bearpaw Meadow

Sequoia National Park

Crabtree

John Muir Trail

To Lone Pine

Rock Creek

Potwisha

Buckeye Flat

Pacific Crest Trail

Foothills

Three Rivers

198

Atwell Mill

Mineral King
Cold Springs

To Visalia

Lookout Point

Hockett Meadow

South Fork

Kern Canyon

lodging facilities (Stony Creek Lodge and Montecito Lake Resort) are just off Generals Highway in Sequoia National Forest between Sequoia and Kings Canyon National Parks.

Reservations: The 3 lodging facilities within the 2 parks are operated by Delaware North Corporation that maintains a common reservation system. DNC Parks & Resorts, PO Box 89, Sequoia National Park, CA 93262. Telephone (877) 436-9615 or visit www.visitsequoia.com. One night's deposit required with a cancellation requirement of 48 hours.

CEDAR GROVE LODGE

86724 Hwy. 180 • Kings Canyon National Park, CA 93633 • (559) 565-3092 • www.visitsequoia.com

Cedar Grove Lodge is a modern two-story wooden building in the isolated and beautiful Cedar Grove area of Kings Canyon National Park. The lodge has the appearance of a ski chalet, with 18 Standard rooms on the second floor and 3 Patio rooms at ground level. The first floor houses a combination market/gift shop, grill, and a small guest registration desk just inside the entrance. The lodge sits among giant cedar and pine trees beside the South Fork of the Kings River. Picnic tables are scattered about the grounds, many near the river. A large, covered second-floor balcony provides a restful place to read and relax while viewing the surrounding tree-covered mountains and listening to the roar of the river. Another large deck, 1 floor below on the same side of the building, has picnic tables outside the grill. The drive to Cedar Grove is the most scenic in either Sequoia or Kings Canyon and worth the time even if you don't plan to stay at the lodge.

All Standard rooms at the lodge have heat, air-conditioning, coffeemaker, and a telephone, but no television. Standard rooms are identical in size and furnishings, with 2 double beds and a private bath with a shower. One handicap-accessible room has a bathtub. Each room has a modest back window but no balcony. Rooms are relatively small with adequate space for 2 people but fairly tight for a family of 4. Second-floor rooms are entered through a narrow inside corridor that connects a ramp at one end and a

wide stairway at the opposite end. Three ground-level Patio rooms are smaller, with 1 queen bed, a full bath with a shower, coffeemaker, and small refrigerator. These rooms each have a private patio with a picnic table a short distance from the river.

Cedar Grove is one of our favorite destinations. Scenery along the drive from Grant Grove to Cedar Grove is as spectacular as anywhere in the country. The Cedar Grove area is quiet and uncrowded, making this a perfect place to unwind and unplug in a beautiful setting. The lodge is 2,000 feet lower and about 10 degrees warmer than Grant Grove. It is off the park's main traffic artery, near the end of a 30-mile road. The remoteness and small size of the lodge reduce visitation to this area, which is not nearly as crowded as Grant Grove Village. The

Cedar Grove Lodge

unpretentious cafe serves the usual sandwiches, hamburgers, fries, and soft drinks. It also offers other selections, including breakfast items, and dinner specials that might include fried chicken, trout, steak, and pasta. Eat on the deck and enjoy your meal while listening to the roar of the river. Afterward walk down the road and across the bridge to browse through the small National Park Service visitor center. Park rangers conduct evening programs at the nearby campground amphitheater.

Rooms: Doubles, triples, and quads. All rooms have private baths with showers. One wheel-chair-accessible room has a bathtub.

Wheelchair Accessibility: One second-floor room is wheelchair accessible. Access is via a long out-side ramp.

Rates: Standard rooms ($133); Patio rooms ($139). Rates quoted are for 2 adults. Children 17 and under stay free unless an extra bed is requested. Each additional person is $12 per night. Rolla-ways are $10.

Location: Thirty-five miles east of Grant Grove Village near the terminus of CA 180, Kings Canyon Highway.

Season: Mid-May to early Oct, depending on weather.

Food: The cafe serves breakfast ($5–$9), lunch ($5–$8), and dinner ($15–$20). Food items including milk, sandwiches, salads, ice cream treats, beer, wine, and drugstore items can be purchased in the market.

Facilities: Laundry, cafe. Gift items are available in the market. A small National Park Service visitor center is a quarter mile away.

Activities: Hiking, fishing, evening campfire programs, horseback riding.

GRANT GROVE VILLAGE

86728 Hwy. 180 • Kings Canyon National Park, CA 93633 • (559) 335-5500 • www.visitsequoia.com

Grant Grove Village includes 50 older wood cabins plus a two-story cedar lodge with 36 rooms. Both the cabins and lodge are off Generals Highway behind a small commercial center that houses a post office, market, gift shop, dining room, and a National Park Service visitor center. The lodge and cabins are within walking distance of the registration desk and dining room.

Cabins are clustered in 2 areas a short distance behind the commercial center. One section, sometimes called "Tent City," is on a hillside overlooking a meadow that separates the cabins from the dining room and registration building. The hillside

Camp cabins at Grant Grove Village

is dotted with numerous large trees. The remainder of the cabins sit in a section called Meadow Camp, a more heavily wooded area across the road from the meadow and a little farther from the commercial center. The lodge is on a hillside a short distance behind and above the cabins. A National Park Service visitor center with exhibits and an information desk is directly across the road. Grant Grove serves as a convenient location for day trips to Cedar Grove and Giant Forest.

Grant Grove offers 4 categories of cabin accommodations plus lodge rooms. Nine cabins have a private bathroom, while occupants of the other 41 cabins must use 1 of 2 central bathhouses. The bathhouse at Meadow Camp includes pay showers and was newly constructed in 2008. All cabins have sheets, towels, and daily maid service. The least expensive rooms are Tent cabins with wooden walls and canvas roofs. Each has 2 double beds (a few also have a twin) in a dark

and stark unfinished interior with a wooden floor. They have no heat or electricity, although a battery operated lamp is provided. One step up (actually, quite a large step) and about $20 more expensive are somewhat larger Camp cabins with propane heat and electricity, but without a bathroom. Most Camp cabins have 2 double beds, although a few also have a twin. A limited number of Oversized Camp cabins have three double beds and cost extra. Each unit has an unfinished interior and a covered patio with a wood stove and picnic table.

Grant Grove also has Rustic cabins that have a similar exterior but much nicer interior than Camp cabins. Rustics have finished paneled interiors, vaulted ceilings, and rent for about $10 per night more than Camp cabins. Parking is directly beside most Camp and Rustic cabins, but some of the cabins are a long walk from the bathroom. Rustic cabin 510 is surrounded by tall shrubs and not far from the bathroom, which makes it a good choice. Rustic 508 is the only cabin to have an inside wood stove. The top cabin accommodations are 9 units with private bathrooms. These have interiors similar in size to the Rustics and are constructed 2 to a building with a shared front porch. Of the 9, cabin 9 is freestanding and classified as Deluxe. It has 1 queen-size bed, sofa bed, refrigerator, coffeemaker, and a front porch. Cabins 1 through 4 are in 2 buildings that sit just up the hill from the parking area, while cabins 5 through 9 are farther up the hill and require more walking.

John Muir Lodge, which opened in May 1999, offers 34 rooms in an attractive two-story cedar building. The lodge does not have an elevator. Each floor has a large balcony with chairs on the west end of the building. The lodge boasts an impressive lobby area with vaulted beamed ceiling and a large stone fireplace. This is a good place to play board games, read a book, or visit with other guests. Furnishings were especially created for the lodge. The rooms have heat, a full bath, a coffeemaker, and a telephone, but no air-conditioning. Rooms classified as Standard have 2 queen beds, while Deluxe rooms have a king plus a sofa bed. Even-numbered rooms on the south side of the building are on the opposite side of the building from the parking lot and offer a better view and less noise.

Grant Grove offers a choice of accommodations at a wide range of prices. Cabin 9 with a bath (called the Honeymoon cabin) is our favorite accommodation. If you don't mind using a community bathroom, Rustic Cabins are the best value. These are especially desirable if you can make use of the outside wood stove that is available for cooking. If you desire modern accommodations, choose the lodge with upscale rooms in an attractive cedar building.

Rooms: Doubles, triples, and quads. Several cabins accommodate 6. Lodge rooms and 9 cabins have a private bathroom.

Wheelchair Accessibility: Two first-floor rooms in the John Muir Lodge are ADA compliant.

Rates: Tent Cabin ($55–$62); Camp Cabin ($80–$89); Oversize Camp Cabins ($95–$103); Rustic Cabin ($90–$94); Cabin with private bath ($122–$129); Deluxe Cabin with private bath ($133–$140); Standard Lodge room ($119–$201); Deluxe Lodge room ($129–$211). Rates quoted are for 2 adults. Rates shown for Tent Cabins, Cabins with private bath, and the Deluxe Cabin include a 10 percent sales tax. Other lodging does not incur the tax. Children 17 and under stay free. Each additional person is $12 per night. Rollaways are $10. Check the website for specials and packages offered throughout the year.

Location: Three miles inside the entrance to Kings Canyon National Park on CA 180 from Fresno.

If you want something to tax your brain, think about this: The complex at Grant Grove spans two California counties. Tulare County on the south side levies a 10 percent hotel/motel tax, while Fresno County on the north side does not. Stay in a cabin on the south side of the complex and you will be charged the tax. Stay in an identical cabin on the north side of the complex and you will not pay the tax. Occupants of the lodge are fortunate because the building sits in Fresno County, which does not levy the tax. Even the concessionaire was confused by this bizarre situation and at one time was charging tax on all rooms. Guests in both the cabins and the lodge are charged a National Park Service impact fee. How can a vacation become so complicated?

Season: Open all year, although the Tent, Camp, and Rustic cabins close during winter.

Food: A dining room offers family dining with breakfast ($3–$10), lunch ($4–$16), and dinner ($4–$22). A pizza parlor (summer only) is attached to the dining room. A market offers limited groceries.

Facilities: Dining room, pizza parlor, market, gift shop, post office, and National Park Service visitor center.

Activities: Horseback riding, hiking, and interpretive programs. During winter months snowshoeing and cross-country skiing are popular.

WUKSACHI VILLAGE AND LODGE

64740 Wuksachi Way • Sequoia National Park, CA 93262 • (559) 565-4070 • www.visitsequoia.com

One of three lodge buildings at Wuksachi

Wuksachi Village and Lodge, named for a Native American tribe that once lived in Sequoia, consists of an attractive cedar registration/dining building and 3 nearby cedar lodge structures that provide a total of 102 guest rooms. Opened in May 1999, the complex is on a hillside amid large cedar, sugar pine, and fir trees. Excellent mountain and forest views are available from the windows of most of the rooms. Parking is down a hill from the buildings, and transporting luggage may require more exercise than you desire. Luggage carts are in the lodge buildings, and bell staff at the registration building are available to assist with luggage. The registration building boasts a handsome lobby under a beamed-vaulted ceiling where guests can talk, read, or just relax in front of a wood-burning stove. A small gift shop is just off the lobby. The dining room on the back side of the building has a large stone fireplace and features a wall of windows providing excellent views of this scenic area of the park. A small lounge is just outside the dining room. Conference rooms are downstairs. The entire complex is attractively done with first-class furnishings.

Paved walkways lead from a central parking lot to each of 3 virtually identical lodge buildings. Each building has 3 floors in a split-level design in which rooms on each floor are accessed from central corridors. Rooms on the bottom floor of each building face the mountains to the east, while rooms on the third floor face the forest to the west. The second floor of each building has rooms on both sides of the corridor. There are no elevators, which means guests may be required to climb 1 or 2 flights of stairs. Two of the buildings, Stewart and Silliman, are entered on the second floor so guests do not have to climb more than 1 flight of steps. The third and largest building, Sequoia, is entered on the first floor, thus requiring third-floor guests to climb 2 flights. If stairs are a problem, request a room on the entry floor of the building to which you are assigned.

Wuksachi Lodge dining room

All 102 rooms at Wuksachi have heat, ceiling fan, full bathroom, hair dryer, refrigerator, television, telephone, coffeemaker, and very attractive furnishings. The rooms are not air-conditioned, but this is seldom needed. Rooms do not have a balcony. Each building offers rooms in 3 classifications. Twenty-four Standard rooms, the lowest-priced alternative, and 60 Deluxe rooms are similar except for a slight difference in room size and furnishings. Standard rooms, each with 2 queen beds, are at least as large as, if not larger than, most nice motel rooms. Deluxe rooms have about 3 feet of extra depth and come with 2 queen beds or a king plus a sofa bed. Eighteen Superior rooms with either 2 queen beds or 1 king bed plus a sofa bed also have a side room with a sofa bed and chair. The extra room can be closed off with 2 sliding wood doors. We suggest a Standard room with a mountain view. Rooms within each classification rent for the same price, so obtaining a room with a mountain view doesn't cost extra.

Wuksachi Village and Lodge is a convenient base from which to explore this impressive national park. The lodge sits alone without stores, a visitor center, or other attractions to serve as magnets to large numbers of park visitors. Despite the secluded location, the lodge is a short distance from several of the park's major attractions. Lodgepole, a major activity area with a large visitor center, market, laundry facilities, mountain shop, deli, and nature center, is only 2 miles away. Giant Forest, with an outstanding museum and trails that offer access to the park's namesake sequoias, is 4 miles south of Lodgepole. A free summer shuttle system connects Wuksachi, Lodgepole, the General Sherman Tree, Giant Forest Museum, Moro Rock, and Crescent Meadow. The shuttles operate from Memorial Day to Labor Day.

The planning for Wuksachi Village and Lodge had been in the works for well over a decade before its May 1999 completion. The major activity and lodging center of Sequoia National Park was for many years at Giant Forest, 6 miles south of Wuksachi. Here there were cabins, motel-type units, and 2 two-story lodge buildings. The area also had a restaurant, market, gift shop, and pizza pub. For a variety of reasons, including an antiquated sewage system, danger from falling trees, high maintenance costs, and harm to reproduction of the area's sequoias, the National Park Service closed all commercial activities here in October 1998 and subsequently began removing most of the structures. The old restaurant/market building currently serves as a museum.

Rooms: Doubles, triples, and quads. Superior rooms can sleep up to 6. All rooms have private baths.

Wheelchair Accessibility: Eight rooms, several in each of the 3 price categories, are ADA compliant. Ramp access is provided to each of the 3 lodge buildings. Keep in mind that rooms are up a hill and some distance from parking. Porters with electric carts are available to assist with luggage and transportation.

Rates: Room rates vary by season and are higher on holidays. Standard ($115–$215); Deluxe ($125–$264); Superior ($155–$277). Rates quoted are for 2 adults. Each additional person is $12 per night. Children 17 and under stay free unless an extra bed is required. Rollaways and cribs are $10 per night. Check the website for specials and packages that are offered throughout the year.

Location: Wuksachi Village and Lodge is just off Generals Highway in the northern section of Sequoia National Park. The lodge is approximately 2 miles west of Lodgepole.

Season: The lodge is open all year.

Food: The restaurant serves breakfast (Continental, $7.50 or full buffet, $13), lunch ($4–$15), and dinner ($5–$34) daily. Reservations are required for dinner. Two miles away, Lodgepole has a market and deli, as well as a snack bar that serves breakfast, sandwiches, and pizza. The lodge offers an evening all-you-can-eat barbecue dinner at Wolverton Recreation Area from mid-June to Labor Day.

Transportation: The National Park Service operates a free park shuttle from Memorial Day through Labor Day. One shuttle operates between Wuksachi and Giant Forest with stops at Lodgepole and the General Sherman Tree. Another shuttle operates between Giant Forest and Moro Rock.

Sequoia and Kings Canyon winter activities include cross-country skiing and snowshoeing during winter months when the area is typically buried in snowfall. Both Wuksachi in Sequoia National Park and Grant Grove Village in Kings Canyon National Park are open all year. Cedar Grove Lodge is closed during winter. Keep in mind that Generals Highway is sometimes closed by snow during the winter, so access to Wuksachi may be limited to the south entrance from Ash Mountain and access to Grant Grove Village may be restricted to CA 180 from Fresno. Call the National Park Service or the lodge where you will be staying prior to leaving home to determine which road to take. Also keep in mind that chains may be required on your vehicle even when a road is open.

Facilities: Restaurant, lounge, gift shop, conference rooms. Snowshoes and cross-country skis are rented in the gift shop during winter months. Two miles away, Lodgepole offers a mountain shop, post office, laundry facilities, deli, market, snack bar, nature center, and a National Park Service visitor center. Most services at Lodgepole are seasonal.

Activities: Hiking, horseback riding, fishing, bird-watching (summer), and guided sightseeing tours. Cave tours are at Crystal Cave, about 20 miles south of Wuksachi. Buy tickets at Lodgepole or Foothills visitor center. Winter activities include cross-country skiing, sledding, snowshoeing, and guided walks.

Yosemite National Park

PO Box 577 • Yosemite National Park, CA 95389 • (209) 372-0200 • www.nps.gov/yose

Yosemite National Park comprises nearly 1,200 square miles of scenic valleys, high-country meadows, and granite peaks and domes in one of America's most spectacular and popular national parks. The 3 major features of the park are beautiful Yosemite Valley, 3 groves of ancient giant sequoias, and the alpine wilderness reached via Tioga Road. The park's main activity area is in Yosemite Valley. Tioga Road is a paved road that winds through the High Sierra and connects on the east side of the park with US 395 at Lee Vining, California. The road is closed from late fall to early spring. Yosemite is in

YOSEMITE NATIONAL PARK

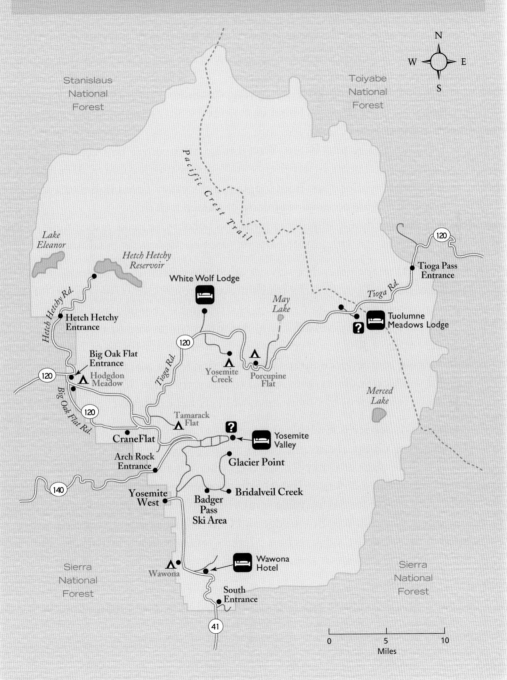

east-central California, approximately 190 miles due east of San Francisco. The southern edge of the park is approximately 60 miles north of Fresno via CA 41.

Park Entrance Fee: $20 per vehicle or $10 per person, good for 7 days.

Lodging in Yosemite National Park: Yosemite has 7 lodging facilities, 4 of which are in Yosemite Valley. Valley accommodations range from the upscale Ahwahnee (many consider this the crown jewel of national park lodges) to bare-bones tent cabins in Housekeeping Camp and Curry Village. A free shuttle stops at each facility as well as other major points of interest in the valley that can be very congested during summer.

Three very different lodging facilities are outside Yosemite Valley. Probably the oldest lodging facility in any national park, the Wawona Hotel, comprises 6 white frame buildings situated in a peaceful setting 4 miles inside the park's south entrance.

Tuolumne Meadows Lodge and White Wolf Lodge offer canvas tent cabins and a few wood cabins on Tioga Road for an overnight experience in Yosemite's high country. Although in the same park, these 2 facilities seem worlds apart from lodging in the valley. Five High Sierra Camps offering backcounty accommodations are accessed via hiking or guided trail rides.

Yosemite is very popular during summer months and holidays, so make reservations on the earliest possible date. Accommodations with private bath are often booked a year in advance.

Reservations: A central reservation office services all lodging facilities in Yosemite. For reservations write or call Yosemite Reservations, 6771 North Palm Ave., Fresno, CA 93704. Phone (801) 559-4884, or visit www.yosemitepark.com. The cost of 1 night's lodging is required as a deposit. Cancellation with a full refund less a $10 fee requires a 7-day notice. Reservations tied to a special event such as the Bracebridge Dinner require a 30-day notice. Stays are limited to a maximum of 7 nights. Reservations for all Yosemite lodging can be made up to 366 days prior to the planned arrival date. If the hotel is fully booked and you lack flexibility with regard to dates, try again 30, 15, or 7 days prior to your intended arrival, when reservations by others are most likely to be canceled.

Food in the Valley: Food service is available at several locations, including all of the lodging facilities other than Housekeeping Camp. The shuttle makes any of the eating establishments easily accessible, so you can choose to have pizza at Curry Village even when staying at The Ahwahnee. Likewise, you can enjoy a memorable evening dining at The Ahwahnee when you have a room at Yosemite Lodge at the Falls. Nearly every type of food is available somewhere in Yosemite Valley. Yosemite Village offers a pizza loft, deli, cafe, and a grill. Yosemite Lodge and Curry Village both offer several different dining experiences listed in the respective lodge section. Markets selling cold sandwiches, alcoholic beverages, soft drinks, snacks, and groceries are at several locations.

Transportation: A free shuttle system within Yosemite Valley serves all the lodges and other popular points of interest. A free daily shuttle operates between Wawona and Yosemite Valley. Another free shuttle offers frequent service between Wawona and Mariposa Grove near the park's south entrance.

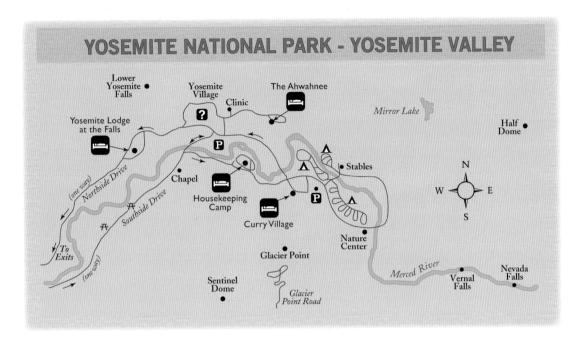

THE AHWAHNEE

Many travelers assert that Yosemite's Ahwahnee is the finest national park lodging facility, a claim that is difficult to dispute. The Ahwahnee, built in the late 1920s with a name Native Americans gave to what is now Yosemite Valley, is both a National Historic Landmark and a world-class facility. Everything about this six-story hotel makes you want to stay, except perhaps the expense, which is rivaled by only a few other national park facilities including Death Valley's Inn at Furnace Creek, Golden Gate's Cavallo Point, and Grand Teton's Jenny Lake Lodge. The hotel underwent a major $12 million historic refurbishment that was completed in 2011. The Great Lounge, with a 24-foot-high beamed ceiling, stained glass windows, and 2 massive stone fireplaces, is the hotel's focal point. The spectacular dining room, with its 34-foot-high vaulted beamed ceiling and floor-to-ceiling windows, is stunning. Baskets, historic photos, paintings, and rugs are placed throughout the public rooms. The Ahwahnee offers 123 rooms in both the main hotel and adjacent cottages. The hotel's location is remote enough to avoid the congestion that typifies much of the valley. Parking is nearby the entrance, and complimentary valet parking is available. Bell staff will assist with luggage.

Lodging is offered in the hotel and in nearby cottages. The main hotel has 99 rooms on 6 floors. Rooms have either 1 king-size bed or 2 double beds. Several also have a sofa bed. Rooms are stylishly furnished and include heat, air-conditioning, television, telephone, small refrigerator, guest bathrobes, coffeemaker, hair dryer, and full tiled bath. Bedding consists of down mattresses, pillows, and blankets. One or

The Ahwahnee

more large windows in each hotel room offer differing views depending on room location. Vistas range from excellent views of Yosemite Falls, Half Dome, or Glacier Point to rooms that look out at a loading dock or under a porch roof. The best views are from corner rooms, which have windows on 2 sides. Hotel rooms fall into 1 of 3 classifications depending on the size, view, and whether a balcony or deck is attached.

The hotel has 2 Junior Suites with extra-large rooms. One has a sunken sitting area and offers the only Jacuzzi in Yosemite. The other has a 4-poster bed used by Queen Elizabeth II during her 1983 stay in this room. Top-of-the-line rooms are 4 suites that have 1 bedroom plus a large, luxuriously furnished parlor with spectacular views. Suites offer varying amenities that can include a fireplace, library, large flat-screen

television, and balcony. Each offers an option of adding a second adjoining bedroom.

The Ahwahnee has 8 separate but nearby single-story frame buildings that house 24 Cottages in a secluded and quiet wooded area of dogwoods and pines near the hotel but away from hotel traffic. Although in a natural setting, most provide minimal views. Cottages are decorated to highlight Yosemite's Native American heritage and most have 1 king bed, while 5 units have 2 double beds. Unlike Hotel rooms, Cottages have ceiling fans, a patio with table and chairs, but no air-conditioning. Cottages 720 and 721 and Cottages 722 and 723 share common patio areas and are probably less desirable. Cottage 716 has a mountain view, while cottages 707 and 718 are more private and offer a view of the Merced River. Cottages 714 and 719 are slightly larger than average and the only 2 with wood-burning fireplaces (wood provided). Cottage prices vary depending upon room size and whether a fireplace is available.

Our suggestion is first-time visitors planning a short stay should choose the hotel to appreciate the delight of staying overnight in such a wonderful place where guests can wander downstairs to read or relax in the Great Lounge. Hotel rooms are not quite as large as most Cottage rooms, but the hotel's common areas are really wonderful. If you plan on staying for more than a couple of days and desire solitude, you may be happier in a Cottage.

The Ahwahnee offers upscale lodging in a beautiful setting. If you are willing to splurge, it is a delightful place to spend several nights while exploring the beauty and enjoying the many activities offered in this spectacular national park. If spending your entire Yosemite stay here will break the bank, consider at least 1 night in this unique hotel. Walk through the lobby and marvel at the Great Lounge. Through the lounge past the second fireplace is the Solarium, where

The Ahwahnee's Great Lounge

massive windows furnish a sweeping view of a grassy area surrounded by trees with a background of granite cliffs. Complimentary afternoon tea and cookies for guests is a tradition. A shuttle operating throughout Yosemite Valley stops at the Ahwahnee entrance, allowing guests to enjoy activities and facilities at other valley locations without using their own vehicles.

Rooms: Singles, doubles, triples, and quads. All rooms can accommodate a rollaway and some have sofa beds. All rooms have a full tiled bath.

Wheelchair Accessibility: Two rooms in the main hotel and 2 Cottages are ADA compliant. Cottages are some distance from parking, although bell service is available.

Rates: Hotel rooms and Cottages: Standard ($417–$471); Classic ($443–$497); Balcony/Fireplace ($469–$523); Junior Suites ($575); Suites ($1,016–$1,149). Children 12 and under stay free in the same room with an adult. Each additional person is $21 per night. A variety of packages are offered during the off season when room prices are often discounted.

Guests who have enjoyed staying in the Ahwahnee since its opening in 1927 can thank Stephen Mather, first superintendent of the National Park Service. Mather facilitated the merger of Yosemite's first concessionaires—Curry Company and the Yosemite Park Company—on the condition the new firm construct an upscale fireproof hotel with the capability of year-round operation. The luxurious hotel was expected to increase tourism (and the park's budget) and attract important people who would provide political and financial support for the National Park Service. The Ahwahnee's architect, Gilbert Stanley Underwood, had previously designed impressive lodges at Zion National Park and Bryce Canyon National Park, and would subsequently design Grand Canyon Lodge on the North Rim and Oregon's Timberline Lodge.

The Ahwahnee has hosted many famous guests since the hotel's opening on July 14, 1927. President John F. Kennedy stayed overnight in August 1962 in what is now known as the Presidential Suite. Presidents Hoover, Eisenhower, and Reagan also stayed overnight, although not during their presidential terms. Winston Churchill, Will Rogers, and Eleanor Roosevelt were guests at the Ahwahnee. Among the numerous Hollywood stars who have stayed here are Shirley Temple, Bing Crosby, Ginger Rogers, Judy Garland, Lucille Ball, Clint Eastwood, Jack Benny, Greta Garbo, Red Skelton, and Humphrey Bogart. Among the hotel's most famous guests were Queen Elizabeth II and her husband, Prince Philip, who stayed 3 nights in March 1983.

Location: North section of Yosemite Valley, at the end of a dead-end road.

Season: Year-round. The hotel is often fully booked a year ahead for busy periods such as holidays and summer months.

Food: An elegant dining room serves breakfast ($10–$19), lunch ($13–$23), and dinner ($31–$46). Dinner reservations are highly recommended, and appropriate attire is required; athletic clothing is not allowed. Sunday brunch ($43) is served from 7 a.m. to 2 p.m. The cocktail lounge serves light meals including sandwiches, salads, and appetizers from 11 a.m. to 10 p.m. Room service is available. Special occasions, such as the famous Bracebridge Dinner, take place throughout the year.

Facilities: Outdoor heated swimming pool, gift shop, cocktail lounge, sweetshop, and full-time concierge service.

Activities: Hiking, swimming, evening programs, guided hotel tours. Winter activities listed under Curry Village.

CURRY VILLAGE

Curry Village is the largest lodging complex in Yosemite Valley, with 503 rooms, mostly canvas tents. The term "village" is certainly appropriate for this facility is much like a small town, with tents, cabins, a buffet, fast-food restaurants, a bar, a sporting goods store, mountaineering school, a market/gift shop, a guest lounge, a post office (summer only), a community shower building, and restrooms.

Curry Village offers 4 types of accommodations. The least expensive are over 400 canvas Tent cabins with a wooden platform and canvas walls and roof. These are available in different sizes, with bedding options that range from 2 singles to a double plus 3 singles. Bedding consists of metal cots, with linens, towels, soap, and maid service provided. A padlock is available for securing the front door. A light is in each tent, although there are no electrical outlets, plumbing, or heat; however, a few heated tent cabins are available at slightly higher cost. Restroom and shower facilities are centrally located.

Curry Village also has wood-frame Cabins, most constructed as duplexes, although a few are quads and some are freestanding. Each Cabin has carpeting, heat, and some have a front porch with a bench. A majority have private baths, mostly with showers but some have a combination shower-tub. Remaining cabins have no bath or running water. Excluding the bathrooms, both types of cabins have approximately the same amount of living space. Cabins with a bath rent for approximately $50 extra and are more widely spaced than Cabins without a bath,

Curry Village Tent cabins

which literally sit on top of one another. Most cabins have 2 double beds, but a few with a bath have a double plus a single. Curry Village also has 1 Deluxe cabin (819) that has a living room with a fireplace, a bathroom, and a separate bedroom. This Deluxe cabin has a king bed plus a sofa bed so the cabin can sleep up to 4 persons and is by far the nicest lodging facility at Curry Village. A single motel-type building, Stoneman House, has 18 Standard rooms with private bath and shower but no tub. These units have heat and a ceiling fan. Beds range from 1 to 3 doubles; the 3 double beds are in units with a loft. Motel units with a loft are an especially desirable accommodation for families, as the loft can be used to separate children from parents, at least temporarily. In addition, they are a good value and rent for the same price as the other motel units.

Lodging facilities at Curry Village are tightly packed, and most units are some distance from parking. Porters with motorized carts can transport luggage to your room. When assigned a room, ask about the distance from parking and whether help from a porter is advisable. The many Tent cabins are among the cheapest of Yosemite's overnight offerings. Guests at Curry enjoy a variety of dining facilities including the Curry Village Pavilion, which serves breakfast and dinner, a grill, a pizza deck, and an ice cream/coffee corner. Evening programs are presented at an outdoor amphitheater. The decision on whether to stay here depends on how much you are willing to spend, what lodging facilities are available when your reservation is made, and, because this area can be very busy in the summer, how well you tolerate crowds.

Rooms: Doubles, triples, and quads; a few units will hold 5 or 6 persons. Most rooms, including all the tent cabins, do not have private baths.

One of Yosemite's best-known activities was the evening Firefall, during which a massive pile of glowing red fir bark embers was pushed over the cliff at Glacier Point near Camp Curry. The practice was begun in the 1870s, abandoned several years later, then revived in 1899 by David Curry, proprietor of Camp Curry. The evening activity became so popular that everything in the valley would come to a halt when the time came for embers to be pushed over the side. The Firefall continued until 1968, when it was permanently halted by park management.

Wheelchair Accessibility: Eight cabins with a bath and 1 motel room with a bath are ADA compliant.

Rates: Canvas Tent cabins ($124–$129); Cabins without bath ($152); Cabins with bath ($202); Deluxe cabin ($339); Standard motel-type rooms ($199). Children 12 and under stay free except in Tent cabins, where an additional child is $6 per night. Rates for an additional person are from $13 to $15. Prices are slightly lower from mid-Nov through mid-Mar, excluding holidays.

Location: Southeast side of Yosemite Valley.

Season: All lodging facilities in Curry Village are open spring through fall. Some are also open during winter.

Food: The Curry Village Pavilion serves breakfast and dinner from spring through fall. Sandwiches, salads, and pizza are served on the patio. An inside coffee corner has specialty coffees, bakery items, and ice cream. A bar serves alcoholic beverages beginning at noon along with hamburgers and a few other items. A small market sells beer, wine, cold sandwiches, and limited grocery items.

Facilities: Gift shop, mountain shop, bicycle rental and river raft rental stands, camp store, outdoor swimming pool, and post office (summer only). In winter an outside ice-skating rink is available and equipment for cross-country skiing can be rented.

Activities: River rafting, hiking, bicycling, swimming, and evening programs. Winter activities include cross-country skiing and ice-skating. Badger Pass, 23 miles from Yosemite Valley, usually receives substantial snowfall and has 4 chair lifts and 1 cable tow to serve 9 ski runs. Ninety miles of marked cross-country ski trails begin here.

HOUSEKEEPING CAMP

Housekeeping Camp is a complex of 266 concrete and canvas structures surrounding several larger wooden support buildings, including a registration desk, public laundry, market, shower building, and several common bathrooms. Rooms are built 2 to a unit, with the back of each room sharing a wall with an identical room. The rooms are constructed of cement on 3 sides (each two-room unit has concrete walls constructed in an H pattern), with a canvas front and a canvas roof that extends over a concrete floor and a front concrete patio area that has a picnic table and a cooking shelf with a light and electrical outlet. A privacy fence partially surrounds the front of each patio. A large food storage box is next to each patio. The canvas entry door cannot be secured, which means valuables should be left in your vehicle.

Each room has 1 double bed and a bunk bed. The interior also has shelving, a mirror, an electric light, and an electrical outlet. Rooms do not have a private bathroom, so guests must use centrally located bathhouses. Guests supply their own sheets, blankets, and pillows, although these can be rented at nominal cost at the registration building. Soap and towels are supplied without charge in the shower building. Most housekeeping units sit close together and offer little in the way of privacy or a view. Many are near a major park road or the crowded parking areas. Units on the bank of the Merced River offer the best views and are a superior choice.

Housekeeping Camp rooms represent national park lodging at its most basic. This area is best suited for groups or families with children, especially those who bring bicycles that can be ridden throughout this large complex. It is the only lodging facility in Yosemite Valley that allows cooking, a major advantage for many families. Actually, Housekeeping Camp is much like a large campground in which the tents are supplied. This is a stop on the valley shuttle, allowing guests to ride to other locations for food, programs, or activities.

Rooms: Rooms are identical, with bedding for up to 4 persons. Two additional cots can be rented. None of the rooms have a private bath.

Wheelchair Accessibility: Four units near a parking area have access to a wheelchair-accessible bathroom. A paved walkway connects the living units and bathroom.

Lodging unit at Housekeeping Camp

Rates: One to 4 persons pay the same price ($99); each additional person is $6 per night. Rates are reduced during the early spring and late fall. Children 12 and under are free.

Location: On the bank of the Merced River in the southeast section of Yosemite Valley, a short distance west of Curry Village.

Season: Spring to mid-Oct.

Food: No food service is at Housekeeping Camp. A small market has limited groceries. A variety of restaurants and snack facilities can be reached via the valley shuttle.

Facilities: Small market, shower, and laundry.

Activities: River rafting, swimming, and hiking.

YOSEMITE LODGE AT THE FALLS

Yosemite Lodge at the Falls is a large complex of wooden buildings with 2 categories of overnight guest facilities, including 1 two-story motel unit and several one- and two-story lodge units. None of the two-story units has an elevator. In all, the lodge provides 245 rooms. Units are scattered about a service area that includes the registration building, located just south of Northside Drive in front of scenic Yosemite Falls. A variety of stores and

Lodge building at Yosemite Lodge at the Falls

restaurants are near the registration building and within easy walking distance of guest rooms. Registration parking is directly in front of the registration building, but overnight guest parking can be a considerable distance from some of the rooms. Bell service is available to assist with luggage.

Nearly all 245 rooms are in 14 one- and two-story frame buildings constructed in the mid- to late-1960s. All these Lodge rooms are virtually identical, with a dressing area, hair dryer, television, mini-refrigerator, telephone, heat, ceiling fan, and a full bathroom with a combination shower-tub. Bedding is available with either 1 king, 2 doubles, or a double plus a bunk bed consisting of a single bed over a double. Each room has a patio or balcony with a table and 2 chairs. The buildings do not have air-conditioning or elevators. Rooms in the 2 one-story buildings and top-floor rooms in the two-story buildings have vaulted beamed ceilings. Bottom-floor rooms have flat ceilings, making the rooms appear less spacious even though they are the same size. Lodge rooms are similar to large upscale motel rooms. Unfortunately, surrounding trees obstruct mountain and waterfall views from nearly all the rooms.

Yosemite Lodge also offers 15 smaller and less expensive Standard rooms in a single

two-story building constructed in the late 1950s adjacent to the registration building. All these rooms, which rent for about $20 less than the larger Lodge rooms, have the same amenities as Lodge rooms. These rooms do not have a patio or balcony. Bedding in Standard rooms varies from 1 double to 2 queens. Four extra-large rooms on the second floor are classified as "Family" rooms that rent for $18 more than Standard rooms but are priced for 4 adults. These rooms each have a mini-refrigerator, TV, dining table, shower (no tub), a separate toilet, 2 sinks, and a king and sofa sleeper plus a bunk bed consisting of a single bed over a double.

Our choice at Yosemite Lodge is a second-floor Lodge room on the back side of the Juniper or Laurel buildings. These rooms offer convenient parking but face away from the road and are relatively quiet. They also face away from Yosemite Falls, but few rooms in Yosemite Lodge offer a view of this picturesque attraction. Our second choice would be any room in one-story Cottonwood. One disadvantage here is the distance from parking. Aspen, Dogwood, and Tamarack, 3 newer buildings with Lodge rooms, are squeezed together on a corner between 2 parking lots. Rooms in these buildings are near parking but offer little privacy. With 2 or more children you may want to try for 1 of 4 Family rooms in the Cedar building.

A variety of tours are offered to Yosemite visitors. These include the 2-hour Valley Floor Tour, the 4-hour Glacier Point Tour, the Mariposa Grove Tour, the Big Trees Tram Tour, the Moonlight Tour, the Stargazing Tour, and the full-day Grand Tour, which combines the Glacier Point and Mariposa Grove Tours with a picnic (extra fee) at the Wawona Hotel. Most tours depart from Yosemite Lodge at the Falls. Tickets can be purchased at several valley locations. Call (209) 372-4386 for information.

Yosemite Lodge at the Falls is in the center of facilities and activities. Food service includes a food court and an upscale restaurant. You will also find an ice cream stand, nature shop, gift shop, and a cocktail lounge. A tour desk is inside the registration building. The shuttle stops across the street from the registration building and provides access to all facilities and activities in the valley.

Rooms: Doubles, triples, and quads, with 6 persons in a limited number of rooms. All rooms have private baths.

Wheelchair Accessibility: Three Lodge rooms and 1 Standard room are ADA compliant.

Rates: Standard rooms ($200); Family rooms with up to 4 people ($218); Lodge rooms ($227). Rates quoted are for 2 adults. Each additional person is $10 per night for Standard rooms, $11 for Lodge rooms. Children 12 and under stay free. Prices are slightly lower from mid-Nov through mid-Mar, excluding holidays. Specials are offered during the off-season.

Location: In the northwest section of Yosemite Valley, near the double waterfall.

Season: The lodge is open year-round.

Food: A food court offers breakfast, lunch, and dinner at moderate prices. Breakfast includes pancakes, french toast, eggs, oatmeal, cold cereals, and bakery items. Lunch and dinner items include pizza, pasta, chicken, fish, salads, and desserts. Lunch and dinner prices range from $5 to $14. Beer and wine are available. In the same complex, the Mountain Room offers an excellent view of Yosemite Falls in a dining room that serves upscale dinners including steaks, seafood, and chicken ($18 to $40). Dinner reservations are recommended. Beer, wine, and other alcoholic beverages are available. The nearby Mountain Room Lounge serves sandwiches and salads from 4:30 p.m. (noon on weekends) to 10:30 p.m. A market behind the registration building sells limited groceries including beer, wine, and snacks.

Yosemite Lodge at the Falls was a substantially larger complex prior to the disastrous flood of January 1997. Three days of rain flooded much of Yosemite Valley, including the Yosemite Lodge complex. The flood was actually similar in intensity to floods that occurred in Yosemite Valley during the previous 100 years. The history of damaging floods caused the National Park Service to order the removal of more than 150 cabins and 2 lodge buildings that were in service prior to January 1997. In all, Yosemite Lodge lost approximately 200 rooms.

Facilities: Gift shops, food court, restaurant, cocktail lounge, branch post office, bicycle rental, tour desk, swimming pool, outdoor amphitheater.

Activities: Evening programs, swimming, biking, hiking. Winter activities are listed under Curry Village.

WAWONA HOTEL

8308 Wawona Rd. • Yosemite National Park, CA 95389 • (209) 375-6556

Wawona Hotel

Wawona (an Indian term meaning "big tree") Hotel is the grande dame of the national parks. While some would argue that Death Valley's Inn at Furnace Creek and Yosemite's own Ahwahnee are more elegant, the Wawona is without a doubt one of the grandest of national park hotels. Wawona Hotel is a complex of 6 white frame, shake-roofed buildings, the oldest of which was built in 1876. The newest building was constructed in 1918. The complex is similar in appearance to a late-1800s western military post.

The 6 buildings at Wawona offer 104 rooms. Each building contains guest rooms, although both building and room size vary considerably.

The main building, which houses registration, a large dining room, and an attractive lounge, has 29 rooms, all but 1 on the second floor. Each floor of this large, two-story building has a wraparound veranda with white railings and posts. Wicker benches, chairs, and tables on the lower veranda offer guests a place to relax while viewing the grassy front lawn that surrounds a stone fountain. Beverages are served here during the late afternoon and early evening. The other 5 buildings are smaller but have a similar architectural style, including verandas with tables and chairs. A nice guest lounge is on the end of 1 building.

All rooms at Wawona have heat but no air-conditioning, telephone, or television. With the exception of second floor rooms in Moore, Washburn, and the Annex, all have ceiling fans. Although rooms vary by size, view, and building, only 2 price categories apply: with or without private bath. Fifty of the 104 rooms have a private bath and rent for about $70 per night more than rooms without a private bath. Guests in rooms without a private bath must use community shower and bathroom facilities. Community bathrooms, accessed from outside porches, can require a walk past up to 8 rooms, depending on the location of your room. Guest rooms in the main building are relatively small and all but 2 are without a private bathroom or in-room sink. Rooms 213 and 220 are much larger than average, while rooms 223 and 224 each have a bathroom with a claw-foot tub. Views vary, with some rooms providing a scenic view toward the front lawn and others in an inside hallway having no view at all. View is not considered in the rate, so request a front room.

If staying in the main building isn't important (and it really shouldn't be because the rooms are quite small) and you want a private bath, request a room in one-story Clark Cottage or Washburn Cottage, but be aware that both cottages have a limit of 2 persons per room. Clark Cottage sits directly beside the main building and offers attractive rooms. Four front rooms in Clark probably offer the best views. Corner rooms have an extra window that provides additional outside light. All rooms have a king-size bed and a private bath. Two-story Washburn Cottage has 16 rooms, all with private baths. First-floor rooms are of nice size with a king bed. Upstairs rooms are smaller, have a queen bed, do not have a veranda, and require climbing a flight of stairs.

Moore Cottage with 9 rooms sits on a hill directly behind the main hotel building and offers the most convenient parking at Wawona. Only 2 of the 9 rooms, both on the first floor,

offer a private bath with a shower. The 4 upstairs rooms are quite small, each with a single dormer window, and no veranda. Guests with an upstairs room must utilize a long, steep stairway to reach the first floor community bathroom and to transport luggage. Try to avoid an upstairs room in Moore.

Our 2 favorite rooms at Wawona are Moore 87, a first-floor room that is quite large and has a private bath, and corner room 89, which has a sink but not a private bath. Little White is a small cottage with only 3 rooms, 2 of which have a private bath and 2 queen beds. The third room with a king bed has connecting doorways to both the other rooms, and the entire building is an excellent choice for family gatherings. The room without a bath (51) is large but requires guests to use bathroom facilities in another building if the room is not rented in conjunction with an adjoining room that has a bath. This building is often booked a year ahead. The two-story Annex has 39 rooms, most of which have a double bed plus a single bed. Half the rooms have a private bath with a claw-foot tub and shower. Other rooms, with in-room sinks only, have connecting doors to rooms with a bath for families that wish to rent 2 rooms. Room 137, with a private bathroom, is quite large and includes 2 double beds plus 1 single bed. All the buildings are clustered closely together, so there should be no concern about the walking distance to the restaurant or lounge.

President Teddy Roosevelt arrived at the Wawona Hotel on May 3, 1903. Assigned room 215, the president dropped off his bags and went off to the Big Trees area to meet with conservationist John Muir. This meeting gave Muir an opportunity to convince Roosevelt to expand the park to include Yosemite Valley. Mariposa Grove and Yosemite Valley were at the time owned by the state of California.

The Wawona dining room retains its Victorian flavor, with tall windows offering views from the front and side of the main building. Although named a hotel, Wawona is actually more of a resort with a swimming pool (the "tank"), a tennis court, and a 9-hole golf course. A practice putting green is on the front lawn. The hotel is adjacent to Pioneer Village, a collection of historic buildings that introduce visitors to events shaping Yosemite's history. Included are a covered bridge, horse-drawn coaches, a homestead, and numerous historic buildings.

Wawona Hotel is a peaceful alternative to lodging facilities in hectic Yosemite Valley. The free daily shuttle to Yosemite Valley allows the hotel to serve as a convenient base for a Yosemite vacation of several days. Why endure the hassle and expense of driving into the valley and searching for a parking place when you can hop a free shuttle and let someone else worry about the driving? A free shuttle also operates between the hotel and Mariposa Grove, site of many giant sequoia trees.

Wawona Hotel has been in continuous operation for over 130 years, longer than any other lodging unit in the national park system. The Wawona had already served travelers for more than a decade before Yosemite National Park was established. In the early days guests enjoyed meals featuring vegetables gathered from a local garden and freshly prepared fish and venison from the nearby streams and woods. The hotel even had its own dairy so guests could enjoy fresh milk and cream. The Wawona, a National Historic Landmark, has its own golf course, which opened for business in June 1918 as the first course in the Sierra Nevada.

Rooms: Mostly doubles, with a few triples and quads. About half the rooms have private baths. Rooms with private baths are often fully booked a year ahead during peak season. Previous guests often request particular rooms, so be as specific as possible about the type and location of the room you desire.

Wheelchair Accessibility: Two first-floor rooms in the Annex have limited wheelchair accessibility.

Rates: Rooms with private bath ($227); rooms without private bath ($154). Rates quoted are for 2 adults and include a buffet breakfast. Each additional person is $14 per night without a bath and $22 per night with a bath. A few rooms can handle a rollaway that costs $11 per night. Children 12 and under stay free. Rates are slightly lower from mid-Nov to mid-Mar, excluding holidays. Several packages are offered for fall and winter.

Location: Twenty miles north of Oakhurst and 4 miles north of the south entrance to Yosemite National Park. The hotel is approximately 25 miles from Yosemite Valley.

Season: Easter through Thanksgiving weekend and 2 weeks around Christmas.

Food: An attractive dining room serves breakfast ($11–$15), lunch ($11–$15), and dinner ($22–$30). Reservations are accepted for dinner only for parties of 6 or more. Alcoholic beverages are served on the front porch, the lobby, and in the dining room. During summer months an old-fashioned barbecue is served Sat night on the front lawn. A snack shop at the golf shop in the bottom floor of the Annex offers sandwiches, chili, and beverages from spring to fall. A market with beer, wine, soft drinks, cold sandwiches, and limited groceries is a short walk from the hotel.

Facilities: Swimming pool, tennis court, 9-hole golf course, putting green, National Park Service visitor center, market, gift shop, post office, gas station, historic Pioneer Village.

Activities: Golf, tennis, horse rides, 10-minute stagecoach rides, nature walks, swimming, fishing, and hiking. Evening entertainment is provided on Tues through Sat evenings by musician Tom Bopp.

TUOLUMNE MEADOWS LODGE AND WHITE WOLF LODGE
Tioga Road • Yosemite National Park, CA 95389 • (209) 372-8413 or (209) 372-8416

Tuolumne Meadows and White Wolf each offer tent cabins and dining facilities along Tioga Road, which crosses Yosemite's high country to the Owens Valley on the east side of the Sierras. White Wolf, the smaller of the 2 facilities with 24 tent cabins, also has 4 hard-sided wooden cabins, each with a private bathroom. Tuolumne Meadows has 69 tent cabins only. Both locations have dining facilities that serve breakfast and dinner. Box lunches are available at Tuolumne Meadows. This is bear country so no cooking or picnicking is permitted near the tent areas. Bear boxes are available for food storage. The facilities are in the High Sierra at between 8,000 and 9,000 feet in altitude, so night temperatures can be quite nippy.

Tioga Road (CA 120), which accesses White Wolf Lodge and Tuolumne Meadows Lodge, was originally built in 1882–1883 as a mining road. It was modernized in 1961. The two-lane paved road climbs to an elevation of 9,945 feet as it winds 75 miles across the Sierra high country from Yosemite Valley to Lee Vining, California. The road closes in winter and, depending on the weather, generally reopens in May. Road and weather information is available from a National Park Service recording at (209) 372-0200.

At an elevation of 8,700 feet, Tuolumne Meadows is a center for summer activities in Yosemite National Park. It is also the main access point for the High Sierra camps—Merced Lake, Vogelsang, Glen Aulin, May Lake, and Sunrise. These hike-in (or ride in on saddle) camps offer canvas cabins with concrete floors and single and double beds. Blankets are provided, but not linens. Breakfast and dinner at each camp are served family-style in a central dining tent. Box lunches for the trail are available at extra cost. The High Sierra camps are very popular, and reservations are made via lottery applications available by calling (801) 559-4909 or visiting www.yosemitepark.com. Applications are accepted Sept 1 to Nov 1, with applicants notified by Jan 15.

The tents are essentially identical to those at Curry Village in Yosemite Valley. They sit either on a cement slab (Tuolumne Meadows) or wooden platform (White Wolf), with an inside wood stove for heat. Each canvas tent is equipped with 4 single beds or 1 double bed plus 2 single beds. Sheets, pillows, and blankets are provided. The tents do not have electricity or plumbing, so guests at both locations must use a common bathhouse with showers. Guests are provided with candles for light, wood for the stove, and towels for the bathhouse. See the photo of a tent cabin at the entry for Curry Village in Yosemite Valley.

The 4 wooden cabins at White Wolf have a small front porch and are constructed as duplexes. They each have propane heat, electricity, 2 double beds, and a full bath. Lodging at both locations is available from late spring to early fall, depending on the weather. Tioga Road did not open in 2011 until June 18 and the 2 lodges did not open until mid-July, so reservations at either location in the late fall and early summer can be iffy. Rates for the tent cabins are approximately $124 per night for up to 2 adults. Each additional adult is $11. Wooden cabins at White Wolf are $156 per night for up to 4 adults. At only $32 more per night, the wooden cabins are a relative bargain, but with only 4 units available, securing a reservation is difficult. Meals are extra and range from $5 to $15 for breakfast and $8 to $28 for dinner.

Conservationist John Muir first visited Yosemite in 1868. Muir recruited Robert Underwood Johnson, editor of *Century* magazine, to use Johnson's influence to protect this area, especially in the high meadows that were being used to graze sheep. Muir and Johnson camped together in Tuolumne Meadows as they planned a strategy to gain national park status for the high country around Yosemite Valley.

Dinner reservations are required at both locations. Dinner is served family-style at Tuolumne Meadows.

COLORADO
State Tourist Information
(800) 265-6723 | www.colorado.com

Mesa Verde National Park
PO Box 8 • Mesa Verde, CO 81330 • (970) 529-4465 • www.nps.gov/meve

Mesa Verde (Spanish for "green table") is our country's outstanding archaeological national park that preserves sites built by ancient Native Americans who are claimed as ancestors by 24 current Native American nations. The magnificent cliff dwellings, pit houses, and other structures, abandoned in the late 1200s, represent the last 75 to 100 years of the 700 years of the Ancestral Puebloans who lived on the mesa tops and sheltered alcoves of the canyon walls. Mesa Verde offers a variety of activities, but most people visit to tour one or more of the park's impressive ruins. Guided tours of ruins are offered seasonally. Tour tickets can be purchased at the new Mesa Verde Visitor and Research Center (open all year), which has exhibits that include prehistoric and historic Indian arts and crafts. Chapin Mesa Archeological Museum offers exhibits and a 25-minute video. The park's entrance road from US 160

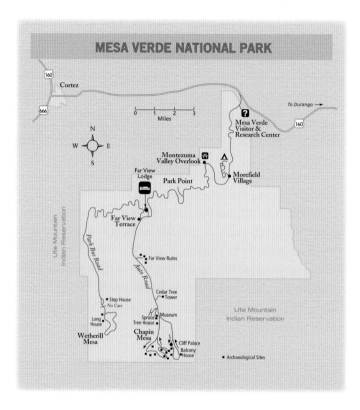

is narrow with steep grades and sharp curves. Trailers must be dropped off at a parking lot near the park entrance station. The 12-mile mountain road to Wetherill Mesa (open summer only) is not open to vehicles over 8,000 GVW and/or longer than 25 feet. Mesa Verde National Park is in southwestern Colorado, 36 miles west of Durango on US 160.

Park Entrance Fee: $15 per vehicle/$8 per individual late May to early Sept; $10 per vehicle/$5 per person the remainder of the year. Entrance fee is good for 7 days.

Lodging in Mesa Verde National Park: Mesa Verde's single lodging facility provides 150 rooms in 17 motel-style buildings. Far View Lodge is 15 miles from the park entrance station, near Far View Terrace. Park ruins are not within walking distance of the lodge.

Far View Lodge
PO Box 277 • Mancos, CO 81328 • (970) 529-4421 • www.visitmesaverde.com

Far View Lodge features an attractive adobe building housing the registration desk, small lobby, dining room, gift shop, and cocktail lounge. Seventeen nearby motel-style frame buildings each contain from 4 to 20 rooms. Paved roads near the lodge lead to park ruins.

Far View Lodge, situated at an altitude of 8,250 feet on a shoulder of the Mesa Verde, offers outstanding views across 3 states: Colorado, New Mexico, and Arizona (hence the name). The lodge has 150 rooms in 2 categories: Standard and Kiva. All have electric heat, bath with a shower or combination shower-tub, coffeemaker, hair dryer, small refrigerator, and telephone, but no television. The bedding ranges from 1 queen or king to 2 doubles or queens. Kiva rooms have been upgraded with air-conditioning, wood or tile floors, new bathrooms, brass bowl sinks, superior mattresses, and Native American and Southwestern artwork and handcrafted furnishings made by local artisans.

Under a new NPS concession contract effective as of 2015, existing Standard rooms are to be upgraded to Kiva rooms by the end of 2017. Following completion of the upgrades the concessionaire will be permitted to increase the rent to that charged for premium rooms.

All 17 lodge buildings are one story except 2 two-story units flanking the registration building. Buildings are situated on a hillside and rooms have large picture windows and private balconies that offer exceptional mesa and canyon views. The best views are in units 131 through 140 and 111 through 120, second-floor rooms of two-story buildings with access that does not require climbing steps.

Far View Lodge is ideally situated for exploration of this fascinating national park. The lodge is a short distance off the main road to Wetherill and Chapin Mesas, a quiet but handy location because guests often visit both areas. The Metate Room, one of our favorite national park dining rooms, offers an attractive decor, scenic vistas, and excellent food. Alcoholic beverages are served in the dining room and in a second-floor lounge that has floor-to-ceiling windows and a large balcony. An extensive wine list is available. A half-mile paved trail connects the lodge with Far View Terrace that offers a food court and large gift shop. Guided bus tours of the park begin at

One of numerous lodge buildings at Far View Lodge

the lodge, where reservations can be made and tickets purchased.

Rooms: Singles, doubles, triples, and quads. Rooms have a private bath with shower or combination tub-shower.

Wheelchair Accessibility: 10 rooms, some in each category, are ADA compliant.

Reservations: Far View Lodge, PO Box 277, Mancos, CO 81328. Phone (800) 449-2288; www.visitmesaverde.com. Deposit required for 1 night's lodging. Cancellation notice of 72 hours is required for refund of deposit.

Rates: Rates vary according to season and occupancy. Standard ($99–$140); Kiva ($130–$175). Rates quoted are for 2 adults. Each additional person is $10 per night. Children 12 and under stay free with adults. Special packages (room plus tour and/or food) are available and Internet specials are frequently offered. AAA and AARP discounts are offered, based on availability.

Location: Fifteen miles inside the park entrance. The nearest major town is Cortez, Colorado, 10 miles west of the park entrance.

Season: Far View Lodge is open from mid-Apr to late Oct.

Food: An attractive dining room has a unique combination of decorations, vistas, and menu items that include Southwestern specialties. Many tables are situated to take advantage of outstanding views provided by large picture windows. Only dinner ($15–$32) is served. During our last visit appetizers included wild boar sliders, prickly turkey, and red chile shrimp. Alcoholic beverages are offered in the dining room and a lounge that serves appetizers and sandwiches. A half-mile away, a food court at Far View Terrace seasonally offers breakfast, lunch, and dinner ($6–$15). Beer and wine are available. Specialty coffees, fudge, and ice cream are also sold.

Facilities: Dining room, gift shop, cocktail lounge. Eleven miles away Morefield Village has laundry facilities, a gift shop, and a store with groceries, beer, wine, and camping supplies. A gift shop and food court are at Far View Terrace and Spruce Tree Terrace. The Mesa Verde Visitor and Research Center and Chapin Mesa Museum each offer exhibits on native tribes.

Ranger-guided tours ($3 per person) at Cliff Palace (1 hour), Balcony House (1 hour), and Long House (90 minutes) on Wetherill Mesa require tickets that are sold only at the Visitor Center or Morefield Ranger Station. Tickets are not available at the sites. Tour spaces are limited, and tickets should be purchased upon arrival in the park. Commercial half-day and full-day guided bus tours ($50 per person for half-day tours) begin at Far View Lodge where tickets are sold. Self-guided tours at the Far View sites (0.75-mile unpaved trail), Spruce Tree House (the park's best-preserved cliff dwelling), and Step House (0.75-mile round-trip) do not require a ticket. Ladder climbing is required during each of the ticketed tours.

Activities: Guided tours of Mesa Verde ruins originate from Far View Lodge. Trails of from 1.5 to nearly 8 miles are available for hikers. Special events, such as Hopi dances and pottery demonstrations, are scheduled May through Oct.

Pets: Small pets are permitted in Standard rooms only and incur a charge of $10 per pet per night in addition to a $50 refundable deposit.

HAWAII
State Tourist Information
(800) 464-2924 | www.gohawaii.com

Hawaii Volcanoes National Park

PO Box 52 • Hawaii Volcanoes National Park, HI 96718 • (808) 985-6000 • www.nps.gov/havo

Hawaii Volcanoes National Park comprises 333,086 acres of active volcanism, including 13,677-foot Mauna Loa and famous Kilauea, where most of the park's activity is centered. An 11-mile paved road circles the Kilauea Caldera and provides access to scenic stops and nature walks. This and other park roads are occasionally closed due to eruption activity. The park is in the southeastern corner of the island of Hawaii. The visitor center and museum are approximately 29 miles southwest of Hilo, on HI 11.

Park Entrance Fee: $10 per vehicle or $5 per person, good for 7 days.

Lodging in Hawaii Volcanoes National Park: Volcano House, with 33 rooms, is the park's only lodging facility. It is just off HI 11 on the north end of Crater Rim Drive. Ten camper cabins are at

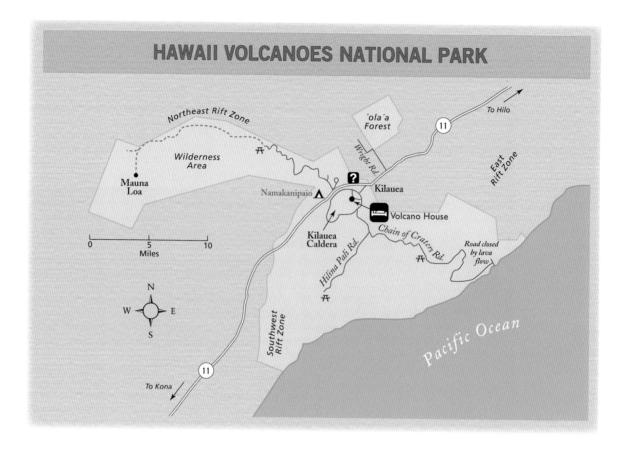

HAWAII VOLCANOES NATIONAL PARK

Namakanipaio Campground, 3 miles west of the park entrance, on HI 11. A city bus operates between Hilo and the park's visitor center, which is across the road from the hotel.

VOLCANO HOUSE

Crater Rim Drive • Hawaii Volcanoes National Park, HI 96718 • (808) 756-9625
www.hawaiivolcanohouse.com

Volcano House is a rustic, two-story wood-and-stone hotel that was constructed in 1941, expanded in 1962, and extensively renovated in 2012–13. The dining room, gift shops, cocktail lounge, snack bar, lobby, and most of the accommodations are in a single building on the edge of Kilauea Crater. Ten less expensive wood cabins without private baths are 3 miles from the hotel, in the Namakanipaio Campground. Volcano House was closed on January 1, 2010 for

extensive seismic and fire safety improvements. The hotel reopened on June 1, 2013 following a $3 million renovation.

The hotel offers 33 rooms, all of which have been refurbished with historic decor. Rooms are furnished with carpeting, heat, telephone, and a private bath, most with a shower. Three rooms have bathtubs. Rooms are divided into 3 classifications, distinguished primarily by size and view. Six Volcano Crater–view rooms in the newer wing are

Volcano House

the largest. Five of these have a king bed, and the other room has 2 doubles. Fourteen Deluxe Volcano Crater–view rooms in the original sections of the hotel have either a king, a queen with 2 twin beds, or 2 double beds. These 20 rooms offer outstanding views of Kilauea Crater. Twelve rooms in the hotel's original section offer views of the ohia and fern forests and have either a king or 2 queen beds. These are classified as Standard rooms.

Ten single-room wood cabins, which look like tiny A-frames, are at Namakanipaio Campground, 3 miles from Volcano House. Each cabin has 1 double bed and 1 bunk bed, an electric light (no outlets), and an outdoor grill and picnic table. Linens, including 1 pillow, sheets, a towel, and 1 blanket per bed, are provided at check-in. You may wish to bring additional blankets, as the nights can be cool at this altitude and the cabins do not have heat. Cabin guests must use community bathroom facilities, which are situated among the cluster of cabins.

Volcano House is a convenient and interesting place to stay when touring the island of Hawaii. The location on the edge of the huge caldera is spectacular. Many visitors like to experience this national park by hiking on a portion of over 150 miles of trails. The hotel provides guests with free use of cruiser bicycles.

Rooms: Doubles, triples, and quads. All hotel rooms have a private bath. Cabins at Namakanipaio do not have private baths.

Wheelchair Accessibility: Wheelchair-accessible rooms are available.

Reservations: Volcano House, Crater Rim Drive, Hawaii Volcanoes National Park, HI 96718. Phone (866) 536-7972; www.hawaiivolcano house.com. First night's lodging is required as a deposit. Cancellation required at least 7 days prior to arrival to avoid loss of the deposit.

Volcano House with a view of Kilauea Volcano

Rates: Deluxe Volcano Crater–view ($385); Volcano Crater–view ($335); Standard ($285); Namakanipaio cabins ($80). Rates quoted are for 2 adults.

Location: Just off HI 11 on the north section of Crater Rim Drive. Volcano House is 30 miles from Hilo.

The original Volcano House was constructed in 1866 of grass and ohia poles. The first wooden hotel was built here 11 years later. This structure is across the road from the hotel and now serves as the Volcano Art Center. The main building of the hotel burned in 1940 and was replaced by the current Volcano House, which opened in November 1941.

Season: Both Volcano House and Namakanipaio cabins are open year-round.

Food: The Rim restaurant serves a breakfast buffet ($18), lunch ($13–$19), and dinner ($21–$39). Uncle George's Lounge offers food service from 11 a.m. until 9 p.m. Limited groceries are available in nearby Volcano Village.

Facilities: Restaurant, cocktail lounge, gift shop, craft gallery, National Park Service visitor center, art center, golf course (1 mile away).

Activities: Hiking, biking, interpretive programs, cultural events, Hawaiian music, golf.

Mammoth Cave National Park

1 Mammoth Cave Pkwy. • Mammoth Cave, KY 42259 • (270) 758-2180 • www.nps.gov/maca

Mammoth Cave National Park covers 52,830 acres of rugged hillsides and beautiful rivers that overlay the longest recorded cave system in the world with over 400 miles having been explored. A variety of guided cave tours are offered throughout the day with tour frequency and variety depending on the season. The park has 70 miles of hiking trails and a gravel bicycle trail. Canoeing, kayaking, and fishing are popular on the Green River. Mammoth Cave National Park is located in central Kentucky, approximately 90 miles south of Louisville via I-65.

Park Entrance Fee: No charge.

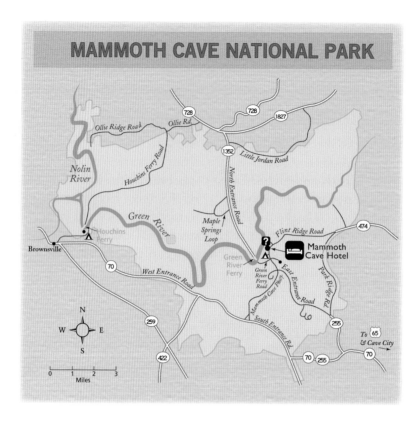

MAMMOTH CAVE NATIONAL PARK

Lodging in Mammoth Cave National Park: A single lodging complex offers a wide variety of accommodations that are close to the visitor center and ticket sales area for cave tours. Buses near the visitor center provide transportation to the cave entrance.

MAMMOTH CAVE HOTEL

PO Box 27 • Mammoth Cave, KY 42259-0027 • (270) 758-2225 • www.mammothcavehotel.com

Mammoth Cave Hotel is actually much more than a hotel. It is a lodging complex consisting of 30 cottages, 4 single-story motel buildings, and a two-story brick hotel. In all, the complex provides 92 guest rooms at reasonable rates. Registration for all lodging is just inside the front entrance of the hotel, which also houses a craft store, gift shop, meeting rooms, and dining facilities. The complex sits in expansive grassy areas near the National Park Service visitor center, where tickets are sold for tours of this world-famous cave. A paved walkway connects the

hotel with the visitor center, where buses leave for scheduled cave tours.

Four types of accommodations are available at Mammoth Cave Hotel. The least expensive lodging is 20 Woodland Cottages, clustered on the north side of the visitor center. These rustic but pleasant wooden structures were constructed in the 1930s and are available mostly in two-bedroom units but also include 4 one-bedroom units, 1 three-bedroom unit, and 1 four-bedroom unit. Beds vary, but the four-bedroom unit can accommodate up to 20 individuals when

Woodland Cottages at Mammoth Cave Hotel

rollaways are added. Each Woodland Cottage has hardwood floors, a vaulted ceiling, ceiling fans, small refrigerator, coffeemaker, and a small private bath with a shower. Two-bedroom units have a sink in each bedroom. Three-bedroom and four-bedroom units each have 2 bathrooms. None of these units have heat, air-conditioning, phone, or a television. Windows and doors are screened to allow ventilation, but consider the lack of air-conditioning if you will be staying when the weather is likely to be hot and humid. These cottages are a nice size and offer more floor space than any other lodging at Mammoth Cave. Two-bedroom units 204/205, 206/207, and 208/209 are at the back of the complex next to a wooded area and offer the most privacy.

Ten Hotel Cottages across the parking lot from the main hotel sit in a semicircle in a large grassy area along the top of a wooded hillside. The small frame cabins, constructed in the 1930s, have electric heat, air-conditioning, television, carpeting, coffeemaker, small refrigerator, and a small private bath with a shower. Each cottage has 1 double bed. The cottages face a wooded ravine, and lawn chairs sit outside the front entrance to each cottage. The Hotel Cottages are situated some distance from the parking lot, so consider the required walk when booking a room.

Sunset Terrace units consist of 4 single-story buildings constructed in the 1960s. These fairly large rooms are designed for families. Each room offers electric heat, air-conditioning, refrigerator, coffeemaker, telephone, television, and a full bath with a combination shower-tub. The rooms are identical, with 2 double or queen beds, and each could easily accommodate a rollaway. Windows across the back side face a wooded area. Cement patios between the buildings have lawn chairs and tables. A large grassy area in front of the buildings is a good place for kids to play.

The main hotel, constructed in 1964–65, has 42 Heritage Trail rooms in a two-story brick

The author reads an interpretive sign on one of the park's many hiking trails.

building adjacent to the registration/restaurant building. This building does not have an elevator, so access to second-floor rooms requires climbing a flight of stairs. Heritage Trail rooms each have a full bath with a combination shower-tub, heat, air-conditioning, small refrigerator, telephone, coffeemaker, and a television. Each room has a private balcony or patio with chairs and a small table. The rooms are small but nicely furnished and have either 1 king or 2 double beds. Rooms on both floors are entered through an interior

Cave tours are the most popular activity at Mammoth Cave National Park. Approximately a dozen different types of tours are offered, depending on the season and demand. Some tours are easy and last about an hour. Others are strenuous and last from 3 to 6 hours. A schedule of each day's cave tours is posted in the visitor center. Cave temperatures are in the 50s, and the paths can be slick, with many steps, so it is important to dress properly. Most tours fill rapidly, so, if possible, make a reservation prior to arrival by mail or phone (877-444-6777) or online at reservations.nps.gov. You will also be able to obtain information about the various tours that are offered. Reservations may be made up to 5 months in advance of the desired tour date. If you arrive at the park without a reservation, be sure to head for the visitor center, where reservations can be made and tickets purchased.

corridor that runs the length of the building. This building is the most convenient to the lobby and dining facilities. We suggest a back room overlooking a wooded ravine.

Mammoth Cave National Park offers more than the cave tours for which it is so famous. In fact, this is one of our favorite parks, both for camping and overnight stays in the lodge. The area in which the lodging facilities are located is very pleasant, with lots of trees and open grassy spaces. Most park visitors have completed their cave tours by the late afternoon, so evenings are perfect for a quiet walk. Hiking trails and ranger-led walks are also available, and an amphitheater with evening programs is a short walk from any of the lodging facilities. Bicycle rentals are available for visitors who wish to take advantage of the park's lengthy bike path.

If you plan to take one of the ranger-led cave tours, be certain to check in at the visitor center behind the hotel as soon as possible after your arrival so that you can reserve a tour time. It is preferable to reserve a tour prior to your arrival.

Rooms: Singles, doubles, triples, and quads. Some units can accommodate more than 4 persons. All rooms and cabins have private baths.

Wheelchair Accessibility: Four rooms near the lobby of the main hotel and 2 Sunset Terrace rooms are fully wheelchair accessible.

Reservations: Mammoth Cave Hotel, PO Box 27, Mammoth Cave, KY 42259-0027. Phone (270) 758-2225, (877) 386-4383; www .mammothcavehotel.com. One night's deposit required. Refund of deposit requires 48-hour cancellation notice.

Rates: Woodland Cottages ($61–$105 depending on the number of guests and the number of rooms); Hotel Cottages ($80); Sunset Terrace units ($105); Heritage Trail rooms ($95). Each extra adult is $7 per night in Woodland Cottages and $9 per night in Heritage Trail and Sunset Terrace rooms. Rollaway beds are $9 per night. The hotel offers packages and seasonal discounts. Call for information.

Location: The lodging complex is near the National Park Service visitor center in the eastern section of Mammoth Cave National Park. From I-65, take exit 53 at Cave City when traveling south and exit 48 at Park City when traveling north. The hotel is approximately 7 miles inside the park entrance.

Season: Heritage Trail rooms and Sunset Terrace rooms are open from early Mar through Oct and weekends only in Nov. Hotel Cottages are open from mid-Mar to late Oct, and the Woodland Cottages are open from mid-May to late Sept. Call for information on exact opening and closing dates.

Food: The Travertine Restaurant serves breakfast ($4–$8), lunch ($4–$10), and dinner ($7–$20). A breakfast buffet may be offered depending on the number of people staying at the hotel. The adjacent Crystal Lake Coffee Shop serves lunch ($4–$10) until 4:30 p.m. when it becomes a bar area that serves beer, wine, and pizza. A fast-food restaurant is open from 10:30 a.m. to 5 p.m. from late spring to early fall. Limited groceries and snacks are available at the gas station.

Facilities: Gas station with convenience store, self-service pet kennels (free to hotel guests), restaurant, coffee shop, fast-food restaurant (summer only), gift shop, craft shop, laundry, post office, canoe rentals, bicycle rentals, nature trails.

Activities: Hiking, cave tours, horseback riding, fishing (no license required), canoeing, kayaking, evening campfire programs (in season), ranger talks.

Pets: Pets are allowed only in the Woodland Cottages. A kennel is available without charge for hotel guests.

The current Mammoth Cave Hotel is near the site of 2 earlier hotels, the first of which burned to the ground and a second that was torn down. The earliest hotel commenced operations in early 1837 when an entrepreneur connected several existing log cabins. This hotel, which was located just east of the current Mammoth Cave Hotel, was upgraded from 1839 to 1849 with a large two-story structure that included a second-floor ballroom. This early hotel was considered one of the state's finest and annually welcomed from 2,000 to 3,000 guests. It burned in 1916 and was replaced in 1925 by a second hotel situated across the parking lot from the current hotel building. The second hotel was expanded 5 years later to include 38 rooms that could accommodate 200 guests plus a dining room that seated 125. This second hotel was near the current Hotel Cottages, hence their name. The hotel was torn down in 1979 after falling into disrepair and being removed from the National Register of Historic Places. A drawing of the first hotel is in the entrance to the current hotel's dining room and a painting of the second hotel is behind the front desk.

Isle Royale National Park

800 East Lakeshore Drive • Houghton, MI 49931 • (906) 482-0984 • www.nps.gov/isro

Isle Royale National Park comprises almost 572,000 acres, including the largest island in Lake Superior. Eighty percent of the park is under water. Isle Royale, approximately 45 miles long and 9 miles wide, is a roadless island of forests, lakes, and rugged shores. There are 166 miles of foot trails and numerous inland lakes on the island, where travel is via foot, boat, canoe, or kayak. Native tribes mined copper here thousands of years before the French claimed possession of Isle Royale in 1671. The island became a possession of the United States in 1783 and was identified as Chippewa Territory until the mid-1800s. Copper mining continued during the latter half of the 1800s, when large areas were burned and logged.

Isle Royale is in northwestern Lake Superior, 22 miles southeast of Grand Portage, Minnesota. No roads or bridges provide access to the island. Pets are not permitted in the park.

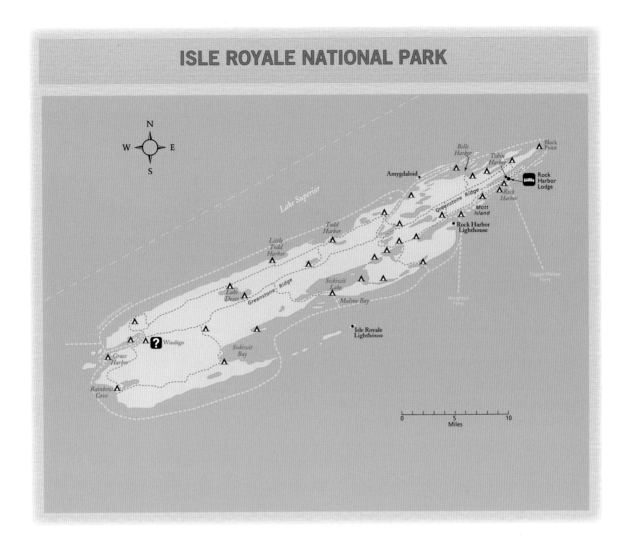

ISLE ROYALE NATIONAL PARK

Park Entrance Fee: A user fee of $4 per person per day is not covered by National Park Service passes. Staying 1 night in the lodge entails paying the user charge for 2 days—the day of arrival and the day of departure. Children 11 and under are exempt.

Lodging in Isle Royale National Park: The only regular overnight lodging facilities inside the park are at Rock Harbor, on the south shore of the northeastern tip of the island. Relatively new one-room rustic camper cabins with electricity but no indoor plumbing are operated at Windigo by the concessionaire at Rock Harbor Lodge. Access to the Rock Harbor Lodge is via seaplane or scheduled passenger boats from Houghton and Copper Harbor in Michigan's Upper Peninsula and from Grand Portage on Minnesota's north shore. The Grand Portage boat stops at Windigo.

ROCK HARBOR LODGE

PO Box 605 • Houghton, MI 49931-0405
(906) 337-4993 or (866) 644-2003 off-season • www.rockharborlodge.com

Two of the Lakeside lodge buildings at Rock Harbor Lodge

Rock Harbor Lodge is a relatively compact complex of 4 motel-type buildings, 20 housekeeping cottages, and various support buildings nestled on a rocky shoreline of Lake Superior. Other buildings include a registration/administration building, restaurant, grill, gift shop, small guest lounge, auditorium, store, National Park Service visitor center, and marina. Lodge buildings and cottages offer a total of 80 guest rooms. Paved walkways weave through the complex to connect all the buildings other than the auditorium, where access is via a gravel trail. Two of the 4 two-story lodges sit side-by-side on each end of an old lodge building with a small meeting room that serves as a gathering place for guests. A deck with tables and chairs faces the lake behind the old lodge. All the lodge buildings are on the shoreline of Lake Superior. Housekeeping cottages are up

a hill in a wooded area somewhat less convenient to the restaurant and grill. Luggage is picked up at the boat and delivered to each guest's assigned room. Luggage for departing guests is picked up in the rooms and delivered to the boat. Arriving guests receive a 5-minute introduction from a park ranger before walking to the registration building to register and pick up room keys.

Four identical lodge buildings with stone-and-wood exteriors were constructed during the early 1960s. The 60 Lakeside Lodge rooms in these buildings are carpeted and have a private bath. Rooms have heat and a coffeemaker, but no telephone, television, or air-conditioning. Bedding is either 2 doubles or a king. Rooms on the first floor enjoy a common wooden deck facing the lake that spans the length of each building. Two chairs are outside each room. Second-floor rooms do not have a deck or balcony, but do offer a much larger window with an excellent lake view. Access to some Lodge rooms requires climbing steps, so mention any mobility issues when making a reservation. Chippewa, with rooms 21 through 35, is closest to the dining room, and first-floor rooms do not require climbing steps.

Ten stone-and-wood duplex buildings offer 20 Cottages in a wooded area on a bluff above Tobin Harbor. Each cottage has electric heat, electric stove with oven, microwave, refrigerator, coffeemaker, dishes, and utensils. There is no telephone, television, or air-conditioning. These units have a double bed and 1 bunk bed (the wheelchair-accessible room has only 1 double bed) with linens and blankets, but no maid service. The double bed converts into a sofa. Rollaways are available and easily fit into the large great room. Cottages are widely spaced to offer privacy and have large windows across the back side and one end, but only a few offer views of Tobin Harbor, and even these views are limited by trees.

Room choice at Rock Harbor Lodge depends on personal taste. Cottages offer more privacy, larger interior space, and include cooking facilities, an appealing combination for families and individuals planning a stay of several days. These units are nearly a quarter mile from the restaurant, a nonissue if you plan to cook most meals. The lodge buildings are closer to the restaurant and offer excellent lake views. Choosing a Lodge room means deciding whether to ask for the first or second floor. Second-floor rooms have some advantages, but we prefer the first floor with deck access. One of the pleasures of staying at the lodge is sitting on the deck waiting for the sunrise, while sipping a cup of hot coffee while listening to the wail of a loon.

Isle Royale is a special place for travelers desiring a different vacation. There are no roads, no vehicles, and few people. You won't pass through the park on your way to somewhere else, and neither will anyone else. Choose to pack in your food and select a cottage, or elect a Lakeside Lodge room and eat in the grill or restaurant. Be ready to hike or canoe, or spend time on one of the many guided tours. Take some food, even if you plan to frequent the restaurant. The restaurant isn't inexpensive, so consider eating a meal or two on your own—perhaps a bowl of cereal or muffins for breakfast or a sandwich for lunch. Also consider a meal or two in the grill, which serves good sandwiches at a reasonable price.

Rooms: Doubles, triples, and quads. Cottages accommodate up to 6 people. All rooms have a private bath.

Wheelchair Accessibility: Three Lodge rooms and 1 Housekeeping cottage are ADA compliant. Trails are not wheelchair accessible.

Reservations: From May through Sept, Rock Harbor Lodge, Isle Royale National Park, PO Box 605, Houghton, MI 49931. Phone (906) 337-4993. From Oct through Apr, Rock Harbor Lodge, PO Box 27, Mammoth Cave, KY 42259. Phone (866) 644-2003 or visit www.rockharborlodge.com. A deposit of the first night's lodging is required. A refund of 90 percent of the deposit for cancellations at least 5 days prior to scheduled arrival.

Rates: Rates are quoted for 2 adults and include a complimentary half-day canoe rental. Peak season (early July to the end of the season)/low season (opening day to early July): Lakeside Lodge rooms ($271/$244), additional adult ($64/$57), additional child under 12 ($19/$17). Cottages ($263/$237), additional adult or child ($55/$50). Rates include a 22 percent National Park Service utility pass-through fee, but do not include state taxes.

Location: South shore on the northeastern tip of Isle Royale.

Season: The end of May through the first week in Sept. Cottages are available from Memorial Day weekend through early Sept.

Food: The restaurant offers 3 meals a day: breakfast ($6–$11); lunch ($9–$13); and dinner ($22–$37). A grill serves breakfast items along with sandwiches, salads, hamburgers, and pizza. Beer and wine are offered in both the restaurant and the grill. Limited grocery items including bread, milk, and ice cream treats (no beer or wine) are sold at the marina store.

Although a number of national parks operate on a seasonal basis, Isle Royale is one of the few that completely shuts down. Every facility is closed and everybody, including all National Park Service personnel, departs the island prior to the harsh Lake Superior winter. The lodge closes to guests in early Sept when the manager and approximately a dozen employees (compared to about 65 during peak season) begin preparing the facilities for winter. Pipes are drained, and the heat is turned off. Canoes and kayaks are stored in the restaurant, while benches are piled in the gift shop. Furniture remains in the rooms and cottages, but moved away from the windows where an errant tree limb might cause damage. The cycle is reversed in mid-May when the manager and about a dozen employees move into the cottages and begin getting facilities ready for an early June opening. This advance group prepares the plumbing and starts the boilers and refrigeration units. Rooms are cleaned and the supplies that were ordered during the winter begin to arrive.

Transportation: Passenger boats to Rock Harbor Lodge depart from Houghton and Copper Harbor, Michigan, and Grand Portage, Minnesota. The Houghton trip takes 6 hours 1 way and operates 2 days a week in each direction. Call (906) 482-0984. The trip from Copper Harbor takes 3 hours, and frequency varies depending on the season. Daily service is offered during high season from July 16 to Aug 15. Call (906) 289-4437. The boat from Grand Portage stops at Windigo and takes approximately 7½ hours 1 way to the lodge. Frequency of service varies with the season, although this boat generally operates 3 times per week from late May to early Sept. For information call (651) 653-5872 in winter and (218) 475-0024 in summer. Check www.rockharborlodge.com for the current schedule for each of the boats. Seaplane service to Rock Harbor (30 minutes 1 way) is offered from Houghton 6 days a week weather permitting. Call Royale Air Service at (877) 359-4753 or visit www.royaleairservice.com for information. A lodge-operated water taxi will pick up hikers, campers, canoers, and kayakers at numerous places on the island. Variable weather can delay boat and seaplane departures to and from the island. Bad weather has sometimes kept lodge guests on the island an extra day or delayed guests with reservations from getting to the island.

Facilities: Restaurant; grill; store with groceries, fishing equipment, and camping supplies; gift shop; and a marina with motorboat, kayak, and canoe rentals. Groceries include bakery items, frozen meats, canned goods, and limited fresh produce and fruit. The marina offers gasoline, diesel fuel, pumping services, and slips for boats up to 65 feet in length. A water taxi service is offered for guests, and their canoes and kayaks.

Activities: Hiking, guided walks, fishing, fishing charters, guided fishing tours, sightseeing tours, National Park Service programs, canoeing, and kayaking.

MINNESOTA
State Tourist Information
(800) 657-3700 | www.exploreminnesota.com

Voyageurs National Park

360 Hwy. 11 East • International Falls, MN 56649 • (218) 283-6600 • www.nps.gov/voya

Voyageurs National Park protects 218,000 acres of forested lake country once inhabited by French-Canadian fur traders who used canoes to transport animal pelts and other trade goods through this area during the late 18th and early 19th centuries. A 1783 treaty established the US–Canadian boundary along the waterway used by the voyageurs. The south side of the Kabetogama Peninsula is dotted with numerous islands, while the north shore is broken with many coves and small bays. One of the park's visitor centers is in its southwest corner, on CR 123. Voyageurs National Park stretches 55 miles along the US–Canadian border, east of International Falls in northern Minnesota. Summer travel within the park is confined to watercraft or floatplane.

Park Entrance Fee: No charge.

Lodging in Voyageurs National Park: Overnight accommodations within the park are available only at the Kettle Falls Hotel and Resort. Kettle Falls, in the northeast corner of the park, is reached via private boat or by private water taxi.

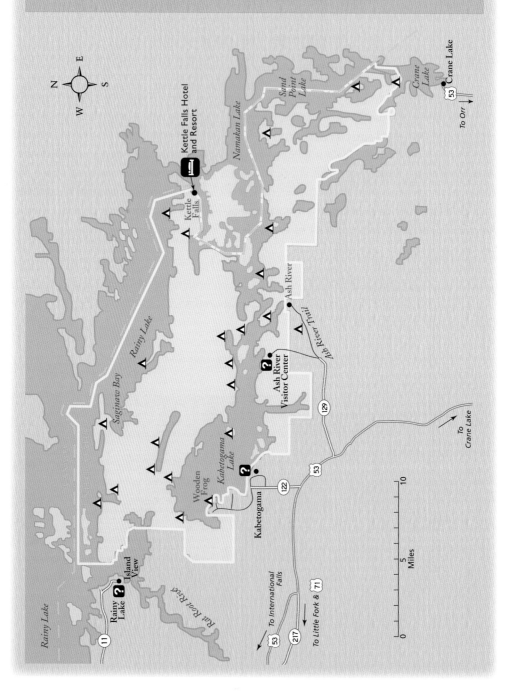

VOYAGEURS NATIONAL PARK

Kettle Falls Hotel

Kettle Falls is a relatively small lodging complex consisting of a historic two-story frame hotel plus 3 newer wooden villas that each contain from 2 to 4 lodging units. The hotel is part of a National Register of Historic Places District that includes the dam, a dam tenders cabin, and other sites and features. The first floor of the hotel houses a lobby, dining room, and saloon with a pool table, working nickelodeon, and antique-covered walls. The hotel is in a small clearing surrounded by woods, while the villas overlook the rocky shore of Rainy Lake. A quarter-mile gravel road leads from the dock to the hotel. Transportation from dockside to the lodging complex is available. Three types of rooms are available. None have a telephone or television. A telephone is in the lobby and televisions are in the lobby and the saloon. The least expensive rooms, all without private bath, are in the hotel.

Twelve second-floor rooms are furnished with antiques and have either 1 double bed or 2 or 3 single beds. All these rooms are approximately the same size. Three modern community bathrooms with showers are also on the second floor. Morning coffee and rolls or muffins are included in the price of a room.

Kettle Falls offers 10 Villas in 3 buildings on the Rainy Lake side of Kettle Falls Dam. Constructed in the early 1990s, the Villas have a screened porch, air-conditioning, and a ceramic-tiled bathroom with a shower. Each has a picnic table, lawn chairs, and an outdoor grill. Two buildings have 2 levels, while the other is a single story. Villas are side-by-side with a connecting door allowing adjacent units to be rented as a suite at a discounted price. One Villa on each level has a full kitchen including a sink, stove, oven, microwave, coffeemaker, toaster, and full-size refrigerator. Pots, pans, dishes, and utensils are included. The connecting Villa on the same level offers a refrigerator, microwave, and coffeemaker. Bedding includes 2 bunk beds or a full bed plus a bunk bed. Villas in the one-story building and top-floor Villas of the two-story buildings have a vaulted ceiling and are considerably larger than bottom-floor Villas. A large entryway offers storage space and the units are at ground level requiring no steps. Villas on the bottom floor of the two-story buildings offer a larger screened porch and direct access to the lake. Access to bottom-floor villas requires descending a series of steps. A 3-night minimum stay is required for Villas.

Although primarily geared to people who love to fish, those with little interest in angling will enjoy the pleasant and relaxing atmosphere of this isolated resort. Spend the early morning on the screened porch sipping a cup of coffee. Take an afternoon stroll down the gravel road and stand where fur traders and trappers once portaged canoes around the falls. Walk to the dam overlook and view Canada, our northern neighbor, while facing south. In the late afternoon stroll into the bar with the sloping floor (resulting from a sinking building foundation) and knock back a cold one before sitting down to a walleye dinner. One afternoon in late August we carried a picnic lunch to the dam overlook where, under cloudless blue skies, we watched a bald eagle circling overhead. Life doesn't get much better.

Rooms: Singles, doubles, triples, and quads. Villas with connecting doors can be converted to suites that accommodate up to 8 people. All villas have private baths. Guests at the main hotel have access to 3 community bathrooms.

Wheelchair Accessibility: Two villas, 1 with a kitchen and 1 without, are handicap accessible. The trail between the hotel and the villas is not paved, but a golf cart is available for transportation. The first floor of the hotel, with a dining room, saloon, and lobby, is wheelchair accessible.

Reservations: Kettle Falls Hotel and Resort, 12977 Chippewa Trail, Kabetogama, MN 56669. Phone (218) 240-1724 or (218) 240-1726 during summer; (218) 875-2070 during the off-season. Reservations require a 30 percent deposit that is refundable (less a 15 percent fee) if canceled at least 30 days prior to scheduled arrival. Cancellation within 30 days of scheduled arrival results in a deposit refund (less a 15 percent fee) only if the dates are filled by another party. Villa reservations require a 30 percent deposit and are refundable (less a 15 percent fee) only if the canceled dates are filled by another party.

Rates: Hotel rooms (single, $60; additional adult, $20; child, $15); Villas per unit (night, $180; week, $850); Villas with kitchenette per unit (night, $210; week $1,050); Suite per unit (night,

The building of Kettle Falls Hotel commenced in 1910. The original hotel included the lobby, kitchen, dining room, and 10 bedrooms spanning the front of the building. The north wing with additional bedrooms and the current saloon was added in 1915. The hotel initially served as a base for stonecutters and masons who worked on the dams, and later for lumberjacks and commercial fishermen. Original owner Ed Rose sold the hotel in 1918 to Bob Williams, reputedly for $1,000 plus 4 barrels of whiskey. The Williams family owned the hotel until being purchased by the National Park Service in 1977. The National Park Service undertook extensive rehabilitation in 1986 when the building was taken apart and reassembled after stabilizing the foundation. The Williams continued to manage the hotel as concessionaire into the 1990s, when the contract was sold to another individual.

$340; week, $1,700). Villas require a 3-night minimum stay. A rollaway is $20 per day.

Location: Kettle Falls Hotel and Resort is in the northeast corner of Voyageurs National Park.

Season: May through Sept.

Food: Breakfast ($5–$12), lunch ($6–$13), and dinner ($17–$25) are served daily in the dining room or on the screened porch. Complimentary coffee and rolls are offered each morning for hotel guests.

Transportation: A hotel-operated boat offers daily service ($45 round-trip) from the Ash River Visitor Center on CR 129. Parking is free. Free docking is available for those who arrive via their own boats.

Facilities: Dining room, saloon, and a trading post with groceries, souvenirs, fishing tackle, live bait, and fishing licenses. Boat docks with fuel, portage service, and motorboat, canoe, and kayak rentals.

Activities: Hiking, bird-watching, boating, and fishing. Kettle Falls is the promised land for those who want a shot at snagging a walleye. The kitchen staff will cook and serve your walleye for a nominal fee. Other frequent catches include northern pike, smallmouth bass, and crappie. Guide service is available when arrangements have been made ahead of time.

Pets: Pets are allowed in the Villas at $10 per night, or $50 per week.

MISSOURI
State Tourist Information
(800) 519-2100 | www.visitmo.com

Ozark National Scenic Riverways

404 Watercress Dr. • Van Buren, MO 63965 • (573) 323-4236 • www.nps.gov/ozar

Ozark National Scenic Riverways cover 80,000 acres of forested hills, mountains, freshwater springs, and caverns paralleling 134 miles of the beautiful Current and Jacks Fork Rivers. The rivers are popular for fishing and float trips in canoes, rafts, kayaks, and inner tubes. The park is in southeastern Missouri, 150 miles south of St. Louis.

Park Entrance Fee: No charge.

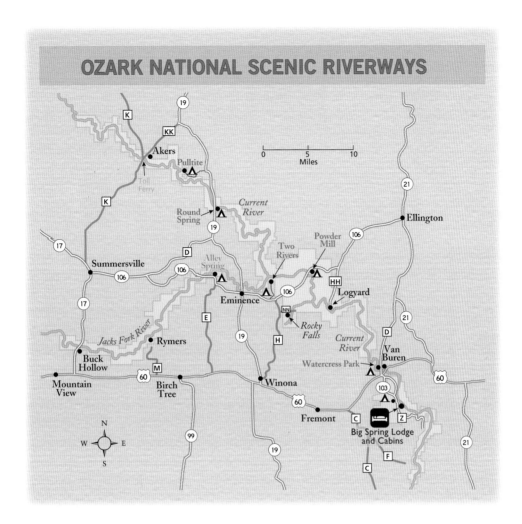

OZARK NATIONAL SCENIC RIVERWAYS

Lodging in Ozark National Scenic Riverways: Big Spring Lodge and Cabins, the park's only lodging facility, is 4 miles south of the town of Van Buren on MO 103. Accommodations are available outside the park in Eminence, Mountain View, Salem, and Van Buren.

Note: Big Springs Lodge and Cabins is expected to close for major repairs for three years beginning with the 2015 season. It is anticipated the lodge will reopen for the 2018 season.

Big Spring Lodge and Cabins

HCR 1, Box 169 • Van Buren, MO 63965 • (573) 323-4423 • www.bigspringlodgeandcabins.com

Big Spring Lodge and Cabins consists of a main lodge plus 14 freestanding cabins. The timber-and-stone lodge building on a bluff overlooking the confluence of Big Spring and the Current River houses the registration desk, dining room, and small gift area. The cozy dining

One of the CCC cabins at Big Spring Lodge

room includes a small wing with windows overlooking the river. The rustic wood-and-stone and frame cabins on a hill above the main lodge provide guest accommodations. A paved road winds up the hill to the cabins. Parking is available for each cabin, but access from parking to a cabin may involve climbing or descending numerous uneven steps. The entire complex sits amid a thick forest of hardwood trees.

Fourteen cabins are in 4 sizes that each sleep 2, 4, 6, or 8 persons. The rate charged includes 2, 4, or 6 occupants depending upon the particular cabin rented. An additional fee is charged for guests that exceed the number included in the rate. Four cabins, 401, 402, 403, and 414, were constructed by the Civilian Conservation Corps

(CCC) of wood and stone. The wood frame cabins were built later by the CCC and the Works Progress Administration (WPA). The cabins are widely spaced to provide relative privacy. They are quite roomy and each has a screened porch, bathroom with a shower, and kitchen facilities that include a 2-burner cooktop, small refrigerator, microwave, toaster, and coffeemaker. Four cabins do not have a kitchen sink. An oven, pots and pans, dishes, and utensils are not provided. A picnic table and fire pit with a grate for grilling are available at each cabin. Some, but not all cabins have an air conditioner, an important issue during July and August, although fans are in all cabins. Cabins 413 and 414, the latter which was originally a CCC laundry facility, do not have a fireplace. When calling for reservations, be sure to discuss the size, bedding, and amenities of the cabin you would like to rent.

Big Spring Lodge and Cabins, a small lodging complex in a quiet rural area of Missouri, is a place to enjoy your own cabin in the woods at a relatively inexpensive price. Plan to read a few books, play some cards, and do a little hiking. Many visitors to Ozark National Scenic Riverways come to float one or both Class II rivers that include 134 miles of clear, spring-fed streams. Numerous National Park Service–authorized concessionaires rent canoes at or near Alley Spring, Big Spring, Paullotite, Round Spring, Two Rivers, and Watercress. Inner tubes are available for rent at several locations. A list of concessionaires is available from the National Park Service.

Rooms: From doubles to 8 persons per unit. Cabins have a private bath with a shower but no tub.

Location: In southeast Missouri, 4 miles south of the town of Van Buren on MO 103.

Big Spring Lodge and Cabins was built from 1934 to 1938, initially by the Civilian Conservation Corps (CCC) and, later, the Works Progress Administration (WPA), in what was then Big Spring State Park. The entrance station, lodge building, and initial cabins were constructed of local oak timbers and cut stone. Later cabins were of frame construction. Local employees started first on tourist cabin 403, classified as a Type A cabin. Next were cabin 402, similar in style to the first cabin, and the considerably larger Type B cabin 401, with 2 large stone chimneys and fireplaces. Nine additional Type E frame cabins with large stone chimneys were constructed, first by the CCC, and later by the WPA. Frame cabin 413, the only unit overlooking the Current River, was built as a residence for the fire-tower keeper. The main lodge, on a hill overlooking the confluence of the Current River and Big Spring branch, and the entrance building were both completed in 1936. The Missouri State Parks Board signed over the state park to the National Park Service in 1969, and the Big Spring Historic District was placed on the National Register of Historic Places in 1976.

Glacier National Park

PO Box 128 • West Glacier, MT 59936 • (406) 888-7800 • www.nps.gov/glac

Glacier National Park is among the most outstanding of America's national parks. Covering more than 1 million acres, it features towering mountains, glacial valleys, sparkling lakes, and more than two dozen glaciers. Visitor centers are on the west side at Apgar, on the east side at St. Mary, and in the high country at Logan Pass. The high country is best seen by driving, taking the free shuttle, or enjoying a Red Bus tour on the Going-to-the-Sun Road, a 50-mile winding two-lane road that bisects the park via the Continental Divide at 6,646-foot Logan Pass. If time permits, drive Chief Mountain International Highway to Canada's Waterton Lakes National Park and the quaint village of Waterton. The 12-mile paved road from Babb to Many Glacier also offers outstanding scenery. The park is in northwestern Montana. The west entrance is 32 miles east of Kalispell, Montana.

GLACIER NATIONAL PARK

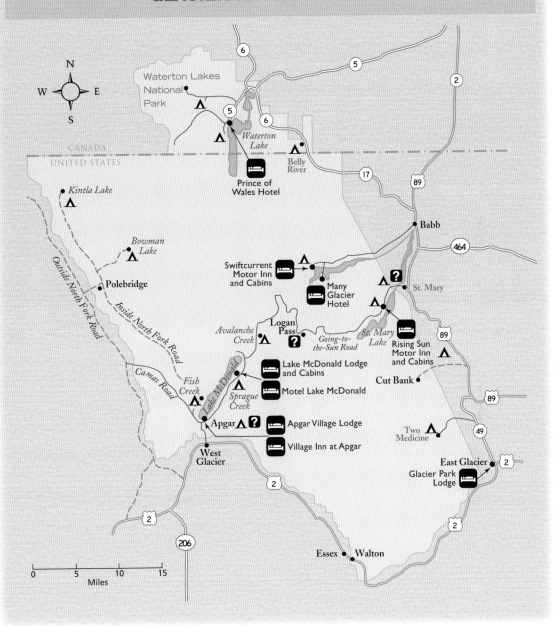

N
W — E
S

Waterton Lakes National Park

⑥

⑤

②

Waterton Lake

Belly River

Prince of Wales Hotel

CANADA
UNITED STATES

⑤

⑥

⑰

Kintla Lake

Babb

89

464

Bowman Lake

Polebridge

Swiftcurrent Motor Inn and Cabins

Many Glacier Hotel

?

St. Mary

Avalanche Creek

Logan Pass

?

Going-to-the-Sun Road

St. Mary Lake

Rising Sun Motor Inn and Cabins

89

Lake McDonald Lodge and Cabins

Motel Lake McDonald

Cut Bank

89

Fish Creek

Sprague Creek

Apgar ?

Apgar Village Lodge

Village Inn at Apgar

Two Medicine

49

West Glacier

②

East Glacier

②

Glacier Park Lodge

②

②

206

Essex • Walton

0   5   10   15
Miles

Park Entrance Fee: $25 per vehicle or $12 per person, good for 7 days. A separate daily entrance fee of $20 per family ($7.80 per adult) is required to enter Canada's neighboring Waterton Lakes National Park, home of the Prince of Wales Hotel.

Lodging in Glacier National Park: Seven lodging facilities are in 4 locations inside the borders of Glacier National Park. Two lodges sit just inside the park's west entrance in the village of Apgar. Apgar Village Lodge is privately owned and offers accommodations in historic cabins and 2 motel-type buildings. Nearby, Village Inn is directly on Lake McDonald and offers excellent lake and mountain views from each room of a two-story motel. A short distance east on Going-to-the-Sun Road, Lake McDonald Lodge has guest rooms in what was once a private hunting lodge plus nearby rustic cabins. A separate lodging facility, Motel Lake McDonald, offers 2 two-story motel buildings adjacent to the cabins. East of the mountain pass on Going-to-the-Sun Road, Rising Sun Motor Inn has motel units and duplex cabins in an uncrowded area of the park's scenic high country. The picturesque Many Glacier area in the park's interior has 2 facilities: historic Many Glacier Hotel, one of the great old national park lodges, and nearby Swiftcurrent Motor Inn, with motel units and inexpensive rustic cabins. We have included 2 additional lodges located a short distance outside the park border, but closely associated with Glacier National Park: Glacier Park Lodge, in the small town of East Glacier on the east side of the park, is a classic lodge with a spectacular lobby. North of the border in Alberta, Canada, Glacier's sister national park Waterton Lakes is home to Prince of Wales Hotel, one of North America's most picturesque national park lodges.

Transportation within the Park: Free shuttles operate July and Aug along the length of Going-to-the-Sun Road and offer the best way to see the park's most scenic areas. The shuttles are especially handy when staying at one of the lodges on or near the road. One shuttle route connects the Apgar Transportation Center (near Village Inn and Apgar Village Lodge) with points of interest (including Lake McDonald Lodge) to the continental divide at Logan Pass. An east-side shuttle connects St. Mary visitor center with Logan Pass and stops at Rising Sun Motor Inn. Riders can change shuttles at Logan Pass and traverse the entire Going-to-the-Sun Road and return the same day. Shuttles run every 15 to 30 minutes depending on the route. A shuttle schedule is available at visitor centers. A separate hikers' shuttle (fee charged) operates within the park during July and Aug between St. Mary and Many Glacier Hotel. This connects at Many Glacier Hotel and the St. Mary visitor center with an east-side shuttle (fee charged) that operates between Glacier Park Lodge and the Prince of Wales Hotel. A variety of scenic interpretive tours in historic red "Jammer" buses are offered daily from each of the hotels except Prince of Wales. These tours are operated by the hotel concessionaire. Sun Tours, operated by the Blackfeet Indian Reservation, offers daily guided tours from East Glacier, St. Mary, West Glacier, and Browning. Call (800) 786-9220 or visit www.glaciersuntours.com for information.

APGAR VILLAGE LODGE

PO Box 410 • West Glacier, MT 59936 • (406) 888-5484 • www.glacierparkinc.com

Apgar Village Lodge is a cluster of rustic wooden buildings including 2 small motel units, 28 cabins, and a registration building. The complex is in a wooded area between McDonald

Creek and the road through Apgar Village, a small commercial district on the west side of the park. The registration building and 1 motel unit are on Apgar Road, and another motel unit and several cabins are on McDonald Creek. The majority of cabins are in a wooded area between these 2 boundaries. None of the buildings sit directly on Lake McDonald, although the complex is no more than half a block from the shoreline. Apgar Village Lodge is near a restaurant and a National Park Service visitor center. The lodge is privately owned and not subject to oversight by the National Park Service other than meeting certain safety and health standards.

Apgar Village Lodge offers a variety of accommodations. All the rooms have electric heat and private baths with showers, but no air-conditioning, television, or telephone. Picnic tables are scattered about the complex. The least expensive rooms are in the motel building on the creek. These units do not have balconies, but back windows offer good views of the creek. These small rooms have 1 double bed, 1 queen bed, or 1 double plus a twin. The beds pretty much fill the room. The front motel building, with 11 rooms, is directly beside the registration building on Apgar Road. Each of the 11 units has 2 rooms, 1 with a queen bed and the other with a queen, a double, or 2 twins.

Most lodging at Apgar Village Lodge is in rustic cabins. The majority are wood-frame, although several older units are of log construction. The cabins are fairly old but well maintained, with interiors that have carpeting and knotty pine walls and many with impressive beamed ceilings. The cabins do not have porches. Larger cabins have both front and back doors. All but 2 of the 28 cabins have a kitchen with refrigerator, stove, oven, sink, toaster, coffeemaker, dishes, utensils, and pots and pans. Cabin sizes vary from a small unit with 1 double bed and no kitchen to a large

Motel unit at Apgar Village Lodge

unit that can sleep 10 and has a bath and a half. The majority of cabins have either 1 or 2 queen beds. Cabins 6, 7, and 8 have kitchens and are situated directly beside McDonald Creek and offer the most desirable location in the complex, with cabin 6 being the most desirable of the 3. Four cabins with kitchens (cabins 10, 11, 12, and 22) face the creek from across a small parking area. Unfortunately parked cars often block views of the creek. Each of the 7 cabins noted above can sleep 4 adults.

Apgar Village Lodge offers rustic lodging in a relatively quiet setting. Walks, wading in the lake, fishing, and kayaking are several of the activities available. The National Park Service visitor center is about half a block away. Although the lodge doesn't have its own eating facility, a restaurant flanks the building.

Rooms: Singles, doubles, triples, and quads. A few large cabins can hold 6 or more persons. All rooms have private baths with showers but no tubs. No rollaways or cots are available.

Wheelchair Accessibility: No rooms at Apgar Village Lodge are wheelchair accessible.

Reservations: Glacier Park, Inc., PO Box 2025, Columbia Falls, MT 59912. Phone (406)

892-2525, or visit www.glacierparkinc.com. A deposit of 1 night's stay is required. Cancellation is required at least 3 days prior to scheduled arrival. A $15 administrative fee is charged.

Rates: McDonald Creek motel units ($95–$110); front motel units ($135); one-bed cabin units ($120–$155); cabins with 2 or 3 beds ($176–$284); three-room cabin with 5 beds ($309). Rates for motel units and small cabins quoted are for 2 adults. Rates on medium and large cabins are for 4 adults. Additional persons are $20 each. Children 12 years and under are free.

Location: In the village of Apgar, Montana, 2 miles from the West Glacier entrance station.

Season: Late May through late Sept.

Food: A restaurant next to the motel on Apgar Road offers breakfast, lunch, and dinner from Memorial Day through Labor Day. Very limited

Milo Apgar, an early homesteader in the area where Apgar Village now stands, arrived soon after the Great Northern Railway reached Belton (now called West Glacier) in the early 1890s. Unable to make it as a farmer, Apgar started offering overnight accommodations for miners and visitors to this beautiful area. Some of Apgar's original cabins are still standing as part of Apgar Village Lodge. Cabin 21 was part of Apgar's first home.

groceries are sold at a gift shop next to the restaurant. The lodge is 2½ miles from a full-service grocery store and several restaurants in the town of West Glacier.

Facilities: The village of Apgar has gift shops, a restaurant, an ice cream shop, boat rentals, and a National Park Service visitor center.

Activities: Nightly ranger/naturalist talks at Apgar campground, boating, swimming (very cool water), fishing, hiking, sightseeing tours. Several hiking trails begin at Apgar.

GLACIER PARK LODGE
East Glacier, MT 59434 • (406) 226-5600 • www.glacierparkinc.com

Glacier Park Lodge is one of the classic national park hotels built in the early 1900s by transcontinental railroad companies to entice people to ride trains to the West. This majestic lodge was constructed in 1912 and 1913 by the Great Northern Railway, which was also responsible for building sister lodges Many Glacier and Prince of Wales. Freight and passenger trains continue to operate a little more than a stone's throw from the impressive hotel entry that is connected to the railway station by a corridor of beautiful flowers. The main lodge was constructed in 1912, and the adjacent West Wing went up a year later. The 2 buildings have a similar outside appearance and are connected by an enclosed walkway beginning at the south end of the giant lobby. The massive three-story lobby, with 40-inch-diameter fir and cedar pillars and surrounded by 2 interior balconies, consumes nearly all of the first floor of the main building. The West Wing is without a lobby and has more than twice as many guest rooms as the main building. A colorful swath of flowers separates a large front lawn. A parking area is near the hotel, but you will want to register and drop off luggage at the front door of whichever building you will be staying in. No elevators are in either building, but bell service is available. Glacier Park Lodge has 160 guest rooms plus a two-bedroom house. Rooms on the west side of both buildings have

Glacier Park Lodge

a view of the Rocky Mountains, while rooms on the east view the front lawn and distant rolling hills. All rooms have heat, telephone, and a private bath with a shower or shower-tub combination. None of the rooms have air-conditioning or a television. Bedding in nearly all rooms varies from 1 double or 1 king to 2 queen beds. Some rooms have balconies, although most are in the West Wing.

All 50 rooms in the main building are on the second and third floors behind wide interior balconies that surround the massive lobby. Rooms in the main building are all carpeted, but differ greatly in size. The hotel has a few Value rooms that are quite small and rent for about $30 less than Main Lodge rooms. Larger rooms in the main lodge include 263, 265, 267, and 269, which share a common balcony on the east (non-mountain) side of the building. Room 252 is also one of the larger Lodge rooms with 2 queen beds and a private balcony that offers a mountain view.

The adjoining West Wing has 110 rooms, most of which are classified Great Northern Wing rooms that are considerably larger than, but rent for the same price as Main Lodge rooms. These rooms have hardwood floors, and the majority have 2 queen beds. Most Great Northern Wing rooms on the first and second floors have balconies. The lodge offers 7 third-floor Family rooms, 4 in the main building and 3 in the West Wing. Each is very large with bedding that ranges from 3 doubles to 4 queens below a sloped ceiling. Family rooms rent for about $50 more and have well over twice the space of a Lodge room. They are also considerably larger than Great Northern Wing rooms. The windows in main building's Family rooms are low, so you must squat to gain any view. Family rooms in the West Wing have regular windows.

Five Deluxe rooms, all in the West Wing, each have 1 king bed, overstuffed chairs, a decorative fireplace, and a balcony. The hotel has 3 suites, 2 on the second floor of the main lodge building and 1 on the first floor of the West Wing. All offer mountain views and large, upgraded bathrooms with a shower. Two Lodge Suites each have a king bed, a sofa bed, and lounge chairs. Suite 264 also has a table and 4 chairs, 3 very large windows, plus a private balcony. In this suite you can lie in bed and still have a good view of the mountains. The first-floor two-room West Wing Suite with decorative fireplace, 2 bathrooms, and a private balcony has a king bed in the bedroom and a sofa bed and chairs in the living room. Situated on the 9th hole of the golf course is a one-story wooden house called the Glacier Golf House. It has a living room, a dining area, a full kitchen (utensils and dishes supplied), 2 bathrooms with a combination tub-shower, and 2 bedrooms, each with 2 queen-size beds. A washer and dryer, telephone, and satellite television with a DVD player are included. The house has an outside deck with a gas grill, flower beds, and a rustic fence.

When choosing a room consider the ambience of walking out your room onto a wide balcony that overlooks the main lobby. This is part of the experience of staying in the main building. On the other hand, no elevator is available, so you must climb at least 1 flight of stairs (24 steps) each time you go to or leave your room. Rooms on the third floor require climbing 2 flights of stairs (another 19 steps). In addition, rooms overlooking the lobby are sometimes a little noisy, especially during the early evening when the lobby is crowded with guests. One advantage of staying in the West Wing is being able to request a room on the first floor at lobby level. In other words, no climbing steps unless you leave the hotel. Another advantage is the larger size of West Wing rooms. If you desire a room in the main building, 2 good choices are 252 or 260, which are large and have balconies. Both rooms have a combination shower-tub. Lodge rooms on the ends of the building tend to offer marginal views, so shy away from these. In the West Wing, rooms 526 on the garden level (1 flight down from the first floor; don't ask us why these rooms have 500 numbers) and 226 on the second floor are very large rooms and have balconies on the mountain side. All even-numbered rooms on the first floor (104 through 124) of the West Wing offer a balcony and mountain view. It is generally best to attempt to reserve a room with extra bedding in either building because these are likely to be larger rooms. For example, request a room with 2 queen beds even if you are reserving a room for 2 people.

Glacier Park Lodge is a fun place to stay, if only to enjoy an evening reading a book and listening to music in the awe-inspiring lobby. It's a popular stop for train travelers who need walk only a short distance along a flower-bordered path from the station to the hotel entrance. A complimentary hotel shuttle waits at the station to pick up luggage and guests who would rather ride. The lodge is a stop for red Jammer buses that carry travelers on narrated tours of the park. It is also a connecting point for the east side shuttle that offers service to St. Mary, where free National Park Service shuttles provide service to Logan Pass on the Going-to-the-Sun Road. The hotel has a 9-hole golf course and a 9-hole pitch and putt. Unlike most other national park lodges, it has a swimming pool and a day spa. Horseback riding is also available. If you plan to stay several days and want variety in your meals, a short walk takes you to several restaurants, including an excellent Mexican restaurant, and a small grocery in the town of East Glacier.

Rooms: Singles, doubles, triples, and quads. Three Family rooms accommodate up to 8 persons. All rooms have a private bath.

Wheelchair Accessibility: Two rooms on the first floor of the West Wing are wheelchair accessible.

Reservations: Glacier Park, Inc., PO Box 2025, Columbia Falls, MT 59912. Phone (406) 892-2525 or visit www.glacierparkinc.com. A deposit of 1 night's stay is required. Cancellation is required 3 days prior to scheduled arrival. A $15 administrative fee is charged.

Rates: Value room ($161); Lodge room ($193–$198); Great Northern Wing room ($198–$208); Family room ($244); Deluxe room ($244); Suite ($386); Golf House ($480). Rates quoted are for 2 adults with the exception of Family rooms and the Golf House, which are quoted for 4. Children 11 and under stay free. Each additional person is $15 per night.

Location: In East Glacier, Montana, at the intersection of US 2 and MT 49. The lodge is at the southeast corner of the park.

Season: Mid-May to late-Sept.

Food: The dining room offers breakfast ($7–$16), lunch ($11–$17), and dinner ($15–$32). Alcoholic beverages are served. The lounge serves snacks and sandwiches. A snack shop in the lobby sells breakfast muffins, cold sandwiches, ice cream, coffee, and cold drinks. Additional restaurants and a grocery are nearby in the town of East Glacier.

Glacier National Park is famous for 33 red "Jammer" motor coaches (frequently called "Reds") that provide narrated tours between the park hotels and sites. The coaches, built between 1933 and 1939 by the White Motor Company, have black canvas tops that can be rolled back for greater visibility by occupants. The colorful coaches derive their name from the drivers who at one time had to "jam" the gears to get up the mountain roads of Glacier. Structural problems caused the fleet to be temporarily retired from service in August 1999. Following a collaborative effort among the National Park Service, Ford Motor Company, and the concessionaire, Glacier Park, Inc., the popular red buses returned to service in summer 2002 with propane-fueled engines and new chassis.

Facilities: Dining room, cocktail lounge, snack shop, gift shop, day spa, swimming pool, golf course, nine-hole pitch 'n putt course. Restaurants, gas stations, and a grocery store are across the road in the town of East Glacier.

Activities: Hiking, horseback riding, shuffleboard, swimming, golf, evening entertainment, sightseeing tours.

LAKE MCDONALD LODGE AND CABINS
PO Box 210052 • Lake McDonald, MT 59921-0052 • (406) 888-5431
www.glaciernationalparklodges.com

The Lake McDonald lodging complex consists of a historic lodge building, 14 structures with cabin accommodations, a dorm-type building and a structure recently converted

Lake McDonald Lodge

into 4 suites. It also includes a restaurant, an auditorium, several support buildings for employee housing, and a store. The main hotel is a rustic Swiss chalet–style lodge with a spacious, open lobby surrounded on 3 sides by upper-floor balconies. The lobby, dining room, gift shop, lounge, and 2 guest rooms are on the main floor, while the second and third floors are devoted to guest rooms. The lodge sits on a small hill facing Lake McDonald, which was used by visitors who arrived by boat until 1920, when the road was built. A huge fireplace with Indian designs in the masonry above the opening dominates the lobby with its large cedar columns in each corner. The balconies, supported by log beams and brackets, provide public areas with tables and chairs where guests can write letters, play cards, or read a book. A covered back patio has chairs and benches for relaxing while viewing Glacier National Park's largest lake.

Lake McDonald Lodge offers rooms of various sizes and bedding in the main lodge, cabins, and two nearby buildings, one a former family home and the other a former employee dormitory. All rooms in the main lodge and in the cabins have heat, a fan, telephone, and a private bath with a shower but no television or air-conditioning. The former home has been converted into suites that each have a television. Rooms in the former dorm have an in-room sink but no private bath.

The main lodge has 32 rooms, nearly all of which are on the second and third floors. Two wheelchair-accessible rooms are on the first floor. The building has no elevator. Bell service is available. Rooms in the lodge are priced the same regardless of size, view, or bedding, which ranges from 1 to 2 double beds. Rooms 202, 212, 302, and 312 are desirable lakeside corner rooms with 2 windows. Rooms 201, 213, 301, and 313 are the largest in the lodge and have windows offering a view of the lake.

Fourteen buildings, some log and some frame, house 38 cabins that sit beside the main lodge and stretch along Lake McDonald. Most of these buildings comprise 2, 3, or 4 cabin rooms, although 1 particularly large building has 6 units. Parking is behind or in front of each cabin. Some of the cabins are entered from the lake side, while others are accessed from the side nearest the parking lot. All cabins have finished interiors and are on the lake, but views tend to be obscured by trees and bushes along the bank of the lake. Cabins are rented and priced in 2 classifications, Small and Large, even though units within each class vary in size and bedding. Twenty-one Small cabins, which rent for about $55 less per day than the Large cabins, have bedding ranging from 2 twins to 2 doubles. Seventeen Large cabins have bedding ranging from a double plus a twin to 2 double beds plus a twin. Most Large cabins offer significantly more floor space than the Small cabins, some of which are very small.

The Cobb House sits in a wooded area near the main lodge. The house was built in 1918 as a family home and only recently converted into guest lodging. The two-story building has 3 two-room suites, each with a sitting area with a sofa bed plus a separate bedroom with one queen bed and a full bathroom. The house also has a large one-bedroom accessible suite. The 4 guest rooms share a large front porch and a common living area with a fireplace. Snyder Hall, which formerly served as employee housing, has 8 small guest rooms on 2 floors. Each room has either a bunk bed or a double bed, an in-room sink, and few furnishings. Guests must use either the common men's or women's community bathrooms on the second floor. These are the least expensive guest rooms in the park.

Our first choice at Lake McDonald is a larger lakeside room (noted above) in the main lodge. These rooms are off the sometimes noisy lobby area. Third-floor rooms are quieter than second-floor rooms but require climbing an additional flight of stairs. Freestanding cabin 8, with a large covered porch facing the lake, is our favorite Large cabin. Cabin 12-B, with a nice covered porch facing the lake, is our favorite Small cabin.

Lake McDonald Lodge is on the site of the earlier and smaller Glacier Hotel, which was built in 1895 by homesteader George Snyder. The property was sold in 1906 to land speculator John Lewis, who built cabins and operated a fishing and tourist camp. In 1913 Snyder hired Spokane, Washington, architect Kirkland Cutter to design a hotel that would compete with the hotels and backcountry chalets being constructed by the Great Northern Railroad. Concrete-and-stone foundations were completed just prior to the winter of 1913, and in June 1914 the hotel opened for business. In 1930 the hotel was acquired by a subsidiary of the Great Northern Railroad, and in 1957 the name was changed from Lewis Glacier Hotel to Lake McDonald Lodge. The lodge was included in the National Register of Historic Places in 1978 and partially renovated in 1988.

Lake McDonald Lodge is the smallest and most intimate of the 4 historic lodges in Glacier National Park. Guests generally smile as they walk through the entrance and glance up at the large colorful lampshades that once hung in the Prince of Wales Hotel. Next their eyes scan the balconies and huge log columns on which old hunting trophies hang. A little farther in and to the left is the focal point of the lobby, a cavernous fireplace that consumes 5-foot logs. Lake McDonald Lodge offers a variety of activities besides sitting in a rocking chair enjoying the fireplace. The lake provides opportunities for boating and fishing, and although the water is a little cool for swimming, you might decide to take a refreshing dip down the hill from cabin 12. Boat tours of the lake leave from a small dock behind the lodge. A classic national park lodge dining room with a large fireplace and a wall of windows providing views of the lake offers evening specialties. An informal restaurant across the road serves pizza and sandwiches in a casual atmosphere.

Rooms: Singles, doubles, triples, and quads. All rooms except those in Snyder Hall have a private bath with shower. Two first-floor accessible rooms in the lodge each have a combination shower-tub.

Wheelchair Accessibility: Two cabins, the only 2 first-floor lodge rooms, and the one-room suite in Cobb House are wheelchair accessible.

Reservations: Xanterra Parks & Resorts Glacier Division, 540 Nucleus Ave., Columbia Falls, MT 59912. Phone (855) 733-4522 or visit www .glaciernationalparklodges.com. A deposit of 1 night's stay is required. Cancellation notice of at least 72 hours is required for a refund.

Rates: Main lodge ($191); Small cabins ($137); Large cabins ($191); Cobb Suites ($331); Snyder Hall ($79). Room rates are quoted for 2 adults.

Each additional person is $15 per night. Children 11 and under stay free.

Location: Ten miles inside the park's west entrance just off the Going-to-the-Sun Road.

Season: Late May through late Sept.

Food: A relatively small but attractive dining room in the main lodge serves a breakfast buffet ($8–$16), lunch ($10–$16), and dinner ($12–$30). Alcoholic beverages are served here and in the adjacent lounge. No reservations are taken. The lounge offers food items from the restaurant's lunch menu all afternoon and evening. Across the road, a "Jammer-themed" pizzeria is open from 11 a.m. to 10 p.m. for pizza, pasta, hoagies, salads, and hamburgers ($6–$25). Beer, wine, and ice cream are sold, and takeout is available.

Facilities: Dining room, gift shop, cocktail lounge, restaurant, post office, general store, boat rental, riding stable.

Activities: Boating, hiking, fishing (no license required), boat tours of Lake McDonald, sightseeing tours, horseback riding, evening ranger programs.

MANY GLACIER HOTEL

PO Box 147 • East Glacier, MT 59434 • (406) 732-4411 • www.glaciernationalparklodges.com

Many Glacier Hotel is one of America's classic national park lodges. The five-story Swiss-themed wooden structure with numerous gables and balconies is situated on the edge of Swiftcurrent Lake. Although it appears as a single structure, the hotel is actually 2 buildings connected by an enclosed walkway. The main floor is highlighted by an outstanding three-story lobby with log beams, interior balconies, and a huge conical metal fireplace suspended from the roof. Many guest rooms offer outstanding views of Swiftcurrent Lake and the surrounding mountains. Parking is on a steep hill above the hotel, so stop at the hotel entrance to register and drop off luggage before parking your vehicle. A small elevator down the hallway near the lounge

A lakeside view of Many Glacier Hotel

is temperamental, but bell service is available to assist with luggage.

The hotel offers a total of 213 rooms of varying size, bedding, and view. All the rooms have heat, telephone, and a private bath but no air-conditioning or television. All but 8 rooms fall into 3 categories: Lakeside, Parkside, and Value. Bedding in these rooms ranges from 2 twins to 2 doubles. The remaining rooms are 2 Suites and 6 Family rooms. Lakeside rooms, the largest category, rent at a premium price and include all but a few of the rooms facing Swiftcurrent Lake. About half these rooms have balconies, but room size and bedding vary, with the largest Lakeside rooms being in the annex. Parkside rooms are similar in size and

bedding to Lakeside rooms but do not offer a lake view, and fewer Parkside rooms have balconies. Value rooms are the least expensive rooms and are generally quite small with 2 twins or 1 double bed. Rooms in this category may also have an obscured view or be located on a main hallway in a heavy-traffic area. Room prices within a category vary according to room size and whether a room has a balcony or recently been refurbished.

Large Lakeside rooms in the main lodge with excellent lake views and balconies are 158, 160, 362, and 364. Larger Lakeside rooms without balconies in the main lodge include 222, 322, 332, 460, and 462. Larger Lakeside rooms in the annex with balconies include 102, 104, 112,

114, and corresponding rooms on the second and third floors. Larger Parkside rooms in the annex with balconies include 105, 205, and 305.

Six Family rooms on the fourth floor of the annex each consist of 2 bedrooms, 1 on each side of a bathroom. Family rooms have various bedding combinations that can sleep either 5 or 6 adults without use of a rollaway. Four of these rooms provide a lake view (rooms 400, 404, 408, and 414), and 2 do not, even though all 6 rooms rent for the same rate. Keep in mind that these are fourth-floor rooms in the annex where no elevator is available. In addition, a sloping roof results in reduced headroom. No Family rooms have a balcony. Two Suites on the second floor each consist of 2 bedrooms and 2 bathrooms. One bedroom has a king bed and the other has a double bed. The Suites are corner rooms, with balconies that provide excellent lake views.

If you request a room category, we think Lakeside annex rooms are probably the best choice. These rooms are a nice size, offer an impressive view, and most enjoy a balcony. In addition, annex rooms are generally quieter than rooms in the main lodge, especially compared to those around the interior balconies, which are subject to lobby noise. The downside to staying in the annex is lack of an elevator, requiring guests on the upper floors to climb stairs. However, there are some excellent room choices in the main lodge. Our favorite room in the hotel is 268, a wedge-shaped room near the elevator that has 4 windows offering views of the lake. Among the Value category, basement rooms 62 and 64 each have an outside door that opens to a small grassy area that fronts the lake.

Many Glacier Hotel is a historic lodge in a scenic mountain setting that is identified by many experienced travelers as their favorite lodging facility in Glacier National Park. The large lobby, with its huge log columns and spectacular vistas, is a gathering place for guests, especially in the evening when its centerpiece, the huge conical fireplace, is lit. The attractive Ptarmigan Dining Room was restored in 2012 to its former glory with a vaulted ceiling and large windows overlooking Swiftcurrent Lake.

Take a few steps outside the hotel and you can begin a hike, kayak, fish, or enjoy a boat tour accompanied by a park naturalist. Or perhaps you would rather relax in one of the Adirondack chairs on the large porch that wraps around 2 sides of the first floor. A stable next to the parking area offers horseback riding. Evening natural history programs are presented in the hotel basement.

Rooms: Singles, doubles, triples, and quads. Six Family rooms hold 4 to 6 persons. All rooms have private baths.

Wheelchair Accessibility: The lodge offers 7 wheelchair-accessible rooms in various categories.

Reservations: Xanterra Parks & Resorts Glacier Division, 540 Nucleus Ave., Columbia Falls, MT 59912. Phone (855) 733-4522 or visit www.glacier

Construction on Many Glacier Hotel commenced in 1914, and the first guests were welcomed on July 4 of the following year. The annex next door was completed 2 years later. The Great Northern Railroad, which built the hotel, erected a sawmill and drying kiln near the site to process timber used in the construction. Trees for the lobby columns were harvested and shipped from Oregon and Washington. Even though most of the other timber and rocks came from the local area, the high cost of fixtures, glass, and boilers resulted in construction costs of $500,000. A swimming pool that sat beside the dining room and a stone fountain near the current gift shop have both been removed. The hotel once had its own hydroelectric plant at Swiftcurrent Falls, but the unit was put permanently out of operation by a 1964 flood.

nationalparklodges.com. A deposit of one night's stay is required. Cancellation notice of at least 72 hours is required for a refund.

Rates: Value rooms ($163–$179); Parkside ($181–$203); Lakeside ($192–$206); Family rooms ($250); Suites ($270). Room rates quoted are for 2 adults with the exception of Family rooms that are quoted for 4 adults. Each additional person is $15 per night. Rollaways are $15 per night. Children 11 and under stay free.

Location: In the northeast section of the park, at the end of Many Glacier Rd., 11 miles east of Babb, Montana.

Season: Mid-June to mid-Sept.

Food: A restaurant offers a breakfast buffet ($15), lunch ($10–$16), and dinner ($13–$32).

Alcoholic beverages are available in the dining room and in the Swiss or Interlaken Lounges just outside the dining room. Soup, salads, sandwiches, and appetizers are available in the lounges. A small store sells specialty coffee, hot dogs, ice cream, yogurt, snacks, drinks, beer, and wine from 6 a.m. to 10 p.m. Limited groceries are available in a general store 1 mile up the road at Swiftcurrent Motor Inn and Cabins. The motor inn also has a moderately priced restaurant.

Facilities: Dining room; cocktail lounge; snack bar; gift shop; tour desk in lobby; horse stable; kayak, canoe, and rowboat rentals.

Activities: Hiking, fishing, boating, horseback riding, naturalist programs, sightseeing tours, boat tours of Swiftcurrent Lake and Lake Josephine.

Motel Lake McDonald

Lake McDonald, MT 59921 • (406) 888-5100 • www.glacierparkinc.com

This Lake McDonald lodging facility consists of 2 two-story motel buildings tucked beside the cabins of Lake McDonald Lodge. Any first-time visitor would assume the motel is operated in conjunction with the lodge, which it was until 2014 when there was a change in concessionaires. The motel was and is privately owned and continues to be operated by the previous concessionaire. Thus it is a separate entity from the lodge and cabins here, even though it sits in the same complex.

The motel offers 28 rooms that each have either 1 or 2 double beds. Parking is between the 2 buildings that are parallel to one another. Neither building has an elevator. The relatively small rooms do not have balconies or offer a view. The larger motel building has paneled rooms that are

entered from outside walkways. The other building with 8 rooms has interior hallways that can be entered from either end of the building. We prefer rooms in the larger unit (rooms 1 through 20). Request Room 20, which has 2 windows, one of which faces the lake.

Motel Lake McDonald

Although the rooms at Motel Lake McDonald don't match those in Lake McDonald Lodge, the facility is in a good location near the store and across the street from Jammer Joe's Grill and Pizzeria. In addition, the dining room, lounge, impressive lobby, and outside deck of Lake McDonald Lodge are a short walk from the motel.

Rooms: Singles, doubles, triples, and quads. All rooms have a private bath with a shower.

Wheelchair Accessibility: None of the rooms are wheelchair accessible.

Reservations: Glacier Park, Inc., PO Box 2025, Columbia Falls, MT 59912. Phone (406) 892-2525 or visit www.glacierparkinc.com. A deposit of 1 night's stay is required. Cancellation is required at least 3 days prior to scheduled arrival. A $15 administrative fee is charged.

Rates: All rooms ($142).

Location: Ten miles inside the park's west entrance just off the Going-to-the-Sun Road.

Season: Early June through late Sept.

Food: The nearby lodge has an attractive dining room that serves a breakfast buffet ($15), lunch ($10–$16), and dinner ($13–$32). No reservations are taken. The lodge lounge offers food items from the restaurant's lunch menu all afternoon and evening. Across the road, a "Jammer-themed" pizzeria is open from 11 a.m. to 10 p.m. for pizza, pasta, hoagies, salads, and hamburgers ($6–$25). Beer, wine, and ice cream are sold, and takeout is available.

Facilities: See Lake McDonald Lodge.

Activities: Boating, hiking, fishing (no license required), boat tours of Lake McDonald, sightseeing tours, horseback riding, evening ranger programs.

PRINCE OF WALES HOTEL

PO Box 33, Waterton, Alberta, Canada T0K 2M0 • (403) 859-2231 • www.glacierparkinc.com

The Prince of Wales Hotel, named after Prince Edward, who later became King Edward VIII, is a seven-story alpine chalet that may be the most picturesque of all the national park lodging facilities. The only Canadian park lodge constructed by the Great Northern Railroad, the hotel sits high on a bluff overlooking Waterton Lake and the charming town of Waterton. Built in 1927, the hotel features two-story windows across the lake side of a six-story lobby. Interior balconies on 3 floors and huge timbers highlight the attractive lobby that is filled with chairs, tables, and sofas. Visitors entering from the United States must pass through a Canadian port of entry, which requires a passport. A Canadian park fee is required to enter Waterton Lakes National Park, in which the hotel is located.

Prince of Wales Hotel has 86 rooms on the 5 floors above the main floor lobby. Although an elevator stops at floors 1 through 4, it is ancient (the oldest in Alberta) and can only be operated by a hotel employee, who must be summoned. This means you will likely be climbing steps during your stay. Consider this when reserving a room because you may want to request a second- or third-floor room and save some steps. Also keep in mind that the elevator does not

Prince of Wales Hotel

go to the fifth and sixth floors, where rooms are offered at a lower rate. Sixteen steps are between the fourth and fifth floors, and another 16 steps are required to climb from the fifth to the sixth floor. Bell service is available to assist with luggage, but a room on the sixth floor will mean lots of steps.

Each hotel room has electric heat, telephone, and a private bathroom but no television or air-conditioning. Most rooms on the second, third, and fourth floors fall into 2 classifications: Lakeside and Mountainside. Lakeside rooms offer a view of Waterton Lake and the surrounding mountains, while Mountainside rooms do not offer as good a view. Rooms in both classifications are priced according to their bedding. Those with a queen or king bed rent for $25 or $40 more, respectively, than a Standard room with a double plus a twin or 2 double beds. Most bathrooms

have a combination shower-tub, although a few have a shower only. All third-floor rooms, but only a few second- and fourth-floor rooms, have balconies. The wind is generally strong enough, especially on the hotel's lake side, that you won't want to spend much time on a balcony, so having one shouldn't be a major consideration in choosing a room. We have visited on a couple of occasions when the wind was so strong it was virtually impossible to even open the door to the balcony. We especially like corner rooms with windows on 2 sides. Lakeside corner rooms with a double plus a twin include 201 and 225 on the second floor, and corresponding numbered rooms on the third and fourth floors, plus 409 and 417 with king beds. Mountainside corner rooms include 200 and 222 with a double plus a twin, and 208 and 214 with a queen, on the second floor, and corresponding numbered rooms on the third and fourth floors.

The hotel offers 20 fifth-floor rooms where the sloping roofline reduces headspace in many of these somewhat smaller rooms. About half face Waterton Lake. Bathrooms have a shower but no tub. Keep in mind the lobby elevator does not provide access to the fifth floor, so these rooms require climbing an additional flight of stairs. On the positive side, all these rooms have queen beds at no extra charge and the fifth floor tends to be quieter. Lakeside rooms 509 and 517 are slightly larger than most other fifth floor rooms.

The sixth floor (yet another flight of 16 stairs to climb) has 4 rooms: 2 Value rooms plus 2 two-room units. The Value rooms are small with 1 double bed and a bathroom with a shower. The two-room units have a double bed in each room and 1 bathroom with a shower. Two-room units have balconies and rent at the standard Lakeside or Mountainside rate, depending on the side of the hotel on which the room is located.

Two upscale suites on the third floor, the Prince and the Princess, each have a living room with a sofa bed, wet bar and refrigerator, coffeemaker, and separate bedroom with a king-size bed. The large bathroom in each suite has a bathtub and separate shower. These suites are expensive and exquisite, with custom-designed furniture.

While standing in the lobby near the registration desk, look up and try to spot a dark ceiling panel. This trap door hides a pulley that was once used to lower a rope to an employee who was hoisted to clean and change burned-out light bulbs in the massive chandelier that hangs between the second and fourth floors. This was a prized job for one of the bellmen who was steered around the chandelier by means of ropes held by 2 of the bellman's colleagues. It is said that people came from miles around to witness the spectacle. Today, a crank is used to lower the chandelier, which is made of aluminum and is relatively light.

View from the lobby in the Prince of Wales Hotel

The Prince of Wales Hotel offers a touch of English tradition. Each afternoon from 1 to 5 (last seating at 4) in the lobby guests can enjoy tea beside windows offering a breathtaking view of Waterton Lake. The hotel's striking lobby is flanked by the Royal Stewart Dining Room on one side and the Windsor Lounge on the other. Both provide outstanding views of the lake and surrounding mountains. The lounge serves the dining room's full lunch and dinner menus and enjoys the hotel's only fireplace. A large gift shop is on the main floor. The town of Waterton, with additional restaurants, clothing stores, and gift shops, is a short distance down the hill. Nearly all businesses accept credit cards and American dollars, although the latter are not always converted at a favorable rate.

Rooms: Singles, doubles, triples, and quads. All rooms have private baths.

Wheelchair Accessibility: The hotel has no wheelchair-accessible rooms.

Reservations: Glacier Park, Inc., PO Box 2025, Columbia Falls, MT 59912. Phone (406) 892-2525 or visit www.glacierparkinc.com. A deposit of 1 night's stay is required. Cancellation is required at least 3 days prior to scheduled arrival. A $15 administrative fee is charged.

Rates: Sixth-floor Value room ($224–$233); Sixth-floor two-room unit ($239–$299); Fifth-floor rooms ($239–$273); Mountainside rooms ($239–$264); Lakeside rooms ($264–$299); Suite ($799). Rates quoted are in Canadian dollars for 2 adults. Each additional person is $15 per night. Children 11 and under stay free with an adult. Rates are reduced 20 to 30 percent during the weeks prior to mid-June.

Location: In Canada's Waterton Lakes National Park, about 48 miles northwest of St. Mary, Montana, and 30 miles south of Pincher Creek, Alberta.

Season: Early June to mid-Sept.

Food: A dining room with carved wood beams and a wall of windows offering a view of Waterton Lake serves breakfast ($9–$15), lunch ($11–$18), and dinner ($27–$35). The lounge serves the full lunch and dinner menus from the dining room. A traditional British tea with sandwiches, pastries, scones, cookies, and other sweets

is served in the lobby each afternoon from 1 to 4 ($30). Several restaurants and a small grocery store are in the town of Waterton.

Great Northern Railroad president Louis Hill originally envisioned the Prince of Wales as a long three-story building similar to the hotel his firm built a decade earlier at Many Glacier. After changing his mind several times, Hill finally settled on the current seven-story rectangular building designed to resemble a Swiss chalet. Construction of the hotel was complicated by high winds and the need to transport materials and supplies the last 25 miles by mules. The winds blew the building off center twice during construction and almost caused the project to be abandoned. The structure is anchored with large cables that run from the loft into the ground. The hotel opened during the summer of 1927, 1 year after construction commenced and 14 years after the site was selected. It was closed for 3 years during the Depression and 5 years during World War II.

Facilities: Gift shop, dining room, cocktail lounge. Additional facilities are in the town of Waterton, a short distance away.

Activities: Hiking, golf, tennis, horseback riding, boat rentals, fishing, lake cruises, and national park programs are offered in Waterton.

RISING SUN MOTOR INN AND CABINS
PO Box 147 • East Glacier, MT 59434 • (406) 732-5523 • www.glaciernationalparklodges.com

Rising Sun Motor Inn and Cabins, opened in 1941 as East Glacier Auto Camp, is a complex of wooden buildings, including a restaurant (added in 1956), general store with attached lodging rooms, 19 duplex cabin buildings, and 2 motel structures. Rising Sun offers 72 guest rooms, approximately half of which are frame cabins dating from 1941. Registration is in the main building, which houses a restaurant and

small gift shop. The general store is across the parking lot, and the cabins and motel buildings are up a small hill but within walking distance of both the restaurant and general store. The motor inn is in a scenic area overlooking St. Mary Lake and surrounded by tall mountains.

Rising Sun offers 3 types of rooms, all of which rent for approximately the same price. Rooms have heat, a fan, and a private bathroom with a shower. No television, telephone, or air-conditioning is in the rooms. The majority of rooms are in 35 rustic Cabins built as duplex units. The Cabins are clustered on a hill behind the store with a few offering a view of the mountains to the south. Parking is directly in front of or beside each Cabin. Interiors are finished with varnished plywood. The small bathroom has a toilet and shower; the sink is in the bedroom. Cabins have small windows, no porch, and beds that range from 2 twins to 2 doubles, although most have a double plus a twin. Cabins 2 through 7 are larger in size and rent for the same price as smaller Cabins. We would choose Cabins 4, 5, or 6, all of which offer a good mountain view and receive morning sun.

The building housing the general store also includes 9 Motel rooms that are accessed from an interior hallway entered from either the front or end of the building. A large covered porch with chairs and tables spans the front of the building, which faces south toward the mountains. The rooms vary in size and bedding, which ranges from 1 double to 2 doubles. Room 31, with 2 double beds, is very large. Corner room 37 has windows on 2 sides and is the most desirable of these rooms.

One of two Motor Inn buildings at Rising Sun Motor Inn and Cabin

Two identical Motor Inn motel-type buildings are up the hill from the restaurant. Each building houses 14 rooms, 7 on each side. A covered walkway runs across each side of the 2 buildings. These rooms are all the same size with bedding that ranges from 2 twins to 2 doubles. Rooms on the south side (rooms 8 through 14 in 1 building and rooms 22 through 28 in the other building) offer good mountain views and a fair view of St. Mary Lake. Corner rooms 8, 14, 22, and 28 have windows on 2 sides and offer a brighter interior.

Rising Sun Motor Inn and Cabins is overlooked by many Glacier visitors who know only about the park's 4 historic lodges. The inn enjoys a scenic location surrounded by towering mountains and up a small hill from the blue waters of St. Mary Lake. The lake is mostly out of direct view of the lodging units, and the surrounding mountains are only partially visible from some of the units. Still, this is a relaxing place to spend an evening. Walk a short distance from your room and gaze at some of the most breathtaking scenery America has to offer. This is a quiet and uncongested area that most travelers on the Going-to-the-Sun Road drive right by. The restaurant, with a vaulted ceiling and large windows

The 52-mile Going-to-the-Sun Road, one of the country's most scenic drives, is the product of more than a decade of work that commenced in 1921. Although several routes were considered, 6,664-foot Logan Pass was chosen, partially because greater exposure to the sun would help clear the road of snow. It takes up to 2 months each spring to clear the road of snow, which in places can reach a depth of 80 feet. The road provides spectacular views of mountains, lakes, waterfalls, and glacial valleys in the heart of Glacier National Park. It is winding and quite narrow and vehicles longer than 21 feet or wider than 8 feet are prohibited from travel between Avalanche Campground and the Sun Point parking area.

facing the lake and mountains, offers meals at reasonable prices. You can hike, fish, take a boat tour of St. Mary Lake, or just experience nature without bumping into hundreds of other vacationers.

Rooms: Singles, doubles, triples, and quads. All rooms have a private bath with a shower.

Wheelchair Accessibility: Four wheelchair-accessible rooms are in 1 of the 2 motor inn buildings.

Reservations: Xanterra Parks & Resorts Glacier Division, 540 Nucleus Ave., Columbia Falls, MT 59912. Phone (855) 733-4522 or visit www .glaciernationalparklodges.com. A deposit of 1 night's stay is required. Cancellation notice of at least 72 hours is required for a refund.

Rates: Cabins ($137); Store Motel rooms ($134); Motor Inn rooms ($142). Rates quoted are for 2 adults. Children 11 years and under stay free. Each additional person is $15 per night.

Location: East side of Glacier National Park, 6 miles west of the park entrance station at St. Mary.

Season: Mid-June to mid-Sept.

Food: A restaurant in the main building serves breakfast ($7–$15), lunch ($8–$15), and dinner ($8–$20). Lunch items are available for dinner. Beer and wine are served. Limited groceries, beer, and wine are sold in the general store.

Facilities: Restaurant, gift shop, general store with camping and fishing supplies.

Activities: Hiking, fishing, boating, boat tour of St. Mary Lake, sightseeing tours, National Park Service evening naturalist program in campground amphitheater.

SWIFTCURRENT MOTOR INN AND CABINS

PO Box 147 • East Glacier Park, MT 59434 • (406) 732-5531 • www.glaciernationalparklodges.com

Swiftcurrent Motor Inn and Cabins offers 95 guest rooms in a complex that has 33 cabins with a central bathhouse, 4 motel buildings, and a registration building that houses a store and restaurant. The cabins and motel units sit behind the registration building, which offers a small lobby and a large covered porch with chairs. Plentiful parking is outside the registration building and directly beside the cabins and motel units.

All accommodations at Swiftcurrent have electric heat, a fan, and coffeemakers (except Pinetop), but no air-conditioning, television, or telephone. The least expensive lodging is in cabins without a private bathroom. A community bathroom has toilets and showers. The cabins, constructed in 1937, are rustic and plain, with painted wooden floors. They are nicely spaced, and all are single units (no duplex units, common among other

Cabins at Swiftcurrent Motor Inn and Cabins

lodges). Eighteen small one-bedroom cabins each have a double bed or a double bed plus a twin bed in 1 room and a sink (cold water only) and small picnic table in a separate room. Two one-bedroom cabins with a private bath rent for about $20 per night more than the one-bedroom units without a bath. Six two-bedroom cabins have a small bedroom with a double bed on each side of a small room, with a sink and picnic table. These cabins do not have a private bathroom. The two-bedroom units rent for $10 per night more than the one-bedroom units without a bath. Cabins in Loop C are closest to the community bathhouse.

Seven new cabins, each with a sitting room that includes a sofa bed, opened in summer 2014. Six cabins are 1 bedroom with 1 double bed, while 1 cabin has 2 bedrooms, each with a double bed. These new cabins have a private bathroom with a shower.

Four one-story wooden motel buildings house 62 guest rooms in 2 price categories. Rooms in all 4 buildings have carpeted floors and a private bath with a shower. Bedding varies from 2 twins to 2 double beds. Rooms with two double beds are generally larger. The three buildings near the back of the complex each have 14 Motor Inn rooms, 7 on a side, that are entered from outside walkways. The fourth motor inn unit, Pinetop, sits toward the front of the complex and has 20 small rooms entered from an interior corridor that can add to room noise as guests enter and leave the building. These rooms have no porch or balcony and are quite a bit smaller and a little less expensive than rooms in the other 3 motel buildings. We stayed in both types of motel rooms and discovered each time that noise from neighboring rooms can be an issue.

Swiftcurrent Motor Inn and Cabins offers economical lodging in what many consider the most scenic area of this magnificent national park. The 1-bedroom cabins without bath are among the least expensive lodgings offered in any national park. These are an excellent value and a good choice if a community bathroom is acceptable. Trees surround all of the lodging buildings, so you won't enjoy great vistas from your room, but good views are available near the registration building. The area is relatively quiet and a pleasant 1-mile walk from fancier and more expensive Many Glacier Hotel. Swiftcurrent is especially popular with hikers and serves as a trailhead for several popular hikes including those to Iceberg Lake, Swiftcurrent Pass, and Ptarmigan Tunnel, the latter of which guides hikers through an unusual 180-foot tunnel. A brochure and map of day hikes are available at the registration desk. Following a day of hiking enjoy an emu burger, buffalo brat, or weasel collar in the restaurant.

Rooms: Singles, doubles, triples, and quads. All motel rooms have private baths. Most cabin guests must use a community bathroom.

Wheelchair Accessibility: Four rooms in one of the motel buildings near the rear of the complex plus the new two-bedroom cabin are wheelchair accessible.

Swiftcurrent Motor Inn is on the site of what was once a tepee camp established in 1911 by the Great Northern Railroad. Here guests slept on army cots in replicas of Blackfoot Indian tepees. By 1933 the tepees had been replaced by 27 cabins and the area was called "Many Glacier Auto Tourist Camp." A year later the Civilian Conservation Corps constructed a campground and additional cabins. The current camp store was built in 1935. The following year a huge forest fire destroyed most of the cabins, which were rebuilt in 1937. In 1940 a central comfort station with showers was added. Three motel-type buildings and an employee dormitory (later converted to a fourth motel building) were constructed in 1955.

Reservations: Xanterra Parks & Resorts Glacier Division, 540 Nucleus Ave., Columbia Falls, MT 59912. Phone (855) 733-4522 or visit www .glaciernationalparklodges.com. A deposit of 1 night's stay is required. Cancellation notice of at least 72 hours is required for a refund.

Rates: One-bedroom cabin without bath ($80); two-bedroom cabin without bath ($90); one-bedroom cabin with bath ($101); new one-bedroom cabin with a bath ($109); new two-bedroom cabin with a bath ($130); Pinetop ($134); Motor Inn ($142). Room rates quoted are for 2 adults. Each additional person is $15 per night. Children 11 and under stay free with an adult.

Location: In the northeast section of Glacier National Park at the end of Many Glacier Rd., 12 miles east of Babb, Montana.

Season: Early June to late Sept.

Food: A restaurant offers breakfast ($7–$15), lunch ($7–$20), and dinner ($14–$22). Lunch items including hamburgers and pizza can be ordered during dinner. Beer and wine are served. Limited groceries, snacks, beer, and wine are available in the general store.

Facilities: Restaurant, laundry, and camp store with gifts, groceries, and supplies.

Activities: Hiking, sightseeing tours, evening campfire programs at the National Park Service campground. Fishing, horseback riding, and boat tours of Swiftcurrent Lake and Lake Josephine are available at nearby Many Glacier Hotel.

VILLAGE INN AT APGAR

1038 Apgar St. • Apgar, MT 59936 • (406) 888-5632 • www.glaciernationalparklodges.com

Village Inn at Apgar is a two-story motel-style building constructed in 1956 with 36 rooms. The inn is at the end of the road, directly on the shore of scenic Lake McDonald. Each room enjoys excellent views of the lake and the mountains beyond. The inn has no food service, although a restaurant is a short walk up the street. The inn offers 4 types of rooms. Each has a coffeemaker, fan, heat, and a full bath but no air-conditioning, telephone, or television. All are wood paneled, and each room has a large window and outside balcony or patio with excellent views of Lake McDonald. Larger rooms on the first floor can be entered from the parking lot behind the building. Unless you specifically desire one of the Kitchen units, we recommend a second-floor room for increased privacy and a somewhat better view of the lake. The 12 least expensive rooms

are small and sit at one end of the building, 6 on the second floor and 6 on the ground floor. Half the rooms have 1 double bed, and the other half have 2 twin beds that nearly fill these rooms.

Ten two-bedroom Family units, all on the second floor, have a double bed in 1 bedroom and either a double plus a twin bed or a double bed plus a sofa bed in the second room. These rooms cost $40 to $50 more per night and are quite a bit larger than the least expensive rooms described above. Eleven first-floor rooms have a bedroom with 2 double beds plus a separate kitchen area with a refrigerator, sink, oven, stove, and all cooking and eating utensils. These are the same size as the two-bedroom units on the second floor, except a kitchen replaces the second bedroom. Village Inn has 3 Suites. Two on the second floor each have a living room and 2 bedrooms, each

Village Inn at Apgar

with a double bed. A sofa bed is in the living room. One first-floor Suite has 2 bedrooms and a kitchen and is wheelchair accessible.

Village Inn is a handy place to spend a night on the west side of Glacier National Park. The inn doesn't enjoy the charm of the park's historic lodges, but the accommodations are comfortable and larger rooms with either 2 bedrooms or a kitchen are a good choice for families. The location at the end of a short road allows guests to avoid crowds while enjoying views of Lake McDonald and the park's scenic mountains. A gravel beach just outside the rooms leads to the cool waters of the lake. The inn is located less than a block from a restaurant that serves meals at reasonable prices, and a short walk from a National Park Service visitor center.

Rooms: Singles, doubles, triples, and quads. Some Family units and 2 Suites can hold up to 6 persons. All rooms have private baths.

Wheelchair Accessibility: A 1-bedroom Kitchen unit and the first-floor Suite are wheelchair accessible.

Reservations: Xanterra Parks & Resorts Glacier Division, 540 Nucleus Ave., Columbia Falls, MT 59912. Phone (855) 733-4522 or visit www .glaciernationalparklodges.com. A deposit of 1 night's stay is required. Cancellation notice of at least 72 hours is required for a refund.

Rates: One-bedroom unit ($146); two-bedroom Family unit ($182–$194); one-bedroom Kitchen unit ($194); three-room Suite ($260). Rates quoted are for 2 adults with the exception of the Suites, which are for 4 adults. Children 11 and under stay free with an adult. Additional adults are $15.

Location: In the village of Apgar, Montana, 3 miles from the West Glacier entrance station.

Season: End of May to mid-Sept.

Food: A restaurant 1 block away on Apgar Road offers breakfast, lunch, and dinner from Memorial Day through Labor Day. Very limited groceries are sold at a gift shop next to the restaurant. The lodge is 2.5 miles from a full-service grocery store and several restaurants in the town of West Glacier.

Facilities: The village of Apgar has gift shops; a restaurant; an ice cream shop; kayak, canoe, rowboat, and motorboat rentals; and a National Park Service visitor center.

Famous western artist Charles Russell had a home built beside Lake McDonald in 1908 by Dimon Apgar. Russell's studio, which still stands, was constructed 8 years later.

Activities: Nightly ranger/naturalist talks at the nearby Apgar campground, boating, swimming (very cool water), fishing (no license required), sightseeing tours. Several hiking trails begin at Apgar.

Lake Mead National Recreation Area

601 Nevada Hwy. • Boulder City, NV 89005 • (702) 293-8990 • www.nps.gov/lake

Lake Mead National Recreation Area comprises nearly 1.5 million acres of beautiful desert landscape that includes Lake Mead and Lake Mohave. The clear water in the lakes is mostly supplied by the Colorado River. Lake Mead is 110 miles long and results from famous Hoover Dam near Boulder City, Nevada. Farther south, 67-mile-long Lake Mohave is formed by Davis Dam near Bullhead City, Arizona. The recreation area is particularly popular for water-related activities such as boating, fishing, and waterskiing. Areas near the lake are often 5 to 10 degrees warmer than Las Vegas, which means summer temperatures frequently rise to 110° Fahrenheit and above. The national recreation area is in southern Nevada and northwestern Arizona. Main access is via US 93, which connects Las Vegas, Nevada, and Kingman, Arizona.

LAKE MEAD NATIONAL RECREATION AREA

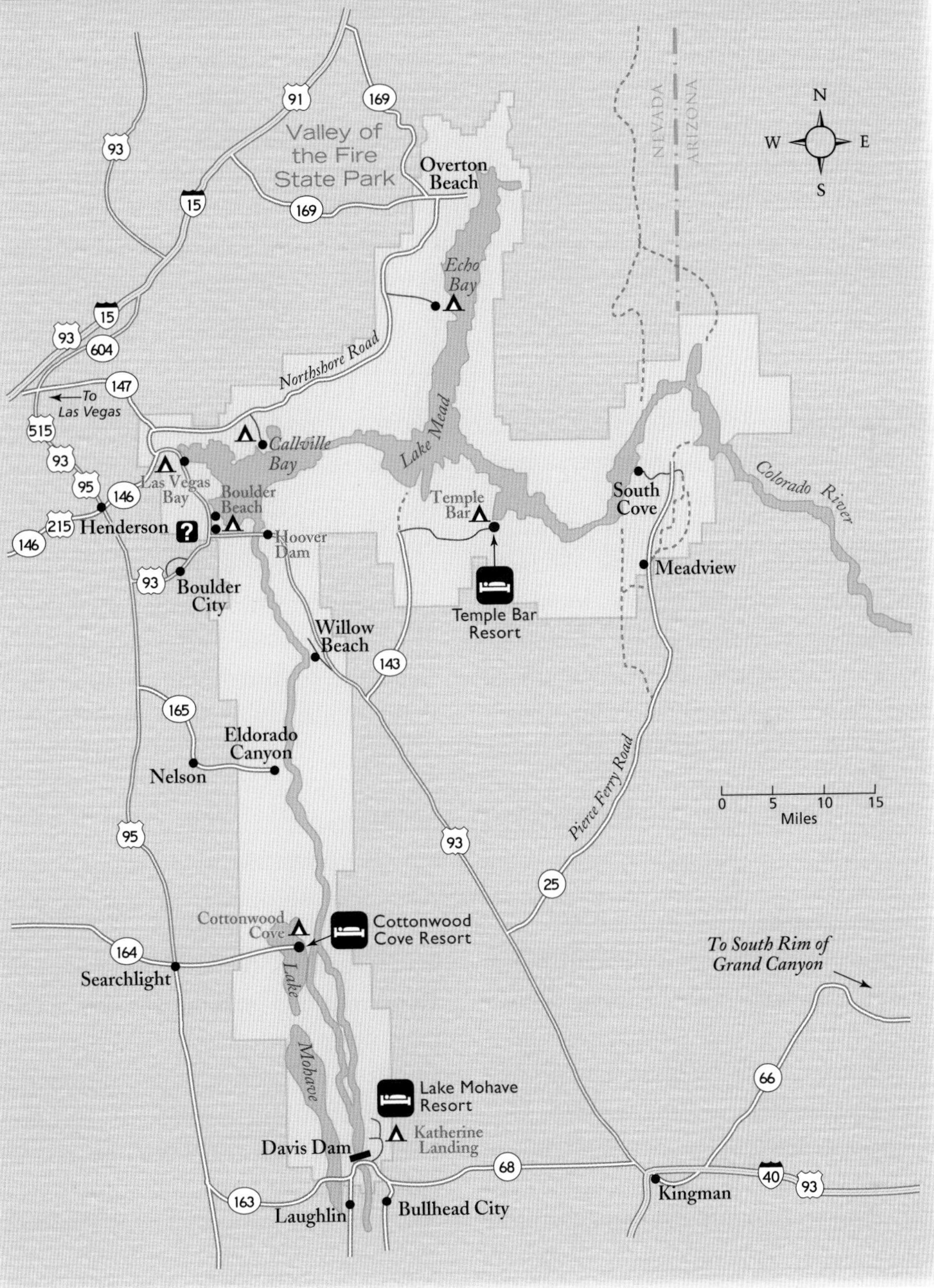

91 · 169

93

Valley of
the Fire
State Park

Overton
Beach

15

169

*Echo
Bay*

NEVADA · ARIZONA

N
W · E
S

93 · 15

Lake Mead

Colorado River

93 · 604

147

← To
Las Vegas

515

Northshore Road

*Callville
Bay*

93

95 · 146

Las Vegas
Bay

Boulder
Beach

South
Cove

*Temple
Bar*

215 · 146

Henderson

?

Hoover
Dam

*Temple Bar
Resort*

Meadview

93

Boulder
City

Willow
Beach

143

165

Eldorado
Canyon

Nelson

Pierce Ferry Road

0   5   10   15
Miles

95

93

25

To South Rim of
Grand Canyon →

Cottonwood
Cove

*Cottonwood
Cove Resort*

164

Searchlight

Lake

66

Mohave

*Lake Mohave
Resort*

*Katherine
Landing*

Davis Dam

68

Kingman

40 · 93

163

Laughlin   Bullhead City

Recreation Area Entrance Fee: $10 per vehicle or $5 per person, good for 7 days. $16 per vessel, good for 7 days.

Lodging in Lake Mead National Recreation Area: The recreation area has 3 lodging facilities. Temple Bar Resort is the only facility on Lake Mead in the northern half of the recreation area, while Cottonwood Cove Resort and Lake Mohave Resort are on Lake Mohave in the southern half of the recreation area.

The 3 lodges are similar in that they are each relatively small and offer basic motel-type accommodations along the shoreline of Lake Mead or Lake Mohave. Guests stay in these lodges primarily to enjoy the lake and water-based activities such as boating, fishing, and waterskiing.

Each property has a restaurant or cafe plus a full-service marina that serves as the primary draw. The resorts serve as alternatives for travelers who become tired of the glitz and crowds of nearby Las Vegas. The 3 facilities are not what most of us envision as national park lodging, but this doesn't make them inferior, only different. Thus, we are presenting a condensed description for the 3 locations.

COTTONWOOD COVE RESORT

10000 Cottonwood Cove Rd. • Searchlight, NV 89046 • (702) 297-1464 or (877) 386-4383
www.cottonwoodcoveresort.com

Cottonwood Cove Resort is an attractive single-story brick building with 24 large guest rooms plus 1 suite. Each guest room has heat, air-conditioning, carpet, cable TV, telephone, and a full bathroom. Most rooms have 2 queen beds, although some have a king plus a sofa bed. A covered patio with table and chairs outside each room overlooks the lake. Room rates range from $79 during value season (Nov through Mar) to $131 the remainder of the year. The suite rents for $176. Cottonwood Cove is 14 miles east of Searchlight, Nevada on NV 164. It is approximately 70 miles southeast of Las Vegas.

LAKE MOHAVE RESORT

2690 E. Katherine Spur Rd. • Bullhead City, AZ 86429 • (928) 754 3245 or (800) 752-9669
www.sevencrown.com/lakes/lake_mohave

Lake Mohave Resort has 2 cement-block motel-style buildings with 51 guest rooms. The buildings are in a large grassy area on a hill above the lake. Each building has a covered walkway with chairs. Rooms have air-conditioning, heat, telephone, television, and a bathroom. Six guest rooms enjoy a private balcony or patio. Fourteen rooms, including 8 suites, have a kitchen. A rental house that sleeps up to 10 persons in 3 bedrooms is also available. Room rates range from $60 to $70 Sept through Apr, and from $95 to $105 the remainder of the year. Rooms with kitchens are $10 to $20 more. The house rents for $275. The resort is 32 miles west of Kingman, Arizona. It is 3 miles off NV 68.

TEMPLE BAR RESORT

1 Main St., Temple Bar, AZ 86443 • (877) 386-4383 • www.templebarlakemead.com

Temple Bar Resort comprises 2 concrete-block buildings with 18 guest rooms plus 4 freestanding cabins. Motel rooms each have heat, air-conditioning, television, and a private bathroom, but no telephone. The larger motel building houses 12 large guest rooms, 6 on a side. Rooms each have 2 double beds and a patio. Lodging rates vary with summer being high season. (Lakeview: $94–$120; Desertview: $85–$110). A separate building offers 6 guest rooms, including 4 with kitchens. The 2 regular guest rooms each have 1 double bed plus a sofa sleeper ($75–$95). Two of the kitchen units have 1 double bed ($98–$115), while the other two larger kitchen units feature 2 double beds in a separate bedroom plus a sofa bed in the combination living room/kitchen ($111–$130). The 4 cabins have 1 double bed plus a rollaway, a stove with an oven, a sink, and a refrigerator ($51–$60). Cabin occupants must use an adjacent community bathhouse. Temple Bar Resort is 78 miles east of Las Vegas, Nevada. It is at the end of a paved road 28 miles northeast of US 93.

Many people who visit Lake Mead National Recreation Area are interested in houseboat rentals at the marinas. Most houseboats are about 14 feet wide, with lengths that range from 50 to 70 feet. Smaller units sleep 6 or 8 persons, while larger units can sleep a dozen. Be forewarned that houseboats aren't cheap to rent. Smaller houseboats often cost $600 per night. Larger houseboats that hold up to 10 or 12 persons rent for $1,400. Rental fees are often reduced during the off-season of mid-Sept to mid-June (excluding Memorial Day weekend). Houseboats are available at 7 a.m. on the first day and need to be returned by 4 p.m. on the last day. Reservations and deposits are required.

NORTH CAROLINA

Blue Ridge Parkway

199 Hemphill Knob Rd. • Asheville, NC 28803 • (828) 298-0398 • www.nps.gov/blri

The Blue Ridge Parkway comprises 93,000 acres in a narrow strip along 469 miles of winding road that follows the crest of the Blue Ridge Mountains. The parkway provides access to craft centers, campgrounds, scenic overlooks, log cabins, rail fences, and striking mountain vistas. Lodges and other points of interest along the parkway can be located using milepost markers alongside the road. Mile marker 0 is at Rockfish Gap near Waynesboro, Virginia, the northern entrance to the parkway. Each mile is numbered progressively southward. Visitor centers offer free parkway maps indicating locations of points of interest. The parkway is in western North Carolina and western Virginia. The north end of the parkway connects with Shenandoah National Park, and the south end leads to Great Smoky Mountains National Park.

Parkway Entrance Fee: No charge.

BLUE RIDGE PARKWAY

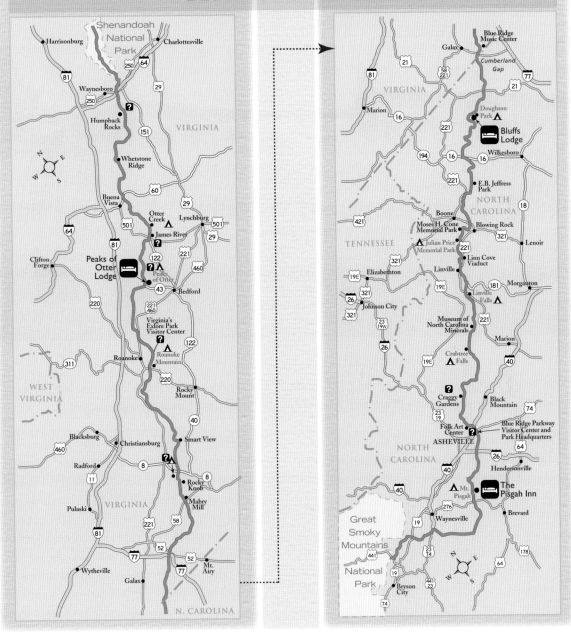

Lodging along the Blue Ridge Parkway: Three lodging facilities are within the boundaries of the Blue Ridge Parkway. Accommodations range from modern two-story lodges to a relatively small rustic lodge with only 24 guest rooms. Lodges are scattered along the parkway from mile marker 86 in the north to very near the south entrance, near Great Smoky Mountains National Park.

BLUFFS LODGE
45356 Blue Ridge Pkwy. • Laurel Springs, NC 28644-9716

Bluffs Lodge

Note: Bluffs Lodge closed following the 2010 season. While the National Park Service continues to search for a concessionaire, it is likely Bluffs will be closed for the 2015 season and, perhaps, longer.

Bluffs Lodge at milepost 241 consists of 2 identical two-story buildings built into a grassy hillside overlooking a meadow and surrounding hills. A coffee shop and gift shop are a quarter mile away on the parkway. Each lodge building contains 12 rooms, 4 on each floor of the back side facing a meadow and rolling hills and 4 rooms on the front facing the parking lot. A spacious, covered second-floor balcony spans the back of each building. A nice rock patio area between the 2 buildings has a large outdoor stone fireplace and many chairs and tables for viewing the scenery or visiting with other guests. The lodge opened in 1949 and has been a favorite for many travelers on the Blue Ridge Parkway. All 24 rooms at Bluffs Lodge are nearly identical except for views and bedding. Each room has heat, a ceiling fan, a coffeemaker, a hair dryer, and a tiled bathroom with a combination shower-tub, but no telephone, television, or air-conditioning. Although not particularly spacious, rooms are clean and comfortable, and each has a large closet to store suitcases, coolers, clothes, and other gear. Several rooms have 1 queen bed, and 2 have a king bed, but the majority have 2 double beds. The best views are from rooms on the back side facing the southwest. Rooms in the front face the northeast, which can be an advantage on particularly hot days when you may not want to deal with the afternoon sun. Remember, there is no air-conditioning. We would choose a second-floor mountain-view room, preferably 203A or 203B, end rooms with an added side window and brighter interior. In addition, other guests will not be walking by when they enter or exit their own rooms. The lodge is built on a hillside, so second-floor rooms do not require climbing stairs.

Bluffs Lodge is as peaceful a place as you will find in any national park or, for that matter, anywhere. It is a quarter mile off the Blue Ridge Parkway, so you won't be bothered by traffic noise, and since no restaurant or visitor center is at the site, there is no congestion of people and vehicles. With only 24 rooms and no televisions, you are likely to strike up conversations with other guests relaxing on the balcony or walkway outside their rooms. In the evening, guests often mingle in front of the large stone fireplace between the 2 buildings. A short walk up a nearby hillside provides an outstanding view of a valley and surrounding mountains. A unique experience when staying here is eating in the nearby old-fashioned coffee shop, which still offers counter service. Both the interior and exterior are virtually identical to when it opened in June 1949. Kathryn Jones, the server who waited on us during a June 2010 visit, had worked in the coffee shop for 59 years! Who says employee loyalty has gone out of style? The coffee shop specialized in regional dishes including pinto beans and cornbread, biscuits and gravy, and country ham. Where else can you order barbecued pork with melted cheese served between 2 golden brown corn cakes topped with cole slaw?

Rooms: Doubles, triples, and quads. All rooms have a private bath.

Location: In northern North Carolina, near the midpoint of the Blue Ridge Parkway at milepost 241.

Peaks of Otter Lodge at milepost 86 consists of a main registration and dining building plus 3 adjacent two-story structures that provide a total of 63 guest rooms. The attractive wood-and-cement block buildings were constructed in the mid-1960s and have a similar appearance. The buildings are on the grassy bank of Abbott Lake, and all the rooms provide an excellent view of this small but pretty body of water.

All but 3 wheelchair-accessible rooms are in 3 two-story buildings connected end-to-end by covered walkways. Each of the 3 buildings sits on a grassy hillside below the parking lot. Because the buildings are built into a hillside, a half flight of stairs gains entry to a walkway that runs in front of the entry doors of either first- or second-floor rooms. Unit 1, with rooms numbered in the 100s, is closest to the main lodge building, although the buildings are close together, so no room is far from the dining room and lounge. The rooms are bright and airy, with a large back window offering a view of Abbott Lake backed by a wooded hillside. Scenic Sharp Top Mountain peeks over the southwest corner of the lake. All but 2 rooms have either a patio or balcony with 2 chairs. Each room has air-conditioning, electric heat, carpeting, television, and a tiled bathroom, but no telephone. The majority of rooms have 2 double beds, while several have 1 king bed. We generally request second-floor rooms, but at this lodge you might prefer a room on the first floor, where you can move patio chairs onto the large grassy hillside leading to the nearby lake.

Peaks of Otter Lodge is a favorite for many travelers on the Blue Ridge Parkway. The rooms are comfortable, and the view from a back balcony is similar to what an armchair traveler might find on a picture postcard. Plan to do a lot of hiking during your visit. A 1-mile paved trail behind the lodge is a pleasant place to stroll as it circles Abbott Lake. Other trails are nearby. Anglers can fish in the stocked lake (artificial lures only). Bus trips to Sharp Top Mountain (fee charged) leave from the nearby nature center building when weather permits. Check the website for departure times. The country-style dining room, with its vaulted, beamed ceiling and large windows overlooking Abbott Lake, serves 3 meals a day, including a Friday night seafood buffet and Sunday brunch buffet. An attractive lounge with a large stone fireplace and great lake views is adjacent to the dining room.

Rooms: Singles, doubles, triples, and quads. All rooms have a private bath.

Wheelchair Accessibility: Three rooms on the ground floor (1 floor below the main entrance) of the main lodge building are accessible. Access to the rooms is via an elevator from the main lobby.

Reservations: DNC Parks & Resorts at Peaks of Otter, Inc., 85554 Blue Ridge Pkwy., Bedford,

Peaks of Otter Lodge

VA 24523. Phone (866) 387-9905. One night's deposit is required. Seventy-two-hour cancellation is required for a full refund, less a $15 fee.

Rates: Mid-Apr through late Nov; weekdays ($110–$130), weekends ($120–$136); some holiday weekends and the month of Oct ($144). End of Nov through mid-Apr, weekends only ($102). Rates quoted are for 2 adults. Each additional person is $11 per night. Children under 16 stay free. Rollaway beds are $11 per night. Check lodge website for specials and packages.

Location: Twenty-five miles north of Roanoke, Virginia, at mileposts 86 of the Blue Ridge Parkway.

Season: Open year-round, but weekends only late Nov through mid-March.

Food: A dining room serves breakfast ($6–$9), lunch ($8–$14), and dinner ($8–$25), including a special seafood buffet on Fri ($28) and a brunch buffet on Sun ($17).

A lodging facility served the Peaks of Otter area as early as 1834, when Polly Woods operated a combination tavern/lodge for nearly a decade. Several hotels followed in this locale prior to the construction of the parkway through the Peaks of Otter area beginning in 1939. The initial development plan envisioned a picnic area and aquatic center at the present lodge site in addition to 22 cabins on the hillside behind the current visitor center. Several proposals followed, including one that called for a lodge and a small lake to replace the aquatic center. The present lodge site was confirmed in 1951 with a plan calling for 1 large structure. This plan underwent several changes, and construction of the present lodge got underway in 1962. Two years later work commenced on the lake.

Facilities: Restaurant, cocktail lounge, gift shop, meeting room, country store, National Park Service visitor center.

Activities: Hiking, fishing, interpretive programs, bus trip to Sharp Top Mountain, National Park Service campfire programs on weekend evenings.

Pets: A $25 fee per pet, per night is charged with a two-pet maximum.

THE PISGAH INN

PO Box 749 • Waynesville, NC 28786 • (828) 235-8228 • www.pisgahinn.com

The Pisgah Inn at milepost 408 consists of 3 two-story buildings with a total of 50 rooms plus 1 suite, a separate restaurant and gift shop, and a nearby country store. Rooms offer excellent views of the distant mountains and are a short walk from the dining room. The inn, constructed in the mid-1960s, is situated at 5,000 feet on the side of 5,749-foot Mt. Pisgah. All rooms have heat, a tiled bathroom, small refrigerator, coffeemaker, ceiling fan, and a television, but no air-conditioning or telephone. Air-conditioning is seldom needed at this altitude. Each room has a private balcony with rocking chairs. Most rooms have 2 double beds, and a few have 1 queen or 1 king bed. The back balcony and windows of each

Mabry Mill, at milepost 176, is a favorite stop for travelers on the parkway. The mill, operated by E. B. Mabry from 1910 to 1935, today serves country ham, barbecue, biscuits, and corn and buckwheat pancakes. Regional handicrafts are available for purchase. A trail leads to the original gristmill, sawmill, blacksmith shop, and other outdoor exhibits. Demonstrations are presented during summer and fall.

Tree Tops is one of three lodge buildings at Pisgah Inn

room generally offer excellent views of the distant mountains, although some first-floor rooms have views partially obstructed by nearby trees and plants. The single suite located above the office is a double-size room with a king bed, 2 televisions, a sitting area with a sofa, a table and chairs, and a gas fireplace.

Pisgah Inn is a place to escape the heat while enjoying mountain views and good food.

The Biltmore Estate near Asheville, North Carolina, is one of this region's major visitor attractions. The 250-room mansion was constructed in the late 1800s by George Washington Vanderbilt, grandson of railroad tycoon Cornelius Vanderbilt. The home, modeled on a 16th-century French chateau, has 34 bedrooms, 43 bathrooms, and 65 fireplaces. Allow at least a half-day for the full self-guided tour of the home, winery, gardens, and greenhouse. Overnight guest rooms are available at The Inn on Biltmore Estate. The Biltmore Estate is 3 blocks north of I-40 (exit 50) on US 25. For information visit www.biltmore.com.

Views from the rooms are the best of any lodging facility on the parkway. At an altitude of 5,000 feet, temperatures are generally cool, even during summer months when the surrounding valleys are hot and humid. Weekends can be busy, so choose a weekday night or 2 if you have the flexibility. The restaurant, with its vaulted ceiling and ceiling-high windows on 3 walls, offers good views from nearly any table. Best of all, the restaurant serves excellent food, with nearly a dozen daily specials for lunch and dinner. On the evening we dined, the menu included sherry-glazed quail with a mushroom and sherry pan sauce over fresh sautéed baby spinach and wild rice. The inn is in an excellent area for hiking, and good fishing is about 10 miles away. National Park Service rangers conduct evening weekend programs across the road at the campground amphitheater.

Rooms: Singles, doubles, triples, and quads. All rooms have a private bath.

Wheelchair Accessibility: Three first-floor rooms are wheelchair accessible.

Reservations: Pisgah Inn, PO Box 749, Waynesville, NC 28786. Phone (828) 235-8228 or visit www.pisgahinn.com. One night's deposit is required. A fee of $25 is charged for cancellations 2 weeks or less from the arrival date. One night's deposit is charged for cancellations 48 hours or less from the arrival date.

Rates: Weekdays ($128); weekends ($135); suite weekdays ($175); suite weekends ($190). Rates quoted are for 2 adults. Each additional person is $12. Rollaways are $9 per night. Children 12 and under stay free. Rates are slightly higher during Oct and holidays. Specials are sometimes available during early spring. A basic breakfast is included when rooms are booked at rack rate.

Location: Southwest North Carolina, 25 miles south of Asheville on the Blue Ridge Parkway.

Season: Apr 1 through Oct 31.

Food: An attractive restaurant serves breakfast ($5–$16), lunch ($8–$18), and dinner ($8–$27). A nearby country store sells limited groceries.

The current Pisgah Inn is immediately adjacent to the location of an earlier inn that was donated by George Washington Vanderbilt, grandson of railroad tycoon Cornelius Vanderbilt. The Pisgah Forest Inn was constructed of wormy chestnut in 1919 by landscape architect George Weston for the Biltmore estate. The inn had 11 rooms, a large dining room, and cabins that were added in the 1940s. Guests arrived via the narrow Buck Spring Trail that was restricted to arriving guests during the morning and departing guests during the afternoon and evening. Following closure to overnight guests during the late 1960s, the lobby of the Pisgah Forest Inn continued to be used for special occasions such as speaking engagements, wedding receptions, and get-togethers. The inn was torn down in 1991. The cabins continued in use as employee housing for several years. Photographs of the Pisgah Forest Inn are in the registration area of the Pisgah Inn.

Facilities: Restaurant, gift shop, laundry, country store with gift items and limited groceries.

Activities: Hiking, mountain biking, evening weekend programs at the nearby campground amphitheater.

Pets: An fee of $40 per night is charged for pets.

OHIO

Cuyahoga Valley National Park

1550 Boston Mills Rd. • Peninsula, OH 44264 • (800) 257-9477
www.dayinthevalley.com • www.nps.gov/cuva

Cuyahoga Valley National Park encompasses 33,000 acres of a rural river valley linking the urban centers of Cleveland and Akron. The park offers a 19-mile Towpath Trail along which visitors can stroll, hike, or bike beside the Ohio & Erie Canal. Winter activities include cross-country skiing and snowshoeing. Cuyahoga Valley includes a restored 1800s farm and village, trails, several visitor centers, and remnants of a company town built in 1906. Throughout the year, the Cuyahoga Valley Scenic Railroad operates the full length of the park and beyond.

Park Entrance Fee: No charge.

Lodging in Cuyahoga Valley National Park: A bed-and-breakfast inn offers the only regular guest accommodations within the park. The Inn at Brandywine Falls is midway between the north and south ends of the park, approximately 4 miles northeast of the crossing of I-80 and I-271. A second lodging facility, Sanford House, is a nine-bedroom, two-bath former youth hostel primarily used for group retreats and large family gatherings. The house is operated by the Conservancy for Cuyahoga Valley National Park and can be reached at (330) 657-2909.

INN AT BRANDYWINE FALLS

8230 Brandywine Rd. • Sagamore Hills, OH 44067 • (330) 467-1812 • www.innatbrandywinefalls.com

The Inn at Brandywine Falls is a pre–Civil War–era farmstead renovated in 1988 by an enterprising couple who operate it as a bed-and-breakfast under a 50-year lease from the US government. The property includes the main house, an adjacent carriage barn, and a nearby stable. Cats, chickens, goats, and an affable dog add to the country atmosphere of the inn.

The inn offers 6 overnight rooms, 4 in the main house and 2 in the carriage barn. All rooms have heat, air-conditioning, a telephone, and a private bathroom. The main house has 3 rooms on the second floor, 1 of which, "Adeline's Retreat,"

has 1 double bed. The other second-floor accommodations include the "Simon Perkins Room," with 2 double 4-poster beds, and "Anna Hale's Garret Suite," comprising a small bedroom with 2 double beds plus a small sitting room that can be utilized as a second bedroom. The single first-floor accommodation, "The James Wallace Parlour," has a double sleigh bed and is wheelchair accessible. More expensive suites in the carriage house each have plank floors, a table and chairs, either a double futon or daybeds, a Franklin stove, a microwave, and a refrigerator, all on the first floor, plus a king bed in the loft. Each suite

CUYAHOGA VALLEY NATIONAL PARK

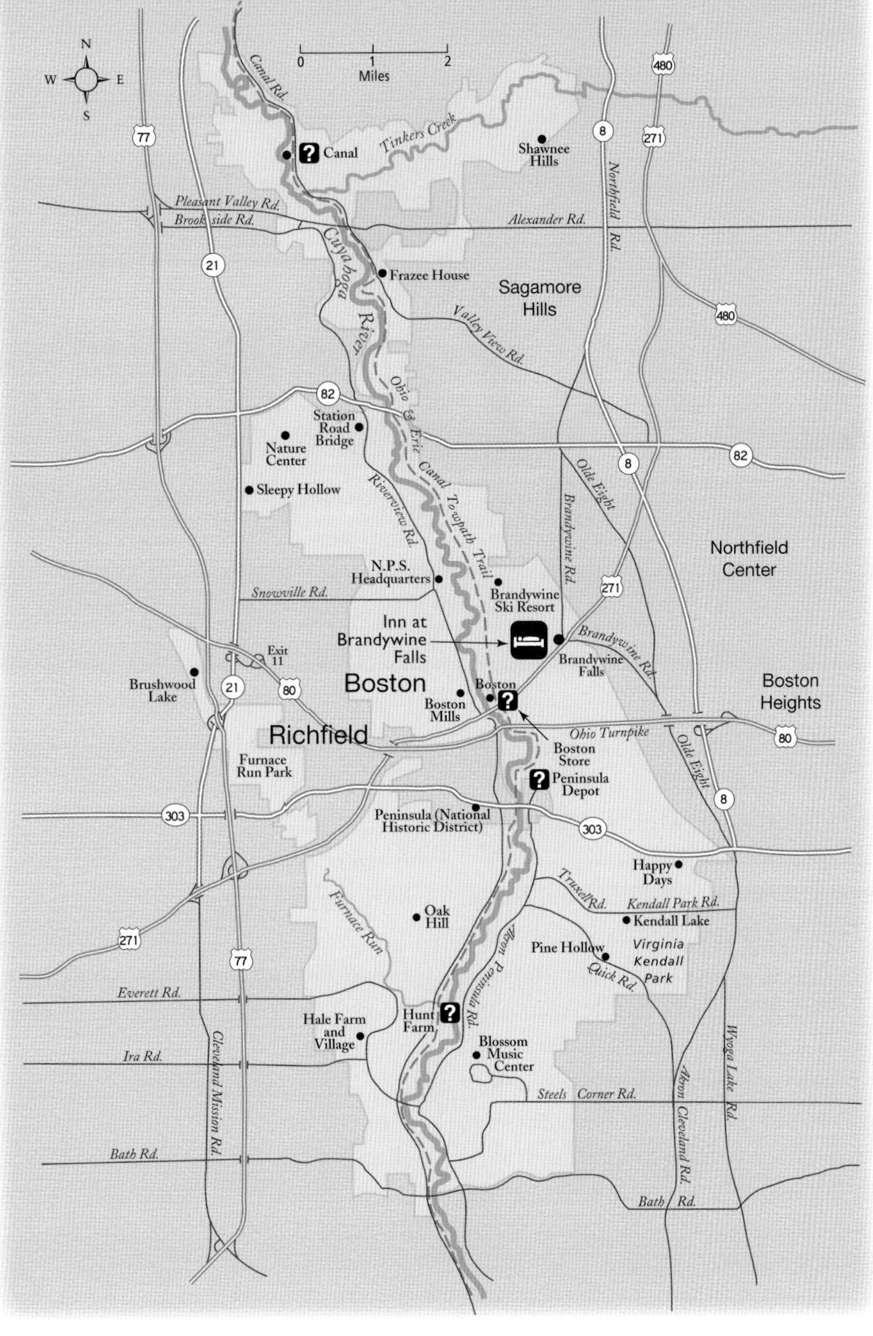

N
W · E
S

0 1 2
Miles

480

77

Canal Rd.

? Canal

Tinkers Creek

Shawnee
Hills

8

271

Northfield Rd.

Pleasant Valley Rd.
Brookside Rd.

Alexander Rd.

21

Cuyahoga River

• Frazee House

Sagamore
Hills

480

Valley View Rd.

82

Station
Road •
Bridge

• Nature
Center

• Sleepy Hollow

Riverview Rd.

Ohio & Erie Canal Towpath Trail

Olde Eight

Brandywine Rd.

82

8

271

Northfield
Center

N.P.S. •
Headquarters

Snowville Rd.

Brandywine
Ski Resort

Inn at
Brandywine
Falls

Boston

Exit
11

Brushwood •
Lake

21 80

Boston •
Mills

? Boston

Brandywine
Falls

Boston
Heights

80

Richfield

Ohio Turnpike

Boston
Store

? Peninsula
Depot

Olde Eight

8

Furnace
Run Park

303

Peninsula (National
Historic District)

303

271

77

Everett Rd.

Cleveland Mission Rd.

Furnace Run

• Oak
Hill

Pine Hollow

Truxell Rd.

Happy •
Days

Kendall Park Rd.

• Kendall Lake

*Virginia
Kendall
Park*

Akron Peninsula Rd.

Chick Rd.

Akron Cleveland Rd.

Wyoga Lake Rd.

Ira Rd.

Hale Farm
and •
Village

Hunt **?**
Farm

Blossom •
Music
Center

Steels Corner Rd.

Bath Rd.

Bath Rd.

The Inn at Brandywine Falls

has a Jacuzzi plus a wall of windows that offers guests a feel of the outdoors. The bathroom in 1 suite is on the second floor, while the bathroom in the other suite is on the first floor.

Located in a rural area of Ohio, the Inn at Brandywine Falls is a place to relax and use as a base from which to explore this diverse national park. You can ride a train, drive to Cleveland and take in the Rock and Roll Hall of Fame, or sit on the front porch and sip tea. Sixty-seven-foot Brandywine Falls is a short walk from the inn, or you can hike the 1.7-mile-long Brandywine Gorge Trail. Guests are encouraged to use the inn's living room, library, dining room, and porch. A full breakfast of fresh-squeezed juice, fruit, fruit-filled oatmeal, homemade bread, and an entree is served each morning from 7 to 10 a.m. (from 8:45 a.m. on weekends).

Rooms: Doubles, triples, and quads. All rooms have private baths.

Wheelchair Accessibility: One room on the first floor is barrier-free. A lift is available for the front entrance.

Reservations: Inn at Brandywine Falls, 8230 Brandywine Rd., Sagamore Hills, Ohio 44067-2810. Phone (888) 306-3381, (330) 467-1812. A 65 percent deposit is required with a reservation. A two-week cancellation is required for a full refund unless the accommodation is subsequently

higher. Prices are for 2 persons and include a full breakfast. Additional persons are $10 to $45 per night, depending on age. A 10 percent discount is offered for stays of 3 days or more, except holidays, and for 2-day stays Sun through Thurs from Jan 15 through Apr. Holidays are excluded.

Location: In northeast Ohio, midway between Cleveland and Akron.

Season: Open year-round.

Food: Breakfast is included. Fruit, homemade cookies, and hot beverages are provided at 4:30 p.m. and after 8:30 p.m. Alcoholic beverages may be brought by guests. Over a dozen restaurants are within 6 miles of the inn.

The James Wallace family came to this area in the early 1800s and built the farmhouse that is now the Inn at Brandywine Falls. Although difficult to visualize from today's serene setting, this was once the thriving community of Brandywine Mills. Wallace built a mill powered by the nearby waterfall and used money earned from the business to purchase 600 acres and build a farmhouse. The farmhouse passed through 5 owners before being purchased by the National Park Service. The property was renovated by innkeepers Katie and George Hoy under an agreement with the NPS.

booked by another party, or the guest purchases cancellation insurance for a modest fee. The innkeepers recommend that reservations be made at least 2 months in advance.

Arrival/Departure: Check-in between 4:01 and 6:45 p.m. and after 8:30 p.m. Checkout at 11 a.m.

Rates: Sun through Thurs non-holiday prices: Main house rooms ($145); main house suite ($165); Carriage house suites ($235). Fri is $25 to $35 higher. Sat and holidays are $50 to $100

Facilities: Dining room for breakfast, library.

Activities: Hiking, biking, and birding. Golf and pond fishing are nearby. Historic attractions include a scenic railroad and museums. Snow tubing, cross-country skiing, snowshoeing, and downhill skiing are popular during winter.

OREGON

State Tourist Information
(800) 547-7842 | www.traveloregon.com

Crater Lake National Park

PO Box 7 • Crater Lake, OR 97604 • (541) 594-3000 • www.nps.gov/crla

Crater Lake National Park encompasses 183,000 acres, including a deep blue lake resulting from the collapse of Mt. Mazama, an ancient 12,000-foot volcano. A 33-mile paved road circles the lake, although heavy winter snowfall averaging 533 inches can keep portions of the Rim Road closed until July. Summer days can be cool and the nights quite chilly. Crater Lake is in southern Oregon, 57 miles north of Klamath Falls. The major road into the park, OR 62, enters through the southwest corner.

Park Entrance Fee: $10 per vehicle or $5 per person, good for 7 days.

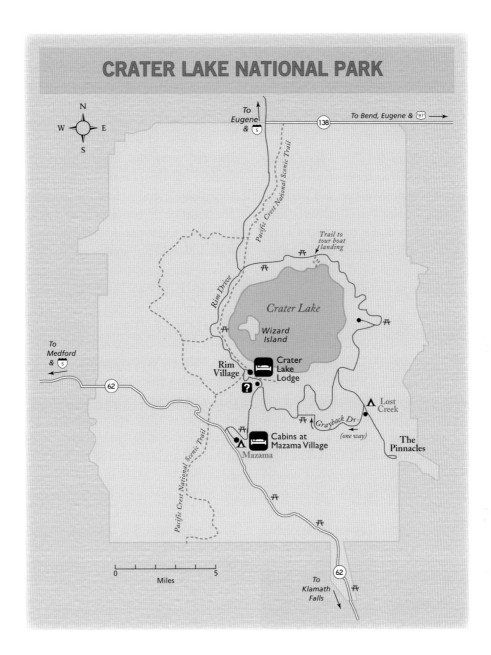

CRATER LAKE NATIONAL PARK

Lodging in Crater Lake National Park: The park has 2 very different lodging facilities. Crater Lake Lodge offers 71 rooms in a historic but completely rebuilt four-story lodge on the rim of Crater Lake. The Cabins at Mazama Village offers 40 basic and less expensive rooms 7 miles south of the rim. Crater Lake Lodge is a classic national park lodge, with a back patio, large lobby, cozy dining room, and 3 large stone fireplaces. Mazama Village is more like a motel unit. Both locations have dining facilities.

Mazama Village offers 40 rooms in 10 modern chalet-style wooden buildings clustered side-by-side in 2 groups of 5. The one-story buildings, constructed in 1983, each contain 4 guest rooms and are situated in a wooded area. Ample parking is directly in front of each building, making it convenient to unload and load luggage. The lodging complex is a short walk from facilities in Mazama Village that include the registration desk, a small market, an attractive family-style restaurant, and a gift shop. Mazama Village is in the southern section of the park, and at an altitude of 6,000 feet, the complex offers warmer conditions than at the higher elevation where Rim Village and Crater Lake Lodge are located.

All rooms at Mazama Village are identical in size, bedding, and layout except for 2 that are wheelchair accessible. This is basic motel-style lodging with 2 queen-size beds and a small table and chairs that pretty much fill the room. The rooms have heat and a coffeemaker, but no air-conditioning or television. The bath has a shower but no tub. Each room has a large window, although no particularly good views are available, so no one room or building is preferable. Each

building has a picnic table near the entrance making it handy to eat a picnic lunch or cook a meal on a propane stove (if you carry one).

Lodging at Mazama Village is a lower-cost alternative to the more upscale Crater Lake Lodge, and the ease of moving luggage between your vehicle and a room at Mazama is a plus. The location is convenient to laundry facilities, a market, and a family-style restaurant. It is also within walking distance of the National Park Service campground where evening programs are presented. An easy 7-mile drive takes you to the rim, where you can explore Rim Village and Crater Lake Lodge. The main National Park Service visitor center is between Mazama Village and Rim Village. We would try for the least expensive ground-floor rooms at Crater Lake Lodge that cost about $25 per night more than rooms at Mazama. Although these lodge rooms are somewhat smaller than rooms at Mazama, the ambience and location of the lodge are worth the difference in cost. If these 4 rooms at the lodge are unavailable, the cost difference between the facilities becomes much greater, which may tilt you toward choosing a room at Mazama.

Rooms: Doubles, triples, and quads. Each room has a full bath with a shower.

Wheelchair Accessibility: Two rooms are ADA compliant with 1 queen bed and a large bathroom.

Reservations: Crater Lake National Park, 1211 Avenue C, White City, OR 97503. Phone (888) 774-2728. A deposit of 1 night's stay is required. A cancellation notice of 48 hours is required for a full refund less a $10 fee.

A lodging unit at Mazama Village

Mazama Village derives its name from the ancient volcano that formed what is now Crater Lake. This dormant volcano is a member of the Cascade Range, a string of volcanoes that extend from Lassen Peak east of Redding, California, to Mt. Garibaldi near Vancouver, British Columbia. Mt. Mazama may once have towered to 12,000 feet above sea level before a violent eruption occurred about 7,700 years ago. After the chamber inside the mountain was emptied, the walls of the volcano collapsed to form a caldera that filled with water from rain and snow and resulted in the nation's deepest lake, at 1,932 feet.

Rates: All rooms ($140). Rate quoted is for 2 adults. Each additional person is $10 per night. Children 11 and under stay free with an adult. Rollaway or crib is $10 per night.

Location: On the south side of Crater Lake National Park, 8 miles from the west entrance.

Season: Late May to late Sept.

Food: A family-style restaurant a short distance from the cabins offers breakfast ($8–$12), lunch ($10–$14), and dinner ($11–$19). A snack bar with soups, salads, and sandwiches is at Rim Village. Crater Lake Lodge has an upscale restaurant.

Facilities: Restaurant, gift shop, market, laundry, self-service gas pump.

Activities: Hiking and evening naturalist programs, depending on snowmelt.

CRATER LAKE LODGE

Crater Lake National Park, OR 97604 • (541) 594-2255, ext. 3200 • www.craterlakelodges.com

Crater Lake Lodge offers 71 rooms in a four-story stone-and-wood building that was originally completed in 1915 and reopened in 1995 following a major 4-year renovation. The lodge is on the rim of Crater Lake, allowing guests to view from the windows of some rooms what many consider America's most beautiful lake. The first floor has a cozy dining room, lobby, and the Great Hall with its massive stone fireplace. Stone fireplaces are also in the dining room and the registration lobby. Two elevators are near the registration area. Parking may involve a short walk, so it is best to unload luggage from a loading zone at the front entrance or the end of the lodge, then move your vehicle to a parking spot. Bell service is available.

Rooms at Crater Lake Lodge are grouped into 6 price classifications depending on size, view, and bedding. Four smaller first-floor rooms without a view are cheapest, and 4 two-story loft rooms on floors 3 and 4 are most expensive. The remaining 63 rooms offer lake views, excellent lake views, or valley views. The remodeled rooms look much newer than the exterior of the lodge would lead you to expect. All are nicely furnished and have heat but no air-conditioning, telephone, or television. Rooms do not have coffeemakers, although complimentary coffee is available each

Crater Lake Lodge

The Great Hall in Crater Lake Lodge

morning in the Great Hall. Most rooms have a full bathroom with a combination shower-tub. A few rooms have claw-foot bathtubs only. Bedding varies from 1 to 2 queen beds. Rooms at the back have views of the lake; those at the front look across the parking lot toward the mountains. Second-floor rooms generally have larger windows and may be the best choice on the lake side. Third-floor windows in many rooms are high (your chin may rest on the windowsill), and fourth-floor windows are smaller but have window seats. The few first-floor rooms have virtually no view. Corner room 401, with 1 queen bed, offers a great lake view including Wizard Island from the claw-foot bathtub. Rooms 301 and 201 also offer this same lake view, just not

from the tub. Room 410 is quite large and has 2 window seats that provide a lake view. Rooms 211 through 220 allow occupants to view the lake while lying in bed. Room 221, a large corner room with 2 queen beds, offers good views of both Crater Lake and Garfield Peak.

The 4 two-level loft rooms have a queen bed on each floor. Loft rooms are entered from the third floor, where guests can view the valley. Lake views are available from the fourth-floor bedroom. Two loft rooms have the bathroom (claw-foot tub) on the third-floor entry level, while the other 2 loft rooms require guests to climb to the fourth-floor bedroom to reach the bathroom. Rooms on both floors are comparatively large. The lodge has 2 second-floor rooms directly above the kitchen that are rented on-site unless specifically requested when a reservation is made. Access requires several steps, and the rooms do not offer a lake view. The Peyton Room is large and in most hotels would be classified as a suite. It has a separate bedroom plus a large living area that can easily accommodate 1 or 2 rollaways. The Garfield Room is smaller with 1 queen bed.

Crater Lake Lodge has always been one of our favorite national park lodges. Situated in a breathtaking location, the lodge provides travelers with a modern facility that radiates the rustic charm appropriate for one of our country's oldest national parks. Rocking chairs on a large back porch that spans the length of the original hotel offer a relaxing (and, often, chilly) place to enjoy a breathtaking view of Crater Lake's deep blue water. Guests often spend much of their time in the Great Hall talking, playing cards and board games, reading, or just sitting in rocking chairs enjoying the flames and warmth of the huge gas log fireplace. Here is a place to make new friends on a lazy afternoon or after a meal in the cozy dining room. The dining room is small, and it is wise to make dinner reservations at the same time you book a room.

Rooms: Doubles, triples, and quads. All rooms have a private bath, most with a shower-tub combination.

Wheelchair Accessibility: Six rooms on the first floor are ADA compliant.

Reservations: Crater Lake Lodge, Crater Lake National Park, 1211 Ave. C, White City, OR 97503. Phone (888) 774-2728. A deposit of 1 night's stay is required. A cancellation notice of 48 hours is required for a full refund less a $10 fee. Consider making dinner reservations at the same time you call for a room reservation.

Rates: Ground floor rooms ($169–$196—4 rooms only); non-lake rooms ($196–$206); Lakeside rooms ($210–$230) two-level loft rooms ($294). Rates quoted are for 2 adults except loft rooms, which are for 4 adults. Children 11 and under stay free in the same room with an adult. Each additional person is $25. Weekend packages are offered in early spring and late fall.

Construction on Crater Lake Lodge commenced about a decade after Crater Lake became a national park in 1902. The building, while impressive from the outside, suffered from many structural faults. Over the years, major maintenance, including the installation of columns to support the ceiling and walls in the Great Hall, was required to keep the lodge in operation. The National Park Service assumed ownership of the lodge in 1967 and in the early 1980s started considering its demolition. The lodge was closed to visitors in 1989, but public and political pressure resulted in congressional support for a $15 million rehabilitation that included everything from a new foundation to a new roof frame. Essentially, the lodge was disassembled and rebuilt from the ground up for a reopening in May 1995.

Location: On the south rim of Crater Lake, 15 miles from the north entrance and 17 miles from the south entrance to Crater Lake National Park.

Season: Late May to mid-Oct. The lodge generally sells out from mid-June to the end of Sept.

Food: A dining room offers breakfast ($7–$13), lunch ($10–$16), and dinner ($21–$37). Alcoholic beverages are served. Reservations are required only for the dinner meal. A snack bar at Rim Village serves some breakfast items plus soups, salads, and sandwiches. A family-style restaurant at Mazama Village offers pizza, pasta, soup, and salads.

Facilities: Dining room. Rim Village, a short walk from the lodge, has a gift shop, snack bar, and small National Park Service visitor center.

Activities: Boat tours of Crater Lake, hiking, fishing, and ranger-guided walks.

Oregon Caves National Monument

19000 Caves Hwy. • Cave Junction, OR 97523 • (541) 592-2100 • www.nps.gov/orca

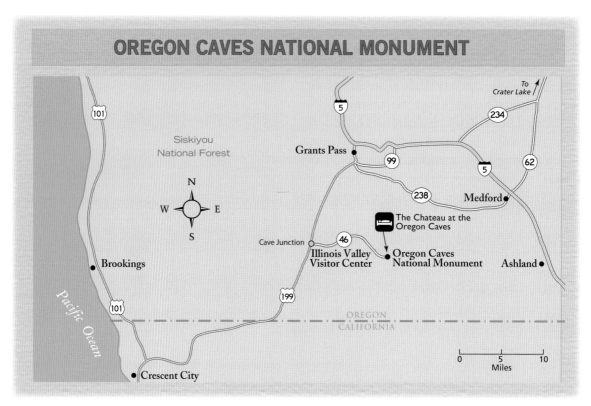

Oregon Caves National Monument was established in 1909 to protect 11 small caves plus a 3-mile-long cave that is home to endangered bats and includes all of the earth's 6 main types of rock. The monument is home to one of the world's few marble caves. The area covers 480 acres of old-growth forest, including part of the most diverse conifer forest in the world. The monument is in southwestern Oregon, 20 miles east of Cave Junction via OR 46. The last 8 miles of the paved highway are crooked and steep. Parking at the monument is limited, especially for motor homes and vehicles pulling trailers. Trailers can be dropped off at the Illinois Valley Visitor Center in Cave Junction or at Grayback Campground on the entry road to the monument.

Guided cave tours operate daily from mid-Mar through early Nov. Tour times and frequency vary by season, with summer tours beginning at 9 a.m. and ending at 6 p.m. Tours last approximately 90 minutes and cover a little over half a mile. The tours are moderately strenuous and include over 500 mostly steep and uneven steps. Frequent bending is required through low and narrow passageways.

The last tour of the day during summer weekends is a flashlight or candle tour. The year-round cave temperature is 44° Fahrenheit, so dress properly and wear shoes suitable for walking and hiking. Jackets are generally available to borrow in the visitor center where tour tickets are sold. Children must be at least 42 inches tall and pass a step test to qualify for a tour. Canes, staffs, walking aids, tripods, and backpacks are not permitted in the cave.

Monument Entrance Fee: No charge for entrance to the monument, but a fee is charged for cave tours.

Lodging in Oregon Caves National Monument: A classic six-story chateau with 23 guest rooms is the only lodging facility in this small national monument. The chateau is at the end of the road near the entrance to the main cave.

The Chateau at the Oregon Caves

PO Box 1824 • Cave Junction, OR 97523 • (541) 592-3400 • www.oregoncaveschateau.com

The Chateau at the Oregon Caves remains an undiscovered national park lodge for even many seasoned travelers. Unlike numerous facilities that call themselves a lodge, but are not, at least in the traditional sense, the chateau is a classic lodging facility. The registration area, lobby, dining room, coffee shop, gift shop, and all guest rooms are in the same alpine-style building that

The Chateau at the Oregon Caves

was constructed in 1934 and became a National Historic Landmark in 1987. The lobby is entered on the fourth floor (which the chateau classifies as the first floor), and guest rooms are on that floor and the 2 floors above. A restaurant, gift shop, and 1930s-style coffee shop are 1 floor below. The six-story chateau retains the look and feel you expect in a national park lodge with a coziness and warmth that modern hotels lack. The exterior is covered with cedar bark sheathing, and wood shakes top the roof with its many gables. The large lobby, with huge log supports and giant ceiling beams, is dominated by a double-hearth marble fireplace that burns real wood, not gas. Most of the original Monterey furniture,

including chairs, card tables, and writing desks, remains in the lobby. Original furnishings are also in a few guest rooms. The chateau often fills on summer weekends, but rooms are likely to be available most weekdays.

All 23 guest rooms offer steam heat and a private bathroom, but no air-conditioning, telephone, or television. Rooms differ with respect to size, layout, view, and bedding, which ranges from 1 queen in a very small Economy room to a Family Suite with two large bedrooms with a queen in 1 room and 2 queens in an adjoining room. The majority of rooms are classified as Standard or Deluxe with either 1 queen or 2 double beds. Several rooms on the top floor are snuggled under gables. The chateau has no elevator. Second-floor rooms require climbing 23 steps, while third-floor rooms require an additional 15 steps. Third-floor rooms are the quietest, in part because the floors squeak. Some rooms offer a view of a tree-covered ravine, while others overlook the parking lot or entrance road. Several Deluxe rooms are among our favorites. We like first-floor corner room 105 with 2 double beds, which is convenient to the lobby and offers a good view of the ravine. Room 205 directly above offers the same good view. Room 201 is quite large, has 1 queen bed, and offers a view and the pleasant sound of the waterfall. Room 312, with 2 double beds, has a unique toilet location. When arriving we suggest you ask to view several available rooms. You may find a room that is larger and/or offers a better view than your assigned room. The Chateau has steam heat which is turned on for about 2 hours in the morning and 2 hours in the evening, when needed. Electric space heaters are available.

The Chateau at the Oregon Caves is one of the most unique lodges in any national park. It is relatively small and yet generally uncrowded, because most travelers have yet to discover it. That is their misfortune. The lodge is operated by a nonprofit organization that helps the community by offering local produce, meats, wines, microbrews, and cheese. The gift shop features local arts and crafts.

The area offers good hiking and a tranquil setting that is ideal for individuals searching for peace and quiet. What a great place for a honeymoon! When is the last time you stayed in a lodge that had a small stream running through the dining room? The chateau does, and you can hear the water ripple through as you enjoy a meal. One night we enjoyed an excellent dinner of stuffed trout before spending the remainder of the evening sitting in front of the glowing fireplace while reading and talking with other guests. Depending on your arrival time, spend the first afternoon taking a cave tour and the next day hiking 1 or more of the monument's several trails. Enjoy an evening reading a good mystery in front of the fireplace.

Rooms: Doubles, triples, and quads. One Family Suite accommodates up to 7 persons. All rooms have a private bath, although 2 on the third floor have only a tub or a shower.

Wheelchair Accessibility: There are no wheelchair-accessible rooms.

The first wooden buildings, including the original chalet, were constructed here in 1923 by a group of businessmen who hoped to profit from curious tourists attracted to the caves. The current Chateau at the Oregon Caves was completed in 1934 at a total of $50,000, half of which was financed by the US Forest Service and half by private investors. The chateau remains relatively unchanged since its construction. A local nonprofit organization, Oregon Cave Outfitters, assumed management of the chateau in 2003 after the National Park Service took over operation of the cave tours in 2002.

Reservations: Oregon Caves Outfitters, PO Box 1824, Cave Junction, OR 97523. Phone (541) 592-3400 or (877) 245-9022. A credit card guarantee is required. Cancellation within 48 hours of scheduled arrival results in a charge of 1 night's stay. A cancellation notice of more than 2 days, but within 30 days, results in a $10 fee.

Rates: Economy ($109); Standard ($145); Deluxe ($170); Suite ($185–$195). Rates are for 2 adults except in Family Suites, where rates are for 4 adults. Children 12 and under stay free with an adult. Each additional person is $15 each per night. Special packages are offered throughout the season.

Location: Twenty miles south of Cave Junction, Oregon, at the end of OR 46.

Season: The lodge is open from early May through late Sept. Cave tours are offered mid-Mar through early Nov.

Food: An attractive dining room with large windows offering views of the ravine is open for dinner only ($14–$35). Reservations are recommended but not required. A retro coffee shop on the same floor serves breakfast ($5–$10), lunch ($6–$12), ice cream, and real milk shakes. The gift shop sells sandwiches, salads, ice cream, and beverages.

Facilities: Gift shop with crafts made by local artisans, restaurant, and coffee shop. A National Park Service visitor center is a short walk from the lodge where cave tours begin.

The Chateau at the Oregon Caves served as the meeting place for 2 men, who together would alter the way people viewed nature . . . and many other things. Harold Graves, a businessman and photographer from Portland, Oregon, was taking photographs in the park one day when he encountered another visitor, William Gruber. Gruber was carrying a tripod on which he had mounted 2 cameras side by side. The 2 men met later that evening in Graves' room at the chateau, where Gruber described his idea for a viewing device that would place the viewer in the middle of the scene. That meeting led to the development of the View-Master, a viewing device familiar to nearly every child.

Activities: Cave tours, ranger programs and nature walks, and hiking. Several hiking trails begin at the lodge.

SOUTH DAKOTA

State Tourist Information
(800) 732-5682 | www.travelsd.com

Badlands National Park

25216 Ben Reifel Rd. • Interior, SD 57750 • (605) 433-5361 • www.nps.gov/badl

Badlands National Park comprises 244,000 acres of prairie grasslands and scenic eroded landscape created millions of years ago by slow-moving streams. An ancient sea once covered this region, which contains a variety of fossilized remains including crabs, clams, and snails. When traveling east on I-90, use exit 110 at Wall to access the Badlands Loop Road and its numerous exhibits, scenic overlooks, and self-guiding trails. Travelers driving west on I-90 access this road using exit 131. Ben Reifel Visitor Center in the park's eastern section opened in 2009 with exhibits and a video presentation that interpret the history and geology of the Badlands. Four other National Park Service units—Minuteman Missile National Historic Site, Jewel Cave National Monument, Wind Cave National Park, and world-famous Mount Rushmore National Memorial—are an easy drive from the park. Information on these and other nearby attractions is available at the visitor center.

BADLANDS NATIONAL PARK

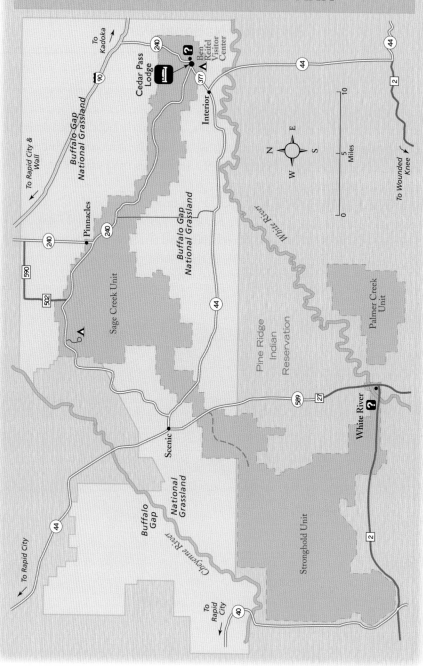

Park Entrance Fee: $15 per vehicle or $7 per person, good for 7 days.

Lodging in Badlands National Park: Cedar Pass Lodge, with 23 wooden cabins plus a large cottage, provides the only overnight accommodations in Badlands National Park. Additional accommodations are along the interstate. A two-story motel just outside the park's boundary is within sight of Cedar Pass Lodge. Cedar Pass Lodge is 8 miles south of I-90 on Badlands Loop Road.

Cedar Pass Lodge

20681 SD Hwy. 240 • PO Box 5 • Interior, SD 57750 • (605) 433-5460 • www.cedarpasslodge.com

Cabin at Cedar Pass Lodge

Cedar Pass Lodge is a complex of small wooden cabins situated on each side of a U-shaped drive in a grassy area behind a registration building that houses the restaurant and a large gift shop. All the cabins are a short walk from the registration building. Adequate parking is directly beside or in front of each cabin. Cedar Pass Lodge sits in an area of grass and small trees at the east end of Badlands National Park, within view of the Badlands.

The lodge offers 23 freestanding and duplex cabins plus a large cottage. Each unit has air conditioning and a TV. The new wooden cabins were brought into the park in 2012 and 2013 as replacements for 21 older stucco cabins that had served the park for many decades. The new cabins are energy efficient with heavy insulation, high-efficiency windows, on-demand hot water, and low-flush toilets. Interestingly, the interior cabin walls are constructed of lumber salvaged from South Dakota pine trees that were killed by beetles. Cabins each have carpeting, 2 queen beds or a king plus a daybed, and a bathroom with a tub and shower. Each cabin has a microwave, mini-refrigerator, coffeemaker, and ceiling fan. One handicap-accessible cabin has a queen bed plus a double bed and a bathroom with a shower only. The cabins measure 16 by 24 feet plus a small covered front porch with chairs.

A large cottage (actually, a complete house) near the registration building has 2 bedrooms, 1 with a queen and the other with 2 doubles. It also has a living room/dining room and a full-size kitchen with a refrigerator, gas range, and washer and dryer. Pots, pans, and eating utensils are included. Try for the cottage if your party includes 4 or more people. The lodge concessionaire also operates Badlands Inn, an 18-room facility a short distance outside the park.

Cedar Pass Lodge is a convenient location from which to explore Badlands National Park. We have found during our stays here that lodge guests enjoy sitting outside at picnic tables or on their porch chairs. This is especially true during the late afternoon or early evening, assuming the temperature cooperates. Thus, it is easy to strike up a conversation, especially about travel experiences. The lodge is a handy stop the night before or after a visit to nearby attractions Minuteman Missile National Historic Site, Mount Rushmore National Memorial, Jewel Cave National Monument, Wind Cave National Park, and Custer State Park. The cabins are a short walk from the park's Ben Reifel Visitor Center and the park campground, where evening programs are presented during summer by National Park Service rangers. Guided walks and other National

Cedar Pass Camp was opened here in 1928 to provide refreshments to the growing number of sightseers to this area. By the 1930s the facility had become an important stop for Badlands travelers. The owner, Ben Millard, died here in 1956, and Cedar Pass Lodge was purchased by the National Park Service in 1964. Cedar Pass Lodge was operated by the Oglala Sioux Tribe of the Pine Ridge Indian Reservation from 1971 to 2002.

Park Service programs are scheduled daily from various points in the park. An 80-mile loop drive through the park to the small town of Scenic and back through Buffalo Gap National Grassland on SD 44 offers an interesting day of sightseeing and hiking. Take a side trip to the town of Wall (north of the Pinnacles park entrance), where funky Wall Drug gives away ice water and sells coffee for a nickel.

Rooms: Singles, doubles, triples, and quads. The cottage holds up to 6 adults. All units have a private bathroom with a combination shower-tub, with the exception of the ADA cabin, which has a shower only.

Wheelchair Accessibility: One cabin is ADA compliant.

Reservations: Cedar Pass Lodge, PO Box 5, Interior, SD 57750. Phone (605) 433-5460 or (877) 386-4383. A credit card guarantee is required. Cancellation requires 24 hours' notice.

Rates: Cabin ($150); cottage ($140). Rates quoted are for 2 people. Additional persons are $15. Children 15 and under stay free.

Location: At the eastern end of Badlands National Park, 8 miles south of I-90 at exit 131. Guests approaching on I-90 from Rapid City should take exit 110 and drive the Badlands Loop Rd. (SD 240), which passes by the lodge.

Season: Mid-Apr to mid-Oct.

Food: A cafe-type restaurant serves breakfast ($6–$8), lunch ($5–$10), and dinner ($8–$19). Menu items include buffalo burgers, trout, and Sioux Indian tacos.

Facilities: Restaurant, gift shop with a large selection of silver jewelry and crafts made by local artisans, National Park Service visitor center.

Activities: Hiking, evening interpretive programs, and guided walks. The park generally serves as an excellent location for star gazing.

Pets: Pets are permitted for an extra charge of $10 per pet, per night, with a two-pet maximum.

TEXAS

State Tourist Information
(800) 452-9292 | www.traveltex.com

Big Bend National Park

PO Box 129 • Big Bend National Park, TX 79834 • (432) 477-2251 • www.nps.gov/bibe

Big Bend National Park covers 801,000 acres of wild and scenic desert, mountain ranges, steep-walled canyons, and ribbons of green plant life along the fabled Rio Grande. Popular activities include bird-watching, hiking, and rafting on the Rio Grande. The park is in southwestern Texas along the Mexican border.

Park Entrance Fee: $20 per vehicle or $10 per person, good for 7 days.

Lodging in Big Bend National Park: Chisos Mountains Lodge in the park's Basin area offers the only lodging within the park. The road to the Basin is not recommended for trailers exceeding 20 feet and RVs exceeding 24 feet. A trailer village at Rio Grande Village is available for visitors with trailers and motor homes.

Chisos Mountains Lodge
1 Basin Rural Station • Big Bend National Park, TX 79834 • (432) 477-2291
www.chisosmountainslodge.com

Chisos Mountains Lodge includes modern motel-type units plus older stone and adobe cottages and lodge units in the scenic Basin area. All lodging units rent for about the same price and are open year-round. The Basin area is approximately 40 miles inside the north park entrance, which itself is 40 miles south of US 90. This is a remote lodge in a very remote park. The Basin area provides breathtaking scenery along with the outdoor experience most people seek in a national park visit. At an altitude of 5,400 feet, the lodge generally experiences moderate summer temperatures while much of the park swelters in the desert heat. Scenery is provided by the Chisos Mountains that surround and tower 2,000 to 3,000 feet above the Basin.

Chisos Mountains Lodge is a combination of a main registration and food-service building

Casa Grande building at Chisos Mountains Lodge

and 4 types of lodging units that provide 72 guest rooms. All rooms have heat, a small refrigerator, microwave, hair dryer, and coffeemaker. About half are in 3 two-story motor lodge–type Casa Grande units that offer semiprivate balconies with a view of the surrounding mountains. Constructed in 1989, these units are along a hillside so that room access may require guests to negotiate a series of steps. The rooms have either 2 double beds or a king, and in the 4 wheelchair-accessible rooms, 1 double bed. Each room has air-conditioning and a full tiled bath.

Two one-story Rio Grande motel buildings constructed in the late 1970s, each have 10 rooms, 5 on a side. Chairs are outside each room along a covered walkway. Rooms on the west side (even-numbered rooms) offer better views than rooms on the backside. Rooms have 2 double

beds, a full tiled bath, and air-conditioning. They are quite a bit smaller and cost about the same as Casa Grande rooms.

Emory Peak Lodge and the Roosevelt Stone Cottages offer a quiet setting a short distance from the other lodging units. One duplex and 4 freestanding stone cottages were constructed in the late 1930s by the Civilian Conservation Corps. Five cottages each have 3 double beds and a bath with a shower. They lack air-conditioning but have ceiling fans. The thick walls, stone floors, vaulted ceilings, and cross-ventilation generally result in a comfortable inside temperature. Most popular with frequent visitors are cottages 103, with a full covered porch, and 102, with a large patio, each of which offers the best mountain views of any of the park's lodging facilities. Cottage 100 is isolated with a king bed and amenities unavailable in other lodging units, making it a nice honeymoon cottage.

Eight 1950s-era Emory Peak Lodge units are in 2 identical one-story buildings situated near the cottages. The upper building, which houses rooms that each have 1 king bed, is up a hillside and requires climbing 35 steps along a gradual slope. The lower building has rooms that each have 1 single and 1 double bed. All 8 rooms have a full tiled bath and a vaulted beamed ceiling with a ceiling fan.

With the exception of cottage 100, none of the rooms have a television. Unless you splurge for cottage 100, 102, or 103, we recommend Casa Grande units in buildings A, B, or C. Rooms in all 3 buildings are large, offer good views, and cost only a few dollars more than rooms in smaller motel units. Second-floor rooms offer better views, more privacy, and avoid noise from upstairs neighbors walking across the floor.

Other than the Roosevelt Stone Cottages and Emory Peak Lodge that are a short distance from the main Basin area, units are arranged in a circular fashion near the building that houses registration, a gift shop, and a dining room. Adequate parking is available near each of the buildings, although a couple of the Casa Grande units require a climb of approximately 30 steps to reach the second floor. Note in your reservation request if stairs will be a problem. Cottages and Emory Peak units are about a quarter mile from other units, but everything in the Basin is within walking distance. The Basin includes a small store, with a limited selection of groceries and camping supplies, a post office substation, and a National Park Service visitor center. A variety of hikes and nature programs are offered in season. A self-guided trail and access to several other trails originate near the lodge.

The Basin is a small part of a very large and diverse park that offers much to attract visitors, especially during spring and fall, when temperatures are mild. The main National Park Service visitor facilities are at Panther Junction. Other major activity areas of the park are Rio Grande Village, 20 miles southeast of park headquarters, which offers hiking, camping, a trailer park, a coin laundry, showers, groceries, general merchandise, gasoline, propane, and a visitor center. Castolon, a historic district 35 miles southwest of the visitor center, offers a campground, ranger station, historic exhibits, and a frontier store that sells picnic supplies, groceries, and general merchandise.

Birders are drawn to Big Bend National Park, where more than 450 species have been identified. Although most are migrants that pass through after wintering in Latin America, occasional rare species end up in Big Bend after wandering off-course. The Chisos Mountains of Big Bend are the only location in the United States where the rare Colima warbler can be observed. Multiday birding seminars are regularly sponsored by the Big Bend Natural History Association. A beautiful blooming desert willow tree beside the back deck attracted a constant stream of hummingbirds, hepatic tanagers, and Wilson's warblers during our most recent stay.

Rooms: Doubles, triples, and quads. A few units sleep up to 6. All have private baths.

Wheelchair Accessibility: Four Casa Grande units are wheelchair-accessible.

Reservations: Forever Resorts, Chisos Mountains Lodge, 1 Basin Rural Station, Big Bend National Park, TX 79834-9999. Phone (432) 477-2291, (877) 386-4383. A deposit of 1 night's stay is required. Cancellation notice of 72 hours is required for a refund. Failure to arrive on the designated date results in forfeit of the deposit and reservation cancellation. Checks are not accepted at checkout.

Rates: Casa Grande ($136); Rio Grande ($134); Roosevelt Stone Cottage ($152–$173); Emory Peak Lodge unit ($132). Rates quoted are for 2 adults. Each additional person is $11 per night. Children under 13 stay free with 2 paying adults. Rollaways are $11 per night.

Big Bend is a huge park where much of the beauty is hidden from casual visitors who drive on the main road to Panther Junction, and, perhaps, to Chisos Basin. The park concessionaire offers several guided excursions in 4-wheel-drive vehicles that hold from 1 to 6 adults. These tours range from 4 hours to all day. The short tour makes a stop near the hot springs where participants can soak beside the Rio Grande. The longer excursion follows the River Road along the remote southern end of the park from Castolon to Rio Grande Village. Customized tours are also available. For information or reservations call (800) 848-2363.

Location: About 40 miles south of the north entrance station and 30 miles east of the west entrance station.

Season: All lodging units are open year-round. Heaviest seasons are spring through Memorial Day and during fall following Labor Day.

Food: A full-service restaurant serves breakfast ($6–$10), lunch ($7–$17), and dinner ($10–$24).

Facilities: Chisos Basin has a store, post office substation, visitor center, restaurant, gift shop, and washer and dryer. A visitor center, gas station, post office, and small grocery are at Panther Junction. A variety of supplies and services are at Rio Grande Village, 20 miles southeast of Panther Junction. A frontier store at Castolon sells picnic supplies, groceries, and general merchandise

Activities: Hiking, bird-watching, guided walks, half- and full-day guided park tours, and National Park Service programs. Big Bend is a Dark Sky Park and offers excellent stargazing. Float trips on the Rio Grande are available with your own equipment (permit required) or through one of the local services approved by the Park Service.

Pets: Pets are permitted only in three Roosevelt Stone Cottages with a $50 nonrefundable fee. Pets may not be left unattended in rooms or vehicles.

US VIRGIN ISLANDS

Tourist Information
(800) 372-8784 | USVITourism.com

Virgin Islands National Park

1300 Cruz Bay Creek • St. Thomas, VI 00830 • (340) 776-6201 • www.nps.gov/viis

Virgin Islands National Park, encompassing nearly 12,850 acres, features quiet coves, blue green waters, and white sandy beaches fringed by lush green hills. The park is on St. John and can be reached via hourly ferry service across Pillsbury Sound from Red Hook, St. Thomas. Ferry service also operates from Charlotte Amalie. Major airlines fly from the US mainland to St. Thomas and St. Croix.

Park Entrance Fee: No charge. A $4 daily user fee is charged at Trunk Bay. Children 16 years and under are free. Inexpensive annual passes are available.

Lodging in Virgin Islands National Park: Although a variety of lodging is available on the island, Cinnamon Bay Campground, with tents and cottages, offers accommodations within the park. Cinnamon Bay is on St. John's north shore, midway across the island via North Shore Road. It is a 15-minute taxi ride from the town of Cruz Bay, where the ferries dock.

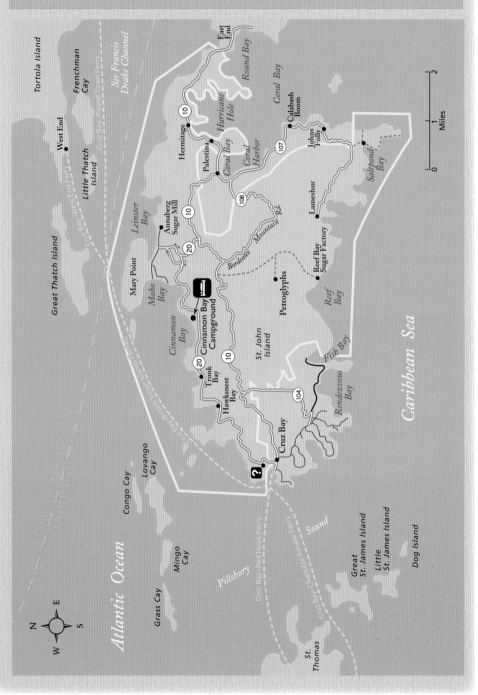

CINNAMON BAY CAMPGROUND

PO Box 720 • Cruz Bay, St. John • US Virgin Islands 00831 • (340) 776-6330
www.cinnamonbay.com

Cottage rooms at Cinnamon Bay Campground

Cinnamon Bay Campground is a complex of cottages, tents, and bare sites, with separate bathhouses. Its main building houses a registration area, restaurant, and general store. The cottages and tents are grouped separately, with bathhouses in each grouping. All the buildings are in a natural area of trees a short walk from half-mile-long Cinnamon Bay Beach.

The 10 cottages comprise 40 rooms that are 15 by 15 feet and constructed of cement sides and floor with front and back screening to allow breezes from the trade winds. Each cottage room has an outside terrace and is equipped with electric lights, a table and chairs, wall fan, picnic table, charcoal grill, propane stove, ice chest, water container, and eating and cooking utensils. The concessionaire provides linens for 4 twin beds in each room. Additional linens can be obtained twice a week at the front desk. The central bathhouse has cool-water showers. Cost varies, with units closer to the beach being more expensive.

Forty-five tents have a wood floor and are 10 by 14 feet. Each tent includes 4 cots, a propane stove, charcoal grill, gas lantern, ice chest, water container, and cooking utensils. A picnic table is under a large canvas flap that extends from the front roof. As with cottage rooms, beds are made on the day of arrival, and fresh linens are available at the front desk twice a week. Three bathhouses scattered throughout the tenting area have cool-water showers.

Cinnamon Bay Campground offers the ultimate national park experience in which accommodations enhance an appreciation for the natural surroundings. Cottages and tents are a short walk from Cinnamon Bay Beach. Phones and coin-operated lockers are near the lodging facilities. A general store carries a wide range of personal and grocery items if you are interested in cooking meals. A restaurant serves 3 meals a day for those who prefer dining out. No laundry facilities are in the campground. Not surprisingly, water-based activities such as snorkeling are popular, and sailboards, sea kayaks, and sailboats are available for rent at a water sports center. Park rangers offer daily activities, which include walks, talks, and snorkeling. Reservations are required only for the Reef Bay Hike (340-776-6201, ext. 238).

Rosewood Hotels & Resorts, the firm that manages Cinnamon Bay Campground, also operates exclusive Caneel Bay on the same island. Although separated by 2 bays and only a few miles, in cost and accommodations these 2 facilities are a world apart. For example, rooms at Caneel Bay run from $500 to $1,700 daily, depending on season and type of accommodation. The 166 rooms include wall safes, personal bars, and handcrafted furniture. Three restaurants provide a choice of formal, eclectic, and casual dining.

Rooms: Doubles, triples, and quads. No rooms have a private bathroom.

Wheelchair Accessibility: One cottage, 1 tent, and the community bathrooms are wheelchair accessible.

Reservations: Cinnamon Bay Campground, PO Box 720, Cruz Bay, St. John, US Virgin Islands 00831-0720. Phone (800) 539-9998; (340) 776-6330. A 50 percent deposit is required. Payment in full required at check-in (personal checks are not accepted). Cancellations are required at least 30 days prior to arrival for a full refund. Later cancellations will be charged the equivalent of a 3-night stay. Reservations for the winter months can be made up to a year in advance.

Rates: Cottage rooms ($81–$105), tents ($67) from May 1 through Dec 14; cottages ($126–$163), tents ($93) from Dec 15 through Apr 30. Rates quoted for 2 adults. Children under 3 stay free with an adult. Each additional person is $20 per night. Maximum occupancy of 4 persons is permitted.

Location: On the north shore of St. John, approximately 4 miles (15 minutes) from the town of Cruz Bay on the island's west end.

Season: All year except Sept and Oct. Peak season is Dec through Apr.

Food: A Caribbean/American bar and grill serves breakfast ($6–$10), lunch ($6–$10), and dinner ($11–$22). Groceries are available at a general store.

Transportation: Ferries for Cruz Bay, St. John, leave from Red Hook ($5 per person) and Charlotte Amalie ($7 per person) on St. Thomas. Baggage ranges from $2 to $4, depending on size. Taxis (about $7 to $9 per person) provide transportation from Cruz Bay to the campground.

Facilities: Restaurant, general store, beach shop, water sports center with boat rentals.

Activities: Swimming, snorkeling, sailing, kayaking, fishing, hiking, National Park Service activities, and commercial guided tours.

UTAH
State Tourist Information
(800) 200-1160 | www.utah.com

Bryce Canyon National Park
PO Box 640201 • Bryce Canyon, UT 84764 • (435) 834-5322 • www.nps.gov/brca

Bryce Canyon National Park comprises nearly 36,000 acres highlighted by numerous alcoves cut into cliffs along the eastern edge of the Paunsaugunt Plateau. The cliffs are bordered by badlands of vivid colors and strange shapes called hoodoos for which this park is most famous. A paved road with numerous scenic pullouts leads 18 miles south from the entrance to Rainbow Point. Trailers are not permitted beyond Sunrise Point, which lies about 3 miles inside the park entrance. The park is in southwestern Utah and most easily reached via US 89 to UT 12 and UT 63.

A free shuttle service that begins outside the park serves the lodge and the northern portion of the park. Lodge guests and other park visitors can hop on and off the shuttle at the lodge and 10 additional

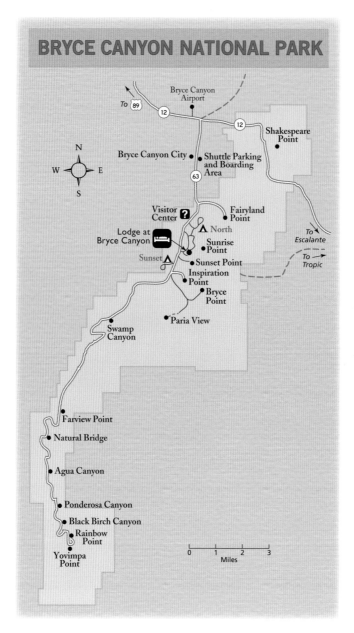

BRYCE CANYON NATIONAL PARK

stops including the NPS visitor center, Inspiration Point, and Bryce Point. The shuttle operates from early May until early Oct.

Park Entrance Fee: $25 per vehicle or $12 per person, good for 7 days.

Lodging in Bryce Canyon: The Lodge at Bryce Canyon, with several types of accommodations, offers the only lodging in Bryce Canyon National Park. All rooms are comfortable and within easy walking distance of both the main lodge and spectacular Bryce Canyon.

LODGE AT BRYCE CANYON

1 Bryce Canyon Lodge • Bryce Canyon National Park, UT 84717 • (435) 834-8700
www.brycecanyonforever.com

Main lodge building at Bryce Canyon Lodge

The Lodge at Bryce Canyon offers a total of 114 rooms in a complex of 2 motor lodge units, 15 multiunit log buildings with 40 cabins, and an impressive wood-and-stone main lodge building that houses the restaurant, registration area, and 3 suites plus a studio. The main lodge was constructed in the 1920s and has been completely renovated. The lodge was designed by Gilbert Stanley Underwood, the same architect who designed the Ahwahnee in Yosemite, Zion Lodge, and Grand Canyon Lodge on the North Rim. The attractive lobby has a huge stone fireplace surrounded by chairs. A large brick porch with chairs and benches stretches across the front

of the building and offers guests a pleasant place to spend idle time. The porch faces a wooded area that separates the lodge from the canyon rim.

Each of the 3 types of lodging facilities is attractive. All rooms have heat, small refrigerator, microwave, coffeemaker, fan, and telephone, but no air-conditioning or television. Forty Western Cabins constructed 2 to 4 to a building each has a gas fireplace, ceiling fan, dressing room with a sink, full tiled bathroom, and 2 queen beds. The Western Cabins were remodeled in 2013–14. The log and limestone cabins, constructed in the 1920s, are quite roomy and half have log-beamed vaulted ceilings. Cabins with vaulted ceilings are

Construction on Bryce Canyon Lodge (the name was changed to Lodge at Bryce Canyon in 2011) began in 1923, and the foundation and skeletal work were completed the following year. The original building, with upstairs accommodations and an office, lobby, dining room, kitchen, showers, and toilets on the main floor, was completed by May 1925. Wings and a rock facade were added the following year, when the lodge was opened for operation. In September 1927, the recreation hall was added, and 67 standard and economy cabins were grouped around the lodge. The few original cabins that remain are currently used by the National Park Service. The other economy cabins were sold and moved. By September 1927, 5 deluxe cabin buildings (the current Western Cabins) had been constructed. The remaining 10 deluxe cabins were completed by 1929. The 15 cabin buildings with 40 Western Cabins remain in use. The wavy pattern of shingles on both the lodge and the cabins was designed to conform to the swaying motion of the surrounding pine limbs. The pattern also enabled snow to slide off the roofs.

constructed 2 to a building with bark remaining on the logs. Each cabin has a semi-private covered front porch with a bench. Cabins 506, 517, 525, 533, and 537 have windows and porches that face a large wooded area but are a longer walk from the parking area.

Two nearly identical two-story motor lodge buildings, Sunset Point and Sunrise Point, were brought into the park and assembled in 1985. The 2 buildings have 70 rooms that were renovated in 2012. Each room has either 1 king or 2 queen-size beds and a full tiled bath. These units each have a private covered balcony with a table and 2 chairs. Rooms are entered through a central hallway that can be accessed at either end or in the middle. These are attractive buildings that resemble upscale two-story lodge buildings. Rooms on the second floor and rim side of each

building provide the most privacy and best views, however the buildings do not have an elevator. The Sunrise building is closest to the main lodge.

Three second-floor Suites and 1 Studio are the only guest rooms in the main lodge. The Suites each have a bedroom with 1 queen-size bed and a separate sitting room; both rooms have ceiling fans. The Suites also have a full tiled bath but no balcony. These rooms are nice and roomy, and it is convenient to stay in the main lodge, where the restaurant and lobby are located. The Studio is a single small room with a private bathroom.

The Lodge at Bryce Canyon is a handy location for exploring this colorful and uncrowded national park. It sits in a heavily treed area with attractive vistas and numerous outdoor activities including hiking and horseback riding. A short walking trail from the front porch of the main lodge leads to spectacular overlooks along the canyon rim. An information desk in the hotel lobby provides information about the area and several tours that originate near the lodge. With only 4 rooms in the main lodge building, your choice will likely be between a Western Cabin and Motel unit. We have always liked the cabins in this park and suggest this as your choice, especially if planning to stay several nights. If you would enjoy a gas fireplace, the cost difference compared to the motor lodge may be worth a splurge, plus the cabins offer more of a national park experience.

Rooms: Doubles, triples, and quads. All rooms have a full bath.

Wheelchair Accessibility: Each of the 2 Motel units offers 2 first-floor end rooms that are ADA compliant, but the rooms are some distance from parking.

Reservations: Forever Resorts, 7501 E. McCormick Pkwy., Scottsdale, AZ 85258. Phone (877) 386-4383, or visit www.brycecanyonforever.com. A deposit of 1 night's stay is required. Cancellation notice of 72 hours is required for a refund.

Rates: Western Cabins ($212); Sunset Point and Sunrise Point units ($185); Suites ($255); Studio ($146). Children 16 and under stay free with an adult. Each additional person is $10 per night. Rollaways are $11.

Location: The lodge is near the north end of Bryce Canyon National Park, about 1.5 miles south of the visitor center that is located near the park entrance station. The lodge is within walking distance of the rim of the canyon.

Season: Late Mar through early Nov. The park is open year-round.

Food: A full-service restaurant serves breakfast ($6–$14), lunch ($6–$16), and dinner ($11–$32). Beer and wine are available. Reservations are recommended for dinner. A pizza restaurant across the parking lot serves coffee and pastries for breakfast with dinner beginning at 3 p.m. Groceries and snacks are available at a general store at Sunrise Point, about 1 mile from the lodge.

The Lodge at Bryce Canyon is the only remaining original lodging facility constructed in this region in the 1920s by the Utah Parks Company, a subsidiary of the Union Pacific Railroad. The Union Pacific was interested in stimulating tourism to the region and competing against other railroads that were building similar facilities in Glacier National Park, Yellowstone National Park, and the South Rim of the Grand Canyon. The "U.P. Loop" consisted of lodges at Zion National Park, the North Rim of the Grand Canyon, Bryce Canyon, and Cedar City, where a spur line connected to the Union Pacific main line in Lund. The Union Pacific in 1972 donated all of the Utah Parks Company's property, including lodges, cabins, curio shops, and service stations, to the National Park Service, which soon signed TWA Services, a subsidiary of Trans World Airlines, as concessionaire.

Facilities: Dining room, pizza restaurant, and gift shop. A general store, 1 mile north of the lodge near Sunrise Point, sells snacks and groceries.

Activities: The National Park Service lectures, nature walks and talks, and slide presentations. Two-hour and half-day mule and horse trips into the canyon are offered daily. Information and reservations are available by calling (435) 679-8665 or visiting www.canyonrides.com.

Zion National Park

SR 9 • Springdale, UT 84767 • (435) 722-3256 • www.nps.gov/zion

Zion National Park comprises approximately 147,000 acres of colorful canyons and mesas that create phenomenal shapes and landscapes. Scenic drives and trails provide access to canyons, sculpted rocks, cliffs, and rivers in one of the most beautiful areas operated by the National Park Service. Zion is in southwestern Utah, with the southwest entrance approximately 150 miles northeast of Las Vegas, Nevada.

The park entry fee includes unlimited access to the free shuttle system, which comprises 2 loops. The Springdale loop connects the town of Springdale with the visitor center and transportation center just inside the park entrance. The second loop operates from the visitor center to the end of Zion

Canyon Scenic Drive. Zion Canyon Lodge is one of several stops on the Zion Canyon Scenic Drive shuttle. The Mount Carmel area on the park's east side remains accessible by vehicle. The drive is beautiful, but often exceedingly slow.

Park Entrance Fee: $25 per vehicle or $12 per person, good for 7 days.

Lodging in Zion National Park: Zion has 1 lodging facility inside the park. Zion Lodge is on Zion Canyon Scenic Drive, 3 miles north of UT 9, which crosses the southeastern section of the park. Driving Zion Canyon Scenic Road to the Zion Lodge requires a permit from Apr through Oct that must be obtained at the visitor center, which maintains a listing of lodge guests.

Zion Lodge
Zion National Park • Springdale, UT 84767 • (435) 772-3213 • www.zionlodge.com

Zion Lodge comprises a central lodge that houses registration and dining facilities, plus 17 separate but nearby buildings that provide 122 guest rooms. No guest rooms are in the main lodge. The lodge is fronted by a large grassy area with cottonwood trees and surrounded front and back by beautiful red sandstone cliffs that make this such a scenic national park. The North Fork of the Virgin River is across the road from the lodge. The wood and Navajo sandstone main lodge building is a one- and two-story, V-shaped, ranch-style structure constructed in 1966 on the site of the original

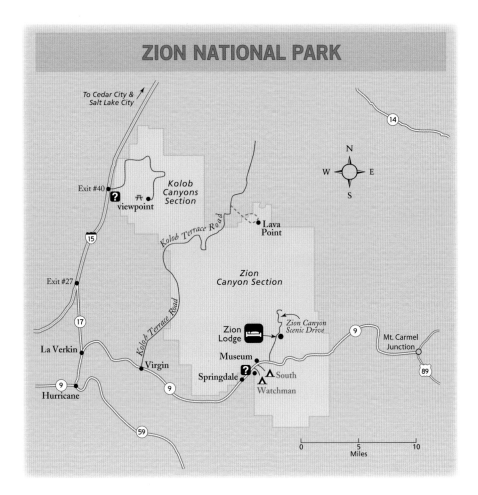

ZION NATIONAL PARK

lodge that burned earlier the same year. The new lodge is attractive but does not have the rustic appearance of its older sister lodges at Bryce Canyon and the North Rim of the Grand Canyon.

Two major types of accommodations plus 6 suites are available. Each room has heat, air-conditioning, telephone, coffeemaker, and hair dryer. Forty Western Cabins each offer 1 queen or 2 double beds, ceiling fan, gas fireplace, wood flooring, and a full tiled bath plus a dressing area with a sink. The cabins were constructed in the 1930s 2 or 4 units to a building, and the interiors were remodeled in 2009 and 2010. The wood-framed cabins with vaulted ceilings and a small porch are

somewhat smaller but similar in design to the cabins in Bryce Canyon and the North Rim of the Grand Canyon. The cabins are closely clustered in the front and at the end of one of the motel buildings south of the main lodge. Cabins that face west are closer to parking and offer a better view of the red cliffs across the river. These include cabins 505, 509, 516, 517, 518, 520, 522, 523, 528, and 529.

Seventy-six Hotel rooms are in 2 large, two-story motor lodge buildings, which were remodeled in 2010 and 2011. A stone fireplace is in the central lobby area of the larger of the 2 buildings. Rooms are quite large and have either 2 queens or 1 king bed and a full tiled bath. Each

Western cabins and hotel rooms at Zion Lodge

room has a large flat-screen TV and a balcony with a table and 2 rocking chairs. The rooms are accessed from an interior corridor. The best rooms for privacy and quiet are on the rear side of the second floor of each building. These are all odd-numbered rooms. Rooms on the front face the parking area but generally offer good views of red cliffs to the west.

Six 2-room Suites on the second floor of the motor lodge buildings have been recently renovated. They have bamboo flooring plus many other amenities that make them eco-friendly. They offer a bedroom with a king bed and a sitting room with a queen sofa bed, chairs, television, wet bar, and a small refrigerator. Each suite includes a full bathroom with a shower-tub and a large covered balcony with table and chairs.

The choice between a Western Cabin and a Hotel room is pretty much a toss-up as both are very attractive and comfortable. Hotel rooms have a TV and offer quite a bit more interior space than the Western Cabins. If the nights will be cool and you enjoy a gas fireplace, paying a few extra dollars for a Western Cabin is probably money well spent. Keep in mind, however, that the cabins are closely spaced and have relatively small front porches.

Zion Lodge's picturesque setting along Zion Canyon Scenic Drive is convenient to hiking trails. The lodge is a stop on the free shuttle that provides service along Zion Canyon Scenic Drive and to the visitor center and nearby town of Springdale. (Be aware that summer months generally bring hot days to Zion, where daytime temperatures often reach 100° Fahrenheit. In fact, the average high temperature in July is 100 degrees.) A large grassy area in front of the lodge is a pleasant place to read a book, eat a picnic lunch, or lie on a blanket under a cottonwood tree. A spacious, wood-paneled restaurant on the second floor has large front windows that offer an outstanding view of the front grounds and colorful canyon walls surrounding the lodge. A large balcony is available

A camp of wood-framed tents opened in 1916 on the site of Zion Lodge. The original lodge, designed by Gilbert Stanley Underwood (1890–1961), was constructed in 1925 for the Union Pacific Railroad, which wanted to promote tourism in southern Utah. The current Western Cabins were constructed in the late 1920s. Fire destroyed the main lodge during renovations in the winter of 1966. The present building, which underwent a major renovation in 1989–1990, was completed only 3 months after the fire.

for outside dining when weather and temperature permit. The lodge also has a lounge, cafe and beer garden, coffee bar, auditorium, and gift shop.

Rooms: Doubles, triples, and quads. All rooms have a full bath.

Wheelchair Accessibility: Four first-floor rooms in the motor lodge building nearest the lodge are ADA compliant. An elevator in the main lodge building provides wheelchair access to the restaurant on the second floor. Shuttle buses serving the lodge are equipped for wheelchair access.

Reservations: Zion National Park Lodge, PO Box 925, Springdale, UT 84767. Phone (888) 297-2757, or visit www.zionlodge.com. A deposit of 1 night's stay is required. A cancellation notice of 48 hours is required for a full refund.

Rates: Western Cabins ($193–$200); Hotel room ($186–$198); Suites ($227–$260). All rates quoted are for 2 adults. Children 16 and under stay free. Each additional person is $10. Rollaway beds are $12. Discount rates are offered Dec to mid-Mar, and special packages are also available in the off-season. Check the website.

Location: Three miles north of the main park highway on Zion Canyon Scenic Drive.

Season: All of the units of Zion Lodge are open year-round. The lodge is often full from early Apr through Oct.

Food: An attractive restaurant on the second floor of the main lodge building serves breakfast ($6–$10), lunch ($7–$14), and dinner ($15–$32). Dinner reservations are required and should be made prior to or immediately upon arrival; otherwise you are likely to end up with a very early or very late dinner. Alcoholic beverages are served. A coffee bar in the lobby is open from 6 a.m. to 1 p.m. A cafe and beer garden at the north end of the main lodge building offers outside dining with pizza, sandwiches, salads, ice cream, soft drinks, and a wide selection of beer from 11 a.m. to 7 p.m. in season. Groceries and restaurants are in the town of Springdale and can be reached via the free shuttle that stops at the lodge.

Facilities: Post office, gift shop, restaurant, lounge, coffee bar, cafe, and beer garden.

Activities: Horseback rides, hiking, and naturalist programs. Horseback rides begin at the corral across the road from the lodge. For information and reservations call (435) 679-8665 or visit www.canyonrides.com.

Concessionaire Xanterra Parks & Resorts in 2010 completed a historic restoration of the 40 Western Cabins. Changes included replacing carpet with fir flooring, installing custom-designed draperies and blankets based on historical photographs, and using custom furniture manufactured by a Shelbyville, Indiana, firm that has a long history of making furniture for national parks. The blankets were woven especially for Zion Lodge by Pendleton Woolen Mills using washable wool. The environmentally friendly cabins include energy efficient water heaters and ceiling fans.

VIRGINIA
State Tourist Information
(800) 847-4882 | www.virginia.org

Shenandoah National Park

3655 US Hwy. 211 East • Luray, VA 22835 • (540) 999-3500 • www.nps.gov/shen

Shenandoah National Park comprises 199,000 acres of forested mountains through an 80-mile stretch of the Blue Ridge Mountains. Most of the park's features lie alongside 105-mile Skyline Drive, a slow but scenic two-lane road that wanders along much of the crest of the mountain range. The road accesses lodges, campgrounds, and overlooks from the north entrance at Front Royal to the south entrance near Waynesboro, Virginia. The park brochure available at entry stations identifies places of interest and park facilities according to mile markers alongside the road. The park has over 500 miles of hiking trails, including a 101-mile stretch of the Appalachian Trail. Shenandoah National Park is in northern Virginia, with the northern entrance some 60 miles west of Washington, D.C. The south entrance connects with the north end of the Blue Ridge Parkway.

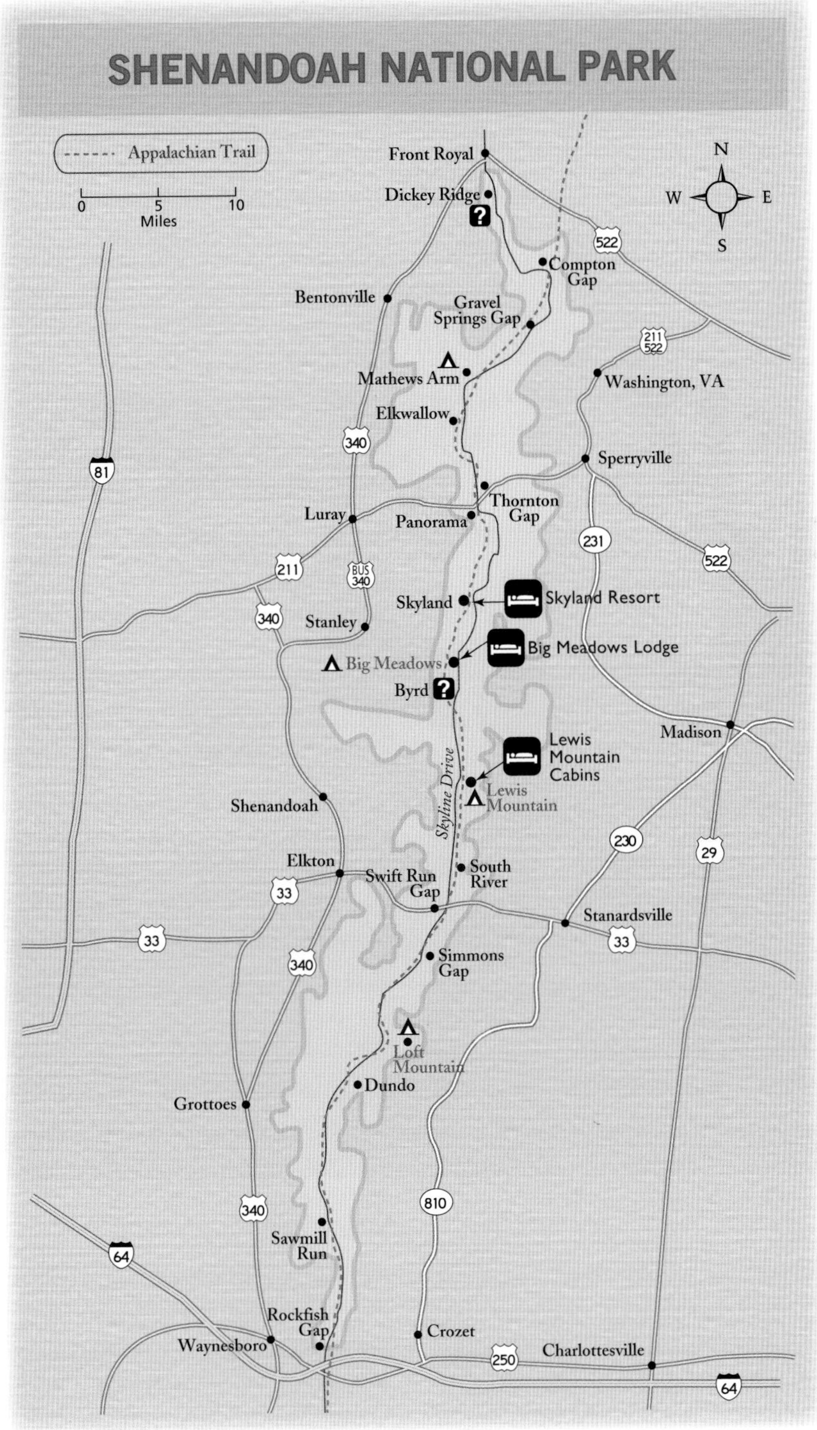

SHENANDOAH NATIONAL PARK

Appalachian Trail

0   5   10
Miles

N
W   E
S

Front Royal

Dickey Ridge

Compton Gap

522

Bentonville

Gravel Springs Gap

211 522

Mathews Arm

Washington, VA

Elkwallow

340

Sperryville

Luray

Panorama

Thornton Gap

231

522

Skyland

Skyland Resort

Stanley

340

211

BUS 340

Big Meadows

Big Meadows Lodge

Byrd

Lewis Mountain Cabins

Madison

Shenandoah

Lewis Mountain

Elkton

Swift Run Gap

South River

230

29

33

Stanardsville

33

340

33

Simmons Gap

Loft Mountain

Grottoes

Dundo

810

340

64

Sawmill Run

Rockfish Gap

Crozet

Charlottesville

Waynesboro

250

64

Skyline Drive

81

Park Entrance Fee: $15 per vehicle; $10 per motorcycle; $8 per pedestrian or bicycle, good for 7 days.

Lodging in Shenandoah National Park: Three locations in the park provide lodging facilities. All are in the central section between mile markers 40 and 60. Big Meadows Lodge and Skyland Resort are relatively large complexes with a historic lodge and cabins and modern lodging units. Lewis Mountain Cabins is a very small facility with cabins only. All 3 facilities are operated by the same concessionaire.

Reservations for All Lodging Facilities: DNC Parks & Resorts at Shenandoah, Inc., PO Box 727, Luray, VA 22835. Phone (877) 847-1919; www.goshenandoah.com. The first night's deposit is required. Refund of deposit less a $15 fee requires a 72-hour advance cancellation. Reservation changes result in a $15 charge.

Big Meadows Lodge

Guest rooms in the main lodge at Big Meadows Lodge

Big Meadows Lodge at milepost 51.2 consists of a historic main lodge building plus 5 cabins, all of which were constructed in 1939, and 6 one- and two-story lodge buildings that together offer a total of 97 rooms. All the buildings are in close proximity so guests have an easy walk from any of the rooms to the main lodge, which houses an attractive dining room, a large great room, a downstairs TV room, and taproom. Excellent views of the Shenandoah Valley are available from the dining room, the great room, and a large stone porch that spans the back side of the main lodge that has overnight rooms on 3 floors. Big Meadows is in a heavily forested area at an altitude of 3,510 feet.

Big Meadows Lodge offers 5 categories of accommodations. In ascending order of price, they include Main Lodge rooms (rooms in the main building), Cabins, Traditional rooms, Preferred rooms, and Suites. All rooms have a private bathroom, wood paneling, heat, and a coffeemaker. None have a telephone. Only the Preferred rooms have a television, and only Preferred rooms in Doubletop and Rapidan have air-conditioning. Suites, Cabins, and some Preferred rooms have a fireplace with wood provided.

The main lodge has 25 relatively small rooms on 3 floors. Most have 1 double or 2 twin beds and will accommodate 2 persons only. Two larger rooms have 2 double beds and 1 room has a queen bed. Each Main Lodge room has a private bathroom with a tub, a shower, or both. Rooms 1 through 6 on the main floor provide good valley views. Rooms on the upper floor have dormers and are entered from an interior hallway accessed from the lobby stairway and also from an outside doorway. An elevator provides access to the bottom floor and the taproom but not to second-floor rooms. As in many older lodges, the main building has some quirky and interesting rooms. One of these, 13 and 14, has 2 separate bedrooms and 2 separate bathrooms but must be rented as 1 room because of a single fire escape. Room 23 on the second floor has a good valley view but is above the kitchen and its associated noises.

Six one- and two-story buildings house 62 rooms in a combination of Suites, Preferred rooms, and Traditional rooms. Rooms in each category have a balcony or patio with a table and chairs. Four one-story buildings sit end to end on a wooded hillside. Three (Piedmont, Blackrock, and Hawksbill) were constructed in the 1940s, while the other, Crescent Rock was built in 1986. Traditional rooms in these one-story buildings have 2 double beds and are relatively small. Rooms each have a private bathroom, most with a combination shower-tub, although a few have only a shower. Two rooms (43/44 and 45/46) in Piedmont have 2 bedrooms and a bath, but rent for the price of a single room.

The newest units at Big Meadows, Doubletop, and Rapidan have 2 queen beds, simulated wood floors, air-conditioning, and ceiling fans. These Preferred rooms on a hillside overlooking the valley are larger, brighter, and nicer than rooms in the one-story units. Each has a private balcony or patio that offers views of a small meadow surrounded by a hardwood forest. Second floor rooms have a vaulted ceiling.

Preferred rooms in Crescent Rock each have 1 large room with a vaulted ceiling, stone fireplace, television, and nice balcony. Eight rooms have a king-size bed plus a sofa bed, while the other 2, which are wheelchair accessible, have 1 double bed and chairs. Six Suites each have 2 rooms, a small bedroom with either 2 double beds or 1 king, plus a large living room with a stone fireplace, sofa bed, small refrigerator, and a private balcony. Suites are at the ends of 3 one-story lodge buildings and connecting doors allow the addition of another bedroom (at an extra charge) to make a two-bedroom suite.

Five wooden duplex buildings house 10 Cabin rooms near the main lodge. The Cabins sit in a grassy area surrounded by trees and offer no particularly good views. Each Cabin has paneled walls, carpeting, a stone fireplace, and connecting doors, so both Cabins in a building can be rented as a single unit. Each has a small bathroom with a shower. All except 1 Cabin have 1 bedroom, most with a double bed, although a few have 2 twins. One Cabin has 2 bedrooms, 1 with a double bed and the other with 2 twins. This unit has a bath and a half but rents for only a little more per night than the one-bedroom units. The Cabins are quite small and only one (120) has a large screened front porch. Cabin units 110 and 111 are next to the playground, a convenient location if you have children, but not particularly desirable if you don't.

With all the lodging options at Big Meadows, which should you choose? All things equal, we like the Preferred rooms in Doubletop and Rapidan. Although more expensive than one-story Traditional rooms, they offer a brighter interior and good views from the balconies and patios. In addition, they have air-conditioning and ceiling fans, desirable amenities during warm afternoons. Second-floor rooms at Doubletop require that guests climb only a half flight of stairs. A disadvantage is that neither unit is directly next to parking. If the season is right and you enjoy a fireplace, choose one of the Cabins. Although relatively small, they are nicely spaced and close to the main lodge. If you want to splurge and desire a fireplace, choose a Preferred room in Crescent Rock. We like these better than the Suites.

Big Meadows Lodge is a place to relax, especially during the fall when the morning air is crisp and trees display their parade of brilliant colors. The great room in the main lodge retains its original 1930s appearance, with a large stone fireplace, a row of rocking chairs, handcrafted furniture including sofas and chairs, and outstanding vistas from large picture windows. Enjoy a good book, play a board game, or just sit and enjoy the scenery. The attractive dining room, with a beamed vaulted ceiling and wall of windows overlooking the valley, is a pleasant place to linger over a morning cup of coffee or an evening trout dinner. Activities include numerous special events such as Virginia wine tasting and craft demonstrations.

Rooms: Doubles, triples, and quads. Suites accommodate up to 6 adults. All rooms have a private bath, although some have only a shower or a tub.

Wheelchair Accessibility: One main lodge room and 2 rooms in Rapidan are ADA compliant. Two rooms in Doubletop are wheelchair-accessible.

Rates: Main Lodge ($101–$114); Cabins ($113–$141); Traditional rooms ($132–$141); Preferred rooms ($175–$196); Suite ($173). Higher rates are charged for holidays and during the fall. Rates quoted are for 2 adults. Each additional adult is $11. Rollaways are $11 per night. Discounts are available Sun through Thurs nights for AAA, AARP, and Shenandoah National Park Association members and for active military personnel. Children under 16 stay free with an adult. Special packages offered seasonally.

Location: Milepost 51.2, about midway on Skyline Drive between the north and south entrances to Shenandoah National Park.

Season: Mid-May to the first week in Nov.

Big Meadows Lodge, named for a nearby grassy meadow, is constructed of stones cut from the Massanutten Mountains across the Shenandoah Valley. Built by Civilian Conservation Corps and mountain labor, the lodge was completed in 1939 and is listed on the National Register of Historic Places. Paneling in the bedrooms and the dining room came from the native chestnut trees that once grew here on the Blue Ridge but were virtually wiped out by the 1930s blight. Beams in the lounge and dining room are native oak. Heavy cement shingles protect the building from the harsh mountain winters.

Food: A full-service dining room serves breakfast ($5–$11), lunch ($8–$14), and dinner ($11–$25). Beer and wine are available. A taproom opens each afternoon to serve appetizers, sandwiches, and chili. A convenience store at the entrance to Big Meadows has limited groceries and a coffee shop that serves breakfast and fast-food items including burgers and fries from 9 a.m. to 8 p.m.

Facilities: Restaurant, gift and craft shop, taproom, TV room, conference room, and a nice playground area for children. A gas station, coffee shop, convenience store, and National Park Service visitor center are at nearby Big Meadows Wayside.

Activities: Hiking and fishing. Nightly entertainment is presented in the taproom. The National Park Service gives frequent programs at the visitor center, the lodge, and throughout the park. The concessionaire offers a variety of guided hikes (fees charged) including one from Skyland Resort to Big Meadows Lodge. Special events are offered throughout the season. Call (877) 847-1919 or visit the website for details.

Pets: Permitted in some Traditional rooms for $25 per pet, per night, with a maximum of 2.

LEWIS MOUNTAIN CABINS

Lewis Mountain Cabins at milepost 57.5 is one of the smallest national park lodges. The complex consists of 1 building with a registration desk and small store, 7 one-story structures that provide 9 overnight rooms, and a hikers' cabin. There is no lobby, dining room, or cocktail lounge. All the cabins are a short walk from the registration building. The complex is in a heavily forested area. The 9 cabins at Lewis Mountain date from the late 1930s and early 1940s, but are well maintained both inside and out. Each has wood paneling, hardwood floors, electric heat, and a private bathroom with a shower. One two-bedroom wheelchair-accessible cabin has an extra-large bathroom with a combination shower-tub. The cabins do not have air-conditioning, telephone, or television. Each cabin has a small front porch with 2 chairs plus a covered picnic pavilion with a table, barbecue pit, electric light, and electrical outlets. Wood is not provided but is available for purchase at the store. Two buildings are constructed as duplexes, with 2 cabin rooms per unit. These 4 cabin rooms each have 1 queen bed.

Five buildings have 2 bedrooms, 1 on each side of a bathroom. The two-bedroom units have 1 double bed in each bedroom and cost the same as one-bedroom cabins. The Hikers' cabin with 2 bunk beds has a potbellied stove but no bath or running water. Public bathrooms are at both the store and the nearby campground. Bunk beds have mattresses, but guests must supply their own linens for the Hikers' cabin.

Lewis Mountain Cabins is the smallest and least expensive lodging option in Shenandoah

In the early 1940s, Virginia still had "separate but equal" facilities for African Americans. The Lewis Mountain area was originally designated for blacks and called Lewis Mountain Negro Area. The National Park Service was responsible for caring for the campground, picnic area, and utilities, while the concessionaire constructed the original 5 cabins. An additional 2 cabins were brought in later. In 1945 National Park Service concessionaires were told by the US government to move to full integration, and Lewis Mountain Cabins was integrated a year later.

Two-bedroom cabin at Lewis Mountain Cabins

National Park. This is an especially inviting place where you can take an evening stroll through the adjacent picnic area or along a stretch of the Appalachian Trail that runs beside the nearby campground. Sitting on the front porch of cabin 8 early one morning, we watched a young bear come out of the woods, scamper up a tree, look around, climb down, and then search the complex for something to eat. What a great way to start the morning! During another stay, this time in cabin 10, we ate dinner at the picnic table while being closely observed by a large owl perched on the dead branch of a nearby tree.

Remember, the small store has limited grocery items so be sure to bring your own food and cooking utensils. The separate covered picnic area in back of or beside each cabin is a great place to grill steaks or roast hot dogs. A restaurant at Big Meadows Lodge and a grill at the wayside beside the National Park Service visitor center are only 6 miles north on Skyline Drive.

Our favorite single cabin is 10 because of its location away from the road. Its picnic pavilion is in the best location of any of the cabins. Cabin 1 and 2 (for whatever reason, each two-bedroom cabin is assigned 2 numbers) has a single neighboring cabin and is the best choice for a two-bedroom unit. If good weather is anticipated and you want to save money, consider choosing the hikers' cabin. The unit is small but has a nearby parking space and a nice covered patio with a picnic table.

Rooms: Doubles, triples, and quads. Each cabin, with the exception of the Hikers' cabin, has a private bathroom.

Wheelchair Accessibility: One two-bedroom cabin is wheelchair accessible.

Rates: Single-bedroom cabins ($114); two-bedroom cabins ($114); Hikers' cabin ($31). Rates are for two adults. Each additional adult is $11. Children under 16 are free.

Location: Between mile marker 57 and 58, near the midpoint of Skyline Drive. Lewis Mountain is about 6 miles south of Big Meadows.

Season: Early Apr to the first week in Nov. Cabins tend to fill on weekends and during July, Aug, and the first part of Oct.

Food: No restaurant or other dining facilities are at Lewis Mountain. A small store with limited groceries is in the registration building.

Facilities: Small store, pay showers (for the hikers' cabin), and laundry facility.

Activities: Hiking.

Pets: Permitted in some of the cabins at a charge of $25 per pet, per night.

SKYLAND RESORT

Skyland Resort at milepost 41.7 is a wide-ranging complex of approximately three dozen one- and two-story structures, including 27 buildings and cabins with guest accommodations. Lodge buildings range from freestanding rustic cabins constructed in the early 1900s to a modern two-story motel-type building with 20 rooms. Some buildings sit on a bluff, others are along a wooded hillside, but most are on a plateau overlooking the beautiful Shenandoah Valley. The registration building at the top of the hill has a small, comfortable lobby with chairs, tables, a television, and a wall of windows offering outstanding views of the valley. An adjacent building has a craft and gift shop, "grab 'n go" snack stand, taproom, small lounge, and a nice dining room with windows offering a valley view. Chairs and tables on a patio between the 2 buildings offer a pleasant place to relax and gaze at the valley.

Lodging structures are scattered about a wide area, although 3 lodge buildings on the top of the hill are near the registration and dining buildings. Many of the remaining buildings and cabins are down a hill and some distance from the dining room. Many, but not all 178 rooms offer good views of the valley. Some have great views from private balconies, while views from other rooms are blocked by trees or nearby buildings. Skyland offers 5 classes of accommodations: Traditional rooms, Preferred rooms, Cabins, Freestanding Cabins, and Suites. All rooms have wood paneling, private bathroom, coffeemaker, and heat, but no telephone. All Preferred and the majority of Traditional rooms have a television. Preferred rooms are the only units with air-conditioning. Most rooms are in a series of 15 one- and two-story lodge buildings that sit on a bluff overlooking the valley.

Buildings vary in size and age, but most have a ceiling fan and hair dryer. Bedding varies from 2 doubles to 2 queens, or 1 king. Two buildings, Laurel with Preferred rooms and Franklin with Traditional rooms, are newer and larger. Each lodge room has a balcony or patio, but views vary depending on the building location and whether trees are between the building and the valley.

The Bushytop building at Skyland Resort

Our favorite building is Shenandoah, with 5 rooms, including 1 Suite, that each offer excellent views of the Shenandoah Valley. Corner room 73 is particularly desirable and less expensive than the Suite directly above. Access requires walking an uphill grade from the parking lot, but this is a small price to pay for staying in this building. Pinnacles is a good choice if you want to be close to the restaurant and registration building. This building sits on a hillside, making entry easier to a second-floor room than a first-floor room. It has recently undergone a complete renovation and now consists of Traditional rooms with televisions, air-conditioning, and upgraded bathrooms.

The least expensive accommodations are Cabins in 9 historic buildings constructed between 1906 and 1922. Most have a small porch with chairs plus a bathroom with a shower. The

Cabins tend to have small windows and dark, paneled interiors. They are scattered among trees, and most do not offer a view of the valley. In addition, most are not close to the registration building or dining room. Cabins differ in size and bedding, ranging from 6 small units with 1 double bed to a large freestanding unit with a separate bedroom, gas fireplace, and large front porch. The latter, Cabin 68, called Byrd's Nest, is our pick of the Cabins, although it doesn't offer a valley view. Cabin 59 has 2 double beds plus a twin bed, and enjoys a large front porch. It is across from the playground making it a good choice for families with children. Adjoining Cabin 60, with identical bedding, can be combined with Cabin 59. Three Cabin rooms in Fell can be rented individually or as a unit, the latter being a popular option for large families. Cabin

173 in Fell has a queen bed and a separate living room fronted by a large picture window offering a commanding view of the valley. This unit does not have a balcony, but a large grassy area with chairs and a picnic table in front of the building offers a pleasant place to relax and enjoy the view.

Three cabins were restored and converted from multiple units back to their original status. Now classified as Freestanding Cabins, these units have either 1 or 2 bedrooms and each features a living room, a large porch with a picnic table, and a kitchenette with a sink, microwave, small refrigerator, and eating utensils. One Freestanding Cabin can sleep 6 adults, while the other two sleep 4. Two of the units have a gas fireplace.

Six Suites each comprise 2 rooms on the end of 4 lodge buildings. Four Suites are near the dining room, and 2 are down the hill. Each Suite offers a living room with a sofa bed and a wood-burning fireplace (wood provided), plus a separate bedroom. An adjoining room with a connecting door can be added at additional cost to provide a second bedroom. Beds vary from a double plus a twin to 2 queens. Suites down the hill offer a view of the valley, while those nearer the registration building each have a balcony with valley views blocked by trees.

Skyland Resort, the largest lodging facility in Shenandoah National Park, offers accommodations for a wide range of tastes, from historic cabins to modern lodge rooms. A conference hall convenient to many of the cabins and lodge rooms can be reserved (fee charged) for gatherings. Lodging units are spread over a fairly wide area, so if location and/or view is an important consideration, state your preference when making a reservation.

Rooms: Doubles, triples, and quads. Some suites sleep up to 5, and one Freestanding Cabin accommodates up to 6 adults. Some rooms, including Suites, can connect with adjacent rooms. All rooms have a private bath with a shower or a combination shower-tub.

The Skyland area was originally developed in the 1850s to mine copper. Surrounding timber was used to make charcoal for a copper smelter. It was not until 1886 that the son of one of the original mine owners considered the possibility of developing the area as a resort. By the early 1900s Skyland had a dining hall, a recreation hall, bathhouses, and bungalows, all paid for by borrowing and the sale of cabin sites. The developer operated Skyland as a concessionaire for the National Park Service until 1937.

Wheelchair Accessibility: Two rooms in Pinnacles (nearest the dining room), 4 rooms in Birmingham, and 4 rooms in Busytop are ADA compliant. Two rooms in Laurel (the newest building at Skyland), and 1 Freestanding Cabin are wheelchair accessible.

Rates: Traditional rooms ($132–$141); Preferred rooms ($175–$196); Cabins ($101–$114); Suites ($173–$248); Freestanding Cabins ($269–$281). The higher rates are charged on holidays and during fall. Each additional adult is $11. Rollaways are $11 per night. Discounts are available Sun through Thurs nights for AAA, AARP, and Shenandoah National Park Association members and for active military personnel. Children under 16 stay free with an adult. Check the website for special packages offered seasonally.

Location: At milepost 42, about midway on Skyline Drive between the north and south entrances to Shenandoah National Park. Skyland is the northernmost lodging facility in the park.

Season: End of Mar to the end of Nov.

Food: An attractive dining room serves breakfast ($5–$9), lunch ($8–$14), and dinner ($11–$25). Beer and wine are available. An adjacent taproom serves appetizers and a limited dinner menu beginning in the early afternoon.

Facilities: Restaurant, taproom, craft and gift shop, "grab 'n go" snack stand, conference hall (fee), large children's playground, stables, trails.

Activities: Hiking, horseback riding, pony rides, rock climbing, and rappelling programs, National Park Service ranger-led programs, nightly entertainment. The park concessionaire offers a variety of guided hikes plus special events throughout the season. Call (877) 847-1919, or visit the website for details.

Pets: Pets are permitted only in Canyon units at an extra charge of $25 per pet, per night.

WASHINGTON
State Tourist Information
(800) 544-1800 | www.experiencewa.com

Mount Rainier National Park

55210 238th Ave. East • Ashford, WA 98304 • (360) 569-2211 • www.nps.gov/mora

Mount Rainier National Park encompasses 235,625 acres, including the greatest single-peak glacial system and one of the most popular mountain-climbing areas in the continental United States. Mount Rainier, the ancient volcano at the center of the park, is surrounded by snow, forests, and subalpine flowered meadows. Visitor centers are at Sunrise, Ohanapecosh, Paradise, and Longmire, the latter being the park's oldest developed area. The road from the Nisqually Entrance in the park's southwest corner to Longmire is considered one of the world's most beautiful forest roads. Mount Rainier National Park is in southwestern Washington, 89 miles south of Seattle. It is 64 miles west of Yakima, Washington.

Park Entrance Fee: $15 per vehicle or $5 per person, good for 7 days.

MOUNT RAINIER NATIONAL PARK

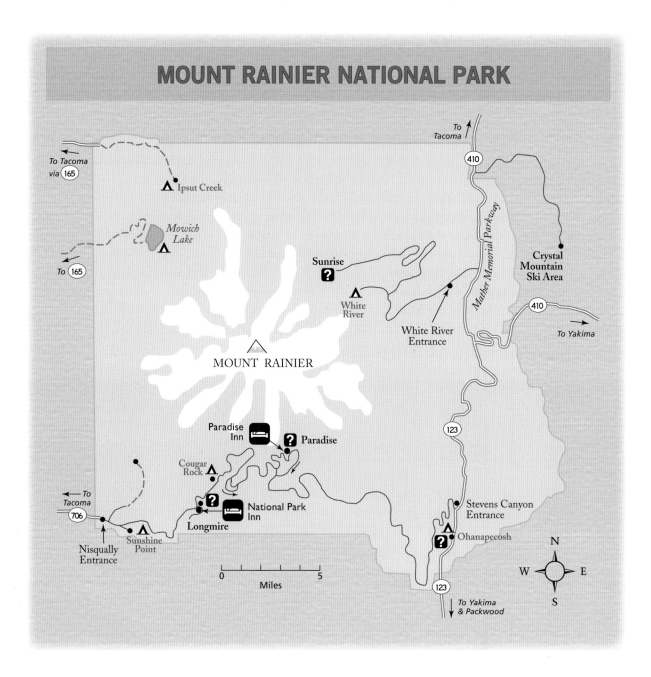

Lodging in Mount Rainier National Park: Mount Rainier has 2 inns that offer very different lodging experiences. National Park Inn is a small, cozy lodge in a heavily forested area with a view of Mount Rainier. The much larger and busier Paradise Inn is at a higher altitude that offers better mountain views in an alpine environment. Despite the different environments, the 2 lodges are both in the southern end of the park and only about 13 miles apart.

NATIONAL PARK INN

Mount Rainier National Park • Longmire, WA 98397 • (360) 569-2411
www.mtrainierguestservices.com

National Park Inn is a small two-story wooden lodge with 25 guest rooms, all but 2 of which are on the second floor. The inn is at an altitude of 2,700 feet, surrounded by an old-growth forest of Douglas fir, western red cedar, and western hemlock. National Park Inn retains the character of an early 1900s lodge even though the building has been completely modernized.

The 25 rooms at National Park Inn are different in terms of size, bedding, and bathrooms. In general, the rooms are comfortable but small. All rooms have heat, window fan, coffeemaker, and hair dryer, but no air-conditioning, telephone, or television. All but 7 rooms have private baths with a tub, a shower, or both. Rooms without a private bathroom have an in-room sink and access to 2 private shower rooms, a men's restroom, and a women's restroom on the second floor. Rooms with a bath cost about $50 per night more than rooms without a private bath. Most rooms have 2 twins, 1 double, or 1 queen bed, although 2 rooms have 2 double beds. Two units each have 2 rooms, 1 with a double bed and the other with 2 twins. Room 7, with a private bath, is much larger than average and has 1 queen plus 2 twin beds. Rooms 6, 8, and 10, with a bath, and 12, 14, and 16, without a bath, are along the front of the building and enjoy a good view of Mount Rainier when it isn't shrouded in clouds. We suggest requesting larger room 16 if using a community bathroom is acceptable. All rooms are entered from an inside corridor accessed via a stairway from the lobby. No elevator is available. Two handicap-accessible rooms, each with 1 queen bed and a private bath, are on the first floor.

National Park Inn is much smaller and cozier, and its rooms are larger and nicer than at its sister

National Park Inn with Mount Rainier in the background

lodge at Paradise. There aren't a lot of people here and activities in the immediate vicinity are minimal, but if you desire a comfortable and quiet place to read a book, get to know your spouse and kids, take a hike, or just recharge your batteries, National Park Inn is a good choice for an overnight stay. A large covered porch with numerous chairs spans the front of the building. A guest lounge off the registration area has a large stone fireplace, sofas, tables, chairs, and a closet full of games, and puzzles. Complimentary tea and freshly baked treats are served here each afternoon. The lounge is where we spend considerable time enjoying the fireplace, reading a book, and visiting with other guests. The general store next door sells gifts, clothing, limited groceries and camping supplies, beer, and wine. A National Park Service visitor center and a museum with exhibits on geology and wildlife are a short walk from the inn.

The current National Park Inn was constructed as an annex of the original three-story, 60-room National Park Inn, most of which burned in 1926. Fortunately the Annex had previously been moved to the opposite side of the road and was spared by the fire. The Annex was subsequently reopened as the National Park Inn and underwent a major remodeling in 1936. Another extensive renovation occurred in 1989, when the inn was essentially rebuilt from the ground up for reopening in May 1990. The adjacent building currently housing the general store was constructed in 1911 as a clubhouse for the first lodge and is the only structure at this location that remains on its original site.

Rooms: Doubles, triples, and quads. Eighteen of the 25 rooms have private baths. Community baths are on the second floor.

Wheelchair Accessibility: The inn has 2 ADA-compliant rooms on the first floor.

Reservations: Rainier Guest Services, PO Box 108, Ashford, WA 98304-0108. Phone (360) 569-2275; www.mtrainierguestservices.com. Credit card guarantee is required when the reservation is made. Any changes incur a $15 fee. Cancellation requires 7 days' notice plus a $15 handling fee. Less than 7 days' notice results in a charge of 1 night's room rate plus tax.

Rates: Rooms without a bath ($122–$158); rooms with a bath ($172–$213); two-room unit with bath ($257). Children under 2 stay free with an adult, using existing bedding in the room. Special winter packages are available Nov through Apr.

Location: Six miles from the southwest entrance to Mount Rainier National Park on WA 706. The inn is 13 miles from Paradise, the park's other lodge.

Season: Open all year.

Food: An informal dining room on the main floor is open for breakfast ($9–$13), lunch ($8–$15), and dinner ($12–$27). Snacks and beverages are sold at the general store.

Facilities: Dining room, general store that sells gifts and some food items, museum, National Park Service visitor center, hiker information center. Cross-country ski equipment and snowshoes are rented during winter months. Lessons are available.

Activities: Hiking, fishing, ranger-guided walks, snowshoeing, cross-country skiing.

PARADISE INN

Mount Rainier National Park • Paradise, WA 98398 • (360) 569-2415
www.mtrainierguestservices.com

Paradise Inn is a large two-story lodge with an attached four-story annex that offers striking views of the park's snow-covered peaks, including majestic Mount Rainier. The inn has 117 rooms, most of which are in the annex that is reached via an enclosed walkway from the lobby of the main building. The primary structure was completed in 1917, and the annex was added in the 1920s. Paradise Inn is at the base of Mount Rainier.

The inn is on a hillside such that entry to the lobby is on the hotel's third floor. Immense stone fireplaces flank each end of the huge two-story lobby, with a vaulted ceiling that spans much of the building's length. The lobby is filled with tables, benches, sofas, and chairs. Massive log

Paradise Inn

beams frame a mezzanine that wraps around the lobby. The parking lot is often crowded (or full of snow), so it is best to temporarily park beside the entrance to unload and load luggage. Assistance with luggage can be requested at the registration desk. There are no elevators, so access to all guest rooms other than those on the third floor requires climbing stairs.

Paradise Inn has several categories of rooms, all of which have heat but no air-conditioning, telephone, or television. The 32 least expensive guest rooms without private bath are all in the main building. Most are quite small (approximately 8 feet by 12 feet, including a small open closet area) with a sink and bedding that ranges from 2 twins to 1 double, to a double plus a single. Room 467 is without a private bath and is quite large with 3 double beds. It is the only guest

room in the hotel that can accommodate 6 people without adding a rollaway. Room 446, also without a private bathroom, is somewhat larger than average and has 2 double beds. It is next to the stairway, which is sometimes noisy. The 32 rooms without a bath share 4 private showers, 1 large men's restroom, and 1 large women's restroom. The restrooms were redone in 2006 and 2007 and are quite nice. Additional restrooms are on the floor below near the stairway. The next room classification includes 77 rooms with bathrooms, nearly all of which are in the annex. Bathrooms have a tub, a shower, or both. Bedding in these rooms varies from 2 twins to 2 doubles, or 1 queen.

Ten rooms have 2 bedrooms and a private bath. One bedroom has either a double or a queen bed, and the other has 2 twins. These rooms rent for about $75 per night more than rooms with

Paradise Inn Lobby

August. Paradise is a heavily visited area of the park, and lots of people, both guests and visitors, browse through the inn's lobby. Tables and chairs on the mezzanine offer a more relaxing place to read, play cards, or just people-watch in the lobby below. Complimentary tea and cookies are served for guests each afternoon. The attractive 200-seat dining room with a beamed ceiling offers several entrees such as Bourbon Buffalo Meatloaf with Jack Daniel's Sauce not found on most menus. The small Tatoosh Cafe with inside and outside seating, serves sandwiches, soups, salads, deserts, beverages, beer, and wine beginning at 6 a.m.

Rooms: Singles, doubles, triples, and quads, with 1 room that can accommodate 6 people. Not all rooms have private baths.

Wheelchair Accessibility: Seven rooms in the passageway between the main lodge and the Annex are ADA compliant.

Reservations: Rainier Guest Services, PO Box 108, Ashford, WA 98304-0108. Phone (360)

1 bedroom and a bath, so consider one of these if you are traveling with children. Paradise also offers 2 Suites, each with a bedroom with a queen bed, a separate sitting room with a futon, and a private bath.

Rooms in both the main lodge and the annex offer varying views, but none enjoy a particularly good view of Mount Rainier. When making a reservation consider that annex rooms are on 4 floors, and there is no elevator. Thus, you may be required to climb 2 flights of stairs each time you go to or from your room. Ask for a third-floor room (the hotel entry level) if you want to avoid climbing stairs.

Choosing a room without a bath will save $60 per night and put you nearer the lobby. These rooms are small but relatively comfortable. If you desire a larger room with a private bath try for rooms 317 or 319, each of which has 2 double beds and a large window area that offers good views of the Tattoosh Mountain Range. Room 411 allows guests to look out the window while taking a bath.

Paradise Inn is a classic national park lodge. At an altitude of 5,400 feet, this area can be quite cool and foggy, even during summer. On the plus side, it is noted for many varieties of subalpine flowers that bloom during July and

The original structure of Paradise Inn, including the existing lobby, dining room, kitchen, 3 storerooms, and guest rooms above the dining room, was constructed in 1917 of Alaskan cedar salvaged from standing dead timber resulting from a nearby 1885 fire. The huge logs were hauled by horse-drawn wagons from an area near Narada Falls and Canyon Rim to the present site. The ceiling-high cedar logs and attached bracing were added later to support the roof under the heavy snowfalls in the Paradise area. The original inn offered 33 rooms, and the attached annex was added in the 1920s. Most of the lobby's woodwork was done by a German carpenter, who used only an adze in his work. He also built an unusual piano and a huge grandfather clock, which remain in the lobby.

569-2275; www.mtrainierguestservices.com. A credit card is required to reserve a room. A charge of $15 is imposed for any change or cancellation of a reservation. Cancellations within 7 days of scheduled arrival result in a charge for 1 night's room rate plus tax.

Rates: Rooms without a bath ($119–$155); rooms with a bath ($178–$221); two-room units with a bath ($267–$286); Suites with a sitting room ($279–$297). Rates are established based on each room's bedding. Children under 2 stay free with an adult, utilizing existing bedding in the room.

Location: Paradise Inn is 19 miles inside the southwest (Nisqually) entrance of Mount Rainier National Park.

Season: Mid-May through the first part of Oct, depending on weather.

Food: An attractive dining room with seating for 200 offers a breakfast buffet ($16), lunch ($10–$16), and dinner ($15–$29), with a special Sunday brunch ($25). Alcoholic beverages are available. Dinner reservations are not accepted. A cafe off the lobby serves soups, salads, sandwiches, beer, and wine. Beverages are served in the lobby starting at 5 p.m.

The need for major structural work resulted in the closure of Paradise Inn during the 2006 and 2007 seasons. Concrete replaced the old frame walls, and a new concrete foundation stabilized the building that was originally constructed on a bed of large rocks. The 3 giant fireplaces, 2 in the lobby and 1 in the dining room, were photographed, taken apart, and rebuilt stone by stone after a concrete base and concrete inner structure had been poured. Parquet flooring was replaced with fir (the original flooring) in the lobby, dining room, gift shop, and cafe, while hall carpeting was replaced, rooms were repainted, and 2 guest showers were added in the inn's older section. Public bathrooms on the first and second floors were redone. The former bar on the main floor was converted to additional handicap-accessible rooms that now line the walkway between the main building and the Annex. The contractor brought in 180 Alaska cedar logs that were used as replacement and additional support beams. Additional renovations planned for the Annex were delayed due to a shortage of funds. Overall, the 2-year renovation cost approximately $22 million. Current plans call for extensive work on the Annex in 2016.

Facilities: Restaurant, cafe, gift shop, hiker information center, nearby National Park Service visitor center.

Activities: Hiking, guided walks, evening programs in the lobby, fishing, mountain climbing, snowshoeing, cross-country skiing, and tubing.

North Cascades National Park Complex
810 State Rte. 20 • Sedro-Woolley, WA 98284 • (360) 854-7200 • www.nps.gov/noca

The North Cascades National Park Complex, covering 1,069 square miles, offers magnificent alpine scenery unmatched in the continental United States. Heavy precipitation has produced alpine lakes, waterfalls, ice caps, more than 300 glaciers, and glacier-carved canyons such as Stehekin (Salishan for "the way through") that sits at the head of 55-mile long Lake Chelan. Compared to many other national parks, this scenic park is relatively wild and uncrowded. The park complex is in northern Washington (the north boundary borders on Canada). Primary access is via WA 20 that bisects the park.

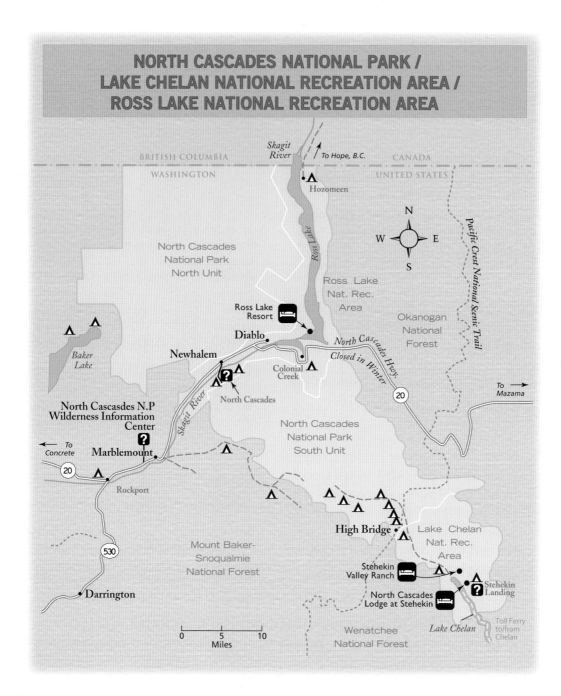

NORTH CASCADES NATIONAL PARK / LAKE CHELAN NATIONAL RECREATION AREA / ROSS LAKE NATIONAL RECREATION AREA

Park Entrance Fee: No charge.

Lodging in North Cascades National Park Complex: Two lodging facilities are in the park. One is in the village of Stehekin at the north end of Lake Chelan, while the other is at the south end of Ross Lake. We have also included a third lodge just outside the community of Stehekin. For information

on other lodging and services, call Lake Chelan Chamber of Commerce at (800) 4-CHELAN (424-3526). The 3 lodges are not accessible via private vehicle. Transportation options are explained in the transportation section for each lodge.

NORTH CASCADES LODGE AT STEHEKIN
PO Box 3 • Stehekin, WA 98852 • (509) 682-4494 • www.lodgeatstehekin.com

North Cascades Lodge at Stehekin consists of 7 wooden buildings, 5 of which house guest rooms. The registration desk is in a kiosk on the dock below the restaurant. The store and restaurant are fronted by a covered wooden deck with chairs and picnic tables. There are also a laundry, post office, a few stores, and a large National Park Service visitor center. Shuttle service and tours for Stehekin Valley begin near the dock.

A total of 28 lodging units of various sizes and configurations are available at the lodge. All have a private bath with a shower or combination shower-tub, heat, and a fan, but no telephone, television, or air-conditioning. Ten Standard rooms, 8 of which are above the store, are the least expensive. These relatively small rooms do not have a balcony or offer a lake view, but a guest lounge with books, games, and puzzles at the end of the hallway has large windows that offer excellent views. Standard rooms 5 and 6 are located on the lower floor of an A-frame building and have nice interiors.

Eleven Lakeview rooms in a two-story motel-style building adjacent to the restaurant are larger than Standard rooms. Each has at least 1 large window and a balcony facing Lake Chelan. Six rooms are larger and rent for more than the other 5 rooms. Five first-floor rooms, 9 through 13,

A view of North Cascades Lodge from the Stehekin dock area

have a significantly larger balcony than upstairs units. Five regular-size Lakeview rooms sleep 2 and the 6 larger rooms sleep from 3 to 7.

Six Kitchen units have a kitchen with a stove, oven, refrigerator/freezer, coffeemaker, toaster, and all utensils including pots and pans. These units are in 4 different buildings. One unit 2 flights above the store (no elevator) has 2 bedrooms plus a living room and sleeps 7. Large windows face the lake and the room can become uncomfortably warm during July and August. A freestanding building with a large deck and wheelchair accessibility, unit 1, has 2 bedrooms plus a living room and can sleep 7. An A-frame building sleeps 6, with a bedroom and living room plus a loft bedroom. The A-frame has a large deck facing the lake on the main floor, 1 flight above ground level. Views from the deck are somewhat

obstructed by buildings. The 3 other kitchen units are in a triplex building. Smaller units 2 and 3 each sleep 3 people while larger unit 4 can sleep 6 in 1 bedroom and a separate living area. All 3 units share a large deck facing the lake.

Lake House is a full-size home that can accommodate up to 12 people. It has 4 bedrooms, a full kitchen, washer and dryer, fireplace, and a hot tub. The home is directly on Lake Chelan and a short walk from other lodging units.

If cost is an important consideration choose one of the Standard rooms above the store. They don't offer a view, but great views from the lounge are a few steps from any of the rooms. Plus, easy lounge access makes it convenient to meet other guests.

Families should consider Kitchen unit 1 with 2 bedrooms, a living room, and kitchen, although some people might prefer the ambience of the A-frame unit. Keep in mind that few grocery items are available at Stehekin, so bring food if you plan to use a kitchen. The Safeway store in Chelan will box and deliver groceries to the boat for customers who purchase goods the day prior to their departure for Stehekin.

North Cascades Lodge at Stehekin is a remote and interesting place to stay after a scenic boat trip up the lake. Settle into your room and then spend part of the afternoon exploring this small village that could well be in Alaska. After dinner at the restaurant, walk out to the dock or up the road and enjoy nature at its finest. Shuttle service is available to Stehekin Valley Ranch, which offers an alternative for dinner. One building at the landing houses a recreation room with a fireplace, a satellite television, and a pool table. This is available as a conference room for retreats.

The lodge serves as the center for Stehekin activities, including boat and bicycle rentals, snowshoe rental in the winter, bus tours, and hikes. Buses for tours of the valley leave from the lodge.

Rooms: Doubles, triples, quads, with a few kitchen units sleeping up to 7. Lake House can accommodate up to 12.

Wheelchair Accessibility: One Lakeview room and the freestanding Kitchen unit are wheelchair accessible. An electric lift on the dock provides wheelchair access to the store, restaurant, and rooms.

Reservations: North Cascades Lodge at Stehekin, PO Box 3, Stehekin, WA 98852. Call (509) 682-4494; www.lodgeatstehekin.com. Payment in full is required to book a reservation. Cancellation of sleeping units requires 14 days' notice. Cancellation of the kitchen units and Lake House requires 30 days' notice. The lodge charges $15 for any change or cancellation of a reservation.

Rates: Standard rooms ($122–$128); Lakeview rooms ($162–$202); Kitchen units ($182–$222); Lake House ($475). Rates quoted are for 2 persons with the exception of 4 larger Kitchen units that are quoted for 4 persons and the Lake House, for which the rate is for 6 persons. Each additional person is $10 per night. Children under 6 stay free. Kitchen units and Lake House require a 2-night minimum. For stays of 5 nights, rates are reduced by 10 percent. Check the website for special packages.

North Cascades Lodge at Stehekin is not the only lodging facility to have served the public at Stehekin. The small Argonaut Hotel with several rooms and a store was under construction, when in 1892 it was sold to Merritt Field, who built a three-story hotel that could accommodate 100 guests in its 50 guestrooms. Faced with flooding as a result of the proposed Lake Chelan Dam, Field sold the hotel in 1915 to the Great Northern Railroad, which continued operations until 1927, when the building was demolished. Timber and beams from the hotel were used to construct the Golden West Lodge farther up the hill, which operated here until 1971, when it was sold to the National Park Service. The former hotel is currently utilized as a National Park Service visitor center. The current lodge is a conglomeration of 2 hotels that were acquired by the National Park Service in 1968.

Location: The north end of Lake Chelan next to the Stehekin boat dock.

Season: Open all year, although services, lodging, and facilities are fully operational only from mid-May through Oct. Four Kitchen units are open year-round. Restaurant hours are reduced, or the restaurant is closed at various times during fall, winter, and spring. Check with the resort about specific dates.

Food: An adjacent restaurant offers breakfast ($6–$11), lunch ($9–$14), and dinner ($14–$26). Dinner reservations are highly recommended. Beer and wine are served. A small store sells very limited groceries plus beer and wine. A shuttle offers transportation to Stehekin Valley Ranch, which is open for dinner. Reservations can be made at the Stehekin Landing kiosk.

Transportation: Stehekin is reached only via floatplanes and commercial boats that depart from the town of Chelan or Field's Point Landing. The largest and least expensive boat (approximately $40 round-trip) takes 4 hours 1 way and leaves Chelan each morning at 8:30. A faster and more expensive boat ($61 round-trip) takes 2½ hours and leaves at the same time. Both boats are operated by Lake Chelan Boat Company. Reservations are recommended. For information call (888) 682-4584, or visit www.ladyof thelake.com. On your first trip to Stehekin, save money and see more by selecting the more leisurely *Lady of the Lake II*. The scenery between Chelan and Stehekin is beautiful, and the captain sometimes approaches the shoreline when wild animals are spotted. For those in a hurry, floatplanes are available for round-trips ($178) or 1 way ($89), with flights taking approximately 30 minutes. Seniors and children rates are reduced by $10 and $30, respectively. Chelan Seaplanes offers several transportation options, including fly/boat trips that allow flying 1 way and taking a boat the other. For information contact Chelan Seaplanes at (509) 682-5555, or visit www.chelanseaplanes.com.

Facilities: Dining room, recreation room, convenience store, craft store, post office, laundry, National Park Service visitor center, marina, boat and bicycle rentals.

Activities: Hiking, fishing, boating, kayak tours, bus tours, river rafting, guided horseback rides, and mountain biking.

Ross Lake Resort

503 Diablo St. • Rockport, WA 98283 • (206) 386-4437 • www.rosslakeresort.com

Ross Lake Resort is an unusual lodging facility consisting of a row of floating cabins, bunkhouses, and support buildings along the shoreline of 22-mile-long Ross Lake. The rustic shake-sided cabins and bunkhouses are constructed on wooden docks attached to huge cedar logs floating on the water and cabled to shore. The floating base allows the cabins to rise and fall with the lake's water level.

Ross Lake Resort caters to people who love to fish, boat, hike, and just relax. The resort includes an office, small marina area, and associated outbuildings. It is in a wild and beautiful region, so don't be surprised if the resort owner's dog scares off an inquisitive black bear that walks out of the woods. Guests do not have access to television, radio, or the Internet, and cell phones are out of range. The isolation alone makes the resort a refreshing place to visit. Lake and mountain views from large windows along the front of each cabin make it even better. *Keep in mind that guests must bring all their own food because no food service of any kind is available at or near the resort.*

Floating cabins at Ross Lake Resort

Four classes of accommodations are offered: Private Bunkhouse rooms, Little Cabins, Modern Cabins, and Peak Cabins. All have woodstove or electric heat, private bathrooms, and kitchens with pots, pans, plates, utensils, a microwave, a coffeemaker, and a toaster. The cabins with woodstoves have plenty of firewood and an axe. Two Adirondack chairs in which to relax and enjoy the fantastic view of the lake and mountains are in front of or beside each cabin. Several gas grills are near the cabins.

Three Private Bunkhouse rooms built in 1982 are reproductions of the bunkhouses used by dam construction crews. Each unit consists of 1 large room with 4 bunk beds (8 total beds), a large table with chairs, and a woodstove. The kitchen area includes an electric stove and oven plus a full-size refrigerator. These are typically rented to large families or groups of 6 or more who come to fish.

Two Little Cabins, constructed as a duplex, each have a bunk bed plus a queen bed in an area separate from the kitchen that includes a stove, oven, small refrigerator, woodstove, and table with chairs. Eight Modern Cabins were constructed over a 10-year period through 1971. All have since been remodeled. Each cabin has an open front room with a kitchen area that includes a stove, oven, a full-size refrigerator, and a large table with 6 padded chairs. Six Modern Cabins have 2 single beds and a woodstove in the front room, while 2 have electric heat (rather than a woodstove) and 3 single beds. A bunk bed is in a very small bedroom between the front room and the bathroom.

The most expensive accommodations are 2 Peak Cabins constructed in 1996. These large, two-story cabins have electric heat plus a wood-stove. They are the only accommodations with a dishwasher in the kitchen, and a full-size bathroom with a combination shower-tub. The front room has a sofa bed and a large table with chairs. A small bedroom includes a single bed and a bunk bed. The loft area, a major attraction for many guests, includes a queen bed and 2 single beds.

Ross Lake Resort is in a beautiful setting with few distractions. Guests typically spend most of their stay boating, fishing, hiking, and reading. Relax in front of your cabin sipping a beverage, reading a book, and taking in mountain views across the lake. Visit when you can stay for several days, because transportation to and from the resort is limited to twice a day. You are unlikely to enjoy much relaxation if you arrive at 4 p.m. one afternoon and leave at 8:30 a.m. the next morning. Even choosing the 2:30 p.m. departure doesn't allow sufficient time to appreciate this beautiful part of Washington.

Ross Lake Resort evolved from numerous floating cabins that were built on the lake to house workers engaged in logging and the construction of nearby Ross Dam. Floating cabins not only allowed the structures to be moved around the lake, it also avoided the need to build structures on the steep terrain surrounding the lake. The dam was completed in 1949, and the power station was added several years later. Although the current cabins are modern, an adventurous atmosphere remains for resort guests.

Choosing among the 4 classes of accommodations is mostly determined by the number of people in your group. All accommodations, except Bunkhouses, have large windows that provide an outstanding view of the lake and mountains. Peak Cabins offer considerably more room and are situated at the far end of the row

so that few other guests will be traipsing in front of your cabin. On the other hand, 2 people are easily accommodated in one of the Little Cabins, which are less expensive and situated such that other guests must walk behind, rather than in front of your cabin.

Rooms: Little Cabins offer bedding for up to 4 guests but are better suited for a couple or a couple with 1 or 2 small children. Modern Cabins can accommodate up to 6 people with the use of a rollaway bed but are more comfortable for 2 to 4 people. Peak Cabins can accommodate up to 9 people but are better suited for 2 couples or a couple with 3 or 4 children. Each Bunkhouse holds up to 10 people, but they had better be good friends.

Wheelchair Accessibility: Each of the 2 Peak Cabins is wheelchair accessible.

Reservations: Ross Lake Resort, 503 Diablo St., Rockport, WA 98283. Phone (206) 386-4437. A required deposit is based on the cabin classification and number of nights requested. Cancellation notice of 30 days is required for a refund, less a $10 fee. A boat rental is required during weekends.

Rates: Private Bunkhouse ($235 for up to 6 people; $8 each additional person); Little Cabin ($165 for 2 people; $10 each additional person); Modern Cabin ($190 for 2 people; $10 each additional person); Peak Cabin ($330 for up to 4 people; $15 each additional person). Children 3 years and under stay free. Specials are offered seasonally.

Location: Approximately 130 miles northeast of Seattle, Washington, via I-5 and WA 20. The resort is on Ross Lake just above Ross Dam.

Season: Mid-June through late Oct.

Food: No stores or restaurants are at or near the resort. Visitors must bring their own food and beverages. Candy, soft drinks, and ice are sold in the office.

Transportation: Ross Lake Resort is reached via WA 20, which bisects North Cascades National Park Complex. Most guests choose to take the combination ferry/truck/speedboat route from near Diablo Dam, 65 miles east of Burlington on WA 20. To access free parking, cross Diablo Dam and turn right to the resort parking lot. A sign on WA 20 indicates the turnoff. The ferry, operated by Seattle City Light and departing each day at 8:30 a.m. and 3 p.m., takes you to the end of Diablo Lake. The charge is $20 per person round-trip, payable in cash. A maximum of 3 carry-ons per person is permitted. You will be met by the resort truck, which transports you and your luggage on a winding gravel road to Ross Lake ($8 round-trip, payable at the resort). From there you transfer to a speedboat that quickly crosses the lake to your assigned cabin. No reservations are necessary for either the ferry or the truck. Guests interested in hiking to the resort can park their vehicle on WA 20 at milepost 134 (the Ross Lake/Ross Dam trailhead). A 1-mile hike down the marked trail leads to the boat docking area across the lake from the resort. A telephone on the last power pole beside the road can be used to call the resort for pickup (dial 18-31974; $2 charge per person).

Activities: Hiking, fishing, kayaking, canoeing, boating. Fishing licenses are sold at the office. Fishing gear is available for rent.

STEHEKIN VALLEY RANCH

PO Box 36 • Stehekin, WA 98852 • (509) 682-4677 • www.stehekinvalleyranch.com

Stehekin Valley Ranch is an isolated lodging complex that includes a two-story dining hall, 15 wooden cabins, and a corral. The buildings sit in a grove of maple trees next to a large pasture and are surrounded by mountains. The cabins are a short walk from the dining hall, which includes a small registration/gift shop area, a loft reading room, separate men's and women's bathhouses, and an attractive log-beamed dining area with 3 massive picnic tables and a wood stove. The location offers outstanding views and access to excellent hiking, kayaking, and fishing in a restful and friendly atmosphere. Three meals a day, including an excellent dinner, are included in the price of a room. There are no televisions or telephones, and cell phones do not work at the ranch. Stehekin Valley Ranch is 9 miles north of the Stehekin boat dock and is reached via a free shuttle.

Lodging at the ranch is in 2 types of cabins. Seven older cabins, constructed in 1983, are wood sided with heavy canvas roofs. These tent cabins have cement floors, screens, and canvas shades (no glass) as window coverings, unfinished interiors, and no heat, electricity, or running water. The 7 differ in size, with cabin 5 with 1 double bed being smallest and cabins 1 and 2 being largest with a double bed plus 3 twin beds. The other 4 canvas-covered cabins each have a double plus 2 twins or a queen plus 1 twin. Community bathroom facilities including shower rooms are on the first floor of the main building, a short walk from all the cabins. A kerosene lantern in each cabin provides the only artificial source of light, so bring a flashlight if you will be staying in one of these cabins. Despite the rustic appearance, these units are clean and comfortable, and

Cabins at Stehekin Valley Ranch

the choice of many regular guests. Five of the 7 cabins (cabins 1 though 5) are directly beside the pasture and provide excellent mountain views. Cabins 11 and 12 are higher on the hill with views obstructed by other cabins.

The ranch has 8 larger wooden cabins with metal roofs, 6 of which were constructed in the mid-1990s. Two newer cabins, each with a kitchen sink, propane stove, and small refrigerator were built in 2006. Each of the 6 older cabins has a painted cement floor, an unfinished interior, and a large front porch with chairs. Sliding windows with screens are on the front and 2 sides. These cabins also have electric lights, an electrical outlet in the bathroom, and a private bathroom with a shower, but they do not have heat. Three of these cabins have 1 queen plus 2 twin beds. Cabins 9 and 10 are larger

with a loft bedroom that has 2 twin beds, while the downstairs has a futon and queen-size bed. The 2 newest cabins have a finished interior, 1 queen bed, a futon, and a private bathroom. The 8 newer metal-roofed cabins are larger, brighter, and more comfortable than the older canvas-covered cabins. They are situated behind 5 of the canvas-roofed cabins, which block their view of the pasture and mountains.

The choice of a cabin depends in large part on whether you want a private bathroom. The metal-roofed cabins cost about $25 per person more per day but offer more interior space and a private bathroom and are likely to be more comfortable in cool or rainy weather. On the other hand, the canvas-covered cabins may offer more of the ambience you seek from this type of vacation. The dining hall and loft reading room are always open to play cards, converse with other guests, or read.

Stehekin Valley Ranch is a place with lots of outdoor activities, including kayaking, horseback riding, mountain biking, fishing, and hiking. Three-hour trail rides leave each morning and afternoon from the nearby corral. Riding lessons are offered to anyone 6 years and older. Mountain bikes are available for rent. Guests at Stehekin Valley Ranch enjoy free use of the shuttle that connects Stehekin Landing with the ranch. The shuttle also stops at the bakery and Rainbow Falls. Hiking trails begin at High Bridge, which is on the route of the Pacific Crest Trail.

The dining room, with 3 large tables with benches, provides a great atmosphere for talking with other guests as you enjoy exceptional meals of fish, chicken, and steak. Best of all are the freshly baked pies served each evening. After dinner relax on the outside deck or climb the stairs to a small loft reading room. Guests often linger in the dining room to chat, read, or play board games.

Rooms: Fifteen individual cabins, most of which sleep up to 4 people. Two larger cabins can sleep up to 6. Seven canvas-roofed cabins have no private bath. Eight cabins have a private bath with shower.

Wheelchair Accessibility: None of the cabins are wheelchair accessible.

Reservations: Stehekin Valley Ranch, PO Box 36, Stehekin, WA 98852. Call (800) 536-0745. A deposit of 50 percent of the total is required at the time the reservation is made. Cancellation via email or in writing must be received at least 21 days prior to the reservation date in order to receive a 75 percent refund. No refunds for later cancellations.

Rates: Canvas-covered cabins ($100 per adult, $70 per child ages 4 to 12, $25 per child ages 1 to 3); cabins with bath (2 adult minimum, $125 per adult, $95 per child age 4 to 12, $45 per child age 1 to 3). A discount of 10 percent is offered for stays of 3 or more nights. Meals are included for all cabins. Packages that include a variety of activities including bicycling and horseback riding are available.

Hugh Courtney, grandfather of the current owners of Stehekin Valley Ranch, homesteaded 52 acres in the Stehekin area in 1916. One of his sons, Ray, subsequently purchased the 20-acre dairy farm where the ranch is currently located and started a successful pack trip business. Six of Ray's children are currently involved in a variety of businesses, including the operation of the ranch. The present lodging operation commenced in 1983 with the construction of the main building and canvas-roofed cabins. Stehekin Valley Ranch is on private land surrounded by Lake Chelan National Recreation Area.

Location: Nine miles north of Stehekin Landing. A free shuttle for guests of the ranch operates 4 round-trips daily between Stehekin Landing and the ranch.

Season: Mid-June to early Oct.

Food: All meals are included in the price of a room. Breakfast includes meat, eggs, pancakes, French toast, oatmeal, and fruit, among other items. Lunch choices include hamburgers, soup, and the makings for cold-meat sandwiches. Guests can make sack lunches after breakfast. The dinner is outstanding, with a choice of steak, chicken, fish, and a daily special. The pies for dessert are world class. Vegetarian meals are available. Alcoholic beverages are not available, but guests may bring their own.

Transportation: Refer to the transportation section for North Cascades Lodge at Stehekin. A valley shuttle system operates every 3 hours beginning at 8:15 a.m. between Stehekin Landing and Stehekin Valley Ranch. The shuttle also stops at the bakery and other points along the road.

Facilities: Dining room, small gift shop, reading room, bicycle rental.

Activities: Fishing, hiking, kayaking, trail rides, riding lessons, guided fishing trips, bicycling, volleyball, horseshoes.

Pets: The ranch charges a fee of $25 per pet per stay. The fee for horses, including a corral and food, is $20 per night.

Olympic National Park

600 E. Park Ave. • Port Angeles, WA 98362 • (360) 565-3130 • www.nps.gov/olym

Olympic National Park covers 1,442 square miles of mountain wilderness that includes active glaciers, 57 miles of scenic ocean shore, and the finest remnant of Pacific Northwest rain forest. The strip of land along the Pacific Ocean includes some of the most primitive coastline in the continental United States. Main access is via US 101, although roads penetrate only the perimeter of the park.

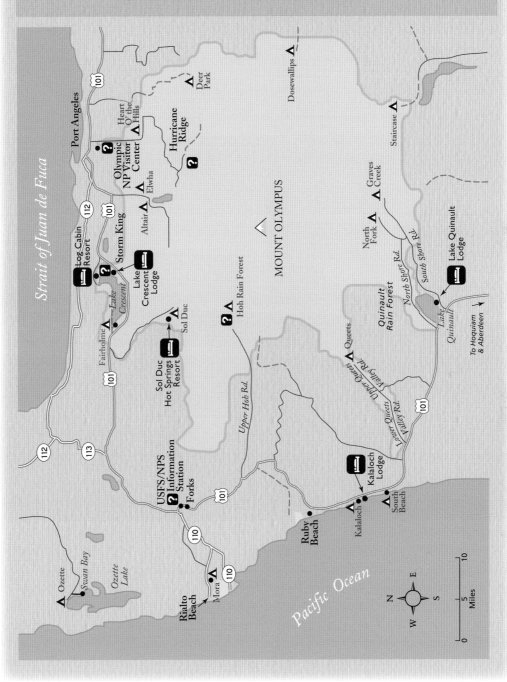

OLYMPIC NATIONAL PARK

Strait of Juan de Fuca

Pacific Ocean

MOUNT OLYMPUS

Port Angeles

Deer Park

Dosewallips

Heart O' the Hills

Hurricane Ridge

Olympic NP Visitor Center

Elwha

Staircase

Log Cabin Resort

Storm King

Altair

Lake Crescent Lodge

North Fork

Graves Creek

Lake Crescent

Fairholme

Sol Duc

Sol Duc Hot Springs Resort

Hoh Rain Forest

Quinault Rain Forest

North Shore Rd.

South Shore Rd.

Lake Quinault Lodge

Lake Quinault

To Hoquiam & Aberdeen

Queets

Upper Hob Rd.

USFS/NPS Information Station

Forks

Lower Queets Valley Rd.

Upper Queets Valley Rd.

Kalaloch Lodge

Ruby Beach

Kalaloch

South Beach

Ozette

Swan Bay

Ozette Lake

Mora

Rialto Beach

N W E S

Miles
0 5 10

Park Entrance Fee: $15 per vehicle or $5 per person, good for 7 days.

Lodging in Olympic National Park: Four facilities offer overnight accommodations. Kalaloch Lodge is directly on the coast and perfect for beach walkers. Sol Duc Hot Springs Resort is an inviting destination for those who want to relax in a hot mineral pool. Lake Crescent Lodge and Log Cabin Resort are situated on the northern edge of the park in heavily wooded areas on opposite sides of beautiful Lake Crescent. We have included charming Lake Quinault Lodge, across Lake Quinault from the park's southern boundary.

KALALOCH LODGE
157151 Hwy. 101 • Forks, WA 98331 • (360) 962-2271 • www.thekalalochlodge.com

Bluff cabins at Kalaloch Lodge

Kalaloch Lodge is a complex of wooden buildings that includes a main lodge, numerous cabins, a motel-style unit, and a store, all situated on a bluff overlooking the Pacific Ocean. Only a few overnight rooms are in the main lodge, whose gift shop includes the registration desk for all guest rooms. This building also houses the restaurant. All of the cabins and other lodging units are adjacent to and within easy walking distance of the main lodge. The lodging complex offers 64 guest rooms in 4 categories, all of which have a coffeemaker, hair dryer, electric heat, and private bath, but no telephone or air-conditioning. Televisions are available only in 2 guest rooms in the main lodge building.

The main lodge has 10 guest rooms, all but 1 of which are on the second floor and accessed from a central hallway reached from the lobby stairway. There is no elevator. All guest rooms in the lodge have a private bathroom with a shower. Two guest rooms, the Becker Room and the Kalaloch Room are relatively large and each has a king bed, television, small refrigerator, and microwave. The Becker Room enjoys a fireplace but is only rented during the summer months. During the remainder of the year it is converted to a library that is available for lodge guests. The size of the remaining rooms varies with 5 having 1 queen bed and the other 3 having 2 queen beds. Rooms 1 (on the first floor), 6, 7, and 8, and the Becker and Kalaloch Rooms provide a view of Kalaloch Creek and the ocean. Five rooms, including 5 and 9 above the kitchen, may be noisy and are only rented on-site.

Two-story Seacrest House, with 6 Studio rooms plus 4 Suites, sits behind 2 Bluff cabins. The 6 motel-style Studio rooms are very spacious with 2 queen beds, a mini-refrigerator, and a private bath with a shower. Each room enjoys its own covered patio or balcony and large windows that face the ocean but do not provide an ocean view. Three Suites have a sitting room with a fireplace (1 bundle of wood provided) and 2 separate bedrooms with 1 double and 1 queen bed plus a sofa bed. One bedroom and the sitting room have large windows. The fourth Suite is 1 large room with a fireplace, queen bed, and futon.

The 20 Bluff cabins are the most popular lodging at Kalaloch. Each has wood siding, tile floors, covered back porch and most offer excellent ocean views. These cabins are offered in different sizes and configurations. Some are duplex units while others are freestanding. Approximately half these cabins have a single room with

2 queen beds or 1 queen plus a futon. The remainder each have either 1 or 2 separate bedrooms with bedding that can sleep from 6 to 8 persons. All but 6 Bluff cabins have kitchens with a sink, refrigerator, stove, oven, pots, pans, and utensils. When reserving a Bluff cabin keep in mind that some have a woodstove or fireplace, some have a kitchen, and larger units have both.

Sitting directly behind the Bluff cabins are 24 Kalaloch cabins with exteriors that have been sided with cedar. Some have interiors that retain exposed log walls. These are comfortable cabins with tiled floors, a woodstove (1 bundle of wood provided), and either a kitchenette or a full kitchen with a refrigerator, stove, microwave, sink, and table with 4 chairs. Larger units also have an oven. Most of these cabins have 1 bedroom with a queen bed plus another queen bed and futon in a separate living area. One large Kalaloch cabin has 2 bedrooms, each with a queen bed plus a living room with a sofa bed. Although these cabins sit back from the bluff, cabins 24 through 27 provide an ocean view when standing by the front windows.

Kalaloch Lodge is for people with a desire to experience the sounds, smell, and ruggedness of the Pacific Coast. Guests can read a book or enjoy the roar of the sea as they walk the beach. A wide sandy beach just below the bluff is reached via a set of steps that begins near the Bluff cabins. The ocean water is relatively cold with potentially dangerous riptides, so you probably won't want to swim, but strolls along the beach are one of the pleasures of staying at Kalaloch. Consider bringing a kite because the ocean breeze makes this a perfect place to hone a skill you probably last used many years ago. National Park Service rangers lead daily walks along the beach and to various points in the park during summer months. The lodge restaurant has large windows that allow diners to gaze at the ocean. Keep in mind that this coastal area is generally breezy and can become quite foggy, so be prepared for the likelihood of winds, mist, and chilly weather that are all part of the experience of a visit to the Pacific Northwest.

Rooms: Doubles, triples, and quads. Several cabins can hold more than 4 persons. All accommodations have a private bath, most with a shower but no tub.

Wheelchair Accessibility: One Bluff cabin and 1 Kalaloch cabin have accessible features but are not fully ADA compliant.

Reservations: Kalaloch Lodge, 157151 Hwy. 101, Forks, WA 98331-9396. Phone (866) 662-9928 or (360) 962-2271; www.thekalalochlodge .com. A deposit of 1 night's stay is required. A cancellation notice of 72 hours is required for a refund less a $25 fee.

Rates: Rates vary depending on day, season, and occupancy. Lodge rooms ($122–$188); Kalaloch room and Becker room ($264–$325); Seacrest House Studio rooms ($132–$209); Seacrest suites ($142–$215); Bluff cabins ($202–$349, depending on size); Kalaloch cabins ($152–$248, depending on size). Rates quoted are for 2 persons. Each additional person is $15 per night. Rollaways are $15 per night. Children 12 years old and under stay free. Special prices and packages are frequently offered on the firm's website.

Location: Directly on the Pacific Ocean, 35 miles south of Forks, Washington, on US 101.

Season: Open year-round.

The current Kalaloch Lodge sits on the site of an earlier lodging facility constructed in the late 1920s by Charles Becker, who had acquired 40 acres just south of Kalaloch Creek. Becker's operation included a home, lodge, and several frame cabins constructed on a bluff overlooking the ocean. Additional cabins were constructed between 1934 and 1936 following completion of US 101. The owner added more cabins and relocated some existing cabins back from the bluff following World War II, during which the resort was occupied by the US Coast Guard. Between 1950 and 1954 Becker erected a new lodge building that remains in use today. In 1978 the National Park Service purchased the Becker operation and renamed it Kalaloch Lodge. Within 4 years a new concessionaire had completed construction of 22 log cabins that have become a major part of the current operation.

Food: A restaurant serves breakfast ($5–$15), lunch and dinner ($12–$35). Dinner reservations are recommended. Alcoholic beverages are served. Limited groceries including beer and wine can be purchased at the store adjacent to the main lodge building.

Facilities: Restaurant, gift shop, and small store. A National Park Service visitor center is a short distance south on US 101.

Activities: Hiking, beachcombing, whale watching, kite flying, surf fishing. Ranger-guided walks are offered each day during summer months.

Pets: Pets are allowed in cabins only for $25 per pet, per stay. A maximum of 2 pets per cabin is permitted.

LAKE CRESCENT LODGE

416 Lake Crescent Rd. • Port Angeles, WA 98363 • (360) 928-3211 • www.olympicnationalparks.com

Historic main building at Lake Crescent Lodge

Lake Crescent Lodge comprises a classic lodge flanked by cottages and one- and two-story motel structures. The main lodge, constructed in 1916 as the Singer Tavern, has 5 guest rooms, all upstairs and without a private bath. Other accommodations are separate from but near the main lodge. The complex is situated on the south shore of scenic Lake Crescent among giant hemlock and fir trees in the shadow of Mt. Storm King. Registration is just inside the main building in a lobby highlighted by a huge stone fireplace. A gift shop, restaurant, lobby bar, and an inviting sunroom are in the same building. Virtually all the accommodations, including the cottages, offer a view of Lake Crescent. All the rooms and most bathrooms at Lake Crescent Lodge underwent extensive remodeling in 2012.

The lodge offers several types of accommodations, each of which has a hair dryer, coffeemaker, and heat but no air-conditioning, television, or telephone. All rooms except those in the main lodge have a private bath. The least expensive accommodations are 5 relatively small but attractive Lodge rooms on the second floor. These rooms are entered from an interior hallway via a lobby stairway. All have a double bed and an in-room sink, but no private bathroom. Shower rooms and bathrooms are in the hallway. All 5 rooms offer a terrific view of Lake Crescent and the mountains on the opposite shore.

Four Roosevelt Fireplace Cottages were constructed from 1945 to 1947. These units are quite nice, with hardwood floors, wood interiors, small refrigerator, microwave, and a stone fireplace (1 bundle of wood provided). The cottages are on the shore of Lake Crescent and at the opposite end of the lodge from the other cabins and motor lodge buildings, a location that provides more privacy and quiet. Two one-room Roosevelt Fireplace units are in a duplex wood-frame building, each with 2 queen beds. Two cottages with 2 rooms are freestanding and have 1 queen in the living area and 2 double beds in the bedroom. These are the most expensive and desirable accommodations at the lodge. With only 4 units available, they are also difficult to reserve and often booked several years in advance.

Thirteen one- and two-bedroom Singer Tavern Cottages are constructed 2 or 3 units to a building. The cottages retain the scale and historic character of the original cabins that were torn down in the 1980s. Each shake-sided cottage has a covered porch with chairs, and all but 1 (cottage 19) offer a good porch view of Lake Crescent. The cottages sit side-by-side in a large grassy area adjacent to the main lodge building. These cottages have large interiors with hardwood floors. The bathrooms, with a combination shower-tub, are quite nice. Ten of the cottages are one-bedroom units with 2 queen beds. The 3 two-bedroom cottages with 1 bathroom have 2 queen beds in 1 room and a queen and small refrigerator in the other room. The two-bedroom units provide double the space but don't cost a great deal more than those with 1 bedroom. Singer Tavern Cottages 20 and 21 sit closest to the lake and parking lot but can suffer from the noise of pedestrian traffic as guests walk between the lodge and parking lot or hiking trails. Cottage 5 is nearest to the main lodge and backs up to a parking area.

Three separate buildings house motor lodge rooms. Marymere Lodge is a one-story motel-type, cement-block-and-wood-frame building with 10 rooms that each have large front and back windows. This building was constructed in 1959 and has direct access to the lake. Most rooms have excellent lake views. A covered porch with chairs spans the length of the building's lake side. Each room is relatively large and has 2 queen beds and a tiled bath.

Two-story wood-frame Storm King Motor Lodge, built in 1962, is situated among trees back from the lake, but its 10 rooms each provide relatively good lake views. The rooms are fairly small, and each has a queen bed, balcony or patio with chairs, and private bath with a tiled shower. Two-story Pyramid Mountain Lodge, constructed in 1991, offers the newest accommodations in the complex. This attractive wooden building sits among trees back from the lake. Each of its 10 rooms has a covered balcony or patio that looks out over a grassy area leading to Lake Crescent. The rooms each have 2 queen beds and a tiled bathroom. Rooms on the top floor have vaulted ceilings. A railing across second-floor balconies obscures views when sitting, so try for a ground-floor room if you choose this building.

The 5 second-floor rooms in the main lodge offer the best value if you don't mind using a community bathroom. Lodge rooms are relatively small, but the front windows offer picture-postcard views of one of the country's most beautiful lakes. Plus, there seems to be a more intimate park experience when staying in the main building of a national park lodge. Room 60 at the end of the hallway has 2 windows and is a good choice. Roosevelt Fireplace Cottages are by far the nicest accommodations and worth the extra cost per night compared to Singer Tavern Cottages. Among the motor lodge units we would choose Marymere, that is closest to, and offers the best lake views. In fact, you can view the lake from bed.

A visit to Lake Crescent Lodge will almost certainly be enjoyable no matter which accommodation you choose. A laid-back atmosphere in a picturesque setting makes this one of our favorite places to stay. Arrive early in the afternoon so you can spend time relaxing in an Adirondack chair on the grassy lawn beside the lake. Here you can read a book or visit with friends or other guests while stealing glances at the scenic lake. If you need to expend some energy, rent a rowboat or kayak and view the lodge and surrounding mountains from a different perspective. Or perhaps hike one of the nearby trails and stand in awe of giant Douglas firs that populate the old-growth forest.

Rooms: Doubles, triples, and quads in most units. Some units hold up to 6 persons. All rooms other than those in the main lodge have private bathrooms.

Wheelchair Accessibility: Two rooms in Marymere and one first-floor room at Pyramid Motor Lodge are handicap-accessible.

Reservations: Lake Crescent Lodge, 416 Lake Crescent Rd., Port Angeles, WA 98363-8672. Phone (888) 723-7127; (360) 928-3211. Visit www.olympicnationalparks.com. A deposit of 1 night's stay is required. Cancellation at least 24 hours prior to scheduled arrival is required for a refund less a $25 fee.

Rates: Rates vary depending upon season and occupancy. Historic Lodge rooms ($112–$122); Singer Tavern Cottages: one-room ($232–$245); two-room ($252–$267); Roosevelt Fireplace Cottages: one-room ($262–$282); two-room ($252–$267); Pyramid, Storm King, and Marymere motor lodge units: ($172–$184). Rates quoted are for 2 persons. Additional persons are $15 extra per night. Children under 12 years of age stay free. Special rates and packages are sometimes available on the firm's website.

Location: Twenty-one miles west of Port Angeles, Washington, on US 101.

Lake Crescent Lodge was completed in 1916 and initially called Singer's Lake Crescent Tavern after owner Avery Singer. The current enclosed porch facing the lake was originally part of a long veranda that wrapped around the north and west faces of the building. The gift shop occupies the former dining room. Singer built a row of 16 cabins the same year and subsequently added a row of frame tents that were later converted to cabins. Lodge guests arrived via boat until 1922, when the road from Port Angeles was extended along the south shore of the lake. The sunroom has a photo of the original lodge, which Singer sold in 1927. Lake Crescent Lodge has hosted luminaries such as Henry Ford, Frank Sinatra, William O. Douglas, Robert Kennedy, and, of course, President Franklin D. Roosevelt.

Season: Open early May through the end of the year. Roosevelt Fireplace Cottages are open during winter weekends and require a 2-night minimum stay.

Food: An attractive dining room on the main floor serves breakfast ($8–$15), lunch ($9–$16), and dinner ($13–$32) during the regular season. The lounge serves appetizers, soups, salads, and sandwiches. Alcoholic beverages are available in both the lounge and dining room.

Facilities: Boat and kayak rentals, restaurant, lobby bar, swimming beach, dock, gift shop.

Activities: Swimming, hiking, boating, fishing.

Pets: Pets are allowed only in the Roosevelt and Singer cottages for $25 per pet, per stay. A maximum of two small dogs is permitted.

LAKE QUINAULT LODGE
345 S. Shore Rd. • Quinault, WA 98575 • (360) 288-2900 • www.olympicnationalparks.com

Lake Quinault Lodge as seen from the back lawn

Lake Quinault Lodge is a complex of 6 shake-covered buildings, including a picturesque two-story lodge that houses the registration desk/gift shop, dining room, lobby, indoor heated swimming pool, and men's and women's dry saunas. The lodge has guest rooms on both floors, but the majority are in 5 buildings on either side of the main lodge. The lodge is in a rain forest, on a hill overlooking the south shore of picturesque Lake Quinault. The beautiful setting includes attractive landscaping, several 88-year-old redwood trees, and a wide lawn that flows from the rear of the lodge to the lake. The lodge is in Olympic National Forest, across the lake from Olympic National Park. We have included this lodge because of its proximity to the park and the fact that the same concessionaire operates 3 additional lodges in Olympic National Park.

Lake Quinault Lodge offers 90 rooms in 4 classifications. All rooms have a coffeemaker, hair dryer, heat, and a private bathroom, but no air-conditioning or telephone. Televisions are only in the Lakeside and Fireplace units. None of the buildings have an elevator. The main lodge was constructed in 1926 and has 30 guest rooms that differ in view and configuration, but are generally smaller than rooms in the 5 other buildings. Lodge rooms have ceiling fans and either 1 queen or 2 double beds. About half the rooms offer a lake view and rent for $20 to $50 extra per night compared to rooms on the opposite side that face the road and front drive. Rooms 102, 104, and 106 on the front side have windows that face a nearby roof and offer absolutely no views. Many returning guests request corner rooms 107 or 223, with 2 windows offering excellent views of the lake.

Adjacent to the main lodge, the Boathouse, constructed in 1923 and the only remaining original building, offers 8 rooms on the first floor that vary in size and view. Rooms are paneled in pine and have bedding that ranges from 1 queen to 2 queens plus a twin-size futon. Each room has a private bathroom with a shower but no tub. This rectangular wooden building with rooms on all 4 sides has a large covered porch on 3 sides and is reminiscent of a western bunkhouse. Room 304, with a lake view, is particularly large, with 2 queens, a twin futon, and a table with 4 chairs. The Beverly Suite (room 309) comprising the entire second floor has a large sitting room with a refrigerator and a separate bedroom with a queen bed. A large bathroom has a shower but no tub. The Boathouse has the only guest rooms (excluding the suite) at Lake Quinault Lodge in which pets are permitted. This is a positive if you have a pet, but can be a negative if your neighbor has a barking dog.

At the other end of the main lodge and connected by a covered walkway are 2 side-by-side attractive two-story buildings constructed in 1972 that house 16 Fireplace units. Fireplace units are the most expensive and considered by most guests to be the nicest rooms at Lake Quinault Lodge. The rooms are quite large, and each contains a gas fireplace, television, 1 king bed, and a full bath with a combination shower-tub. Fireplace units each have a large private balcony or patio facing the lake, but views from the first floor of both buildings tend to be obstructed by trees and bushes, giving guests the feeling of being in a private garden. Second-floor rooms 226 through 230 offer outstanding lake views. Try for a second-floor room if you don't mind climbing a flight of stairs. Among ground floor rooms, we like corner room 111, which offers a reasonably good lake view combined with some privacy provided by nearby bushes. Patio chairs can be moved to the surrounding grassy area.

On the far side of the Boathouse are 2 shake-sided modern-style buildings that house 36 Lakeside units. These three-story buildings were constructed in 1990, and guest rooms were refurbished in 2011. Rooms in 1 of the 2 buildings were completely renovated during 2013 and rent for approximately $60 more per night. The rooms are nicely furnished and spacious, although not quite as large as the Fireplace units. Rooms have either 2 queens or a king plus a sofa bed, television, and small private balcony that faces the lake. These units are closest to the lake, although lake views from some rooms are mostly blocked by nearby cedar and fir trees. Rooms 414, 415, and 416 offer the building's best lake views. Some Lakeside rooms have connecting doors. Noise can filter through the closed doors, however, so you may want to avoid rooms with connecting doors if you only require 1 room. Lakeside rooms are entered from an outside walkway on each floor, reached from either a stairway or a series of ramps. Neither Lakeside building has an elevator, so a room on the third floor will require climbing 2 flights of stairs or toting luggage up an extended ramp system.

Lobby in Lake Quinault Lodge

Lake Quinault Lodge's main attraction is its scenic lake setting. The dining room has 2 walls of large windows that offer excellent lake views. The rustic lobby with its hardwood floor, large brick fireplace, comfortable furniture, and windows that overlook the lake, is the focal point of the lodge. It is perfect for reading, playing board games, completing jigsaw puzzles, conversing with friends, or just enjoying the fireplace on a rainy day. A lobby bar sells coffee, espresso, beer, wine, cocktails, and other beverages. When the weather clears, move to a chair on the spacious back porch or lawn. Activities range from games such as badminton and bocce ball, to swimming in the lake or indoor pool, to kayaking. Sporting equipment can be borrowed from the lodge. A 30-minute loop drive around Lake Quinault offers excellent views of the rain forest and the possibility of an elk sighting.

Rooms: Doubles, triples, and quads. A few rooms sleep more than 4. Each room has a private bath, with the majority having a combination shower-tub, although some have either a bathtub or a shower, but not both.

Wheelchair Accessibility: Two first-floor Lakeside rooms are ADA compliant.

Reservations: Lake Quinault Lodge, 345 S. Shore Rd., Quinault, WA 98575-0007. Phone (800) 562-6672 or (360) 288-2900; visit www.olympicnationalparks.com. First night's payment is required. A 24-hour cancellation notice is required for full refund less a $25 cancellation fee.

Rates: Rates vary depending on day, season, and occupancy. Lakeside rooms ($129–$229); Renovated Lakeside rooms ($189–$279); Main Lodge lake view ($129–$249); Main Lodge woodside ($109–$194); Fireplace units ($189–$279); Boathouse lake view ($119–$204); Boathouse woodside ($99–$184); Boathouse suite ($219–$309). Rates quoted are for 2 adults; each additional person is $15. Children under 12 stay free. Rollaways are extra. Check the website for special packages offered throughout the year.

Location: On the south shore of Lake Quinault, 2 miles east of US 101 on South Shore Road.

Season: The lodge is open year-round.

The first log structure to accommodate travelers to Quinault was built in the 1890s. Another facility, Lakeside Inn, was constructed here in 1923. The inn eventually changed its name to The Annex (now the Boathouse) following construction of Lake Quinault Lodge in 1926. Even though lumber, glass, fixtures, and furniture had to be hauled over 50 miles of dirt road, the lodge was completed at a cost of $90,000 in only 53 days. Guests can still view original stenciled designs on the beamed ceiling of the lobby. Lake Quinault Lodge's most famous guest was President Franklin D. Roosevelt, who visited here in 1937, 1 year before signing legislation that created Olympic National Park. He did not stay overnight at the lodge.

Food: The dining room serves breakfast ($8–$14), lunch ($9–$15), and dinner ($15–$32). Reservations are required for dinner. A service bar in the lobby offers drinks and appetizers during the afternoon. A general store across the road (open seasonally) serves hamburgers, pizza, sandwiches, ice cream, and beverages including espresso and milk shakes. It also sells groceries, beer, and wine.

Facilities: Heated indoor pool; men's and women's dry saunas; game room; canoe, kayak, sea cycle, and boat rentals; swimming beach; auditorium; dining room; lobby bar; gift shop; gas station; museum; general store. A US Forest Service visitor center is next door.

Activities: Guided walks, rain forest van tours, canoeing, kayaking, boating, badminton, bocce ball, croquet, horseshoes, and evening programs are popular during summer. Fishing, hiking, swimming, Ping-Pong, and board games are available year-round.

Pets: Pets are allowed only in the Boathouse at $25 per pet, per stay.

Log Cabin Resort

3183 E. Beach Rd. • Port Angeles, WA 98363 • (360) 928-3325 • www.olympicnationalparks.com

Registration building and lodge rooms at Log Cabin Resort

Log Cabin Resort is a complex of freestanding cabins and linked A-frame chalets scattered in front of and alongside a main lodge that houses motel-type rooms. The one-story wooden lodge, constructed in the 1950s, houses the registration desk, restaurant, deli, and small store. Nearly all the cabins and rooms offer excellent views of beautiful Lake Crescent and the mountains on the southern shore. The resort offers 4 types of accommodations. All rooms have electric heat, but no air-conditioning, television, or telephone. No cooking or eating utensils are provided in units with kitchens. The main lodge has 4 attached Lodge rooms that each have 2 queen beds, a private bath with a shower, and a kitchen area with a sink, coffeemaker, microwave, and small refrigerator. Rooms are paneled and have large back windows that provide views of Lake Crescent. A table and 2 chairs are beside the window and a back door opens to a private patio with table and chairs.

West of the lodge along the shoreline are 2 buildings, each with 6 attached A-frame structures called Lakeside Chalets. The first floor has a bathroom with a shower, double bed, futon, kitchen sink, coffeemaker, microwave, and small refrigerator. A second double bed is in the loft reached via a stairway. Back windows allow good lake views. A cement patio across the back of both buildings has a picnic table and grill for each room.

Eight Rustic cabins constructed in 1928, 3 with kitchens, are available in a variety of sizes, with several types of bedding that range upward from a double plus a single bed. The cabins have a private bath with either a shower or tub. Each cabin has a covered front porch with chairs that allow guests a good view of the lake and mountains. Three cabins with kitchens each have a stove, oven, sink, coffeemaker, and refrigerator. Six cabins are arranged in a semicircle on a grassy hillside overlooking the lake. A picnic table is in front of each cabin. The least expensive accommodations are 4 camping log cabins with electricity but no plumbing. Each cabin has 2 double

Log Cabin Resort is on the site of the former Log Hotel (also known as Log Cabin Hotel or Hotel Piedmont), the first hotel built on Lake Crescent. The two-story Log Hotel was constructed of peeled cedar logs and had an attached observation tower built of logs. The hotel burned in 1932, and the present Log Cabin Resort was built in the early 1950s on the same site. A large photo of the old hotel is in the resort lobby.

beds, but guests provide their own bedding or it can be rented. A picnic table and fire barrel are outside each cabin and a community bathroom with showers is nearby.

Log Cabin Resort is a popular choice for families who enjoy water-based activities in a magnificent mountain and lake setting. Guests have plenty to do, with a roped-off lake swimming area just beside the lodge, boat rentals (canoes, paddleboats, kayaks, and rowboats), and fishing. Guests can often be seen reading a book in the grassy area beside the lake. A 4-mile-long trail along an old railroad bed beside the lake passes by the resort. The restaurant has a wall of windows that offers diners excellent lake views. A patio area directly behind the main lodge is available for outside dining.

Rooms: Singles, doubles, triples, and quads. A-frame chalets can hold up to 6 persons.

Wheelchair Accessibility: No wheelchair-accessible rooms are available.

Reservations: 3183 E. Beach Rd., Port Angeles, WA 98363. Phone (888) 896-3818 or (360) 928-3325; visit www.olympicnationalparks.com. A deposit of 1 night's stay is required. Cancellation notice of at least 24 hours is required for a full refund less a $25 fee.

Rates: Rates vary by season and occupancy. Lodge rooms ($122–$127); Lakeside Chalets ($163–$168); Rustic cabins ($94–$99); Rustic cabins with kitchen ($117–$122); Camping log cabins ($66–$71). Rates quoted are for 2 adults. Each additional person is $15 per night, with the exception of the camping cabins, where each additional person is $7. Children 5 years and under stay free.

Location: Eighteen miles west of Port Angeles, Washington, on US 101, 3.5 miles on East Beach Road along the north shore of Lake Crescent.

Season: Mid-May to late Sept.

Food: An attractive restaurant serves a breakfast buffet ($14), lunch ($6–$13), and dinner ($10–$22). Pizza is available for lunch and dinner ($15–$22). Alcoholic beverages are served. A deli serves hot dogs, burgers, fish-and-chips, espresso, other beverages, and ice cream from 11 a.m. to 4 p.m.; microwaveable foods are sold in the store and a microwave is available for use.

Facilities: Swimming beach, boat rental, boat launch, gift shop, limited groceries, laundry, fishing supplies.

Activities: Fishing, hiking, boating, swimming.

Pets: Pets are allowed in the cabins with a $25 fee per pet, per stay.

SOL DUC HOT SPRINGS RESORT

12076 Sol Duc Hot Springs Rd. • Port Angeles, WA 98363
(866) 476-5382 • www.olympicnationalparks.com

Sol Duc (a Quileute term meaning "sparkling water") Hot Springs Resort includes a single two-story lodge constructed in the 1980s and 29 modern wooden buildings with guest rooms. The former owner's home (the River Suite) is available for group rental. No overnight accommodations are in the main lodge, which houses the registration desk, small lobby, gift shop, small convenience store, and restaurant. The resort is known primarily for more than 20 hot mineral springs that feed 3 pools located immediately behind the lodge. A large swimming pool is in the same complex. The resort is situated in the Sol Duc River Valley, surrounded by the heavily treed mountains of Olympic National Park.

The resort offers 32 cabins plus 1 suite. Twenty-six cabins are freestanding, while the other 6 are in 3 duplex buildings immediately beside the lodge. The freestanding cabins are clustered about a grassy lawn with porch swings and picnic tables. The cabins are in 2 categories; those with a kitchen and those without. Except for kitchens and bedding, all the cabins are virtually identical, with finished interior walls, carpeted floors, electric heat, table and chairs, a full bathroom with a combination shower-tub, hair dryer, and coffeemaker. None of the cabins have a telephone, air-conditioning, or television. Bedding ranges from 1 king to 2 queens and cabins without a kitchen include a twin-size sofa bed. Interiors are similar to, but perhaps a little larger than, most motel rooms. Three duplex units and 5 freestanding cabins with a kitchen are each furnished with a sink, microwave, full-size refrigerator, stove, oven, toaster, pans, dishes, and eating utensils. These units rent for about $35 per night more than cabins without a kitchen. Parking is near each of the cabins, so handling luggage isn't

Cabins at Sol Duc Hot Springs Resort

a problem. The River Suite, a three-bedroom house with 2 baths, full kitchen, living room, dining room, family room, sunroom, and a deck overlooking the river, is available for group rental. All of the living space is on the second floor.

People generally visit Sol Duc to enjoy the natural hot springs that have made this area a popular tourist destination for nearly 100 years. The resort has 3 circular pools of hot mineral water and a regular heated swimming pool, all located immediately behind the main lodge. The largest hot-water pool and a small shallow pool for children each have mineral water at a temperature of 99° to 101° Fahrenheit. Another small pool has mineral water at a temperature of 104° Fahrenheit. These pools are relatively shallow and designed for sitting, not swimming. A larger swimming pool has heated regular water, rather than mineral water. The larger mineral water pool and the swimming pool have ramps for wheelchair access. Guests have free use of

the pools; other visitors can use the facilities for a fee.

Sol Duc Hot Springs Resort is a place to unwind. You can hike in the morning on one of the hiking trails near the resort that lead into the rain forest and to beautiful Sol Duc Falls, soak in a mineral water pool after lunch, get a professional massage in the late afternoon, take a nap in your cabin, and then walk to the lodge for supper.

According to Quileute legend, dragon tears are the source of the hot springs at Sol Duc. Whether dragon tears or natural phenomena, the hot springs have drawn people to this area for many years. In the early 1900s the springs were claimed by Theodore Moritz, who said the hot mineral water helped him recuperate from an injury in the woods. In the early 1920s the third owner of this property built 2 pools, a 50-by-150-foot freshwater pool without heat and a 50-by-60-foot hot springs pool. The sides of these pools were knocked out in 1984 and replaced by the 4 pools currently in use.

A restaurant in the main lodge serves breakfast and dinner, while lunch is available at a deli beside the pool. If your cabin includes a kitchen, you may prefer to fix a meal and eat on your front porch or at one of several picnic tables scattered about the lawn. Evening programs are occasionally offered by rangers at the nearby National Park Service campground. After that it's time for a good night's sleep so you can start all over again the next morning.

Rooms: Doubles, triples, and quads. The River Suite with 2 full bathrooms can sleep a maximum of 14 people.

Wheelchair Accessibility: Three freestanding cabins, 1 with a kitchen, are ADA compliant. Wheelchair access is available to 1 hot mineral pool and the freshwater pool. Wheelchairs are available for loan.

Reservations: Sol Duc Hot Springs Resort, 12076 Sol Duc Hot Springs Rd., Port Angeles, WA 98363. Phone (866) 476-5382. A deposit of 1 night's stay is required. A cancellation notice of 72 hours is required for a full refund less a $25 fee.

Rates: Rates vary depending on day of the week and season. Cabin without kitchen ($153–$173); cabins with kitchen ($190–$210); River Suite ($353–$373). Rates quoted are for 2 persons except for the suite, which is quoted for 4 persons. Each additional person is $23 per night. Children under 4 years of age stay free. Children 4 to 11 years of age are each an extra $9. Special rates and packages are sometimes available on the firm's website.

Location: Twelve miles southeast of US 101. The resort is in the northern part of Olympic National Park, 42 miles from Port Angeles, Washington.

Season: Late Mar to mid-Oct.

The first hotel at Sol Duc Springs was opened in 1912. The elaborate hotel, constructed by a man who claimed the mineral springs had cured him of a fatal illness, included tennis courts, bowling alleys, golf links, a theater, and a three-story sanatorium with beds for 100 patients. Unfortunately, sparks from the fireplace ignited the shingle roof and burned down the hotel only 4 years after its completion. According to legend, the fire short-circuited the hotel's wiring, causing the organ to begin playing Beethoven's "Funeral March" while the building was burning.

Food: A restaurant in the main lodge building serves a breakfast ($9–$15) and dinner ($12–$32). Beer and wine are available. Sandwiches and beverages are available at the poolside deli from 11 a.m. to 4 p.m. during summer. A few groceries, beer, and wine are sold near the registration desk.

Facilities: Heated swimming pool, hot mineral pools, restaurant, deli, gift shop, convenience store, and licensed massage practitioners.

Activities: Swimming, hiking, fishing, and soaking in mineral water. Occasional evening National Park Service programs.

Pets: Pets are allowed in the cabins for $25 per pet, per stay. Pets are not allowed in the pool area or on the trails.

Grand Teton National Park/John D. Rockefeller Jr. Memorial Parkway

PO Drawer 170 • Moose, WY 83012 • (307) 739-3300 • www.nps/gov/grte • www.nps.gov/jodr

Grand Teton National Park covers nearly 310,000 acres including the famous Teton Range, considered by many to be America's most beautiful mountain range. The park's 3 visitor centers are at Moose, Jenny Lake, and Colter Bay. A visitor center jointly operated by the US Forest Service and the City of Jackson is at the north end of Jackson. The 24,000-acre John D. Rockefeller Jr. Memorial Parkway is a 7.5-mile corridor linking the south entrance of Yellowstone National Park with the north entrance to Grand Teton National Park. The Snake River flows through both parks and offers excellent float trips. The parks are in northwestern Wyoming, directly south of Yellowstone National Park.

Park Entrance Fee: $25 per vehicle, $20 per motorcycle, or $12 per person, good for 7 days. This fee also covers Yellowstone National Park.

Lodging in Grand Teton National Park: Grand Teton National Park and the John D. Rockefeller Jr. Memorial Parkway have 7 lodging facilities. Headwaters Lodge & Cabins at Flagg Ranch is the only

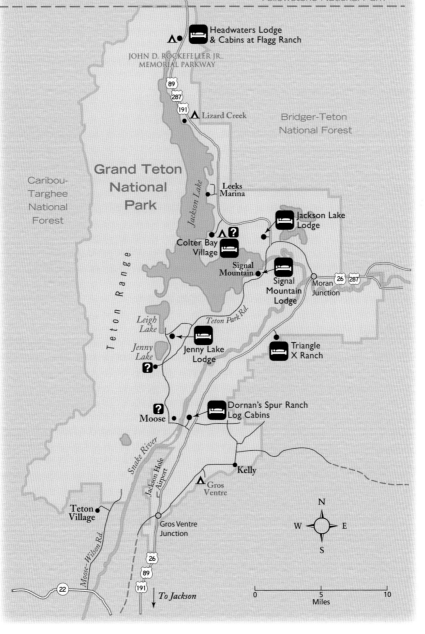

GRAND TETON NATIONAL PARK /
JOHN D. ROCKEFELLER JR. MEMORIAL PARKWAY

Yellowstone National Park

Headwaters Lodge
& Cabins at Flagg Ranch

JOHN D. ROCKEFELLER JR.
MEMORIAL PARKWAY

89
287
191

Lizard Creek

Bridger-Teton
National Forest

Grand Teton
National
Park

Caribou-
Targhee
National
Forest

Jackson Lake

Leeks
Marina

Jackson Lake
Lodge

Colter Bay
Village

Signal
Mountain

Signal
Mountain
Lodge

Moran
Junction

26 287

Teton Range

*Leigh
Lake*

Teton Park Rd.

*Jenny
Lake*

Jenny Lake
Lodge

Triangle
X Ranch

Moose

Dornan's Spur Ranch
Log Cabins

Snake River

Jackson Hole Airport

Kelly

Gros
Ventre

Teton
Village

Gros Ventre
Junction

N
W   E
S

26
89
191

To Jackson

0   5   10
Miles

22

lodge in the parkway. Triangle X Ranch, the only working dude ranch in a national park, is the most unusual lodging facility in the park—maybe in any park. The least expensive facilities are at Colter Bay. The view rooms at Jackson Lake Lodge are some of the most upscale accommodations. Signal Mountain Lodge also offers its guests excellent mountain views. Jenny Lake Lodge, with a 4-diamond rating, is a quaint facility but quite expensive, even considering that horseback riding, bicycles, breakfast, and a 5-course dinner are included in the price. Dornan's is a private facility offering very nice cabins in a quiet area near Moose.

COLTER BAY VILLAGE
PO Box 240 • Moran, WY 83013 • (307) 543-3100 • www.gtlc.com

Colter Bay Village, a major recreation center for Grand Teton National Park, includes a grocery store, gift and tackle shop, Laundromat, 2 restaurants, National Park Service visitor center, marina, and a gas station. The lodging facility at Colter Bay consists of 166 rooms in log cabins plus 66 tent cabins. A small cabin rental office handles registration for the log cabins, while a separate office farther down the road takes care of registration for the tent cabins. The 2 types of accommodations are in separate areas, but both are near the restaurants and other facilities.

Colter Bay has 2 very different types of accommodations. The least expensive lodging is in 66 tent cabins. This lodging is about as basic as you will find outside your own tent. The tent cabins are constructed from 2 canvas walls and a canvas roof connected to 2 log walls. The cabins each contain a woodstove (wood is not provided but can be purchased), electric lighting, and 2 sets of bunk beds with thin vinyl-covered mattresses. A picnic table is on a canvas-covered porch just outside the front door. Guests are responsible for everything else, including sheets, blankets, pillows, and utensils. Sleeping bags, cots, blankets, and pillows can be rented at the registration office. Two restroom facilities without showers are in the immediate area. Showers (fee) are available at a nearby laundry facility. The tent cabins are on a hill and offer views of

Cabins at Colter Bay Village

pine trees, and a few sites have limited views of the Tetons.

Colter Bay also has 166 log cabins clustered on a hillside of pine trees, grass, wildflowers, and weeds along paved roads behind the commercial center. All cabins have electric heat and, other than 2 semiprivate dorm units, a private bath with a shower. They do not have a telephone, television, or air-conditioning. The well-maintained cabins are of varying size and age, with vaulted log-beamed ceilings, attractive log or wood interiors, and linoleum floors.

Most one-room cabins are constructed as duplex units, although a few are freestanding, and 1 particularly long building includes 6 cabins. Only a few cabins have a front porch. Bedding ranges from 1 double to 2 doubles plus a single. Cabins 637 and 639 are each freestanding with a nice porch overhang. Cabin 212, with floor to ceiling windows on 1 wall, was once an artist's studio and is the most unusual cabin at Colter Bay. One-room cabin 471 was constructed more than 100 years ago and is the oldest cabin in the complex.

Forty-two cabins each have 2 rooms, most with a bedroom on each side of a common bathroom. Most two-room cabins are freestanding with a very small front porch. About half have a double bed in 1 room and 2 twin beds in the other room. Units 617 and 810 in this group sit on a hill and offer more privacy than most other cabins, although staying in either unit will involve some climbing. The other two-room cabins are a little larger, have 2 double beds in each room, and are priced somewhat higher, but the price includes up to 4 adults. Cabins 1031, 1035, 1039, 1043, and 1055 in this group are particularly desirable because they are on a dead-end road and back up to a wooded area.

Two log buildings in the cabin area offer 9 rooms without private baths. These semiprivate dorm rooms are nice, but occupants must use a community bathroom. Four units in 1 building each have 2 twin beds and 2 hallway bathrooms. Five units in a nearby building behind the restaurant are smaller, with 1 double bed. Bathrooms here must be entered from the outside. The building with twin-bed units is far more desirable because of bigger rooms (especially rooms 460 and 466), an inside bathroom, and a quieter location. A guest lounge with couches, chairs, and game tables is next door. The major drawback is that these buildings have no insulation, so guests are likely to hear conversations in adjacent rooms.

Colter Bay Village offers some of the least expensive lodging in Grand Teton National Park.

Although the main village area, with a marina, restaurants, gift shops, grocery store, laundry facility with showers (fee), and the National Park Service visitor center, is generally bustling with people and vehicles, the lodging is far enough away to escape most of the noise and congestion. At the same time, it is close enough that guests can easily avail themselves of the facilities. If you don't mind a room without a private bath, the semiprivate dorm rooms are by far the best value, at about half the price you will pay for the smallest cabin and about $20 more than a tent cabin, where you must supply your own bedding and pay for a shower that is some distance away. Colter Bay Village offers a variety of activities, including horseback riding, raft trips, fishing, lake cruises, and boating. Walking down to the lakeshore in the early evening is one of the pleasurable experiences of staying here. A pool at Jackson Lake Lodge is available to Colter Bay guests.

Most buildings at Colter Bay Village were moved here from other locations around the Jackson Hole area. At one time Jackson Hole had many small dude ranches and tourist resorts, typically consisting of a central lodge building and 5 to 30 log cabins. After Grand Teton National Park was expanded in 1950 with a gift of 34,000 acres from John D. Rockefeller, Jr., most of the old lodges were closed and many of the cabins were moved via flatbed truck to Colter Bay, where the cabins were modernized with new roofs, electricity, and plumbing. In fact the existing Colter Bay cabin office was once the old store at Square G Ranch located just north of Jenny Lake. The ranch also supplied many of Colter Bay's cabins. Other cabins came from the old Teton Lodge at Moran, the old Jackson Lake Lodge, and the Circle H Guest Ranch. Cabins from several other old resorts were moved to Colter Bay during the 1960s. A written history of each cabin is framed and posted inside the cabin. Guests may ask the front desk for a keepsake history of the cabin in which they stayed.

Rooms: Doubles, triples, and quads. A few two-bedroom units can accommodate up to 10 persons. All but tent cabins and semiprivate dorm cabins have a private bath.

Wheelchair Accessibility: Three wheelchair-accessible cabins with asphalt paths to the doorway are ADA compliant.

Reservations: Grand Teton Lodge Company, PO Box 240, Moran, WY 83013. Phone (800) 628-9988, (307) 543-3100; or visit www.gtlc.com. A deposit of 1 night's stay is required. A cancellation notice of 3 days is required for a refund less a $15 fee.

Rates: Tent cabins ($59); semiprivate dorm cabins ($77); one-room cabins ($141–$185); two-room cabins ($206–$239). Rates quoted are for 2 persons with the exception of the larger two-room cabins, where rates are quoted for 4 adults. Each additional person is $6 per night in tent cabins, $10 per night in log cabins. Children 11 and under stay free with an adult.

Location: North section of Grand Teton National Park, 40 miles north of Jackson, Wyoming.

Season: Late May to late Sept for log cabins. Late May to early Sept for tent cabins.

Food: Colter Bay has 2 eating establishments. The Ranch House Restaurant serves breakfast ($6–$15), lunch ($10–$13), and dinner ($12–$22). The Cafe Court serves salads, sandwiches, and wraps ($6–$10). A grocery store in the village sells bakery items, deli sandwiches, and ice cream in addition to a fairly extensive line of groceries, beer, and wine. The concessionaire also offers meals as part of boat cruises, raft trips, and wagon rides. Inquire at the lodge reservation desk about tickets.

Facilities: Restaurant, food court, grocery store, gift shop, tackle shop, stables, marina, boat rental, service station, Laundromat, National Park Service visitor center with museum and gift shop.

Activities: Hiking, fishing, guided fly-fishing, boating, boat cruises, horseback riding, float trips, bus tours to Yellowstone National Park and through Grand Teton National Park, ranger/naturalist talks and walks during the day, evening campfire programs. The swimming pool at Jackson Lake Lodge is available to registered guests from Colter Bay Village.

Pets: Pets are allowed in some cabins at a fee of $15 per night.

Dornan's Spur Ranch Log Cabins
PO Box 39 • Moose, WY 83012 • (307) 733-2522 • www.dornans.com

Dornan's Spur Ranch is a complex of 1 ranch house plus 12 modern cabins constructed in 6 log duplex buildings clustered in a courtyard of grass and wildflowers. The ranch house, cabins and registration building are down a hill from a small but busy commercial center that includes a grocery, bar and pasta restaurant, gift shop, sporting goods store, wine shop, gasoline pumps, and chuckwagon restaurant. The hill protects lodging guests from the noise of people and vehicles visiting the commercial area. The development rests in a scenic basin next to the Snake River. Parking is beside the registration building and a short distance from the cabins. Two-wheel

Cabin area at Dornan's Spur Ranch

carts kept near the registration building allow guests to transport luggage along walkways leading to each cabin. The ranch house and cabins sit on a portion of a little less than 10 acres of Dornan family land surrounded by Grand Teton National Park. Dornan's is located near the south end of the park, at Moose Junction.

The ranch house, with 3 bedrooms and 2½ bathrooms, sits beside the Snake River with great mountain views. It has a living room, dining room, full kitchen, screened porch, and a patio with a barbecue grill. The house has a washer and dryer and can accommodate up to six people.

The 12 modern log cabins, constructed in 1992, are well maintained both inside and out. Each cabin has a combination living room–kitchen, a full bathroom with a combination shower-tub, and either 1 or 2 bedrooms. The kitchen has a table and 4 chairs. Bedrooms have 1 queen bed with a down comforter, and the living room includes a sofa bed. A door off the living room leads to a small covered wooden deck with table and chairs. A charcoal grill (but

no charcoal) is beside each porch. The cabins sit near the famous Snake River and have been sited so most decks offer a view of the Tetons. One duplex unit houses Cascade and Garnet, 2 one-bedroom cabins that are next to the river and provide excellent mountain views. Larkspur, a two-bedroom unit, has a patio that faces the river.

Although the cabins are duplex units, we experienced minimal noise from our neighbors. The cabins are roomy with hardwood floors in the living room–kitchen, nice tile in the bathroom, and fully carpeted bedrooms. The kitchen is equipped with a full-size refrigerator, stove, oven, coffeemaker, toaster, dishes, and all utensils. All you need to bring is the food, or you can stroll up the hill to the grocery and purchase some nice sirloins and that special bottle of wine. All this makes for a very pleasant stay.

Dornan's cabins are among this area's nicest accommodations. The food is good, the people are nice, and the scenery is magnificent. Enjoy breakfast while sipping a cup of coffee and taking in the mountain views from your deck. If you are around at noon, walk up the hill and select from a variety of sandwiches at the deli. In the evening enjoy an all-you-can-eat outdoor western dinner after knocking back a cold one from the outdoor deck connected to the bar. A short path beside the bar leads to the historic landing of Menor's Ferry, where the National Park Service offers rides across the Snake River to the house of a former homesteader. One evening after dinner we walked to the landing and exchanged greetings with rafters and kayakers as they floated the Snake.

The land on which Dornan's now welcomes travelers is a little less than half the 20 acres Evelyn Dornan homesteaded in the early 1920s. Evelyn, a divorcee who was born and raised in Philadelphia, first visited Jackson Hole in 1918 with her 16-year-old son, Jack. In the 1930s, Jack developed a portion of the property into a dude ranch that was deeded to him in 1941 by his mother. Evelyn, who lived to be 83, sold her remaining 10 acres to the National Park Service in 1952. Although the park service attempted to purchase the remaining acreage, Evelyn's strong-willed son stood his ground and, with wife Ellen, continued to operate Dornan's until their retirement in 1972, when the business passed to their sons.

Rooms: One-bedroom cabins can accommodate up to 4 persons. Two-bedroom units hold up to 6. All cabins have a full bath and full kitchen. The ranch house can accommodate up to six adults.

Wheelchair Accessibility: One cabin is wheelchair accessible.

Reservations: Dornan's Spur Ranch Log Cabins, PO Box 39, Moose, WY 83012. Phone (307) 733-2522. A deposit of 3 nights' stay is required during high season, and a deposit of 1 night's stay is required for low season. All cancellations result in a $50 charge plus forfeit of deposit if received less than 30 days prior to arrival. The owner requests a minimum 6-night stay and 50 percent deposit for the ranch house.

Rates: Rates are seasonal. High-season rates apply mid-May to mid-Oct and Christmas through New Year's Day with a 3-night minimum: one-bedroom cabin with 1 to 2 persons ($185), with 3 to 4 persons ($215); two-bedroom cabin with up to 6 persons ($265). Low-season rates for mid-Oct to mid-May with a 1-night minimum: one-bedroom cabin with 1 to 2 persons ($125); with 3 to 4 persons ($150); two-bedroom cabin with up to 6 persons ($175). The ranch house is $395 per night.

Location: South end of Grand Teton National Park, at Moose Junction. The cabins are 12 miles north of Jackson, Wyoming.

Season: Open year-round.

Food: A chuckwagon outdoor restaurant serves breakfast ($10), lunch ($8–$12), and all-you-can-eat dinner ($17–$20) Mon, Tues, Wed, and Sun only, prime rib or 12-ounce steak ($25) during summer. A bar/restaurant serves salads, pizza, and pasta for lunch and dinner (hours vary); inside and outside seating are available for both the chuckwagon restaurant and the bar/restaurant. Groceries are available at the store.

Facilities: Grocery; bar/restaurant; wine store; outdoor restaurant; gift shop; fly-fishing store; gas station; and a sports shop with sporting equipment and bicycle, canoe, and kayak rentals. A National Park Service visitor center is nearby.

Activities: Hiking, fishing, scenic and whitewater float trips on the Snake River, canoeing, kayaking, mountain biking. Winter activities include cross-country skiing, downhill skiing, and snowmobiling.

Cabin at Headwaters Lodge & Cabins at Flagg Ranch

Headwaters Lodge & Cabins at Flagg Ranch encompasses a modern log-style main lodge, 92 nearby modern log cabin rooms, a service station, and a campground with hookups. Cabin registration is just inside the front door of the lodge, which itself has no guest accommodations. The lodge is quite attractive, with a small lobby separated from the dining room by a large double-sided stone fireplace. In addition to the dining room and lobby, the lodge houses a gift shop, tour desk, small grocery, lounge, and front desk. Thirty wooden buildings constructed in 1995 with metal roofs and log-style exteriors house 92 cabin-style rooms. The cabin complex sits on a bluff overlooking the Snake River Valley approximately a quarter mile from the lodge. The river itself is visible from only a few of the cabin patios. The buildings, constructed as either duplexes or quads, are clustered in a natural

setting of rocks, dirt, weeds, grass, and wildflowers. The cabins are insulated and nicely spaced, so you are unlikely to be bothered by noise from guests in an adjoining cabin. A series of cement walkways lead from the parking area, where 2-wheeled luggage carts are kept. The cabins are far enough from the lodge and restaurant that many guests drive between the 2 locations.

All the cabins are rented in 1 of 3 classifications: Standard, Deluxe, or Premium. All 92 cabins are the same size, with some having 1 king bed and others 2 queen beds. All Standard cabins have two queens. Each cabin has a private bathroom with a combination shower-tub (with the exception of 4 wheelchair-accessible cabins), gas heat, a vaulted ceiling, and a finished interior similar to that found in a large and nicely furnished motel room. Each cabin also has a coffeemaker and telephone. None of the rooms have air-conditioning, television, or a kitchenette. Cabins have a covered cement patio with rocking chairs.

Premium cabins rent for nearly $100 per night more than the Standard cabins and are in the back of the complex nearest the bluff and most distant from the parking area. Premium cabins each have a sliding glass door and patio facing the Snake River Valley. Deluxe cabins are in the middle of the complex and, like the Premium cabins, have been recently renovated and include a mini-fridge and microwave. Standard cabins are nearest the parking lot but most distant from the Snake River Valley.

The cabins at Headwater Lodge are modern, clean, and comfortable. When choosing a cabin keep in mind that those with a view are most distant from the parking lot, but with the availability of luggage carts, the difference in distance isn't really a problem if you don't mind a modest walk from your vehicle. We enjoyed sitting on the patio of one of the Premium cabins, reading a book, and being able to see the beauty of the Wyoming landscape uninterrupted by other cabins. Whether this is worth the extra cost is something you and your bank account must decide. A trail behind the cabins leads along the edge of the bluff and down to the Snake River.

Headwaters Lodge & Cabins at Flagg Ranch offers modern, comfortable lodging at a convenient location between Yellowstone and Grand Teton National Parks. The cabins are relatively large, and the lodge has an attractive western decor. Several activities are available for guests, including interpretive tours to Yellowstone and Grand Teton National Parks, guided trail rides, scenic float trips, and whitewater rafting trips. The road between the town of Jackson and Headwaters Lodge is open during winter months, although the lodge is open only from mid-Dec through early Mar. Snowmobile and snowcoach tours of the area stop at the lodge. Snowcoaches from Yellowstone provide transportation between the lodge and the Old Faithful area, where Old Faithful Snow Lodge is open during winter months.

Rooms: Doubles, triples, and quads. All rooms have a private bath with a combination shower-tub.

Wheelchair Accessibility: Two Standard and 2 Deluxe cabins nearest the parking area are ADA compliant.

Reservations: Headwaters Lodge & Cabins at Flagg Ranch, PO Box 187, Moran, WY 83013. Phone (800) 443-2311 or (307) 543-2861; or visit www.gtlc.com. A deposit of 1 night's stay (or 2 nights' stay for multiple nights) is required. A cancellation notice of 7 days is required for a full refund, less a $30 cancellation fee.

Rates: Standard ($190), Deluxe ($235), Premium ($275). Rates quoted are for 2 adults. Each additional person is $11 per night. Children 11 and under stay free.

Location: North end of John D. Rockefeller Jr. Memorial Parkway, 2 miles south of the south entrance to Yellowstone National Park.

Headwaters Lodge & Cabins at Flagg Ranch is in a location believed to have been a favorite camping spot for both native tribes and fur trappers. The ranch was established between 1910 and 1916 at its present location by an early guide and pioneer in this area and is the oldest continuously operating resort in the upper Jackson Hole area. It has served as both a dude ranch and a lodging facility, offering overnight accommodations to early trappers and present-day travelers. The ranch name is derived from the flag that flew from the Snake River Military Station, once located here.

Season: Summer from June through Sept; winter from mid-Dec through early Mar.

Food: A full-service restaurant offers breakfast ($7–$12), lunch ($9–$20), and dinner ($11–$32). Alcoholic beverages are served in the dining room. A cocktail lounge adjacent to the dining room serves burgers, sandwiches, and appetizers. Groceries are available at a small store in the lodge.

Facilities: Restaurant, cocktail lounge, gift shop, grocery store, gas station, coin laundry, small National Park Service visitor center.

Activities: Hiking, whitewater rafting, float trips, trail rides, guided fishing trips, interpretive tours to Yellowstone National Park and Grand Teton National Park. Winter activities include cross-country skiing although the lodge does not rent skis. Tours on snowmobiles and in snowcoaches are offered by Scenic Safaris; phone (888) 734-8898 or visit www.scenicsafaris.com.

Pets: Pets are permitted only in the Standard cabins at an additional fee of $17 per day, per pet.

JACKSON LAKE LODGE
Grand Teton Lodge Company • PO Box 240 • Moran, WY 83013 • (307) 543-3100 • www.gtlc.com

Jackson Lake Lodge includes a very large central lodge flanked by numerous multiple-unit cottage units partially hidden by surrounding trees. Guest rooms are also on the third floor of the lodge. The three-story concrete lodge rests on a bluff overlooking a large willow meadow and Jackson Lake, both of which are highlighted by the spectacular Teton Mountain Range. The lodge has a large second-floor lobby with 2 corner fireplaces, many comfortable chairs and sofas, Native American artifacts scattered throughout, and a two-story wall of windows offering a picture-perfect view of the Tetons. The lodge also has a dining room, grill, cocktail lounge, gift shop, apparel shop featuring fine western and adventure wear, and T-shirt shop—all on the second floor; an art gallery on the third-floor balcony has tables and chairs and the same great view. A large parking lot is just behind the lodge, and plentiful parking is near each of the cottages. Arriving guests can use the entrance drive to register and, for guests who will be staying in the lodge, drop off luggage. An elevator is in the lodge.

The back side of Jackson Lake Lodge

Jackson Lake Lodge offers 4 types of rooms: View lodge rooms and cottages, Nonview lodge rooms and cottages, Nonview Patio cottages, and Suites. All rooms have heat, telephone, hair dryer, coffeemaker, ceiling fan, and a private bath, but no television or air-conditioning. Cottages comprise the vast majority of the 385 rooms at the Jackson Lake complex. Thirty-seven rooms in the main lodge, all on the third floor, are similar except for the view. Rooms on the west side of the building, with large windows that provide great views of the Tetons, cost nearly $100 more per night than rooms on the east side. The more costly View rooms also have a small refrigerator, wet bar, and down comforters on the beds. All rooms in the lodge have 2 queen beds and are quite large and attractively decorated, but none have a balcony. The main lodge has a Suite with 2 bathrooms including a whirlpool bathtub, a living/dining area furnished with a kitchenette and full-size refrigerator, and a separate bedroom with 1 king bed. The Suite offers a panoramic view of the mountains.

The 347 cottages each have either 2 queens or a king bed (patio units), comfortable furniture, and a full bath. Cottages are quite roomy (bigger than rooms in the main lodge) and attractively decorated. Most have a vaulted beamed ceiling and are considerably nicer than a typical motel room. Most cottages are in a series of one-story wood-frame buildings of 8 to 20 rooms that back up to one another. The buildings are in a nicely landscaped area with lots of vegetation including fir and aspen trees. Many cottages have a front porch but do not offer a mountain or lake view. One two-story and 5 one-story buildings offer cottages with a king bed, a private back patio or balcony, and rent for $10 extra per night. Cottages 123 and 125 in this category each have a patio that offers a partial view of the Tetons. Three two-story cottage buildings house 46 View cottages that have 2 doubles or a king bed, small refrigerator, and a great view of the Tetons. Rooms on the second floor each have a balcony and a vaulted ceiling, while first-floor rooms have a regular ceiling and a back patio fronted by a small grassy area. Other than 3 corner Suites in 1 building, these are the premier cottage units. Three Suites in one of the two-story

view buildings each have a double-size room, full kitchen, living area, and a king bed. Suite 911 has a wraparound balcony. There are no elevators in the two-story cottage buildings.

Staying in a Nonview room in the lodge allows you to enjoy a great view of the Tetons by walking down 1 flight of stairs (an elevator is available) to the second-floor lobby. If you want to splurge for a room with a view, we suggest choosing one of the View cottages, which have a private balcony or patio facing the mountains. One of the great pleasures of staying in these units is sitting on your back patio or balcony and enjoying the magnificent panorama of Jackson Lake against a background of the Tetons. The View cottages each have a large back window that allows a similar view. The back patio or balcony, along with the ease of getting your luggage into the room, makes these a better choice than View rooms in the lodge.

Jackson Lake Lodge is a place to enjoy spectacular scenery and abundant wildlife. The highlight of a visit is sitting in the upstairs lobby and looking out enormous windows at America's most beautiful mountain range. All rooms in the complex are relatively large and comfortable. Several choices are available for dining, and the main dining room on the second floor has large western-theme murals and large windows with views that rival those of the lobby. The cocktail lounge, on the opposite side of the lobby from the dining room, has 2 walls of windows with views of the Tetons. The lodge offers more stores than are typically found in a national park lodge. A variety of activities are available, including swimming in a heated pool, horseback riding, float trips, and narrated bus tours of Grand Teton and Yellowstone National Parks.

Rooms: Doubles, triples, and quads. All rooms have a private bath.

Wheelchair Accessibility: In the lodge, 1 Nonview and 1 View room are ADA compliant. An elevator operates from the registration area on the lower floor to the third floor, where lodge rooms are located. Eighteen cottage units, both View and Nonview, are ADA compliant.

Reservations: Grand Teton Lodge Company, PO Box 240, Moran, WY 83013. Phone (800) 628-9988, (307) 543-3100; or visit www.gtlc .com. Main lodge rooms and suites can only be reserved by phone. If staying 2 or more nights, a 2-night deposit is required. A 7-day cancellation is required for deposit refund less a $30 fee.

Rates: Nonview lodge rooms and cottages ($259); Nonview cottages with patios ($269); View ($325–$355); Suites ($705–$845). Rates quoted are for 2 persons. Each additional person is $11 per night. Children 11 and under stay free.

Location: Jackson Lake Lodge is located on the eastern shore of Jackson Lake, 5 miles northwest of Moran Junction, about 24 miles north of the town of Moose.

Season: Mid-May through early Oct.

Food: The main dining room serves a breakfast buffet ($16), breakfast menu ($6–$14), lunch ($11–$19), and dinner ($20–$43). Next door, the Pioneer Grill, with U-shaped counters, serves breakfast ($5–$10), lunch/dinner ($6–$23). A

The Amoretti Inn, the original lodge constructed in 1922 at this site, included a main lodge building and 30 cabins. The lodge, which stood near where the 900 building of the current lodge is located, boasted of indoor plumbing in its log cabins. The name was changed to Jackson Lake Lodge in the late 1920s. The old lodge continued to provide overnight rooms until the new Jackson Lake Lodge was completed in June 1955. The current lodge was designed by Gilbert Stanley Underwood, who also designed Yosemite National Park's Ahwahnee. The old cabins were moved to Colter Bay, where they were renovated and remain in use.

pool grill with sandwiches, pizza, and ice cream is open for lunch during July and Aug. An all-you-can-eat barbecue ($23) is offered Sun through Fri evenings, weather permitting. Soups, salads, sandwiches, and appetizers are available in the lounge. A cappuccino/espresso cart is open during the morning hours in the lobby.

Facilities: Dining room, grill, cocktail lounge, gift shops, apparel shop, newsstand, tour desk, outdoor heated swimming pool, service station, stable, medical clinic, conference facilities.

Activities: Horseback riding, swimming, Snake River float trips, hiking, evening ranger/naturalist programs, boat cruises on Jackson Lake, narrated bus tours to Yellowstone National Park and through Grand Teton National Park.

Pets: Pets are allowed in some cottages with a fee of $17 per night.

JENNY LAKE LODGE

PO Box 240 • Moran, WY 83013 • (307) 733-4647 • www.gtlc.com

Jenny Lake Lodge features a main log lodge plus 37 log cabins. The complex is at the base of the Tetons, near beautiful Jenny Lake. The main building, with hardwood floors and vaulted ceilings, houses the registration desk, dining room, and a cozy lobby with comfortable furniture and

Cabin at Jenny Lake Lodge

a large stone fireplace. Lobby and some dining room windows provide good mountain views. A wooden front deck has chairs and benches that face the mountains. A few cabins are freestanding, but most are duplex units. The cabins are nicely spaced in an area of pine trees. The facility is quaint, quiet, well maintained, and expensive. Unlike at most national park facilities, the rates here include breakfast, a 5-course dinner, the use of bicycles, and, for those so inclined, horseback riding on a first-come, first-served basis. Lunch is available for an extra charge. Jenny Lake Lodge has been awarded 4 diamonds by the American Automobile Association, indicating that it is one of the more upscale lodging units in the United States, let alone a national park. Each cabin is named for a wildflower, beds are covered with handmade quilts and down comforters, and robes are provided in each cabin.

Two types of accommodations are available. Each cabin has a log-beamed vaulted ceiling, hardwood floors, heat, ceiling fan, small refrigerator, coffeemaker, hair dryer, telephone, and a private bath with a combination shower-tub, but no air-conditioning or television. Thirty-one 1-room cabins vary somewhat in decor, view, and bed configuration, which ranges from 1 queen bed, to a queen plus a twin, to 1 king bed. Each cabin has a covered front porch with 2 rocking chairs. Some cabins face the mountain range and offer good views from the front porch. Six cabins designated as Suites each have a woodstove (wood provided) and sofa bed in the sitting area or living room and an in-wall safe. Five have 2 rooms, a living room, and a bedroom. One Suite consists of 1 very large room with a whirlpool tub and a large private patio. The Suites have either a king or 2 queen beds.

At Jenny Lake Lodge guests enjoy the sights and activities of Grand Teton National Park in luxury. You can relax, hike, bike, and sightsee while staying at the national park lodge that is nearest to the beautiful Tetons. The rustic nature of the lodge and cabins provides a taste of the West, but with style. Two meals a day, bicycles, and horseback riding are included; the chef will cook any fish you catch; and a valet will take care of your laundry for a nominal charge. Fly into Jackson and the staff will, with prior notice, pick you up. The downside is the expense, for Jenny Lake Lodge is one of the most costly lodging facilities in any national park. For the price of a night at Jenny Lake Lodge, you can stay 2 nights and eat well a short distance up the road at sister facility Jackson Lake Lodge. On the other hand, if cost isn't a factor, Jenny Lake Lodge is your place to enjoy the beauty of the Tetons, and do it in comfort.

Rooms: Singles, doubles, triples, and quads. All cabins have a full bathroom.

Wheelchair Accessibility: Two cabins are wheelchair accessible.

Reservations: Grand Teton Lodge Company, PO Box 240, Moran, WY 83013. Phone (800) 628-9988 or visit www.gtlc.com. Up to a 3-day deposit is required for stays of 3 days or more.

Forty-five-day cancellation is required for a refund less a $40 fee.

Rates: Cabin: 1 person ($589); 2 persons ($689); Suites: 1 or 2 persons ($869–$959). Each additional person is approximately $170 a day. Children 3 years and under stay free with an adult. Breakfast and dinner are included in the price of a cabin.

Location: Midsection of Grand Teton National Park, approximately 20 miles north of Jackson, Wyoming.

Season: End of May to early Oct.

Food: A cozy dining room serves breakfast, lunch, and a five-course dinner. Breakfast and dinner are included in the price of a room. Lunches range from $11 to $14. Nonguests are charged $85 per person for dinner.

Jenny Lake Lodge is the descendant of a small 1920s dude ranch called Danny Ranch on the same site. Five cabins and a portion of the original main lodge building remain as part of the existing complex, which gained its current name in 1952. The original log building now houses the lodge dining room. Cabins have been modernized and added to over the years. A major restoration was undertaken in the late 1980s, and 4 new cabins were added in 1993.

Facilities: Dining room, stables, bicycles, gift shop, concierge service. Guests have free use of the swimming pool at Jackson Lake Lodge. A National Park Service visitor center is 3 miles away.

Activities: Hiking, fishing, horseback riding, Snake River float trips, bicycling. Guided walks and evening campfire programs originate at the National Park Service visitor center. A different guest activity is offered daily.

Signal Mountain Lodge
PO Box 50, Grand Teton National Park, Inner Park Road • Moran, WY 83103
(307) 543-2831 • www.signalmountainlodge.com

Signal Mountain Lodge is a medium-size commercial and lodging complex with 79 cabin units plus support structures that include a registration building, restaurant/gift shop, marina with rental boats, and a gas station/general store. The back side of the registration building houses a comfortable lounge with couches, chairs, tables, a stone fireplace, and large windows that offer excellent views of Jackson Lake and the Teton Range. A separate and somewhat smaller room has a television, small library, computers with Internet access, and a collection of games and puzzles. An adjacent building houses an attractive restaurant and grill, both of which offer lake and mountain views. The same

building includes a cocktail lounge, T-shirt shop, and nice gift shop.

The lodge offers 6 types of cabins constructed 2, 3, or 4 to a building with the exception of 1 large freestanding unit. All cabins have a fully tiled bathroom with a combination shower-tub, carpeting, electric heat, telephone, and a porch with chairs or a picnic table, but no television. Only the 4 new Premier Western Rooms offer air-conditioning. The cabins are within easy walking distance of the registration building, restaurant, and store. The least expensive rooms are one-room Rustic cabins with beds that range from 1 double to 2 doubles plus a sofa bed. Five units with 1 double bed have a gas fireplace. Two-room Rustic cabins

Two-room Rustic log cabin at Signal Mountain Lodge

can accommodate from 4 to 6 guests with bedding that ranges from 2 to 3 double beds. Both one- and two-room Rustics are priced according to the number of beds in the cabin. Some cabins have a good view of the lake, while other cabins have views obstructed by trees or other cabins. Two-room Rustic cabins 136, 138, 142, 143, and 144 sit a short distance from the lakeshore and offer excellent lake views from the porches. Avoid one-room cabin 107 and two-room cabin 112, which each have a porch directly on the road.

Sixteen larger Country Rooms offer more modern motel-style lodging with 2 queen beds or 1 king, a small refrigerator, a microwave, and a coffeemaker. Three Deluxe Country Rooms, all in the same building, have a king bed and a small sitting area with a gas fireplace. All but 1 of the Country Rooms sit back from the lake and offer minimal views. Country Room 137 is sandwiched between 2 two-room cabins and enjoys a private porch that offers a good lake view. We would choose this over the other 12 units in this classification. Two new duplex cabins housing

Premier Western Rooms were completed in 2013. These rooms each have 2 queen beds, a microwave, small refrigerator, coffeemaker, and are the only air-conditioned guest rooms at Signal Mountain. The new buildings are designed to be energy efficient and the bathrooms have granite countertops and slate tile.

Twenty-eight Lakefront Retreats are constructed 4 units to a building, with 2 up and 2 down with a shared balcony or patio. These large two-room units that were completely remodeled for the 2014 season have a living room–kitchenette with a sofa bed, microwave, 2-burner stove, coffeemaker, refrigerator, and limited cookware and utensils. A separate bedroom has either 2 queen beds or a king. These face Jackson Lake and are the only accommodations at Signal Mountain Lodge that offer excellent views of both Jackson Lake and the Tetons. The upper units of each building are closer to parking, offer more privacy, and are priced about $20 per night more than bottom units. Request upper Lakefront unit 152 or lower unit 151, both of which offer superior views.

Larger groups can be accommodated in a Family Bungalow with 2 units that are available for rent either separately or as a whole. One unit has a bedroom with 2 queen beds, as well as a separate kitchenette/living room equipped with a sofa bed, microwave, stove top, oven, coffeemaker, full-size refrigerator, and limited cookware and utensils. The attached one-room unit has a king bed, sofa bed, small refrigerator, microwave, and coffeemaker. The building has a large deck with chairs and a picnic table. One large "Home Away from Home" cabin has 3 rooms including a bedroom with 2 queen beds, a living/dining room with a sofa bed and gas fireplace, and a kitchen with limited cookware and utensils. This unit also has a washer and dryer.

Signal Mountain Lodge is a quiet facility situated directly on Lake Jackson in a beautiful area of Grand Teton National Park. Rooms here have a more rustic appearance and are less expensive than at nearby Jackson Lake Lodge, but the vistas are equally impressive. The cabins are similar to those at Colter Bay, but the Signal Mountain complex is much smaller. All the cabins are near the lake, allowing guests to walk a short distance to enjoy a swim or rent a canoe or kayak. The location approximately midway between the town of Jackson and Yellowstone National Park makes this a good base from which to explore this scenic area.

Rooms: Doubles, triples, and quads. Several rooms with a sofa bed can accommodate up to 6 persons. All rooms have a private bath.

Wheelchair Accessibility: Two Premier Western Rooms are ADA compliant. The restaurant, grill, and lounge are wheelchair accessible.

Reservations: Room reservations can be made either at the lodge website or by phone. It is recommended that travelers desiring more than 1 night make their reservations by phone. Phone (307) 543-2831 Mon through Fri from 8 a.m. to 5 p.m. MST. The reservation line is open 24 hours daily from May through early Oct. A deposit of 1 night's stay is required. Cancellation notice of 14 days is required for refund of deposit less an administrative fee of $20 per room. Reservations of 4 or more rooms are subject to a 28-day cancellation policy.

Today's Signal Mountain Lodge was a small fishing camp that went through several owners before being purchased in 1932 by Charles Wort, a homesteader who had plans to make this a fishing resort. His dream was at least partially fulfilled by his 2 sons. The Worts sold the lodge in 1940 in order to build an upscale hotel that continues to welcome guests in the town of Jackson. The new owners financed construction of the current guest cabins, general store, and registration building during the 40 years they owned the property.

Rates: One-room Rustic log cabins ($163–$202); one-room Rustic log cabin with a fireplace ($189–$199); two-room Rustic log cabins ($195–$232); Country rooms ($201–$211); Deluxe Country rooms ($242–$264); Premier Western rooms ($270–$284); Lakefront Retreats ($275–$325); one-room Family Bungalow ($201–$219), two-room Family Bungalow ($297–$324); Home Away from Home ($335–$366). Rates are by the room and not the number of occupants. Rollaways are $20 per night with a maximum of 1 per unit.

Location: On Jackson Lake, 7 miles west of Moran Junction and 35 miles north of Jackson.

Season: Early May to mid-Oct.

Food: The Peaks Restaurant serves dinner only ($15–$32). The adjacent Trapper Grill offers breakfast ($6–$12), lunch and dinner ($9–$18). Food from the grill is also served in the lounge and on the outside deck. Limited groceries, snacks, beverages, and beer are available in the general store. Eleven miles north, Leeks Pizzeria serves pizza, pasta, and sandwiches.

Facilities: Restaurant, grill, cocktail lounge, gift shop, clothing store, general store, Laundromat, and gas station. Marina with runabout, pontoon boat, canoe, and kayak rentals.

Activities: Boating, canoeing, kayaking, fishing, hiking, guided lake and river fishing trips, guided Snake River float trips.

Pets: Pets are permitted in all of the units except the Upper Lakefront Retreats and the Premier Western Rooms for a charge of $20 per night.

TRIANGLE X RANCH
2 Triangle X Ranch Rd. • Moose, WY 83012 • (307) 733-2183 • www.trianglex.com

Cabins at Triangle X Ranch

Triangle X Ranch, the only operating dude ranch in a national park, includes all the buildings you would expect at a working ranch, as well as freestanding cabins that provide guest accommodations. The ranch offers excellent views of the Teton Mountain Range from a rise overlooking Jackson Hole. Its authenticity and scenic location have resulted in the ranch serving as a location for several movies, including John Wayne's first film and the classic western *Shane.* The cabins are a short walk from the dining room. During peak season of June through August Triangle X requires a minimum stay of 1 week beginning and ending on Sunday. Reduced minimum stays are required other times of the year. The ranch is particularly appealing to people who enjoy horseback riding, a major activity for most guests.

Twenty log or wood-frame cabins each have electricity, heat, and a private bathroom with a combination shower-tub, but no telephone or television. Cabins are available with 1, 2, and 3 bedrooms. Two- and three-bedroom units each have 2 full bathrooms. Most bedrooms have either 2 twin beds or 1 queen bed. While the cabins have a rustic exterior, interiors are quite nice, with paneled walls and heavy pine furniture. Most ceilings are slightly vaulted. Each cabin has a covered front porch with chairs, and most enjoy views of the spectacular Tetons.

If you are looking for a complete national park western experience, Triangle X is your place. Guests enjoy mountain scenery, horseback riding, and evening activities with a western theme. Spending an entire week at the ranch means it is a certainty you will make new friends. Three meals a day, each announced by the ringing of a dinner bell, are served family-style and included in the price of a room. Daily horseback riding (except Sun) is included in the cost of lodging. Each guest is assigned his or her own horse at the beginning of the week's stay. Each evening has a different scheduled activity, including square dancing, ranger talks, cookouts, and campfire gatherings. Triangle X offers float trips and pack trips at extra cost.

Children 5 to 12 receive special attention. They eat in a separate dining room from teenagers and adults, and activities, including horseback riding, are especially designed for their age group.

Winter brings a new environment with different activities. The required stay is reduced to 2 nights, and rates decline. Complimentary cross-country skis and snowshoes are provided. Guided snowmobile trips can be arranged (fee). An outdoor hot tub is available for guests. Winter is accompanied by more formal gourmet meals including dinners with 3 to 4 courses and several entree choices. Wine-pairing and beer-pairing dinners are offered as special events.

Rooms: One to 3 persons in a one-bedroom unit; 3 to 5 persons in a two-bedroom unit; 5 to 6 persons in a three-bedroom cabin. All cabins have a private bath with a combination shower-tub.

Wheelchair Accessibility: One cabin is wheelchair accessible.

Reservations: Triangle X Ranch, 2 Triangle X Ranch Rd., Moose, WY 83012. Phone (307) 733-2183. Minimum stay of 1 week from early June to late Aug, 4 nights at other times during the summer season; a 2-night minimum is required during the winter season. The required deposit is 35 percent of total cost. Credit cards are not accepted during the summer season. When a cancellation occurs, a refund is given if the cabin can be filled.

Triangle X Ranch has served as home to 4 generations of the same family. The ranch was purchased in the summer of 1926 by John S. Turner, who started construction of his home and welcomed guests the same summer. The ranch was self-sufficient, with refrigeration provided by ice cut from nearby beaver ponds and stored in piles of sawdust. In the late 1920s Turner sold the property to a land company owned by John D. Rockefeller, who eventually donated the property to the federal government. Today the grandsons of John Turner operate the ranch as a concession of the National Park Service.

Rates: All rates are per person per week. One-bedroom cabin (1 person $2,520, 2 persons $2,130, 3 persons $1,820); two-bedroom cabin (3 persons $2,250, 4 persons $1,970, 5 persons

$1,820); three-bedroom cabin (5 persons $2,045, 6 persons $1,820). Prices reduced prior to mid-June and after late Aug. Winter rates are $140–$150 per night per person. A 15 percent service charge for gratuities is added to all bills. Summer rates include meals, horseback riding, and all ranch activities.

Location: East side of Grand Teton National Park, 25 miles north of Jackson, Wyoming. The ranch is 6 miles south of Moran Junction, on US 26, 89, and 191.

Season: Summer season: mid-May through Oct. Winter season: Dec 26 to mid-Mar.

Food: Three daily family-style meals are served in the ranch dining room. A typical dinner includes a main entree, green salad, several vegetables, home-baked bread, and dessert. Meals are included in the quoted rates for both summer and winter seasons.

Transportation: Triangle X provides shuttle service from the Jackson airport for $40 per trip regardless of the number of riders.

Facilities: Corrals, dining room, laundry, gift shop.

Activities: Summer—horseback riding, breakfast and dinner cookouts, square dancing, fishing, hiking. Optional services offered (fee)—float trips, guided-fishing trips, pack trips (minimum of 4 days), and hunting trips (10 days). Winter—cross-country skiing, snowmobiling, snowshoeing, wildlife viewing, relaxing in the outdoor hot tub. Downhill skiing is available at 3 area resorts.

Yellowstone National Park

PO Box 168 • Yellowstone National Park, WY 82190 • (307) 344-7381 • www.nps.gov/yell

Yellowstone, the world's first and probably best-known national park, comprises nearly 3,400 square miles of lakes, waterfalls, mountains, and some 10,000 geysers and hot springs. The park has almost 300 miles of roads. Most major attractions are near Grand Loop Road, which makes a figure eight in the park's central area. The road's east side provides access to canyons, mountains, and waterfalls, while the west side leads to areas of thermal activity. The park is mostly in the northwestern corner of Wyoming, with overlapping strips in Montana and Idaho.

Park Entrance Fee: $25 per vehicle, $20 per motorcycle or snowmobile, and $12 per person, good for 7 days. The fee covers Grand Teton National Park and the connecting parkway.

Lodging in Yellowstone National Park: Yellowstone has 9 lodging facilities scattered about the park. One is near the north entrance, 1 is in the northeast section, 1 is in the canyon area, 2 are in Lake Village on the north shore of Yellowstone Lake, 1 is 20 miles inside the south entrance, and 3 are in the Old Faithful area. The lodges offer a wide choice of accommodations that range from rustic cabins without a private bathroom to a modern upscale lodge with handcrafted furniture. Likewise, prices range from what you are likely to pay for a Motel 6 in rural America to the price of a nice hotel room in a major city. Much of Yellowstone's lodging consists of cabins in 4 categories. In ascending order of quality and cost, cabins are classified as Budget (rustic, small, no private bathroom), Pioneer (rustic, small, private

YELLOWSTONE NATIONAL PARK

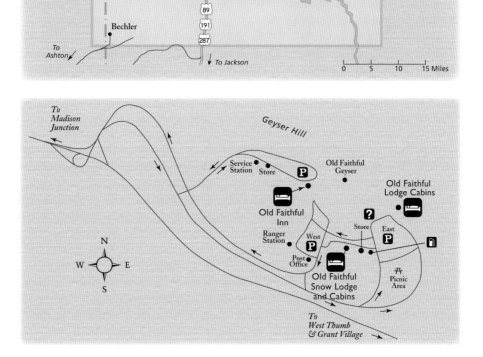

To Livingston
89
Gardiner

To Bozeman

191

MONTANA
WYOMING

Silver
Gate

Mammoth
Hot Springs

Pebble
Creek

212

Mammoth
Hot Springs
Hotel and
Cabins

Roosevelt
Lodge
Cabins

Slough
Creek

**To Quake
Lake**

287

Indian Creek

Tower Fall

Lamar Valley

**To
Red Lodge**

To Ashton

Norris

Canyon

Canyon Lodge
and Cabins

20
West
Yellowstone

Madison

Fishing Bridge

MONTANA
WYOMING

Lake Village

Lake Yellowstone
Hotel and Cabins

IDAHO
WYOMING

Old
Faithful Inn

Bridge
Bay

Lake
Lodge
Cabins

14 16 20

West
Thumb

To Cody

Lewis
Lake

Grant
Village

Yellowstone
Lake

89
191
Bechler

287

**To
Ashton**

To Jackson

0   5   10   15 Miles

**To
Madison
Junction**

Geyser Hill

Service
Station   Store

Old Faithful
Geyser

Old Faithful
Lodge Cabins

Old Faithful
Inn

Store

East

Ranger
Station

West

Post
Office

Old Faithful
Snow Lodge
and Cabins

Picnic
Area

N
W   E
S

**To
West Thumb
& Grant Village**

bathroom), Frontier (small or mid-size, nicer interior, private bathroom), and Western (nicest, larger than Frontier, private bathroom). Cabins are quite old, but interiors have often been refurbished. We generally find the cabins to have nicer interiors than indicated by their exterior appearance.

Mammoth Hot Springs Hotel and Cabins, near the north entrance, offers a historic hotel plus two classes of rustic cabins. Both have rooms with and without private bathrooms.

Roosevelt Lodge Cabins, in the northeast section of the park, has rustic cabins with and without private bathrooms. Roosevelt is the park's smallest lodging facility with some of the least expensive accommodations.

Canyon Lodge and Cabins, the park's largest lodging facility, is centrally located midway between the east and west entrances. Canyon includes modern lodges plus Western cabins.

Lake Village, on the park's east side, has 2 neighboring lodging facilities. Lake Yellowstone Hotel and Cabins provides Frontier cabins plus an elegant historic hotel that was recently renovated. Nearby, Lake Lodge Cabins offers cabins that range from rustic to reasonably modern.

Grant Village, 20 miles from the park's south entrance, has 6 relatively modern motel-type buildings with nearly 300 rooms.

The Old Faithful area has 3 lodging facilities, including famous Old Faithful Inn, with rooms in the original structure, or "Old House," plus larger and more upscale rooms in 2 newer wings. Nearby, Old Faithful Lodge Cabins offers cabins with and without private bathrooms at relatively inexpensive rates. Old Faithful Snow Lodge and Cabins, behind its more famous sister hotel, has 2 classes of cabins plus 100 rooms in one of the newest and nicest hotels in the park. Cabins at Snow Lodge are larger and less closely clustered compared to the cabins at Old Faithful Lodge Cabins.

When deciding upon lodging consider that Yellowstone encompasses nearly 3,500 square miles and visiting different sections of the park can entail unexpectedly long driving times. Distances are substantial, but planning to visit another area of the park on the basis of mileage alone will almost certainly underestimate the travel time required. Traffic can be heavy, animal watching causes bottlenecks on the roads, and the park seems to be in an endless cycle of road repair that often slows traffic to a standstill. Consider staying in multiple locations, especially if you will be visiting more than a couple of days.

Three good choices for a stay of a week are Old Faithful, Mammoth, and Lake Village. First-time visitors to Yellowstone will want to spend time in the Old Faithful area, a good base for exploring the park's geyser country. Staying at Mammoth offers time to learn about the park's history and explore what was once an Army fort for soldiers who protected Yellowstone. Either Canyon Village or Lake Village can serve as a base for exploring the park's canyon country and viewing beautiful Yellowstone Falls. Although Canyon Village is nearer canyon country, our choice would be the Lake Village area, which enjoys a more relaxed atmosphere. Lake Yellowstone Hotel is our favorite place to stay in the park. If you are planning a short visit and want to stay in a single place, Canyon Village offers the most convenient location to all the park's features.

Yellowstone is very busy, so it is important to make reservations as early as possible. If you are unable to obtain a reservation when you first call, it may pay to call periodically, because openings may become available due to cancellations. You may be able to obtain a room as a walk-in, although there may not be much choice regarding the location, facility, or cost. All 9 lodging facilities are operated by the same firm, so the registration desk at any of the lodges can determine whether vacancies exist anywhere in the park.

Reservations: Yellowstone National Park Lodges (operated by Xanterra Parks & Resorts), Reservations Office, PO Box 165, Yellowstone National Park, WY 82190. Phone (866) 439-7375 or visit www.yellowstonenationalparklodges.com. A deposit equal to the first night's lodging is required at each location where you will be staying. Cancellation notice of 48 hours during the summer season required for refund of deposit. Fourteen days' advance notice required for cancellation of winter reservations. Check Xanterra's website for special packages that include lodging, activities, tours, and/or food.

Transportation: Snowcoaches operate during winter months between Old Faithful and Mammoth (4 hours 1 way), and Headwaters Lodge & Cabins at Flagg Ranch (3½ hours 1 way). Within the park, only Old Faithful Snow Lodge and Mammoth Hotel are open during winter months. The road from

Livingston to Mammoth and then on to Cooke City is open year-round. All other roads in the park are closed. Transportation is available between Jackson and Headwaters Lodge Cabins at Flagg Ranch during winter months. Most transportation mentioned above operates only once per day.

Pets: Pets are limited to dogs and cats that are permitted in cabins only if they are quiet and housebroken. They are limited to 2 per cabin and may not be left unattended at any time. A fee of $25 is charged for each stay.

CANYON LODGE AND CABINS

Cascade Lodge at Canyon Lodge and Cabins

Canyon Lodge and Cabins is Yellowstone's largest lodging complex and includes a registration building, approximately 100 Western cabins, and modern lodge buildings adjacent to a large commercial center. The Canyon Village center includes a large general store/coffee shop, registration building, restaurant, cafeteria, deli, lounge, sporting goods store, gas station, post office, gift shops, and an impressive National Park Service visitor education center. This is a busy commercial center, but most rooms are far enough away that guests are able to enjoy a relatively quiet stay. It is also distant enough that

you will have a hike, or you may prefer driving, to the restaurant, depending on the location of your room. Canyon Village takes its name from the Grand Canyon of the Yellowstone River, half a mile away.

Canyon Lodge and Cabins has 2 classes of accommodations. All rooms have heat and private baths but no telephone, television, or air-conditioning. The Canyon facility is undergoing a $70 million redevelopment with the goal of replacing all the Frontier cabins with a series of multistory lodge buildings similar to the Dunraven and Cascade structures described further on. The redevelopment commenced in 2014 and will take place over several years.

Ninety-nine Western cabins are constructed 4 or 6 units to a building. These were constructed in 1969 and extensively refurbished from 2005 to 2007. Each Western cabin has 2 queen beds, a bathroom with a combination shower-tub, coffeemaker, and upgraded furniture.

Two newer rustic-style lodges, Dunraven and Cascade, with steep shake roofs and dormers offer 81 nearly identical guest rooms, each with 2 double beds (except for 7 wheelchair rooms and 2 rooms on the fourth floor of Dunraven), a carpeted floor, attractive pine furniture, coffeemaker, and a bathroom with a combination shower-tub.

Public telephones, vending machines, and ice machines are in each of the buildings that are connected by a short walkway. The oldest of the two, Cascade Lodge, was constructed in 1993 and has 37 rooms on 3 floors. Newer Dunraven Lodge was completed in 1999 and has 44 rooms on 4 floors. Dunraven is built on a small hillside and entered on the second floor. The first floor has rooms on only 1 side. Only Dunraven has an elevator, plus an attractive second-floor lobby that is available for use by guests of both buildings. Three additional lodge buildings similar to Dunraven and Cascade are scheduled to open in 2015, while 2 more are scheduled be added the following year.

Visitors seeking a more authentic national park experience should probably choose a Western cabin. If you typically prefer a nice motel, choose a room in one of the lodges. Of the 2 lodges select the newer Dunraven that has an elevator. Try for second- or third-floor rooms on the south side (odd-numbered rooms) that face the woods rather than the parking lot. Dunraven rooms on the fourth floor are somewhat smaller than rooms on the other floors. Rooms on the third floor of Cascade, especially 305 and 307, are larger and offer views of the woods.

Canyon Lodge and Cabins is a convenient place to stay if you plan to explore Yellowstone from a single base. It is a large and busy complex, but the strategic location near the center of Yellowstone may trump any negatives, especially if you plan to spend most of every day touring this large park. The lodge is situated in the canyon district, one of the park's most scenic areas. Canyon Village, in which the lodge is located, has anything you will need after a long day of sightseeing.

Rooms: Doubles, triples, and quads. All rooms have a private bath.

Canyon Lodge is within walking distance of the North Rim of the Grand Canyon of the Yellowstone. A half-mile trail leads to the North Rim's Grandview Point. From here North Rim Trail leads either 1 mile northeast to Inspiration Point or 1 mile southwest to the Lower Falls. The entire North Rim Trail, which begins at South Rim Drive Bridge and ends at Inspiration Point, is slightly less than 3 miles, and a portion of it is paved. A variety of trails are also on the south side of the canyon.

Wheelchair Accessibility: A total of 7 rooms in the 2 lodge buildings and 5 Western cabins are ADA compliant.

Rates: Western cabins ($194); Lodge rooms ($194). Rates are for 2 adults. Each additional person is $15 per night. Children 11 and under stay free.

Location: Near the middle of Yellowstone National Park, 40 miles from the west entrance at West Yellowstone.

Season: Early June through the last week in Sept.

Food: Several eating options are available in the Canyon commercial center, which is a long walk from most of the lodging. A dining room offers a breakfast ($6–$12), lunch ($9–$19), and dinner ($12–$24). A less expensive cafeteria serves 3 meals a day with dinner costing from $7 to $15. The deli serves sandwiches, salads, drinks, and ice cream. A coffee shop in the general store serves breakfast, salads, sandwiches, hamburgers, ice cream, and beverages. A lounge serves appetizers.

Facilities: Restaurant, cafeteria, deli, coffee shop, lounge, gift shop, laundry, general store with groceries, sporting goods store, post office, gas station, stables, National Park Service visitor education center.

Activities: Horseback riding, hiking, narrated excursions, evening ranger programs at the campground amphitheater.

GRANT VILLAGE

Grant Village includes a registration building, 2 restaurants, and 6 modern two-story lodge buildings, each with approximately 50 rooms. A general store, service station, and National Park Service visitor education center are nearby. The wooden lodge buildings, constructed from 1982 to 1984, sit staggered across a hillside above the south shore of the West Thumb of Yellowstone Lake. There are no elevators, but assistance with luggage can be requested at the registration building. The lodge buildings and rooms are similar to what you are likely to find in a Holiday Inn Express or Comfort Inn. Rooms on both floors of each building are entered from long central corridors. Although half the rooms in each of the 6 lodge buildings face toward the lake, views are obscured by pine trees. All of the rooms have electric heat, a coffeemaker, a hair dryer, a telephone, and a private bath. About half the bathrooms have a shower only, while the remainder have a combination shower-tub. None of the rooms have air-conditioning, a television, or a balcony. Each building has a small first-floor lobby with tables and chairs.

The building you are assigned shouldn't be a major concern. Building A is closest to the

One of the six lodge buildings at Grant Village

dining room, so this may be a factor. Ask for a room with 2 double beds, because the few rooms with 1 queen bed (other than ADA rooms) are quite a bit smaller. You might also consider asking for a room that doesn't face a parking lot. The 8 corner rooms in buildings A, D, E, and F enjoy an extra side window.

Grant Village primarily appeals to people traveling between Grand Teton and Yellowstone after a long day of driving and sightseeing. In other words, it is a place to spend a night rather than a base from which to explore the park. Being away from the park's heavily visited tourist areas means the village is quiet and free from the traffic and crowds found in much of the rest of Yellowstone. In addition, it is only 19 miles from the park's main attraction, Old Faithful. Stay at Grant Village and you can beat the crowds by arriving at Old Faithful early the next morning. Three eating establishments with varying menus and prices are a short walk from the lodge buildings. The Grant Village dining room near Lodge A is in an unusual building, with windows that offer lake views and a high vaulted ceiling supported by large beams. A small cocktail lounge, The Seven Stool Saloon, is just off the entrance area. An informal and less expensive restaurant, Lake House, is directly on the lake and serves a buffet breakfast and sandwiches and salads for dinner. Large floor-to-ceiling windows on 3 sides of the building provide excellent lake views. A general store near the registration building houses a grill that serves breakfast, sandwiches, ice cream, and beverages.

Rooms: Doubles, triples, and quads. All rooms have a private bath with shower or combination shower-tub.

Wheelchair Accessibility: Two rooms on the first floor of each building are ADA compliant.

Rates: All rooms ($155). Rates are quoted for 2 adults. Each additional person is $15 per night. Children 11 and under stay free.

Location: At the south end of the park, 20 miles north of the south entrance.

Season: The end of May through late Sept.

Food: Grant Village Dining Room serves a breakfast buffet ($12), breakfast menu items ($7–$12), lunch ($9–$14), and dinner ($12–$30) in an attractive building. Lake House serves a breakfast buffet ($10) and a dinner menu ($9–$19). A grill in the general store serves breakfast, salads, sandwiches, and beverages. The store also has a good offering of groceries.

Facilities: Dining room, restaurant, cocktail lounge, grill, general store, gift shop, service station, boat ramp, post office, Laundromat, National Park Service visitor center.

Activities: Hiking, fishing, narrated bus tours, evening ranger programs at the campground amphitheater.

LAKE LODGE CABINS

Lake Lodge Cabins is a complex consisting of a large log building with a registration desk and support services, plus 186 cabins situated on a hill overlooking the lodge. No guest rooms are in the main building, which has a cafeteria, gift shop, bar, and a large lobby area with 2 impressive gas fireplaces. The main building has a long covered front porch. This is a pleasant place to relax in one of the many rocking chairs while enjoying a view of Yellowstone Lake and the surrounding mountains. The entire complex sits back from the lake, and the cabins offer no lake views. Lake Lodge Cabins offers 3 types of cabin accommodations. All have heat and private bath with shower, with some Western cabins having a combination shower-tub. There is no air-conditioning, telephone, or television in any of the cabins. Most cabins are constructed 4 to a building, although a few buildings have 2 units and others have 6. The least expensive alternative is 66 Pioneer cabins that sit in an area devoid of trees. The smallest Pioneer cabins have 1 double bed; larger units have 2 double beds. These cabins look very rustic on the outside, but the interior is fairly nice, with paneled walls and carpeting. One level up are 20 Frontier cabins that are the same size as the Pioneers but were extensively refurbished in 2010 with a new foundation, a new interior, and the removal of ceiling tiles to reveal the original vaulted ceiling.

One hundred Western cabins are identical to those at Canyon Lodge and Cabins. All are the same size and come with 2 queen beds. These cabins are quite a bit larger and cost over $100 more per night than Pioneer cabins. Layouts differ from building to building, but a majority of Western cabins have windows in 2 walls. Western cabins have been extensively renovated with brighter interiors, upgraded furniture, and new bathrooms. Those toward the rear of the complex (loops G, H, and J) are spaced farther apart and surrounded by trees. Cabins in loop J offer the most quiet.

Lake Lodge Cabins provides both modestly priced and more upscale accommodations in a scenic and relatively quiet section of the park. Renovated Frontier cabins offer comfortable accommodations and are a good value. This is the nearest lodging complex to Fishing Bridge and Bridge Bay Marina. Guests can enjoy a leisurely stroll across a wide grassy area to beautiful

Frontier cabin at Lake Lodge Cabins

Yellowstone Lake, frequently in the presence of a grazing bison or two. The nearby historic ranger cabin and the first gift shop opened by Charles Hamilton are a short walk from the lodge. The gift shop was recently rehabilitated and retains fountain equipment that was installed in 1938. Dining options range from a relatively inexpensive cafeteria in the registration building to an elegant dining room in nearby Lake Yellowstone Hotel. Make reservations as early as possible if you want to eat dinner in the hotel dining room.

Rooms: Doubles, triples, and quads. All cabins have private baths.

Wheelchair Accessibility: Ten Western cabins are ADA compliant.

Rates: Pioneer cabins ($79); Frontier cabins ($125); Western cabins ($194). Rates quoted are for 2 adults. Each additional person is $15 per night. Children 11 and under stay free with an adult.

Location: On the north shore of Yellowstone Lake, in the east-central section of Yellowstone National Park. The lodge is approximately 30 miles from the east park entrance and 43 miles from the south entrance.

Lake Lodge was constructed during the 1920s to provide mid-level accommodations to travelers who didn't want to tent camp but who couldn't afford the more expensive hotels. The East Wing was added as a dining area (currently the cafeteria) in 1926, and the West Wing was built as a dance hall (now an employee recreation hall) in the same year. The front porch of Lake Lodge was added in 1929.

Season: Mid-June to late Sept.

Food: A cafeteria is open for breakfast ($5–$11), lunch/dinner ($6–$20). A nearby general store has limited groceries and a lunch counter that serves breakfast, salads, sandwiches, soups, ice cream, and beverages. Nearby Lake Yellowstone Hotel has a lovely dining room and a small deli.

Facilities: Gift shop, Laundromat, cafeteria, lobby bar. A general store is a short walk from the lodge. Nearby Lake Yellowstone Hotel offers additional facilities.

Activities: Hiking, fishing. Nearby Bridge Bay Marina offers boat tours on Yellowstone Lake, boat rentals, and narrated tours.

LAKE YELLOWSTONE HOTEL AND CABINS

Front of Lake Yellowstone Hotel

Lake Yellowstone Hotel and Cabins comprises a three- and four-story hotel building, an adjacent two-story Sandpaper Lodge, formerly called the "Annex," and 110 closely clustered cabin units located behind the hotel. The hotel, adjacent lodge, and cabins offer a total of 300 rooms. The hotel underwent $25 million of structural work and renovations during 2013 and 2014. The first floor houses the registration desk, lobby, dining room, lobby bar, gift shop, and a few rooms. The popular sunroom has large windows that overlook Yellowstone Lake. The dining room has large windows on the south and west walls. Although most guests enter the hotel from the large back parking lot, driving under the hotel's front lakeside portico provides more convenient access for registration and dropping off luggage.

The hotel, often called Lake Hotel, has 154 rooms in 2 wings, 1 on each side of the main lobby. The hotel's only elevator is in the East Wing, and bell service is available. All rooms are attractively decorated and each has heat, full tiled bathroom, fan, coffeemaker, bathrobes, hair dryer, and a telephone, but no air-conditioning or television. Room size and beds vary, but the largest rooms are in the three-story West Wing, while the best lake views are from end rooms of the East Wing. The East Wing elevator makes it easy to haul luggage to fourth-floor rooms that enjoy the best views and where nobody is walking on a floor above. We recommend even-numbered rooms 430 to 460.

> Construction on Lake Yellowstone Hotel began in 1889 in an area once populated by native tribes, fur trappers, and mountain men. The first guests arrived 2 years later. Additions engineered by the architect of Old Faithful Inn in the early 1900s nearly tripled the number of rooms at the hotel to 210. The East Wing, with 113 additional rooms, was completed in the early 1920s, and the sunroom was added in 1924. The hotel had fallen into disrepair by the 1980s, when a decade-long renovation was initiated to return the building to its glory years of the 1920s.

Bedding ranges from 1 queen or king to 3 queen beds. Rooms in the hotel are priced according to bedding and whether they face the lake or are on the back side of the hotel. Rooms on the lake side rent for an extra $10 to $20 per night, which is money well spent. Four Lakeside Suites consist of a living room with a sofa sleeper plus a wet bar and a mini-refrigerator, and a separate bedroom with a king bed. The Presidential Suite on the corner of the second floor has a queen bed in each of 2 large bedrooms, 2 full

bathrooms, and a large living room with a wet bar and refrigerator stocked with snacks and sodas. In the West Wing, room 100 with 1 queen bed is a good choice.

Two-story Sandpiper Lodge, once used as employee housing, has 36 rooms that rent for significantly less per night than rooms in the hotel. Sandpiper rooms have heat, telephone, coffeemaker, hair dryer, bathrobes, and a private bathroom with a combination shower-tub (except for 6 wheelchair-accessible rooms that each have a roll-in shower), but no air-conditioning or television. A small lobby with several comfortable chairs is on the first floor. Beds in these rooms consist of either 1 or 2 doubles. Rooms with 2 double beds are generally larger but rent for the same price. None of the rooms in Sandpiper Lodge offer particularly good views, although those on the east side provide views of pine trees, while rooms on the west side overlook the parking lot. Lodge rooms probably offer a better value than rooms in the hotel, especially if you can get a larger room with 2 double beds on the east side. If you book a room in Sandpiper, this is what you should request.

The Frontier cabins were built in the 1940s and renovated from 2002 to 2005. They are closely clustered in an area devoid of trees behind the hotel and away from the lake. Most cabins are constructed as duplex units, with rooms that back up to one another. The remaining cabins are freestanding. All cabins are approximately the same size and have a nicely finished interior with carpeting, 2 double beds, and a private bathroom with a shower. If you decide to book a cabin, request freestanding units 49, 50, or 51, which sit at the far end of the complex and face the lake and trees. In addition, you will avoid noise from guests in an adjoining room.

Lake Yellowstone Hotel and Cabins is our favorite place to spend several nights in

Yellowstone National Park. It is in a peaceful setting on a beautiful lake, and you can't go wrong with any of its lodging options. The hotel captures the ambience of an earlier period, with a bright, airy sunroom that serves as a pleasant place to read a book or talk with friends, while stealing occasional glances at the lake. A pianist or string quartet entertains here most evenings. The hotel has a delightful dining room and a small deli and is a short distance from neighboring Lake Lodge Cabins, which offers laundry facilities and a relatively inexpensive cafeteria. If you are unable to secure a room on the lake side of the hotel, or if you prefer not to pay over $300 per night, consider a room in Sandpiper Lodge. It isn't as nice as a hotel room, and it doesn't have the view and atmosphere, but you can still enjoy a walk along the lake and a dinner at the hotel dining room. The Frontier Cabins, especially the freestanding units, offer the best value at this location. Choosing a cabin makes it easier to transport luggage because parking is close to each of these units. Sandpiper Lodge is immediately adjacent to the hotel, and the cabins are nearby, so staying in the lodge or cabins allows guests to enjoy the hotel's sunroom and dining room.

Rooms: Doubles, triples, and quads. A few rooms sleep up to 6. All rooms, including cabins, have private bathrooms.

Wheelchair Accessibility: Eleven rooms in Lake Yellowstone Hotel, six rooms in Sandpiper Lodge and 4 Frontier Cabins are ADA compliant.

Rates: Frontier Cabins ($149); Sandpiper Lodge ($155); Hotel—back ($319–$349), front ($339–$359), Lakeside Suite ($545); Presidential Suite ($629). Rates are quoted for 2 adults. Children 11 and under stay free. Each additional person is $15 per night.

Location: East-central section of the park, on the north shore of Yellowstone Lake. The hotel is 30 miles from the park's east entrance.

Season: From mid-May to early Oct.

Food: A 1920s-era hotel dining room serves a breakfast buffet ($15) and menu items ($7–$15), lunch ($9–$16), and dinner ($13–$35). A deli on the first floor is open from 10:30 a.m. to 9 p.m. for sandwiches, soups, and beverages. A cafeteria at nearby Lake Lodge Cabins serves 3 meals a day. A general store close to the hotel has limited groceries and a counter that serves breakfast, sandwiches, soups, salads, ice cream, and beverages.

Facilities: Clinic, dining room, lobby bar, small deli, gift shop, post office. Nearby is a general store. Lake Lodge Cabins has a cafeteria and laundry facilities.

Activities: Hiking, fishing, photo tour, sunset tour, narrated park tours, evening music in the hotel lobby. Nearby Bridge Bay Marina offers boat tours on Yellowstone Lake, boat rentals, and fishing guides.

MAMMOTH HOT SPRINGS HOTEL AND CABINS

If you have ever wanted to stay at an old Army fort, then Mammoth Hot Springs Hotel and Cabins is your place. The hotel is adjacent to buildings that were once part of a small military post that served as headquarters for the US Army when it was in charge of this park. Some of the original Army buildings are still in use as housing and administrative offices for personnel

Cabins at Mammoth Hot Springs Hotel and Cabins

of the National Park Service. The current lodging complex at Mammoth comprises a four-story hotel plus 115 cabin units that together provide 212 rooms.

Registration for all lodging is in the first-floor lobby of the hotel. Bell service is available at the front desk. Cabin units each have their own parking area and are clustered along the roads and in grassy areas behind the hotel.

The lodging complex offers various types of rooms, both in the hotel and the cabins. Ninety-six hotel rooms each have steam heat and a telephone, but no air-conditioning or television (with the exception of the Suites). An elevator is near the registration desk. The hotel has 66 rooms with a private bath that rent for about $30 per night more than 30 rooms without a private bath. Community bath and shower rooms are on each floor. Rooms without a bath have 2 queen beds. Regular hotel rooms with a bath have either 1 or 2 queen beds. Some bathrooms have a tub, some have a shower, and some have both. Corner rooms 230, 231, 330, and 331 each have a full bath and rent for the same price but are quite a bit larger than other rooms with a bath. The hotel has 2 Suites, 1 each on the third and fourth floors. These are about the size of 2 regular rooms and have a bedroom plus a separate sitting room with a couch and a single trundle bed.

Suites each have a television and coffeemaker, and guests receive a gift basket, stocked mini-fridge, and a newspaper. The fourth-floor Suite has 2 bathrooms, 1 with a shower-tub combination. The third-floor Suite has 1 bathroom with a shower.

The cabin units, both with and without a private bath, are either freestanding or duplex units. All cabins have nearly identical living space (not counting the small bathroom in Frontier cabins), finished interiors, 1 or 2 queen beds, a sink with hot and cold water, and a covered front porch with chairs. A limited number of Budget cabins have 2 bedrooms but no bathroom. Frontier cabins have a shower and toilet and rent for about $55 extra per night compared to Budget cabins without a bath. Four Frontier cabins with 1 queen bed each have a large hot tub on a private porch and rent for approximately $100 extra per night. These hot tubs can be rented by the hour during winter months. All cabins front either on a road or around a grassy area. The latter are preferred, and we recommend Budget cabins C26, C27, and C30. Frontier cabins B14, B15, B16, C46, and C49 are recommended if you desire a private bath. Each of these cabins is freestanding, fronts on a grassy area, and enjoys morning sun.

Mammoth Hot Springs Hotel and Cabins is in a unique and interesting section of Yellowstone. It's fun to walk through the surrounding area and view the historic buildings of this former Army post. A National Park Service visitor center in one of the old military buildings has exhibits on the park's early history. Trails to the upper and lower thermal terraces begin near a picnic area just down the road from the hotel. Mammoth is a handy location for visitors planning a trip to Lamar Valley in an attempt to view the park's elusive wolves. Mammoth guests enjoy the flexibility of eating in a large art deco–style dining room or at the nearby grill.

We prefer the cabins listed above to rooms in the hotel even though the former are a little more expensive. The cabins allow you to relax on your own front porch, and parking beside each cabin makes loading and unloading luggage less of a chore. The major downside of staying at Mammoth is its location at the extreme north end of the park, some distance from Old Faithful and many of Yellowstone's other popular sites. Choosing to stay only at Mammoth will result in substantial driving while going to and from other features of the park. This isn't an issue if you will be utilizing several lodging locations during your visit.

Rooms: Doubles, triples, and quads. Many hotel rooms and cabins have private baths.

Wheelchair Accessibility: Two rooms in the hotel and 4 cabin units are ADA compliant. The restaurant across the street from the hotel is wheelchair accessible, with access through the grill on the opposite side of the building.

Rates: Budget cabins ($89); two-room Budget cabins ($172); Frontier cabins ($145); Frontier cabins with hot tubs ($239); Hotel rooms without a bath ($90); Hotel rooms with a bath ($129); Suites ($479). Rates quoted are for 2 persons except Suites, which are for up to 4. Each additional person is $15 per night. Children 11 and under stay free. Special packages are offered during the winter season.

Location: North end of Yellowstone National Park, 5 miles south of Gardiner, Montana.

Season: Summer season is from early May to early Oct. Winter season is from mid-Dec to early Mar. During winter months, only the hotel is open. The hot tub cabins are open to rent by the hour.

Food: A large dining room across the street from the hotel offers breakfast ($5–$14), lunch ($8–$16), and dinner ($11–$30). Dinner menu items include bison slider, bison taco, bison meatballs, and bison top sirloin. A grill next to the dining room offers breakfast items, a variety of fast food, soups, salads, and ice cream. A general store sells ice cream, beverages, limited groceries, and alcoholic beverages.

The hotel and cabins currently operating at Mammoth are only the latest chapter in a long history of lodging in this area. The first crude hotel in the park was built at Mammoth in 1871. The much larger and more elaborate National Hotel was constructed here in 1883. An annex that was added to the National Hotel in 1911 serves as the main lodging section of today's Mammoth Hot Springs Hotel. The remainder of the old National Hotel was torn down. The current hotel's front section containing the lobby, a map room, and a gift shop was added in 1936 and 1937, 1 year before the first 96 cabins were completed behind the hotel.

Facilities: Restaurant, cocktail lounge, espresso bar in lobby, grill, gift shop, auditorium, general store, post office, National Park Service visitor center. Winter season: ski shop, ice-skating rink, and skate and snowshoe rental.

Activities: Walks along the boardwalk through the hot springs area, walking among the historic buildings at Mammoth (printed guide available), hiking, evening programs. Winter activities include ice skating, guided snowshoe touring, cross-country skiing, snowmobiling, guided snowmobile touring, and snowcoach rides.

Old Faithful Inn

Old Faithful Inn is America's most famous national park lodge. Think of national parks, and both Yellowstone and this historic hotel will almost certainly come to mind. The large lobby, with log beams and a vaulted ceiling that soars 77 feet above the first floor, has multiple overhanging balconies. A mezzanine with chairs, tables, and sofas wraps around the entire second floor. Oddly shaped logs are used as decoration and for support of the railings and log beams. A huge clock projects from the front of a massive, 4-sided stone fireplace that highlights the lobby. An attractive restaurant and lounge are entered from the back of the lobby. The hotel is well maintained, and all of the facilities, including the rooms, are clean and comfortable.

The inn doesn't directly face Old Faithful, but arriving guests are likely to discover that the famous geyser is the first thing they see as they arrive at the entrance to unload luggage. Good views of Old Faithful are obtained from several locations in the hotel, including the large second-floor porch and a few of the guest rooms. Guest rooms are in the older main section and 2 attached wings. No cabins or separate buildings are part of the hotel, although 2 other lodging facilities with cabins are nearby. The registration desk for Old Faithful Inn is to the left as you enter the lobby. Bell service is available to assist with luggage. A large parking area is in front of the hotel, a relatively short walk from the entrance. Guest rooms are on 3 floors in the

Old House (the original structure) and the East Wing, and on 4 floors in the West Wing. One elevator is in each wing, but these are relatively slow during busy periods, so you may end up climbing several flights of stairs depending upon where your room is located.

The inn offers over 300 rooms that vary in size, views, bathroom facilities, and configuration. Accommodations range from restored Old House rooms without private bath in the original central log building to relatively large rooms with a private bath in each of the wings. Room rates vary accordingly. All rooms have heat, but none have air-conditioning or television. Only rooms in the wings have telephones.

The least expensive rooms in Old Faithful Inn are in the original Old House section of the building. Although these rooms tend to be dark and can be noisy if located near the busy lobby, the log or rough-hewn wood hallways and interior walls provide the ambience of a rustic national park lodge. Most rooms in the Old House are without a private bathroom. Guests in these rooms must use one of the community bathrooms located on each corridor of this section of the building. The community bathrooms are quite nice as they were recently renovated with tile and marble. Rooms in the Old House are all different and interesting. Some are small with 1 queen bed, while a few are quite large and have 3 queen beds. First-floor rooms have interior log walls, while rooms on the second and third floors have walls of rough-hewn pine. Bathrooms often have claw-foot tubs, but none have a shower. A few have pull-chain toilets. If requesting an Old House room, keep in mind there is only 1 shower on the first floor, and guests staying in first-floor rooms without a bath may end up using the larger second-floor shower rooms. Some of the best Old House rooms are without a private bathroom, such as corner room 229, which offers the best view of Old Faithful geyser, and room 46, a large, rustic corner room with corner window seats. Room 243 has a unique shape and is entered from a short private stairway. The best rooms with a bath are 8 and 108, both of which have 2 bedrooms. Room 127 is large, offers a view of the geyser basin, and has a unique bathroom. President Clinton stayed in room 127 during his visit to Old Faithful. It is best to avoid rooms 1 through 6, which are in a hallway with a bathroom that is heavily used by nonguests.

Rooms in the East Wing are generally larger with either 1 or 2 queen beds. These rooms also have tiled bathrooms, a coffeemaker, and a hair dryer. Rooms 1012, 1020, 1024, and corresponding rooms on the second and third floors offer good views of Old Faithful geyser. Three L-shaped Semi-suites in this wing each have 2 queen beds and a sitting area with a coffeemaker, daily newspaper, and refrigerator stocked with snacks. Six two-room Suites with windows facing Old Faithful each have 2 queen beds and a separate sitting room. Suites offer the same amenities as described for the Semi-suites, including upgraded bathrooms.

Renovated West Wing rooms have a nice tiled bathroom, coffeemaker, hair dryer, and bedding is either 1 or 2 queen beds. Rooms facing the front of the hotel (even-numbered rooms) are somewhat larger and more expensive than rooms on the opposite side of the hallway. Although they entail a longer walk from the elevator and lobby, we like corner rooms 2073 and 2074, and corresponding rooms on the third and fourth floors. These rooms are at the end of the corridor and subject to less noise and foot traffic. They also provide additional light and better views by having windows on 2 walls.

Old Faithful Inn is the classic national park lodge in which every visitor to Yellowstone should stay at least 1 night. That first entry into the marvelous lobby often brings a child's sense of wonderment to the most experienced traveler. Guests gather on the porch over the front portico for an excellent view of Old Faithful geyser doing its thing. The inn is convenient to the Upper and Lower Geyser basins and a good base for exploring thermal activity in this section of the park. Be aware that, during the summer, the inn is a busy place and the Old Faithful area is congested during the day. Both guests and visitors constantly roam the lobby, mezzanine, and second-floor porch, so if you are seeking quiet, this isn't the place. On the other hand, you've got to see Old Faithful, so you might as well do it from where you are staying.

The Northern Pacific Railroad financed the construction of Old Faithful Inn, which provided lodging for the large number of tourists coming to this area by train. The hotel that would cost approximately $140,000 was to replace the Upper Geyser Basin Hotel, which had been lost to fire. Old Faithful Inn was constructed in 3 phases: the original Old House along with the dining room, kitchen wings, small guest room wings, and the magnificent seven-story lobby was completed in 1903. The East Wing was constructed from 1913 to 1914, while the Y-shaped West Wing was added in 1927. Numerous modifications have taken place over the years, including an expansion of the lobby (timber columns supporting the balconies replaced the old north wall), additions to the dining room, and construction of the cocktail lounge.

Rooms: Doubles, triples, and quads. A few rooms in the Old House can sleep up to 6 persons. Most but not all rooms have a private bath.

Wheelchair Accessibility: Four rooms are wheelchair-accessible.

Rates: Old House rooms: 1 room without a private bath ($103); 2 rooms without a private bath ($189 for up to 6 persons); 1 room with a private bath ($159); 2 rooms with a private bath ($254 for up to 4 persons). West Wing rooms ($174–$221 depending on location). East Wing rooms ($230–$260 depending on location). Semi-suites ($425); Suites ($525). Most rates quoted are for 2 persons. Semi-suites and Suites are quoted for 4 persons. Each additional person is $15 per night. Children 11 and under are free when staying with an adult.

Location: Southwest section of Yellowstone National Park, 30 miles from the entrance station at West Yellowstone.

Season: Early May through early Oct.

Food: A dining room on the main floor serves a breakfast buffet ($14), a breakfast menu ($6–$14), a lunch buffet ($15), a lunch menu ($8–$17), a dinner buffet ($28), and dinner ($13–$28); reservations are required for dinner. The deli offers sandwiches, fast-food items, and ice cream; the bar sells sandwiches and appetizers; a lunch counter in the adjacent general store serves breakfast, salads, sandwiches, hamburgers, soup, ice cream, and beverages. Other eating facilities, including a food court and a grill, are nearby.

Facilities: Dining room, mezzanine lounge, mezzanine espresso shop, deli, bar, tour desk, gift shop. Many additional facilities, including a gas station, gift shops, stores, and restaurants, are in the immediate area. The National Park Visitor Education Center is nearby.

Activities: Walking through nearby geyser area, guided tours of the inn, narrated bus tours, hiking.

OLD FAITHFUL LODGE CABINS

Old Faithful Lodge Cabins consists of a rustic lodge building plus 97 cabins, mostly constructed 2 to 4 to a building. The main lodge was built in the late 1920s and has no guest accommodations. The cabins are behind and to one side of the lodge, which houses the registration desk. The impressive lobby has large windows that provide an excellent view of Old Faithful. A big stone fireplace is surrounded with chairs and tables for eating, visiting, and viewing. The main building also has a food court, ice cream shop, bake shop, and gift shop. It is a short walk from the better-known Old Faithful Inn.

The lodge offers cabins in 2 classifications, Budget and Frontier. All cabins have finished interiors, heat, electricity, and carpeted floors, but only Frontier cabins have a private bathroom. Keep in mind that the cabins are not insulated, so the small electric heaters may prove inadequate when the outside temperature is low, as may be the case in the spring and fall. The cabins are clustered closely together behind the lodge in an area with much paving and few trees. A few cabins front on a river, while several others face the geyser basin. Most, however, offer no particularly good views. Cabins in either classification are the best values in the Old Faithful area.

The least expensive rooms in the Old Faithful area are 35 Budget cabins, which have a hot-and-cold water sink but no bathroom facilities. Toilets and sinks are in 2 community bathrooms and also in the main lodge. Shower facilities are only in the community bathroom nearest the lodge office. Bedding in Budget cabins is a double bed plus a twin bed or 2 double beds. Cabins in this classification are all the same size, so units with 2 doubles have less floor space for you and your belongings. All except 2 of the Budget cabins are constructed as duplex units with

Frontier cabins at Old Faithful Lodge Cabins

connecting doors, a feature that may appeal to families. If you plan to choose a cabin without a bath, we suggest units 221 through 225, which sit on a small bluff overlooking the river in the back of the complex. These offer more privacy and a good view but are some distance from the showers. Budget cabins 200, 201, 203, 205, 207, and 209 are nearest the geyser basin, but trees obstruct views of Old Faithful. Budget cabins 226 and 235 are the only freestanding units in this classification, which means you will probably enjoy more quiet. Both are away from the river but close to a community bathroom.

Sixty-one Frontier cabins are mostly constructed as duplex units. These units have a sink in the room and a private bathroom with a toilet and shower. Bedding is 1 double or a double plus a twin. Frontier cabins with a double and a twin are somewhat larger in size but priced the same as cabins in the same class with 1 double bed. Essentially, most Frontier cabins are the same size as Budget cabins but have a private bathroom. Frontier units 114, 141, and 144 are the only freestanding cabins in this classification. Cabin 114 faces Old Faithful geyser but is in the front of the complex and subject to heavy traffic flow. ADA cabin 228 is about twice the size of a regular cabin.

Old Faithful Lodge Cabins offers basic but relatively inexpensive accommodations near Old Faithful geyser and the geyser basins. This lodge is in essence a low-cost alternative to the 2 nearby lodges. Cabin rooms here are certainly not as nice as rooms in Snow Lodge or Old Faithful Inn, but they are convenient to the thermal areas of this section of the park. The main lodge is a comfortable place to relax and watch Old Faithful do its regular business. The food court serves relatively inexpensive lunch and dinner items, while a small bakery sells muffins, cinnamon rolls, and other baked goods, as well as coffee. More upscale meals plus snacks are available at the other 2 lodges, while a nearby general store offers sandwiches, soups, and other light items.

Rooms: Doubles, triples, and a few quads. More than half the cabins have a private bath.

Wheelchair Accessibility: One double-size Frontier cabin, 228, is ADA compliant. One Budget cabin has ramp access.

Rates: Budget cabins ($74); Frontier cabins ($124). Rates quoted are for 2 persons. Each additional person is $15 per night. Children 11 and under stay free with an adult.

Location: Southwest section of Yellowstone National Park, 30 miles from the entrance station at West Yellowstone.

Season: Mid-May to early Oct.

Boardwalks and unpaved paths meander through Upper Geyser Basin, near Old Faithful Lodge Cabins. A boardwalk that begins near the lodge leads around Old Faithful geyser and through a large area of pools, geysers, and hot springs. One path is designated for both people and bicycles. One 3-mile loop leads to Morning Glory Pool and returns to the lodge. Both shorter and longer trails are in the basin area.

Food: A large food court offers the same menu for lunch and dinner ($6–$14). Two snack shops serve bakery goods, packaged sandwiches, ice cream, yogurt, and espresso. Upscale dining and a grill are available at the 2 nearby lodges. Two general stores each have a lunch counter and sell limited grocery items.

Facilities: Food court, snack shops, tour desk, gift shop. Many stores and restaurants are in the immediate vicinity.

Activities: Walking through the geyser area, hiking, ranger-guided walks, narrated tours.

OLD FAITHFUL SNOW LODGE AND CABINS

Old Faithful Snow Lodge and Cabins consists of a single three-story main lodge plus 34 nearby wooden cabins. The lodge offers a dining room, grill, cocktail lounge, gift shop, and an impressive two-story lobby with huge wood beams and a large gas fireplace. A second-floor mezzanine with chairs and a table overlooks the lobby. Craftsmen created many of the furnishings in the lobby, lounge, and restaurant. Lamps and chandeliers throughout the building and guest rooms feature animal motifs. Even much of the woodwork includes inlaid animal figures. The rustic design of the lodge fits in well with better-known Old Faithful Inn, which is nearby. Registration for the lodge and the cabins is at the main desk of the lodge building.

Old Faithful Snow Lodge

Snow Lodge is the first full-service hotel (dining rooms, lobby, gift shop, etc.) built in Yellowstone National Park since Canyon Lodge was completed in 1911 (and has since burned). The new lodge building replaces the previous Snow Lodge that was demolished in 1998. The complex has 100 similar but not identical rooms that are all rented at the same rate. Each room in the new lodge has 1 queen bed plus a twin, 2 queens, or 1 king bed. Heavy wooden shutters swing out to cover the windows. A padded window seat is in a few of the rooms. All rooms have a full bath with a combination shower-tub, bathrobes, telephone, small refrigerator, coffeemaker, and heat, but no air-conditioning.

The complex is in a relatively quiet section of the Old Faithful area, but the location does not lend itself to great views from any of the rooms. The lodge has elevators and bell service is available to assist with luggage. We recommend that you try to book rooms 2037, 2039, 2041, and the 3 corresponding rooms on the third floor, which are larger but rent for the same rate as all other rooms in the lodge. Rooms on the second floor have larger windows than third-floor rooms.

Two categories of cabins are rented at Snow Lodge. All sit in a gravel area of sparse vegetation. The least expensive are 10 Frontier cabins with 1 or 2 double beds. Units 706 and 707, each with 1 double bed, are quite a bit smaller than the other 8 Frontier Cabins. They all rent for the same price, so try to get 2 doubles if you book a Frontier cabin. These cabins are roomy and nicely finished. They do not have a porch. Each cabin has a private bath with a shower but no tub. Twenty-four Western cabins are somewhat larger and nicer than the Frontier units. These are constructed 4 to a building. Each cabin has a small covered porch, 2 queen beds, and a full bath with a combination shower-tub. We believe Frontier cabins with 2 double beds are a better value than Western cabins.

Old Faithful Snow Lodge and Cabins offers something for everyone. Those on a tight budget can choose an inexpensive Frontier cabin. If you are willing to spend more, spring for a room in one of Yellowstone's nicest lodges. Although the lodge is relatively new and doesn't have the aura of nearby Old Faithful Inn, Snow Lodge is a first-class place to stay. The location of Snow Lodge is both an advantage and a disadvantage. While convenient to the boardwalks and trails of the area's geyser basins, the lodge rooms and public areas do not enjoy any really good views of the thermal features that make this area so popular. For those seeking quiet, Snow Lodge is away from the high-traffic areas of Old Faithful. While the lobbies of Old Faithful Inn and Old Faithful Lodge Cabins are often full of people and noise, the lobby at Snow Lodge is generally uncrowded and quiet.

Old Faithful Snow Lodge and Cabins and Mammoth Hot Springs Hotel are the only 2 park facilities that offer winter accommodations. Reservations should be made well in advance of your planned arrival. Only Mammoth is accessible by private vehicle. Old Faithful Snow Lodge is accessible only by over-the-snow vehicles from West Yellowstone, Mammoth, and, from the south, Headwater Lodge and Cabins at Flagg Ranch. Cross-country skiing, snowshoeing, and ice skating (Mammoth) are popular activities. Ski rentals, waxes, trail maps, and other equipment are available at both locations. A winter visit to Yellowstone is a unique experience that we enjoyed immensely.

Rooms: Doubles, triples, and quads. All rooms have a private bath.

Wheelchair Accessibility: Five first-floor rooms in the lodge and 1 Western cabin are ADA compliant.

Rates: Frontier cabins ($99); Western cabins ($155); Snow Lodge rooms ($229–$239). Rates quoted are for 2 persons. Each additional person is $15 per night. Children 11 and under stay free.

Location: Southwest section of Yellowstone, 30 miles southeast of the west entrance at West Yellowstone.

Season: Summer season is from early May to mid-Oct. Winter season is from mid-Dec to early Mar. No roads are open to the Old Faithful area during winter months.

Food: An exceptionally attractive dining room with a western motif has a large gas fireplace and handcrafted furniture. The dining room serves a breakfast buffet ($13), a breakfast menu ($6–$14), and dinner ($15–$32). Lunch is served only when Old Faithful Inn is closed for the season. A grill serves breakfast items and hamburgers, hot dogs, and sandwiches for lunch/dinner. Another dining room, a food court, and a general store with limited groceries and a grill are nearby.

Facilities: Dining room, grill, cocktail lounge, gift shop, laundry facilities, and bicycle rental. Other nearby facilities include a clinic, general store, National Park Service visitor center, and post office. Winter sports equipment rental is available during winter months.

Activities: Hiking, walking through the nearby geyser area, guided walks, biking, and narrated tours. Winter activities include snowcoach tours, guided ski tours, cross-country skiing, snowshoeing, and snowmobiling.

Named for an area that served as a favorite campsite for President Theodore Roosevelt, Roosevelt Lodge Cabins includes a log registration and dining building and an adjacent small store. The 2 structures are surrounded on 3 sides by rustic wood cabins that were constructed mostly in the 1920s. The complex is situated on a hill surrounded by pine trees and overlooking a valley with a background of mountains. The relatively isolated location places the lodge away from congestion that plagues other such facilities in the park. Roosevelt Lodge Cabins provides 80 wood-frame cabins in the smallest lodging complex in Yellowstone. All overnight accommodations are in freestanding cabins, which have vaulted ceilings, shake roofs, and wood floors. None have air-conditioning, television, telephone, or a porch. Cabins are closely clustered in an area of trees, grass, gravel, and weeds, surrounded by hills. They are near a small store and the log registration building that houses the dining room. Parking is in front of the dining room and beside or near each cabin.

The least expensive units at Roosevelt Lodge Cabins are 66 Rough Rider cabins, which have no water or private bathroom. The concessionaire supplies complimentary manufactured (Presto) logs for the woodstove that serves as the only source of heat. Three modern community bathrooms with toilets, sinks, and showers are scattered among the cabins. Most Rough Rider cabins are small freestanding buildings with wood floors and 1 double bed. The interior has adequate space for luggage and other belongings. The cabins come in different sizes and have small screened windows to provide ventilation and outside light, which results in relatively dark interiors. Some Rough Rider units are in larger cabins that have either 2 or 3 double beds. Rough Rider cabin 5, with 3 double beds, is the only

Rough Rider Cabins at Roosevelt Lodge Cabins

cabin in the complex with 2 rooms. All cabins in the Rough Rider classification rent for the same price regardless of size and bedding.

Fourteen Frontier cabins with a private bath and heat have nicely finished interiors. They are the same size as larger Rough Rider cabins and have a much nicer interior appearance than you would expect from viewing the cabin exterior. Each Frontier unit (other than 2 wheelchair-accessible Frontier cabins) has 2 double beds and 4 windows that admit more exterior light than the Rough Rider units. Frontier cabins are in a small cluster among the Rough Rider cabins.

The choice between the 2 types of cabins will depend primarily on how much you are willing to pay for a private bathroom and a heater. If you don't think they are worth $50 extra, request a less expensive Rough Rider cabin. Rough Rider cabin 5 is a bargain, with 2 rooms and 3 double beds. This unit also has a front porch and is the end unit in a row of cabins. We especially like the location of Rough Rider cabin 115, bordered on 2 sides by a creek. Cabins 109, 111, 113, and 114 are also on the creek but not in quite as good a location as 115. These are 5 smaller cabins, each with 1 double bed. You might also consider requesting a Rough Rider cabin with 2 double

The location of Roosevelt Lodge Cabins has served as a home for previous lodging facilities. John Yancy, an early entrepreneur to this area, built the Pleasant Valley Hotel in 1884 near the site where today's Old West Cookout takes place. Yancy died in 1903, and the hotel burned 3 years later. This same year saw the construction of Roosevelt Tent Camp, which had wood-floored, candy-striped canvas tents. The current lodge was completed in 1920, and the cabins were added during the same decade.

Wheelchair Accessibility: Two Frontier cabins are each ADA compliant.

Rates: Rough Rider cabins ($74); Frontier cabins ($124). Rates quoted are for 2 persons. Each additional person is $15 per night. Children 11 and under stay free.

Location: Northeast section of Yellowstone, 23 miles southeast of the north entrance.

beds, in which case you are likely to end up with one of the larger cabins in this classification. Rough Rider units 80, 88, and 89 each have 3 double beds and are near the bathroom and the creek. None of the Frontier cabins are preferable to any other, although all have finished and comfortable interiors that make them considerably nicer than most of the Rough Rider cabins. Frontier cabins generally fill quickly and must be reserved well in advance.

Season: Early June through early Sept.

Food: A dining room serves breakfast ($5–$10), lunch ($8–$14), and dinner ($11–$25). An Old West Cookout via horseback ($76 for 1 hour, $85

Roosevelt Lodge Cabins offers basic accommodations at nominal cost in a quiet area near the Lamar Valley, where wolves are frequently sighted. The Frontier cabins are comfortable, and Rough Rider cabins are among the lowest-cost accommodations in the park. The main registration and restaurant building, of log construction, has an attractive lobby with a hardwood floor and a large stone fireplace. A lobby bar in 1 corner serves alcoholic beverages beginning in the late afternoon. The covered porch is a great place to sit in a rocking chair and watch the sun rise, spend part of an afternoon, or relax after an evening meal. The informal country-style dining area specializes in BBQ ribs and fish. Horseback riding and stagecoach rides are available at the nearby corral.

Roosevelt Lodge Cabins is well-known for its "Roosevelt's Old West Cookout." Participants depart for Pleasant Valley from the Roosevelt Corral each day in a wagon or on horseback. Different rates are charged depending on whether you choose the wagon ride, the 1-hour horseback ride, or the 2-hour horseback ride. The cookout includes a steak dinner plus entertainment and is very popular, so reservations should be made well in advance, especially if you choose 1 of the 2 horseback rides. Reservations for the cookout can be made when you reserve a room.

for 2 hours) or covered wagon ($57) is offered each evening, rain or shine. Limited groceries are sold at a small store.

Facilities: Store, dining room, lobby bar, gift counter, stables, gas station.

Activities: Hiking, guided trail rides, fly-fishing guide service, stagecoach rides, half-day and full-day guided tours to Lamar Valley.

Rooms: Doubles, triples, and quads. A few cabins hold up to 6 adults. Most cabins do not have a private bath.